American Art:
1750-1800
Towards Independence

Charles F. Montgomery and Patricia E. Kane,
General Editors

With Essays on American Art and Culture
by J. H. Plumb, Neil Harris,
Jules David Prown, Frank H. Sommer
and Charles F. Montgomery

Published for
Yale University Art Gallery, New Haven
and The Victoria and Albert Museum, London
by the New York Graphic Society, Boston

American Art: 1750-1800 Towards Independence

This book is published in connection with the exhibition held at Yale University Art Gallery, New Haven, Connecticut, April 3–May 23, 1976 The Victoria and Albert Museum, London, July 15–September 26, 1976.

This project is supported by grants from the National Endowment for the Arts and the National Endowment for the Humanities, federal agencies.

Designed by Esther and Christopher Pullman

First Edition

New York Graphic Society books are published by Little, Brown and Company. Published simultaneously in Canada by Little, Brown and Company (Canada) Limited

Printed in the United States of America

General Editors
Professor Charles F. Montgomery,
  Curator of the Garvan
  and Related Collections,
  Yale University Art Gallery
Patricia E. Kane,
  Associate Curator of the Garvan
  and Related Collections,
  Yale University Art Gallery

Contributors
For the essays in "A Display of American Arts" and for the Catalogue draft typescripts were prepared by the following:

Paintings
Jules David Prown,
  Professor, History of Art,
  Yale University
Frank H. Goodyear, Jr.,
  Curator, Pennsylvania Academy of the Fine Arts, and
  Acting Curator of American Painting, Yale University Art Gallery (academic year 1974–1975)
David Nathans,
  National Endowment for the Humanities Museum Intern
William T. Oedel,
  National Endowment for the Humanities Museum Fellow
Richard H. Saunders,
  Doctoral Candidate,
  Department of History of Art
Professor Theodore E. Stebbins, Jr.,
  Curator of American Painting,
  Yale University Art Gallery

Prints
David Nathans
Patricia Rubin,
  National Endowment for the Humanities Museum Fellow

Furniture
Patricia E. Kane
Margaretta M. Lovell,
  Curatorial Assistant,
  Yale University Art Gallery
Oswaldo Rodriguez,
  National Endowment for the Humanities Museum Fellow
Robert Trent,
  National Endowment for the Humanities Museum Fellow

Silver and Gold
Oswaldo Rodriguez
Patricia Rubin

Pewter
Charles F. Montgomery

Brass
Charles F. Montgomery

Ceramics
Margaretta M. Lovell
Robert Trent

Glass
Robert Trent

Textiles
Gerald W. R. Ward,
  National Endowment for the Humanities Museum Intern

Bibliography
Gerald W. R. Ward

Library of Congress Cataloging in Publication Data
Main entry under title:

American art, 1750-1800.

"Grows out of the great bicentennial exhibition organized by the Yale University Art Gallery and the Victoria and Albert Museum."
  Bibliography: p.
  Includes index.
  1. Art, American—Addresses, essays, lectures. 2. Art, Modern—17th-18th centuries—United States—Addresses, essays, lectures. 3. United States—Civilization—English influences—Addresses, essays, lectures. I. Montgomery, Charles F. II. Kane, Patricia E. III. Victoria and Albert Museum, South Kensington. IV. Yale University. Art Gallery.
N6507.A54 1976   709'.73   75-24591
ISBN 0-8212-0692-3

Contents

Committees for the Exhibition

England

The Rt. Hon.
The Lord Harlech, K.C.M.G.
Chairman

The Lord Astor of Hever
Vice-Chairman

H. E. The American Ambassador
  to the Court of St. James's
H. E. The British Ambassador
  to the United States
The Director of the Victoria
  and Albert Museum
The Director of the Yale University
  Art Gallery
The Chairman of the Arts Council
  of Great Britain
The Hon. Walter H. Annenberg
Mr. J. Carter Brown
Mr. Hugh Bullock, K.B.E.
Mr. C. Douglas Dillon
The Lord Gore-Booth, G.C.M.G., K.C.V.O.
Mr. Henry J. Heinz II
Mr. Thomas Hoving
Mr. Paul Mellon
Sir John Pope-Hennessy, C.B.E.
Mr. Robert L. Sigmon
Mr. John Walker

United States

Kingman Brewster, Jr.
President, Yale University
Honorary Chairman

Henry Chauncey, Jr.
Secretary, Yale University
Honorary Vice-Chairman

Alan Shestack
Director, Yale University Art Gallery
Chairman

Prof. Charles F. Montgomery
Prof. Jules David Prown
Prof. Theodore E. Stebbins, Jr.

Sponsors

England

The Pilgrims
in association with The Arts Council
of Great Britain and
The Victoria and Albert Museum

The Pilgrims and Organizers wish
to express their gratitude to the
following donors who have made the
exhibition in England possible:

The Lord Astor of Hever
The Bank of England
Bank of Scotland
Barclays Bank Limited
The Baring Foundation
C. T. Bowring & Co. Limited
British Airways
The British Petroleum Company
    Limited
Commercial Union Assurance
Members of the English-
    Speaking Union
Sir Charles Forte
Mr. Alan P. Greenaway
Sir Derek Greenaway, Bart., C.B.E.
Guinness Mahon & Co. Limited
Harris Trust and Savings Bank
Mr. Henry J. Heinz II
Kleinwort, Benson Limited
Legal & General Assurance Society
    Limited
Lloyds Bank Limited
Midland Bank Limited
Morgan Grenfell & Co. Limited
Morgan Guaranty Trust Company
National Westminster Bank Limited
Pearson Longman Limited
Pitt & Scott Limited
Rio Tinto Zinc Corporation Limited
The Royal Bank of Scotland Limited
Shell International Petroleum Co.
    Limited
Singer & Friedlander Limited
Sotheby, Parke-Bernet & Co.
Strauss, Turnbull & Co.
Sir Bernard Waley-Cohen, Bart.
Mr. George S. Warburg
Wells Fargo Limited
Williams & Glyn's Bank Limited

United States

Yale University and the
Yale University Art Gallery

The President and Fellows of
Yale University wish to express their
gratitude to the following donors
who have made the exhibition in
the United States possible:

The Annenberg Fund, Inc.
The English Speaking Union
Mrs. Francis P. Garvan
Mr. and Mrs. Henry J. Heinz II
The L.A.W. Fund
Mr. and Mrs. Robert L. McNeil, Jr.
Mr. Paul Mellon
National Endowment for the Arts
National Endowment for the
    Humanities
Miss Josephine Setze
Mr. and Mrs. John Hay Whitney
Mr. Stanley Woodward

Prefaces

**Preface by Roy Strong, Director,
Victoria and Albert Museum**

The collaboration of the Victoria
and Albert Museum and the Yale
University Art Gallery is for me
a particularly happy event, evoking
in concrete form a long, personal
relationship with the Mellon
Centres for British Art in London
and New Haven. Yale has been
and is a major centre for British
scholarship in America, embracing
the whole spectrum but with a
special emphasis on the literature
and fine arts of eighteenth-century
England. It is therefore appropriate
that the Victoria and Albert
Museum's celebration of the American Bicentennial, organized jointly
with the Yale University Art Gallery, should take the form of a
panorama of the visual arts during
the reign of America's last king,
George III. Compared with the
American passion for eighteenth-
century art, British knowledge and
interest in American art has always
been minimal. The exhibition
therefore presents us with the
unique opportunity of filling this
gap in our knowledge by seeing
gathered together the very best of
the American achievement in the
fine and applied arts of that time.

The London end of the Exhibition originated as long ago as 1970
with an approach to my predecessor, Sir John Pope-Hennessy, from
the Hon. Treasurer of The Pilgrims, a society for the promotion
of Anglo-American friendship
under the patronage of The Queen
and The President of the United
States. Holding an exhibition to
mark the bicentenary of the American Declaration of Independence
was discussed, and an initial
Steering Committee was set up
under the Chairmanship of Lord
Harlech and an Executive Committee under the Chairmanship of
Lord Astor of Hever to explore
the possibilities. Through the me-
diation of John Walker, former
Director of the National Gallery
of Art in Washington, it was subsequently agreed to join forces with
Yale University Art Gallery. In this
way, we have benefited from the
expertise of a first-rate team of
American art historians, headed by
Charles Montgomery, Jules David
Prown and Theodore Stebbins,
who as a steering committee have
planned the exhibition and have
selected the exhibits.

Another project for a bicentennial show under the sponsorship of
the *Times* and the *Sunday Times*
has developed into an Exhibition
entitled "1776," which is being held
at Greenwich. Designed to tell the
story of the War of Independence
from the British end, it is complementary to the exhibition at the
Victoria and Albert; it is my hope
that those who have enjoyed the
one show may be encouraged to
visit the other.

The Exhibition at the Victoria
and Albert Museum could not have
taken place without a generous
contribution from the Arts Council

and very active participation from members of its staff, among whom it is a pleasure to name Robin Campbell, Joanna Drew, Andrew Dempsey, and Janet Holt. After the sad death in January 1975 of Anthony Gishford, Robert Sigmon energetically assumed responsibility for raising funds for the exhibition on behalf of The Pilgrims, and has been generous with his advice and time over many other matters. Nor should the work by members of my own staff be overlooked, notably John Physick, Keeper of Museum Services, Madeleine Mainstone, Keeper of the Education Department, John Mallet, who had the onerous task of overall coordination, Michael Darby, Assistant Keeper, Exhibitions, and Sue Runyard, Information Officer. Ivor Heal and Paul Williams, with a limited budget, undertook the design of the installation at this end. Especial gratitude is due to those institutions and owners who have parted with their treasures for so long. To all of these and to many others, I extend thanks. Through this happy collaboration on both sides of the Atlantic a major exhibition has been created, enabling the British public to see early American art *en masse* for the very first time and through this visual experience respond to its unique vigour and idiosyncrasy. Above all, it is an expression of good will between two countries over two centuries of history.

Preface by Alan Shestack, Director, Yale University Art Gallery

In 1972 the Yale University Art Gallery was invited by Sir John Pope-Hennessy and The Pilgrims to organize a comprehensive exhibition of early American art to be shown in 1976 at the Victoria and Albert Museum to commemorate the American bicentenary. Our response was immediate and enthusiastic. We were pleased by the opportunity—the first in history—to share some of the greatest treasures of eighteenth-century America with the British public. It seems especially appropriate that this exhibition, consisting as it does of a wide variety of art forms—silver, furniture, glass, ceramics, and textiles in addition to paintings—should be shown at the Victoria and Albert, which houses Britain's national collection of applied art. It is equally fitting that it should fall to Yale to organize such an exhibition, since the university has been a leader in the collection of American arts since about 1750. In 1832, as a direct result of Yale's acquisition of John Trumbull's famous paintings of American Revolutionary subjects, the university was the first in America to establish an art museum. Since 1930, Yale has had extensive holdings of eighteenth-century American art as well as a distinguished faculty and curators in the American field.

Although some of the objects in the current exhibition were drawn from Yale's own collections, especially the Mabel Brady Garvan Collection, the show is primarily an ambitious loan exhibition, with works assembled from sixty-seven public and private collections all over America. Our goal was to bring together over two hundred works of art to demonstrate the excellence and variety of artistic production in America during the years of transition from the late colonial period to that of independence, and also to suggest how certain characteristics intrinsic to American art reflect some different aspects of the American national character.

We are indebted to Roy Strong, who, after assuming the directorship of the Victoria and Albert, carried on the planning and arrangements for the exhibition with his usual imagination and flair. Throughout the planning period our two museums were aided by the efforts of John Walker, former director of the National Gallery of Art in Washington, who served as courier, fund-raiser, liaison officer, and helpful friend to both institutions. Obviously, the exhibition could not have been realized if the lenders had not agreed to part with their cherished possessions for the extended period of the show, or if we had not enjoyed the great generosity of a small number of American patrons, whose names appear on a special page, to say nothing of the moral and financial support of the English-Speaking Union as well as of the two federal agencies: the National Endowment for the Arts and the National Endowment for the Humanities. We are grateful to all of them.

American Art: 1750-1800, Towards Independence was conceived as a three-part undertaking, with exhibition, catalogue, motion picture and slide show supervised and coordinated by Charles F. Montgomery, Professor of Art History and Curator of the Garvan and Related Collections of American Art. The preparation of this exhibition has been a cooperative effort of the American Arts Office of the Yale University Art Gallery, the History of Art Department and the Program in American Studies. Planning of the exhibition and selection of objects was carried out by a committee consisting of Henry Chauncey, Jr., Secretary of the University, Mr. Montgomery, Jules David Prown, Professor of Art History and Director of the Yale Center for British Art and British Studies, and Theodore E. Stebbins, Jr., Curator of American Painting and Sculpture (who also served as Acting Director and head of this committee during my leave of absence for the first half of 1975), as well as Frank H. Goodyear, Jr., Acting Curator of American

Painting (1974-1975), Patricia E. Kane, Associate Curator of American Arts, and myself.

Special thanks are due the writers and editors of the book to accompany the exhibition: Professors Neil Harris and J. H. Plumb, and Dr. Frank H. Sommer. In particular thanks are due to Professor Prown for his vital role in preparing the essay on paintings, drawings, and watercolors. Professor Montgomery and Patricia Kane acted as general editors as well. Others to whom we are indebted for writing and research are listed on page 4. In the spring of 1974 in a graduate seminar, *American Arts, 1700-1800: Native Trends, Themes and Qualities,* given by Charles Montgomery, the following students carried out rigorous research on the kinds of objects included in the exhibition: Louise Bloomberg, John Caldwell, Helen Cooper, Patricia Fischer, William Howze, Katherine Menz, William T. Oedel, Oswaldo Rodriguez, Stewart Rosenblum, Patricia Rubin, and Richard H. Saunders. Their work made a valuable contribution to the catalogue. Margaretta Lovell, Curatorial Assistant, was in charge of the complex arrangements for loans, photographs, and catalogue data. David Nathans assisted with gathering information and illustrations for paintings and prints. Plans for the collection and

transportation of loans were made by Nan Ross, registrar of the Yale University Art Gallery. Much of the voluminous correspondence was handled by Dorothy Hooker, former secretary to the director, Galina Gorokhoff, and Constance Clement, assistant to the Curator of American arts, while much of the final typescript was carried out by Marion Sandquist. June Guicharnaud and Norman Ross undertook the task of editing the multi-authored text of this book to achieve stylistic unity. The exhibit in New Haven was brilliantly designed by Vincent Ciulla; the extensive cabinetwork and carpentry was carried out in our own workshop by Robert Soule and his staff. A film by Charles Eames entitled "The Look of America, 1750-1800" and a multiprojector slide show by Charles Belson and William Howze were made possible by a grant from the National Endowment for the Humanities.

Exhibitions, however beautiful or edifying, are temporary, and if they do not provide an occasion for serious scholarship, they are soon forgotten. We trust that this book, which is intended to be more than a record of the exhibition, will be a lasting contribution to the literature on American Art in the Age of Independence.

Alan Shestack

Lenders

Her Majesty The Queen

Mary Allis
American Numismatic Society
The Athenaeum of Philadelphia
Bennington Museum, Inc.
Mrs. Alfred Elliott Bissell
The Boston Athenaeum
Bowdoin College Museum of Art
The Trustees of the British Museum
The Brooklyn Museum
Chicago Historical Society
Mrs. Thomas M. Cole
Colonial Williamsburg Foundation
Columbia University
The Connecticut Historical Society
The Corning Museum of Glass
The Currier Gallery of Art
Department of State, Diplomatic
    Reception Rooms
The Detroit Institute of Arts
Dietrich Brothers Americana
    Corporation
Mr. Peter W. Eliot
The Fine Arts Museums of
    San Francisco
The Fogg Art Museum, Harvard
    University
Fordham University Library
Benjamin Ginsburg
Girard College, Estate of Stephen
    Girard, deceased
Mr. and Mrs. Christopher
    Ireland Granger
Greenfield Village and Henry Ford
    Museum
Mr. and Mrs. James H. Halpin
Harvard University Portrait
    Collection
The Historical Society of
    Pennsylvania
Mr. and Mrs. Walter M. Jeffords, Jr.
Kahal Kadosh Mikveh Israel in
    the City of Philadelphia
Mr. and Mrs. George M. Kaufman

Mr. and Mrs. Edward A. Kilroy, Jr.
Mr. and Mrs. William S. Kilroy
Mr. and Mrs. Bertram K. Little
Mr. and Mrs. Robert L. McNeil, Jr.
Dr. and Mrs. Robert Mallory III
Massachusetts Historical Society
Mr. and Mrs. Paul Mellon
The Metropolitan Museum of Art
The Secretary of the Navy and Mrs.
    J. William Middendorf II
Helen and Harvey Muehlenbeck
Munson-Williams-Proctor Institute
Museum of the City of New York
Museum of Fine Arts, Boston
National Gallery of Art
Nelson Gallery–Atkins Museum
Old Gaol Museum, York, Maine
Old Salem, Inc.
The Paul Revere Life Insurance
    Company
Philadelphia Museum of Art
Mr. and Mrs. John Paul
    Remensynder
Mr. and Mrs. Raymond V.
    Shepherd, Jr.
Smithsonian Institution, The
    National Museum of History and
    Technology
The Society for the Preservation of
    New England Antiquities
Mr. and Mrs. Richard Stiner
The St. Louis Art Museum
Mr. and Mrs. Stanley Stone
Mr. Charles V. Swain
Mrs. H. Gordon Sweet
The Trustees of the Tate Gallery
Valentine Museum
Wadsworth Atheneum
The Whitney Museum of
    American Art
Dr. and Mrs. Melvyn D. Wolf
Mr. and Mrs. Eric M. Wunsch
Yale University Art Gallery
Yale University Library
Private Collections

American Art
and American Culture

America and England: 1720-1820
The Fusion of Cultures
by J. H. Plumb

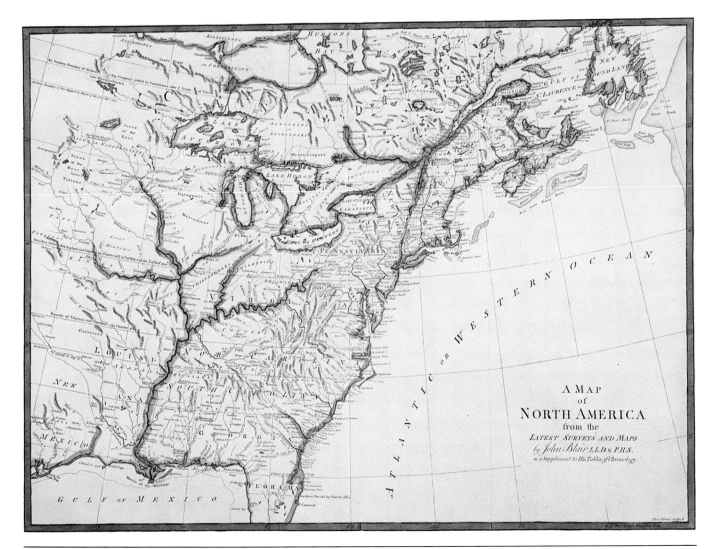

Fig. 1
John Blair
A Map of North America from the
Latest Surveys and Maps
1760. Map Collection, Sterling
Memorial Library, Yale University.

For an Englishman driving about New England, there is an acute sense of cultural confusion. It is not that Leicester is but a suburb of Worcester, or that Epping is only a stone's throw from Portsmouth, which itself is impossibly close to Manchester; the feeling of confusion goes far deeper than the place-names. The same is true strolling about Charleston or walking around Savannah. The broad avenue of Bull Street, leading from Johnson Square to Forsyth Park in Savannah, is curiously disturbing. Again, it is not the occasional foreign names—Chippewa, Monterey—for most of the rest are English enough. Nor is it the iron lacework balconies and railings, although they are ornate by the standards of England. Like the place-names of the squares and avenues, a little off-center maybe, but not critically so. The trees in Savannah and Charleston, the live oaks, the Spanish moss, the freestanding magnolia grandifloras, are exotic, strange, disturbing, perhaps, like the heat and humidity, to an Englishman. In Charleston the houses themselves are not English, not truly English, with their vast balconies and their setting of semitropical gardens. And the same is true of the churches of New England. There they are built in gleaming white-painted wood, which makes them odd. All of these things give a touch of fantasy, of difference, but they do not explain the fundamental disquiet. To go into a well-preserved house, full of furniture of its period, such as the Owens Thomas House in Savannah or the Sword Gate House in Charleston, the sensation almost of anxiety becomes even more acute—beautiful eighteenth-century furniture, some imported, some locally made: Wedgwood's creamware; Boulton and Watt's silver plate; but alongside these there are paintings, pottery, stools, and chairs, bedcovers and curtains, curiously primitive and very American, bringing a powerful echo of an England long dead by 1800. The confusion arises, I think, not because of the superficial differences or the exoticisms created by climate or the inertia of fashion and taste caused by distance. One may be astonished to find a house, like the Isaiah Davenport House of Savannah, built in 1820, when it might have graced Salisbury, Wiltshire, in 1750, but it remains truly English. The explanation lies in the fact that New England, and much of the Southeast as far as Georgia, is so deeply English, at least in what remains of the houses and furniture of the eighteenth and early nineteenth centuries. The English eighteenth century lives as powerfully in Savannah and Charleston and in scores of towns like Leicester and North Oxford in New England as it does in Bath or Tunbridge Wells, or the great Georgian terraces of Edinburgh. But what is disturbing is that these powerful vestiges of eighteenth-century England live in what, for an Englishman, is the alien ambience of twentieth-century America—with the hideous revolving, neon-flashing advertisements, and used-car lots, with their odd fluttering flags.

American eighteenth-century buildings, furniture, even paintings, cannot be regarded as mere country cousins of Britain. In Copley and West, America produced artists of European, let alone British, reputation. Many American craftsmen were of the highest distinction. Surely America did not produce a Paul de Lamerie or a Thomas Chippendale, but a silver coffeepot by Paul Revere or Jacob Hurd or Charles Le Roux was every bit as fine as any by Thomas Whipham, E. Wakelin, or Pezé Pilleau, or any other first-class London silversmith. Chests of drawers by Jonathan Gostelowe or card tables by Thomas Affleck were as good as could be found in the warehouses of the best English cabinetmakers. Of course, the farther one got away from Boston, New York, Philadelphia, or Charleston, the more clumsy were the decorative arts, but the same may be said of Britain or, for that matter, France; they, too, had plenty of provincial furnishings of moderate quality, even in the eighteenth century.

The closeness of the artistic bond between America and England in the eighteenth century was not, however, inevitable. In the seventeenth century the craftsmen of the American colonies had been touched by changes of English fashion, but often very lightly, and they had persisted with styles and forms for many generations, and by and large they had satisfied their market. Only the very rich, and they were not numerous, had imported works of art or decorative porcelain, silver, and furniture of high fashion. Nor in the seventeenth century had England itself been swarming with silversmiths, cabinetmakers, painters, and carvers, or even chinamakers of high distinction and genius. There was not, in fact, a great deal in England to entice the guineas from an American middle-class pocket. It was affluence in both England and America, and in America a fantastic surge in the size of the middle class, that had so profound an influence on the development of a common culture in the eighteenth century.

The jump in the population of the American colonies was dramatic between 1700 and 1770. As Thomas Malthus wrote years later, it was "a rapidity of increase almost without parallel in history," from a mere 629,000 in 1700 to 2,148,000 in 1770. By 1800, 5,000,000. Of course, this might seem a trivial population, considering the immensity of the thirteen states, but the population was not unduly scattered; much of it was highly concentrated. Philadelphia, in 1770, had become the second largest city in the British Empire. And although the proportion of this growing population that lived in the cities was actually falling, the growth of the major cities was great enough and rapid enough to sustain a prosperous and cultured society. Without cities, a highly sophisticated culture is not possible. Nor, in eighteenth-century terms, was it possible without a class rich enough to indulge in conspicuous consumption or without the leisure to read, to watch plays, to listen to concerts, or even to build their houses and adorn them, of which nothing is more time-consuming. By 1750 the five major seaports—Boston, Newport, New York, Philadelphia, and Charleston—already possessed a very prosperous class of commercial gentry, and it was a class that was growing fast and becoming richer. The wars against the French and the Indians of the 1740s and fifties made many fortunes, as did the buoyant trade in tobacco, rice, and indigo. Although he began as a bookseller and graduated to be a paper-maker, the bulk of Thomas Hancock's fortune was made out of supplying British forces in America, engaged in war against the French and the Indians, and it was Hancock who, in 1737, built on Beacon Hill the most distinguished house that Boston had seen, with its flanking pavilions to contain the ballroom and the domestic offices; the house was typically that of an English country gentleman of moderate means. From London came Hancock's marble chimney-pieces, his blue Delft tiles, his looking glasses, and his wallpaper; likewise, he imported his fruit trees and his walnut trees and yews, but the rest of the house and its furnishings were supplied by American craftsmen. With burgeoning population and wealth, there were never enough American craftsmen, or craftsmen sufficiently ahead of fashion, to supply the needs of the rich middle class. Pattern books flew across the Atlantic and were rapidly reprinted. So buoyant a market became a magnet for young professional architects or English master craftsmen who had too small resources for the severe competition of the London market. As always in colonial society, the goods imported from England, and to a lesser extent from Europe, possessed a cachet in American eyes that no similar home-produced goods could rival. Also, as fashions changed in England with novel speed (the patterns of textiles did every year), American craftsmen and manufacturers tended to be forever a step behind; the lag enhanced the chic of the imported goods and made the making of quick copies of English fashions a surer way to a profit than an attempt at originality. In England the emphasis was on modernity; the pressure on men such as Josiah Wedgwood and Matthew Boulton to invent and explore new materials and new shapes in order to capture the market was intense. In America, therefore, a copy which could pass as just imported might have a readier sale, but it always proved exceptionally difficult to defeat the true imports. This is beautifully illustrated by the first porcelain produced in America, the soft-paste wares of Bonnin and Morris of Philadelphia. The few pieces that remain are all pastiches of English factories—Bow, Worcester, and the rest. Neither this firm nor Batchem in South Carolina survived for long. They could not secure sufficient skilled workmen, nor could they produce so economically as Wedgwood or other English potters who continued to dominate the china trade for decades and therefore were responsible for setting the style of American decorative arts.

The Revolution caused little break with the flow of fashion or the emigration of professional craftsmen from Britain to America; indeed, British culture remained dominant for the early decades of the nineteenth century. From 1830, however, America became more strongly influenced by European styles and also began to develop—in literature, in painting, in the applied arts—a culture that was markedly her own. Nevertheless, the impress of Georgian England goes very deep. From Bar Harbor to Savannah, the Englishman today is constantly reminded, in one visual image after another, of the most beautiful age of British architecture and art.

But culture is more than art, and to sustain a sophisticated way of life requires new attitudes, conscious commitment in men and women, as well as novel social institutions; in cultural activities there must be a sense of worth and of aspiration. In eighteenth-century Britain there was a great expansion of cultural activity. Young aristocrats like Horace Walpole were bred to think of art and literature as the natural occupations of a gentleman, along with building, gardening, and the support of the theatre and music. The same passions, the same interests were seeping down through every gradation of the middle class. Much of this culture was sought after because of its self-improving nature—an aspect that quickly caught the attention of Benjamin Franklin. Indeed, in many of his interests, Franklin was as typical of the newly emerging British middle-class culture as he was of Philadelphia's. Both Englishmen and Americans were busy forming discussion clubs, founding book-subscription libraries, schools, and hospitals, and attending the lectures of itinerant lecturers on science—except here there was one startling difference between England and America. Franklin bought the scientific apparatus of Dr. Spence, who visited Philadelphia, and made far better use of it than the lecturer! Nevertheless, the emerging culture of Philadelphia, in which Franklin was so deeply involved, was typical of many provincial towns of England, particularly the new manufacturing towns of Birmingham, Manchester, and Leeds. But it was to London that the Philadelphian Subscription Library sent for its first consignment of books, and indeed it would be books written and published in London that would provide the bulk of the library's reading for the rest of the century and beyond. There was, of course, a growing range of publications of purely American origin printed in Philadelphia, as well as a great deal of piracy of British books. Nevertheless, English publishers and English publications dominated the market. And that was true, too, of the subscription rooms and reading rooms such as that at Charleston, which so quickly followed Philadelphia's example. Books and itinerant science lecturers flowed across the Atlantic; so, too, later in the century, did plays and actors, music and musicians.

The traffic was, of course, not all one way, for Benjamin West came to be George III's favorite painter, and he acquired a dominant authority in the art world of London. And in many ways, some obvious, some obscure, America contributed to the culture of Britain. One influence that is often neglected is how America enriched the British flora in the eighteenth century. Englishmen developed a consuming passion for their gardens, and were soon ransacking America for new trees, new shrubs, and new flowers. By the 1730s it was possible to buy, at the chief nurseries in England, tens of thousands of native American trees; plants of every kind from America had been acclimatized and often hybridized. And men such as Thomas Hancock were quick to raid, in return, the British nurseries for their exotics: after all, the camellia, "the Japanese rose," reached America via Britain at this time. At all cultural levels, from the breeding of flowers or horses to natural philosophy, literature, and the arts, the two countries were almost as one.

There were, however, deeper resonances than in art or literature or architecture or science, or in the planting of gardens or the furnishing of houses. England in the 1740s, fifties, and sixties witnessed a mounting sense of political unease that quickly developed into active discontent. There was a great expansion of political comment in the daily newspapers, in the political press, in the pamphlets and broadsheets that festooned the taverns and coffeehouses. Great issues of peace and war and of taxation were violently debated, often with a satirical bitterness that included the royal family as well as the chief ministers—a freedom of satire that astonished foreign observers. A new type of urban radicalism began to take root, first in London and then in the major provincial cities, particularly those that were concerned with commerce and industry. There was a growing feeling that the high hopes, bred by the success of Parliament in the seventeenth century against the Crown, for a society based on liberty and freedom had been betrayed; that the power, wealth, and patronage had passed into the hands of a narrow oligarchy and that Parliament was no longer representative of the people, but an institution riddled with corruption and self-seeking, and one in which the deeper needs of the nation were ignored. It was a mood of incoherent distrust and criticism that knew what it was against, rather than what it was for, but it was a mood that resonated in Boston, in Philadelphia, in New York, that showed the same feelings of frustration, of exclusion from true power, of being used. It was a mood that was easy to ignite by a specific act of obvious injustice, as London, and then all England, was ignited by Wilkes, or as America was inflamed by the Stamp Act.

Although many Englishmen, like Americans, believed that their country enjoyed a degree of freedom unparalleled in history, nevertheless, many of the more sensitive and intelligent critics considered that freedom to be in jeopardy. From the 1720s, let alone the thirties, an impressive literature of opposition grew up in Britain of which the most persuasively argued were *Cato's Letters* and *The Independent Whig* by John Trenchard and Thomas Gordon, and the essays of *The Craftsman*, many of which were written by Bolingbroke. These essays, either verbatim, paraphrased, or just cribbed, were immediately published in American newspapers from Massachusetts to South Carolina. Once again it was as if America were but an extension of England—not, however, of official England, of the men of power and authority, but of their critics. As Bernard Bailyn has written,

The political culture of colonial America—the assumptions, the expectations, patterns of responses, and clusters of information relevant to the conduct of public affairs—was thus British, but British with a peculiar emphasis. It was not simply a miscellaneous amalgam of ideas and beliefs common in eighteenth century England, nor, most emphatically, was it simply a distillation of the thought of a few great minds, particularly Locke's. It was, rather, a pattern of ideas, assumptions, attitudes, and beliefs given distinctive shape by the opposition elements in English politics.

And likewise, when the great struggle was joined in the 1760s and 1770s, pamphlets attacking the ministerial actions, printed in Boston and Philadelphia, were rapidly reprinted and extensively sold in England, as, indeed, were those of the English defenders of American freedom, such as the pamphlets of Jonathan Shipley, of John Cartwright, and the rest, in America. Nor is it surprising that the most powerful of all propaganda weapons printed in America—Tom Paine's *Common Sense*—was the work of an Englishman.

American discontents were English discontents, giving rise to a common rhetoric of political opposition. And America and England adopted common political heroes. John Wilkes, in jail, received presents from Boston and from Virginia. All propaganda material, which with Wilkes amounted almost to an industry—the prints, the punch bowls, the mugs, the buttons, all proclaiming "Wilkes and Liberty"—had as ready a sale in the American colonies as in provincial England. After the Revolution the political experience of America and England began to diverge. America developed its own patterns of political discourse, its own style of parties; nevertheless, vestiges remained of its ancient political attitudes. The substantial ghost of George III, king and tyrant, stalked through the school history books generation after generation; there was bred an immediate, instinctive, and often wrongheaded sympathy for all movements in the British Empire which could be dubbed anticolonial, so deep was the memory, or so frequently refreshed was the memory, of its own struggle against monarchy and the British Parliament.

Although the paths of politics began to diverge most sharply after 1800, the institutions of government created by the British proved to be incredibly strong and completely acceptable to the American people. It is often forgotten that the pattern of local government in American states, as well as in American towns, stems directly from British practice. Even the town meetings of New England communities have much in common with the open vestry meeting of the English parish, while the county system is as undeniably British as the grand jury and the sheriff and his posse. Many of these institutions, such as the grand jury, long moribund in Britain, still enjoy a vigorous life in America. America's legal system, which, of course, it shared with Britain in the eighteenth century, has, in many aspects, displayed an inertia, an avoidance of change that is in marked contrast to England. Even in the most fundamental concept of all—namely, de-

mocracy—America owes more to seventeenth- and eighteenth-century Britain than is commonly supposed. Few realize how very widespread the county franchise was in England in the eighteenth century—that is, those who possessed the right to vote in the election of the members of Parliament for the county seats. It embraced far more of the adult male population than had the right to vote *after* the Reform Bill of 1832. The forty-shilling freehold had become so trivial by 1700 that it was scarcely possible to question the vote of any adult male who turned up at the hustings. The same had been true of seventeenth-century New England, when many of the states were creating the franchises for their own assemblies: the broad suffrages adopted by the states had their roots deep in the English tradition. And so did the methods of the management of the electorate. In neither country was it possible to dominate totally so broad an electorate and form it into a political machine, but that did not mean that influence lacked weight. In Virginia, as in Yorkshire, the gentry families—one has only to think of the Byrds—maintained a permanent political position generation after generation, as did the Fitzwilliams in Yorkshire. Again, the method of patronage employed feebly, and not very successfully, by the royal governors and officials in colonial days were not cast away by the Revolution. The use of the post office service as a source of political patronage was not an American invention. It was the common English practice of the eighteenth century. The irony of history lies in the fact that while England rejected many of its eighteenth-century political habits, America did not; rather was the system extended. Nor were the machine politics of Tammany Hall devoid of a British ancestry. They were a commonplace of urban politics of eighteenth-century England, and particularly deeply embedded in the treacherous poverty-ridden suburbs of London, such as Stepney.

Even the American Constitution is indelibly English, rooted in what the opposition to the English political establishment of the eighteenth century believed to be the pure form of the English constitution, in which the separation of powers was the keystone. And it was this false interpretation to which Montesquieu had given a wider currency—false because English legislature and the executive had never been separated; only politicians out of office believed that they had been and should be. The Founding Fathers, however, adopted what they felt to be the pure form of the English constitution. Again the senators—two from each state—reflected the English knights of the shire, always thought to be the wisest and most independent of members of Parliament. Tiny Rutland had as many knights of the shire as vast Yorkshire, just as Rhode Island was to have as many senators as New York State. And the powers of the president were those of an English monarch, deprived certainly of the capacity to give honors or create aristocrats, but in other ways more powerful, one might say more absolutist, than the English king, who, by 1782, could not choose even his junior ministers. Indeed, the American Constitution was the result of eighteenth-century British political attitudes and constitutional interpretations.

For more than two centuries America and Britain enjoyed a common political and social culture. When divergence came, it was brought about by the vast immigrations of the nineteenth century, but two centuries of common culture cannot be obliterated, particularly when it was the foundation upon which subsequent generations had to build. And already this common culture had learned how to assimilate what might so easily have become symbiotic enclaves of alien cultures. The great German influx in the 1740s and fifties into Pennsylvania, with its full complement of churches, schools, and newspapers, had made Franklin aware of what might happen. Although the German language and traditions lingered, and small communities persisted in maintaining their German culture, the majority were within a generation or two absorbed into the Anglo-American culture of Philadelphia; for success in trade, in manufacture, in banking and finance was possible only through the English language, a fact that ambitious young Germans quickly realized. And so by 1820 it was already clear, come Germans, Dutch, Italians, Greeks, Russians, and Armenians, that the language of government, the language of commerce, the language of culture would be English. Just as there would be no Balkanization of government, so there would be no Balkanization due to language. And language remains the basis of culture: it is, and must remain, the foundation of that special relationship between America and Britain, making for a natural cultural interchange that no other European nation can enjoy with America. An Englishman driving about America may feel confused, but he is quickly aware that he is a part of the English-speaking peoples and all that implies.

The Making of an American Culture: 1750-1800

by Neil Harris

The population of little more than one million who hugged the eastern coastline of North America in 1750 cannot be easily described. At a distance of two hundred years they seem equally remote and homogeneous, but it was a diverse grouping of people. The native American population had declined dramatically before the expansion of the Europeans, but the whites and the black slaves themselves represented a variety of cultures. The majority of whites, of course, were British in origin, although as Scots, Irishmen, Welshmen, and Englishmen, they retained strong traces of their ancestral identities. The remnants of older Dutch and Scandinavian settlements kept many of their special habits, while the Germans and Swiss, frequently members of pietistic religious sects, dominated whole regions.

Daily experiences bolstered distinctions. However small the area of the American colonies appears in relation to the present size of the United States,

A VIEW of NEW ORLEANS TAKEN FROM THE PLANTATION OF MAR

89

John L. Boqueta de Woiseri.
A View of New Orleans Taken from the Plantation of Marigny
Aquatint printed partially in color (only known state), 1803.

The Secretary of the Navy and Mrs. J. William Middendorf II.

it was considerable by eighteenth-century standards, with an enormous coastline stretching more than a thousand miles, or the distance from London to Rome. Natural obstacles—mountains, swamps, forests—and primitive roads made movement and communication difficult, even when colonists were separated by relatively small distances. Travel from Boston to New York, which today can be covered by automobile in four hours, required days of effort and heroic fortitude. Movement along the coast and on the many rivers that flowed inland was naturally easier than on land, but the coastline was treacherous, sometimes even impossible.

And yet, despite their ethnic diversity, regional isolation, and a range of differing occupational experiences, the white population of the American colonies did share certain traits that distinguish it from the contemporary world. In 1750 no rigid lines of separation compartmentalized the people's lives, cutting off the fine from the applied arts, high scholarship from folk culture, work from play, or religion from politics. At this distance it is the wholeness of their culture that seems most striking—the assumption that men of capacity and education could move across politics, medicine, business, law, farming, and even religion. Common concerns and relationships were localized and decentralized. Oral communication was more common than written; bureaucracies were small; work, even when nonagricultural, took place in informal and paternalistic settings; colleges and schools were few in number; land ownership was diffused; and religious uniformity, if no longer a legal principle, remained strongly attractive as an ideal.

But by 1750 there were signs that this traditional culture was about to experience change. Religious disputes, the dispersion of competence among large portions of the population, considerable experience with the possibilities of self-government, increasing economic wealth and complexity: all were beginning to produce their effects. In the next fifty years spheres of specialists and a new compartmentalization of human activities would come into being. Not only was a new nation-state to be created, presenting on its surface a novel definition of communal identity, but a new society was to accompany it. Its rules and ideals were to signal the development of modernization as a social process, of new rationalized attitudes toward work, politics, religion, and art. These countervailing strains—toward specialization of role and function, on the one hand, and toward homogeneity of belief, on the other—make up the counterpoint that dominated the institutional and intellectual life of

Americans in the second half of the eighteenth century. And this counterpoint is reflected in their material culture as well.

When they talk about culture, scholars mean many things. An old anthropological division of culture into three categories may be helpful here. There are, first, the artifacts of a people, the material constructions and technology that supply goods and services. Artifacts include tools, machines, clothing, furniture, housing, and ships—the shaped resources that sustain human life and contacts. Next, there are the sociofacts, those institutions and rituals that govern interpersonal behavior. Among a culture's sociofacts one finds its educational systems, its religious ceremonies, its political, legal, marriage, economic, status, and administrative systems, its philanthropy, and its codes of manners. Finally, there are the mentifacts, those attitudes, values, and abstractions that help to create religious belief, political philosophy, music, art, and ethics. Objects, rituals, and beliefs, together, form much of the substance of cultural history. Relationships tie these categories to one another, but do not guarantee their identical or even complementary evolution. Discrepancies among the mental and organizational attributes of a people, as well as among their artifacts, account for many of those moments of crisis that are labeled revolutions.

By 1750 such discrepancies had already appeared in North America. New experiences challenged inherited beliefs. Paradoxes abounded. Despite the material bounty of the continent, violence, hunger, warfare, and massacre had been major elements in daily living. Food seemed abundant, but people had starved; land was plentiful, but men fought bitterly over it; government, religious and secular, was all but invisible compared with its European counterparts, yet it was frequently challenged and occasionally overthrown. Mobility—economic, social, and geographic—was widespread, but it was also limited by specific and seemingly arbitrary decisions made thousands of miles away.

To a large extent, the strains were caused by the very strength of the English inheritance. Despite the undeniable contributions made by the aboriginal, black, and continental populations, it is remarkable how complete the dominance of British cultural values became. In establishing their towns, farms, and congregations, the first groups of British coastal settlers had managed to establish a spiritual hegemony over those who came after them, while swamping the small groups of continentals already on the scene. By 1750 the language the colonists spoke, the political traditions they referred to, and the physical ideals they set for themselves had become almost entirely British. And as the decades passed in the second half of the century, they became even more so.

This Britishness posed a problem which would never completely be outgrown by Americans. For revolutionary nationalism was bred in a setting of cosmopolitanism, nourished by the values and ideals that were best exemplified in the home culture of Great Britain. Again and again, patriots explained that they were rebelling in the name of British history and British freedom, that the goals they sought were the same goals that had animated loyal Englishmen since Magna Carta, and more recently, since the Glorious Revolution of 1688.

The arguments and the examples that Americans drew upon to defend their revolutionary actions were transmitted to them, in large part, through the pamphlets, sermons, tracts, and histories of Englishmen, aided, to be sure, by continental and classical sources.

The mother culture was as rich in material goods as it was in ideas. Try as they would, over the next centuries, to create their own physical forms, Americans would remain alternately impressed and angered by the achievements of a world they were trying to outgrow. Colonial cultures often fluctuate between defiance and adulation; simultaneously, they can resent and emulate the centers of power that dominate their own provincial existence. This ambivalence was clear during the eighteenth century. In 1750 western Europe—London and Paris more particularly—represented the acme of material achievement. In clothing, architecture, furniture, and painting, what was produced or consumed by Londoners and Parisians set the standard for the colonists; almost by definition such products seemed superior to their own. If the New World were adding content to human experience, style apparently remained the prerogative of the Old, for proper forms developed only through choice, and choice required a surplus of goods. Connoisseurs demonstrate their taste through selection; without a surplus of producers, they could not honor the best. American consumers were better at meeting basic needs than desires. London remained the great mart, the supermarket across the sea. And the colonists were mail-order customers, who often lacked even the most elementary of catalogues.

To those colonists who wished to associate themselves with the cosmopolitan culture of Europe, there were two routes open. One was to go to the Old World directly to make their purchases, or sometimes to rely on traveling friends and relatives. The correspondence of the gentry is filled with requests for objects described in trade advertisements or depicted in prints and pictures. In 1750 such purchases were seen to be individual affairs, dependent only upon ambition and one's pocketbook. There was assumed to be a correspondence between a large income and the display of fine objects. It was natural for wealthy colonials to own larger homes, better clothing, and finer horses than their less fortunate countrymen. In their daily lives rich Americans appropriated the traditional evidences of luxury. Before 1760 the character of this private taste stimulated little discussion. With British and continental examples so plentiful and polished, many colonists simply imported, or ordered copies. Originality was not necessarily a value to be cultivated for itself. If there was any overriding concern, it was value for money. And given the commercial or business-oriented background of many extravagant purchasers, such a concern was appropriate.

Of course, not all objects were imported. Artisans worked in the eastern cities, producing their own silver, glass, and furniture. Colonial printing presses produced not only newspapers and pamphlets but editions of the European philosophers and historians. This second route to expenditure, however, did not differ markedly from the first. Most colonial artisans were recent emigrants from Europe themselves, parading, in their advertisements, a knowledge of the latest modes that were capturing the fancy of European customers. The presence of a cabinetmaker in Newport or Philadelphia, or a silversmith in Boston, could mean only that European goods were being made at home, not that a novel provincial style was about to impose itself on the products of the atelier.

There were exceptions, of course. Creativity and innovation were not absent in American workrooms. The chief sources for American furniture designs, as the furniture historian John Kirk has concluded, were not the elaborate plans that master furnituremakers like Chippendale put in their pattern books, but simpler English objects. New materials, earlier training, and even purchaser preferences were factors in the creation of the American pieces. But these differences, as Kirk has pointed out, are often subtle and thus more apparent to the specialist than to the layman. Such creativity, however vibrant, was largely unselfconscious in character, the pride and talent of individual craftsmen whose commitment to quality and sense of personal skill led to interesting variations. But even those artisans faced problems. Given the lure of cheap, abundant land, it was difficult to attract apprentices or maintain craft skills within one's own family, which was the traditional way to guarantee a firm's survival and protect the standards and secrets of human callings.

By 1750 there were many levels of production and consumption in the colonies. Isolated farmers often made their own tools and furniture or purchased them from country carpenters, whose imitation of European styles resulted in original and interesting vernacular variations. But they did not buy the vernacular pieces out of pride in their originality. Rather, rural Americans acquired such pieces because the more expensive and elegant European or European-style furniture was not available to them. By general consent, the most sophisticated consumers of goods (and the few patrons of the arts) tended to be centered around the mercantile communities of the Atlantic coast or on the plantations of the Chesapeake and the Tidewater. What few colonial collections of books, paintings, and music existed were likely to be found in Boston, Newport, Philadelphia, New York, and Charleston, or on isolated plantations in Virginia and South Carolina. Southerners, whose rivers and cotton shipments put them in direct contact with city merchants, were producing an exotic but recognizable modification of the English squirearchy, while northern merchants were discovering new and exciting roles for themselves to play.

Eighteenth-century merchants had a lively sense of their social significance, not simply as economic men but as spearheads for international communication and supporters of polite culture. Because merchants benefited so heavily from the advantages of specialization—involved, as they were, with insurance brokers, lawyers, bookkeepers, shipbuilders, sailing crews, and retailers—they were quintessentially urban types, congregating in coffeehouses or in the exchanges they had built for their needs, eager for the latest newspapers, for reports of peace or war, gluts or shortages, storms and natural disasters. As merchants, they served many economic functions, from retailing to wholesaling to supplying capital for local improvements or manufacturing enterprises. The mercantile career put a premium on wide knowledge, good judgment, and varied experiences. In sum, flexibility and ingenuity often spelled the difference between bankruptcy and fortune-making.

Commerce also permitted its practitioners a good deal of free time. When ships were gone for months or years at a time, with retail outlets few and small, many merchants discovered they had time on their hands. Since they were familiar, either through travel or correspondence, with the traditional devices that their foreign counterparts had developed for making use of such time, they became enthusiastic supporters of libraries, cotillions, tea dances, clubs, debating and philosophical societies, coffeehouses, and the other institutions that resolved the problem of leisure in the eighteenth-century city.

There were, however, prouder traditions than this. Not so long before, the merchant princes of the Italian city-states, the burghers of the Netherlands, and the great men of the City of London had hired architects, painters, goldsmiths, and sculptors to enshrine their corporate glory and the mercantile independence that emblemized freedom. In England and America merchants drew upon the legacy of predecessors like the Medici and proclaimed themselves the friends of liberty and culture. But despite traditions connecting commerce with the arts, merchants faced problems. Artists were few in colonial America; the scale of wealth, the religious context, the diffusion of population, the absence of schools, all discouraged the development of the graphic and plastic arts. There was, in the colonies, wealth, ambition, and cultivation. The outlet they took, then, aside from the occasional commission of a portrait or the purchase of a landscape, was to create an art of living. Handsome houses, fine tables, wine cellars, silver, china, good horses: these formed the aspiration of northern merchants and southern planters. High achievers, resourceful, and self-confident, the colonial elites lived a life that was enhanced and softened by the artist, the upholsterer, and the dancing master.

Certainly those coming of age in the 1750s and sixties would form a revolutionary generation, but they nevertheless managed to attain a unique combination of heroism and domesticity. Whatever glorious achievements were soon to be wrought on the battlefield and in the cabinet room, the participants remained civilians; they moved through drawing rooms, taverns, and assembly chambers without, on the whole, changing their clothing, their manners, or their speech. Their sense of proportion remained constant through great events and small, and were once again a product of the nonspecialized world of preindustrial society. As civilians, however, what distinguished them from their military or royalist counterparts across the ocean was a commitment to comfortable living, excluding, on both ends of the scale, enormous pomp and desperate privation. Domestic artifacts, like domestic virtues, embodied a reasonable ideal. Objects of daily use provoked delight, perhaps because the physical civilization of America seemed so recent and so vulnerable. Wallpaper, carpeting, and linen were homely luxuries, but they represented the dual aspect of American commitments: to comfort, but to comfort within bounds.

There were dangers, of course. However domestic the scale of such pleasures, they were clearly intense. The purpose of accumulating money was to spend it on objects of luxury, and primitive passions for elegance were apt to produce a bondage to materialism. Indeed, before the Revolution, no other European society enjoyed as much comfort as Americans did.

But the appeal to arms in the 1770s cut across this realm of good living. Both in England and America men were convinced that the colonial desire for material pleasure and money-making provided both a cause for rebellion and the reason for dooming its success. The materialistic American was not born with the traveling millionaires of the nineteenth century or the middle-class tourists of the twentieth. In the 1760s and seventies the British government interpreted early resistance to legislation like the Stamp, Paper, Tea, and Hat acts as indications of selfish greed. Secure in the protection of British military power from the ambitions of the French and the assaults of the Indians, the colonists still seemed to resent making contributions to the staggering budget of the military establishment. The home government found the elaborate legal and historical arguments developed by colonial pamphleteers to be empty rationalizations; mercenary ambition seemed a more convincing cause for colonial actions.

In the colonies themselves, opponents of the trade and revenue acts despaired of weaning their countrymen away from devotion to the finer things of life. The most successful tactics for opposing the home government in the days preceding armed rebellion seemed to be those of nonimportation, refusal to consume the delights that British merchants and manufacturers dangled before hungry colonial eyes. Many individuals responded positively, opting for American instead of English producers. In 1765, when Samuel Powel, a colonial visiting England, decided to purchase some furniture there, his uncle, Samuel Morris, attempted to discourage him. "Household goods may be had here as cheap and as well made" as any England produced. And "in the humour the people are in here, a man is in danger of becoming Invidiously distinguished who buys anything in England which our Tradesmen can furnish."[1] Tories or stubborn consumers who insisted on their right to buy from England had their names published in newspapers and pamphlets, and occasionally suffered even worse fates. But the basic question remained. Would a population of comfortable merchants and farmers, whose chief feature had, until the 1770s, been a higher standard of living than most other parts of the world, accept the discipline and austerity that resistance demanded? And would that experience, even if successful, work a permanent change in colonial habits and values? Could a culture be created that was built on both a commitment to prosperity and a restraint in consumption?

The answers, as usual in historical inquiry, were ambiguous. Clearly, the American Revolution was a cultural as well as a political and military event. Clergymen and political leaders appealed for support on idealistic and unselfish grounds; the language of the Declaration of Independence echoed, in its concern with historical principles and legal rights, much of the discussion of the previous ten years. The new republic declared itself a rescue operation in the name of human liberty, pursued and tortured throughout the world. Americans ticked off the litany of departed republics one by one: Athens, Holland, Venice, Denmark, and now England. The presence of a king did not automatically invalidate republican government; but with a king above the laws, whose subjects were not secure in their historic and constitutional rights, a government would certainly lose its republican status. When Americans sought explanations for the death of freedom, in the ancient as well as the modern world, they found them not in the actions of tyrants, for such were always to be expected, but in the manners and morals of the population itself. Virtue, Americans argued, was the cement of liberty. No people could mount a revolution without it; and no people could retain a free government unless they remained virtuous. The word *virtue* implied a constellation of personal qualities—honesty, forbearance, prudence, piety, bravery—but a free government, in its collective manifestations, also demanded restraint and temperateness. Mercenary ambitions could and did make men slaves of their passions, as well as easy victims for a despot's bribes. The revolutionary and the republican had to be singleminded in their pursuit of liberty, even to the point of sacrificing those elegances of life for which colonials had so much affection. Before the Revolution what distinguished Americans from Europeans was a level of material opportunity, an abundance of natural resources, and room for small farmers and mechanics to make a living. After the Revolution the distinguishing marks were supposed to be different: a dedication to certain ideas, a holy conformity to

virtuous goals and behavior, a collective will that could demonstrate the possibilities of self-government and popular sovereignty. True revolutionaries, then, sought cultural reformation, the exaltation of spiritual values, and the abandonment of materialism as a natural trait.

The easiest way of demonstrating adherence to this goal was through denial. The nonimportation agreements of the seventies were only a rehearsal for the sacrifices entailed by wartime interruptions of trade. The British cornucopia no longer poured out its wares. Necessities as well as luxuries were in short supply, and to bolster morale, revolutionary leaders paraded simple poverty as a badge of determination and difference. In choosing republicanism as a political ideal, Americans discovered a style of life as well, a form that comprehended not merely their way of government but their mode of dress, of building, of furnishing, and of writing.

Since restraint was not enough to indicate the power of this new style of thinking and its influence upon artifacts as well as sociofacts, a more active principle was necessary. And so, into fashion crept the iconography of the new republicanism—the eagles, the stars and stripes, the mystical "13," the pantheon of heroes headed by Washington, the rattlesnakes and beavers, the corncobs and tobacco husks, the fasces and arrows—a compound of domestic, military, classical, and natural symbols that found expression also in the flags, seals, coinage, and ceremonies of the young state. No sanctuary was too private, no arena too public to be immune from physical evidences of commitment to the cause: theatre curtains and proscenium arches were decorated with revolutionary scenes; silver and china, wallpaper and tavern signs, all bore the marks. For a brief moment during and after the Revolutionary War, it seemed that style and substance had united in America. The success of the Revolution revealed to the colonies a unity that, if more apparent than real, had nonetheless survived the strains of war and occupation. The cause that required sacrifice had triumphed; the first generation of leaders had proven equal to the task, both militarily and diplomatically. A sense of new beginnings lay everywhere in the early 1780s— newness in politics, religion, education, even in spelling and natural science.

But gradually it became clear that newness was not easily preserved, that the success of the Revolution was more complex than the slogans of the early patriots. British merchants, who hurriedly shipped their goods to the reopened ports, found their old customers hungrier than ever for the trappings of luxury. Although Britain was the enemy country, British craftsmen and British culture were equally admired, and newspaper advertisements again proclaimed the eagerness of New York and Philadelphia cabinetmakers and upholsterers to associate themselves with European sophistication. So far as stylistic change was concerned, the American Revolution seemed a minor matter. Much more dramatic were contemporaneous developments in France. The presence of not only an artist community but a rich supply of the relics of the *ancien régime* made possible more fundamental and radical departures from the styles of the past. The revolutionary fêtes, the paintings of David, the neoclassical furniture and coiffures, all put America's paltry efforts at redesigning to shame. American efforts were less dramatic, less comprehensive, and less rapid. Both as a nation and as a cause, America had to choose between a new stylistic uniformity and an older, more tolerant, and more heterogeneous pattern. Would the American style, in fact, be something novel and unprecedented? Or would it simply be a selection of the best the world could offer, combined and synthesized with a freedom appropriate to a democratic republic?

For a time, romantic revivalism, particularly the neoclassical, provided a meeting place for the varied interests and groups that made up the young country. The need for unified symbols was great. Regions grew farther apart in their economic organization, class lines became more recognizable, governmental establishments grew, wealth and poverty increased, and concentrations of men and capital replaced the smaller organizations of commerce and manufacturing. While all this was happening in the early and mid-nineteenth century, homes, banks, public buildings, and even churches displayed common stylistic elements. How could one eat one's cake and remain on a diet simultaneously? How could the nation consume objects of luxury and proclaim its allegiance to restraint? By suffusing the material world with moralism and nationalism, by insisting on the search for a national style in every segment of its culture, and by arguing that artists, writers, and craftsmen must bend their efforts to meet didactic needs. As the decades passed, these demands became more strident. In the eighteenth century such didacticism had not yet reached its apogee. Men like Jefferson wished their countrymen to learn more about art and architecture in order to exhibit good taste and avoid barbarism. A display of sensibility could redeem republicanism from charges of vulgarity and indicate a commitment to universal truths.

Thus, during the eighteenth century, physical culture in America remained harnessed to traditional values. The Revolution was tied to a worldwide enlightenment that did not yet require a specific American style in order to be validated. In this realm—in the objects and art works that can be displayed in exhibitions—the fact of the American Revolution is not easily observable. Apart from a few obvious symbols that creep into art and artifacts, older European orientations do not disappear. However much values and ideas changed, objects and, to a slightly lesser extent, the social structure remained tied to an earlier period.

Certainly the connoisseur's eye and the historian's vision can both detect stylistic unities in the American objects. It would be arbitrary to deny *any* evidence of a national orientation. Students of painting, furniture, architecture, and technology have all pointed to certain elements that can be said to mark America's early national arts and crafts. But the distinctiveness, compared with others in the national experience, is muted, and the varying rates of change—among artifacts, mentifacts, and sociofacts within American culture—are suggestive. They point to patterns that were to become characteristic of American life. For during the past 150 years there has been a special intensity in the American search for stylistic forms in literature, architecture, painting, and drama. This intensity was a legacy of the Revolutionary disjunction, the contrast between the newness of the political ideology and the inescapable continuity of art and design. Such continuity was spatial as well as temporal. American forms changed as fashion dictated. But since the changes were often tied to European modifications, foreign visitors, however biased, frequently found them derivative and superficial.

In retrospect, then, Americans seem materialists manqués, ironically enough damned as voracious consumers by cultures whose devotion to appetite was even greater. The moment when form and content seemed about to correspond—during the seventies and eighties—had apparently fled forever. The Revolution That Never Was is the label that might well be applied to declarations of our cultural independence.

And yet there was newness, there was innovation, there was a distinctiveness in American manners and institutions. When it came to education, penology, family structure, and religious behavior, Americans were in fact shaping a new culture. Its expressions, however, were often subtle and occurred in places where historians and commentators were slow to look. Moreover, it took some time for the results to become clear. The making of an American culture, unlike the making of an American political philosophy, could not be the work of a single generation. In 1800 this revolution still lay in the future. But its impact and its character combine to form a subject perhaps as important as the political event which this bicentennial is meant to celebrate. We stand, perhaps, at a new disjunction in American life; only now it is the ideology that has not moved as fast as the artifacts. And it is, again, a question of whether it should.

Style in American Art: 1750-1800

by Jules David Prown

The most complete and dramatic stylistic change in the entire history of American art occurred during the period covered by this exhibition, the years divided by the watershed of the War of Independence. In general terms, the transition in style was from rococo in the third quarter of the eighteenth century, the end of the colonial period, to neoclassical during the years of the establishment of the Federal Republic in the last quarter of the century. This stylistic shift, almost a purge, was intensified by the abnormal delay in the transmission of styles from Europe to America caused by the war. Acceptance after the war of the neoclassical style, shockingly different from what conservative Americans were accustomed to, was eased by the fact that it was fashionable in Europe and represented a renewal of transatlantic cultural links. Moreover, and perhaps more important, moral fervor and intense political feelings in post-Revolutionary America created a receptive intellectual climate for the new style.

The English colonies in America during the third quarter of the eighteenth century enjoyed at last prosperity and security. Force of arms in the French and Indian War, and the Treaty of Paris (1763), provided secure borders. Flourishing commercial activity generated wealth that added to the sweetness of life, especially for the urban rich, who were the primary patrons of art. The dominant rococo style was derived from European (mostly English) pattern books and imported art objects, or promulgated by immigrant artists and craftsmen. American rococo objects differ from their European prototypes in their greater simplicity, a penchant for planarity, an emphasis on the expressive quality of form itself, and a reluctance to let surface decoration override or disguise structure. Even the most elaborate rococo pieces made in America, such as the Joseph Richardson teakettle and stand (146), seem simple in comparison with high-style French or English examples.

The rococo style in America as in Europe revels in the curve and reverse curve. Surfaces move in and out; outlines are irregular; objects penetrate and are penetrated by ambient space. A Philadelphia Chippendale chair of the third quarter of the century (103) has a pierced splat through which space flows, while its knees protrude and the ears of the crest thrust up and out rather than flow directly into the back posts. The facade of an American Georgian house such as Mount Pleasant in Philadelphia (fig. 2) or the Craigie-Vassall-Longfellow House in Cambridge, Massachusetts, (fig. 3) is marked by a forward projection of the central bay which gives a sense of plasticity and mass, reinforced by strong articulation of the window and door surrounds and by quoining or pilasters at the corners. In American colonial art and architecture of the third quarter of the century there is delight in the substantiality of things—weight, mass, texture, and solidity.

John Singleton Copley's portraits of *Mr. and Mrs. Isaac Smith* (13 and 14) epitomize the values of the American colonies on the eve of the Revolution in their celebration of worldly goods and success. The mahogany side chair Isaac Smith is seated in, his plum-colored suit, the silver standish on the baize-covered table and damask curtain in the background, represent goods this successful Boston merchant has accumulated. In a Puritan-descended society getting rich was no sin; it remained a positive sign of God's favor. In the painting the style informs the meaning; deeply saturated colors enhance the sense of richness and *luxe;* sober hues bespeak seriousness of purpose; crisp contrasts of light and dark suggest decisiveness of character. The white-clad legs form an arrow directing the viewer's attention to Smith's head, as do the lines of gold buttons and the arc of the quill pen. The head, the central fact of the portrait, is turned away, and Smith stares off into space rather than back at the viewer. Here is a man to be looked up to, to be respected. Mrs. Smith is also imbedded in luxurious materials, and the colors are fully as rich as in her husband's portrait, although brighter and more lively. The feeling is more open and relaxed. She sits in an upholstered armchair rather than a spare sidechair, her dress is informal, the background opens up to a lush river landscape, and the ripe bunch of grapes in her lap suggests fecundity. The sitter makes eye contact with the viewer, and there is greater warmth and intimacy than in the pendant portrait. Like her husband, Mrs. Smith is productive and successful, but her arena is the home rather than the world of commerce, and her image is that of the *materfamilias.*

Reflecting similar worldly values, colonial domestic arts were solidly constructed with a delight in the materials used. Silver and furniture are substantial and weighty; silver is hammered in and out, furniture is heavily carved. Decorative details are three-dimensional, existent plastic facts in their own right. Motifs are often organic forms derived from nature—leaves, shells, ropelike

Fig. 2
Mount Pleasant, Philadelphia,
ca. 1761.

Fig. 3
Craigie-Vassall-Longfellow House
Cambridge, Massachusetts, 1759.

13
John Singleton Copley
Isaac Smith
Oil on canvas, 1769. Yale
University Art Gallery; gift of
Maitland Fuller Griggs, B.A. 1896.

14
John Singleton Copley
Mrs. Isaac Smith
Oil on canvas, 1769. Yale
University Art Gallery; gift of
Maitland Fuller Griggs, B.A. 1896.

gadroons, claw and ball feet—replicating in wood or silver solid, natural shapes.

Benjamin West's *Agrippina Landing at Brundisium With the Ashes of Germanicus* (**19**) of 1768 stands as the prophet and the paradigm of the change that was to befall the arts in America in the last quarter of the eighteenth century. Born and raised in Philadelphia, West left America in 1760 at the age of twenty-two to study art in Italy. He was there during the stimulating years when direct contact was being made with the past through the excavations at Herculaneum and Pompeii, the digging up of antique sculpture at sites throughout Italy, and the measuring and publication of Greek and Roman architectural ruins and reconstructions. West's *Agrippina* reflects the influence of the new knowledge of antiquity and its significance within the context of Enlightenment thought.

The painting represents the scene described in Tacitus when Agrippina returns home carrying the ashes of her assassinated husband in a cinerary urn. Accompanied by her children and entourage, Agrippina bears herself with dignity, composure, and grace. Although Germanicus was a hero who gave his life for his country in a far-off land, Agrippina is the heroic figure here. Her calm courage is presented by West as an inspiration and model for the eighteenth-century viewer. The picture is a sermon in paint. In order to make the scene as realistic as possible, West tells the Roman story in Roman terms. The central grisaille group of Agrippina and her children is derived from a detail of the procession of the senators and their wives from the *Ara Pacis* relief of 14 B.C.[1] The building in the background is based on the

palace of Diocletian, published in accurate measured drawings by Robert Adam only a few years before the picture was painted. By being as realistic as he could, West stressed that what is depicted had really happened to real people, and could be emulated by eighteenth-century man. He demonstrated in his painting the Enlightenment conviction that man is inherently good; that in ancient days human beings had achieved a high level of morality, justice, courage, beauty, and so on; that it was possible in the eighteenth century to re-create a society as admirable as ancient Rome and Greece. Thus *Agrippina* was not as innocuous as it seems. The picture suggested the possibility of social improvement, social improvement implied political change, and political change could mean, and in the case of America and France did mean, revolution.

West drove his message home forcefully in *The Death of General Wolfe* (1771) (**20**). Wolfe has given his life in the service of Great Britain. *Dulce et decorum est pro patria mori.* The knowledgeable English viewer would not miss overtones of martyrdom implicit in the composition of the central group, suggesting traditional Christian scenes of the Deposition and Lamentation, or compositional elements recalling the Crucifixion, such as the wounded officer on the left recoiling like a swooning Virgin Mary or the grieving figure like John the Evangelist in the right foreground.[2] Nor would the point have been missed of the red Indian, a "noble savage," a natural and uncorrupted man who contemplates and understands Wolfe's sacrifice. Of primary importance is the fact that the figures are in modern dress. West did

19
Benjamin West
*Agrippina Landing at Brundisium
with the Ashes of Germanicus*
Oil on canvas, 1768.
Yale University Art Gallery;
gift of Louis M. Rabinowitz.

20
Benjamin West
The Death of General Wolfe
Oil on canvas, 1771.
Her Majesty The Queen.

not follow tradition by putting Wolfe in a toga to indicate that he was worthy of the ancients. Rather, he inverted the argument, emphasizing that acts as heroic and noble as those of the ancients did in fact occur in the eighteenth century, that it was possible to equal in modern times the deeds and accomplishments of antiquity.

The America that emerged at the end of the War of Independence brought into being a political system based on Enlightenment thought, imbued with veneration for man's reason and his capacity through its use to create a better world, and with a vision of classical antiquity as the prototype and model of that world. In independent America after the Revolution, Thomas Jefferson considered a Roman temple in France, the Maison Carrée at Nîmes, the appropriate model for a seat of government of the new regime, replicating it for the State Capitol of Virginia at Richmond. The Republic may have lacked an emperor, but it had senators; the landscape eventually became peppered with place names like Athens, Rome, Sparta, Corinth, Troy, and Syracuse; clothing, hairstyles, and of course the arts were transformed into antique modes: all testify to the intensity and completeness of the transformation in American thought and values that took place in the wake of independence.

American neoclassical objects, things made in the last quarter of the century, for the most part after the war had ended, reflect a value system dramatically different from that of the colonial world. The neoclassical style had developed vigorously in England and France during the third quarter of the century, but made virtually no headway in far-off and stylistically conservative America prior to the Revolution. After the war, however, the new style was embraced in America, cautiously at first and only by the most sophisticated, but eventually the flood of neoclassicism was in full tide. American neoclassicism differs from its European sources not in kind but in degree. The broad sweep of stylistic change and the purity of style that emerged echo the remarkable thoroughness of America's transition from colony to nation. As Bernard Bailyn has observed, "the political and social ideas of the European Enlightenment [were] more universally accepted in eighteenth-century America than in Europe, they were more completely and more permanently embodied in the formal arrangements of state and society."[3] The same is true of the acceptance of neoclassicism; indeed the stylistic change illuminates and makes more immediately real for us the nature and sweep of the political and social change. Curves give way to straight lines, substance to abstraction. Decorative details on furniture and silver shift from natural to geometrical forms—circles, rectangles, squares, ovals, et cetera. These designs spring from the mind of man; they are the artifacts of reason. Where identifiable objects do appear, they are pregnant with ideology—eagles, urns, helmets, and shields all carry classical connotations. Inlay replaced carving in furniture. The palpable replication of natural forms gave way to two-dimensional abstractions—an eagle (fig. 4), an urn, a bellflower (130)—pictures of things were used in place of the thing itself. Carved gadrooning on the skirt of a table, which breaks light striking it into highlight and shadow, was replaced by bands of alternating bits of light and dark wood inlay that

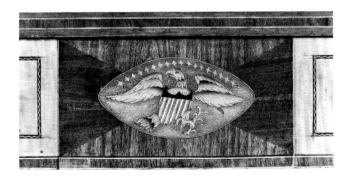

Fig. 4
Inlaid eagle from a card table
Boston, ca. 1800. Yale
University Art Gallery; Mabel
Brady Garvan Collection.

are an abstraction, a picture, of the same visual effect. In silver, three-dimensional repoussé elaboration yielded to plain surfaces embellished with two-dimensional engraving or bright cutting along the rims, doing for silver what inlay does for furniture. The surfaces of silver objects became smooth and taut, eventually with assistance from technology when sheet silver became available that could simply be bent into shapes and joined. A similar clear and precise surface effect was achieved by sliced veneers applied to furniture, and even by the planar brick facades of houses like Gore Place in Waltham, Massachusetts (fig. 5), into which apertures for windows and doors were cut directly without the heavy enframements of Georgian architecture.

The intellectualizing and abstracting process affects the very substantiality of American neoclassical objects. A rolled silver vessel is much lighter than its hammered predecessor. A neoclassical chair is much easier to lift and carry than a rococo chair. It also breaks more easily, but for Americans after independence the value of having a chairback shaped like an urn or a shield outweighed practical considerations.

American neoclassical art is a ballet of geometrical shapes: square and round plinths, oval inlays, rectangular doors, triangular pediments. The smooth surfaces of all categories of neoclassical objects created closed forms sealed off from their surrounding space. Geometrical forms by definition had precise boundaries, as did the recurring urn, shield, and helmet shapes. The unbroken surfaces not only isolate each object from its surrounding space, but also keep it aloof from the viewer as well.

The Founding Fathers of the American Republic, their thinking shaped by the Enlightenment, the Age of Reason, had a deep distrust of the sensuous and emotional appeal of art. For example, John Adams's "emotional response to the arts, his driving, uncontrollable, sensuous appreciation of the physical things around him . . . was immediate, it changed according to his mood, it surprised him, and more than anything else it frightened him." Adams associated "the love of the sensuous, to which he was himself prone, with decadence and frivolity."[4] In 1778 he wrote his wife from Paris, commenting on the richness and magnificence of Paris and Versailles, "I cannot help suspecting that the more elegance, the less virtue, in all times and countries."

A taste for art could lead to a taste for luxury and the unleashing of the emotional and irrational side of life. This imposed upon Adams and his contemporaries the need for rigid self-restraints in order to focus on the important business at hand. The difference between a late colonial world that celebrated the physical or material things of life and the Federal Republic's more austere value system is suggested even in picture frames. The original carved and gilded rococo frame on the Isaac Smith portrait (fig. 6) penetrates and is penetrated by the space in which it exists, linking the painted world of Isaac Smith and the real world in which the painting and the viewer exist. A classical frame (fig. 7) is characteristically a perfect geometrical form, cutting off with a sharp clean line the painted figure from his or her surroundings. The portrait is aloof, and the interaction between the painted figure and the surrounding world is only visual, not physical.

Fig. 5
Gore Place
Waltham, Massachusetts, 1805.

The austere surfaces of classical objects—silver, furniture, architecture, even picture frames—offer little in the way of tactile or seductive sensuous appeal; they are to be embraced by the eye rather than the hand. Their appeal is more abstract, intellectual, and rational—geometrical shapes and iconographically loaded motifs—directed to the mind rather than to the emotions. Whereas the third quarter of the century reveled in the material stuffs of the world, the fourth quarter feared the debasing effects of luxury; it opted for appeal to the eye and mind in preference to touch and "feeling." The essential opposition between the ornate rococo of the third quarter of the century and the restrained neoclassicism of the last quarter of the century resides in the polarity between emotion and reason. The exuberance of rococo objects increasingly disturbed the post-Revolutionary sensibility, suggesting reliance upon feelings, instability, possible irrationality, whereas the intellectually controlled aloofness of neoclassical objects represented the dominion of the mind. They embodied the premise that as in furniture or silver or architecture man could apply his rational powers to solve problems of design, so too could he use his mind to create an ideal society. The task of building a new nation, with reference to the model of classical antiquity, stood at the top of the list of American priorities. And American art was transformed from a source of sensory gratification during the late colonial period into a safe and controlled form of visual expression as the neoclassical style was enthusiastically embraced during the early years of the Republic.

Fig. 6
John Singleton Copley
Isaac Smith, 1769.
Yale University Art Gallery;
gift of Maitland Fuller Griggs,
B.A. 1896, L.H.D. 1938. (Color, p. 34.)

Fig. 7
Gilbert Stuart
Mrs. Richard Yates, 1793-1794.
The National Gallery of Art;
Andrew W. Mellon Collection,
1940. (Color, p. 110.)

The Metamorphoses of Britannia

by Frank H. Sommer

I think of both the art historian and the archaeologist as essentially the same combination of detective, solicitor, barrister, and judge, the great difference between them, of course, being their clientele. This essay—which might be called a case study, rather than a survey—concerns the investigation into a particular example of the interrelationship of the art and thought of Great Britain and her colony of Massachusetts in the eighteenth century. The case is that of the English Whig and art patron Thomas Hollis (the fifth of that name) and his attempts to promote the civil and religious liberties of the English-speaking Protestants of the eighteenth century through iconographic propaganda—in other words, to spread what I have called "the Gospel of British liberty" in Massachusetts. For in this episode lay some little-known but important seeds of the American Revolution.

In 1753 Thomas Hollis V and his friend Thomas Brand returned to England from the Continent, where they had spent some four years on two Grand Tours. Both were rich dissenters who, in all but their religion, led the life of the wealthy English gentlemen of their day. Both had country estates. Both lived, at least part of the year, in London. Both collected works of art—especially Roman and Greek antiquities—and both were patrons and friends of contemporary artists and architects. In their circle were architects Sir William Chambers, James Stuart, and Robert Adam, the sculptor Joseph Wilton, Sir Joshua Reynolds, and the Florentine painter John Baptist Cipriani. However, Hollis and Brand differed from most of their wealthy contemporaries not only in their failure to belong to the Established

Church but also in their politics. They were radical Whigs, or what Professor C. Robbins has called "Commonwealth Men." That is, their thinking, especially Hollis's, was based on the works of the leading writers on politics in the period of the British Commonwealth—and, primarily, on Algernon Sidney and John Milton.

It was Hollis's firm conviction that there were only three countries in all Europe in which civil liberty flourished in his day: the Netherlands, Switzerland, and—above all—England. For him the British constitution and the Protestant succession of the House of Hanover were the safeguards of what he called "the principles of British Liberty," and for many years he both idolized William Pitt as the guardian of those principles and detested the memory of Robert Walpole as their corruptor.

After his return to England from his tour, Hollis set out on a deliberate campaign of propaganda on behalf of the principles of British liberty. He did so not only by editing and republishing many of the classic "Commonwealth" and Whig texts on the subject (most notably John Locke's *Two Treatises on Government*) but also by "planting" squibs and news stories in the press, by employing writers (the best known was Samuel Johnson) to produce pamphlets of a political nature, and by attempting to sponsor legislation favorable to his cause in Parliament. My concern here, however, is not Hollis's verbal propaganda but his self-conscious efforts to design visual material on behalf of British Liberty. To do so, he enlisted the help of Chambers, Wilton, and Cipriani, and formed a "stable" of less well-known artists and craftsmen to carry out his plans. That is,

he himself conceived the "Idea" of the work (in G. P. Bellori's sense of that term) and then used the skills of some of his artist friends (and/or employees) to execute his concepts—under his own very close supervision. The style he encouraged and helped to develop for his purposes was in part "Burlingtonian," but also in part a style transitional to neoclassicism.

While Hollis did all he could to promote British Liberty at home, in Holland, and in Switzerland, he firmly believed that it would flourish best in British North America. His greatest efforts, therefore, were devoted to its promotion in what are now the United States. In 1754 his interest had been aroused by a sermon published by a young Congregational minister of Boston named Jonathan Mayhew. On "The Lord's Day after the 30th of January, 1749–50," Mayhew had preached a sermon called *A Discourse concerning Unlimited Submission and Non-Resistance to the Higher Powers* . . . (Boston, 1750). It was preached soon after the feast of the martyrdom of King Charles I, and its theme was that resistance to the tyranny of the British Monarch was justified if he violated the principles of British Liberty. In that American sermon Hollis found inspiration for one of the main themes of his visual propaganda. A second major theme was supplied by two ancient Roman coins—both commemorating the efforts of Caesar's murderer, Brutus, to restore Roman republican liberty. A third theme, the image of *Britannia-Libertas*, was inspired first by two coins—the ordinary English penny of Hollis's day, and a British sestertius of Antoninus Pius—as well as by a painting of Roma found on the grounds of the

Fig. 8
Lorenz Natter
Design for the Hollis cameo of
"British Liberty Triumphant"
Pen and ink. Houghton Library,
Harvard University.

Palazzo Barberini in Rome.

To celebrate his loves—England, its land, its language, its literature, its accomplishments "by deeds of peace," its Protestantism, and, above all, its tradition of liberty—Hollis composed not poems but pictures. He, as I said, invented the "Ideas," "images," or symbols, and his various artist-assistants made the actual, physical works of art. He provided the *theoria*, they the *practica*. For example, Lorenz Natter, a German gem-cutter, provided the first physical icon for the Hollis cult of British Liberty, a seated goddess triumphant over Charles I (fig. 8). At an unknown date before 1759, Hollis had an engraver cut some book-binding tools to stamp leather-bound volumes with decorative figures in gold, which, to Hollis's mind at least, symbolized in one way or another the contents of the pages inside the bindings. The first of the *Britannia* symbols of this kind was based on the contemporary penny (a design that originated during the reign of Charles II). With an olive branch in her right hand and a spear in her left, *Britannia* sat on a barely visible globe with a shield by her side, bearing on its field the crosses of Saints George and Andrew placed on an asymmetrical scrolled cartouche.

Between 1759 and 1761 his friend Cipriani designed a set of nineteen bookbinding tools for Hollis (fig. 9a). Cipriani seems to have based the *Britannia* in this set directly on a sestertius of Antoninus Pius, which clearly showed a female figure seated on a large globe, accompanied by an oval shield and holding a military standard in her right hand and a staff or scepter in her left. The first Cipriani design used the olive branch of the

penny in Liberty's right hand, but capped the rod of her left with the *pilleus libertatis* (liberty cap) of the ancient Romans. In this image, then, like the Natter *Britannia*, the attributes of Britannia and Liberty were fused, but an image of Liberty (fig. 9b) based on a coin of Nerva was used as a separate personification as well. By 1761 Cipriani had changed the image of Britannia once again. In this version Britannia's hand was made to hold a trident, whereas Liberty continued to hold a staff, or *hasta*, in her left hand and a liberty cap in her right, as in the coin of Nerva.

The most elaborate of the images of *Britannia* and *Libertas* worked out by Hollis and Cipriani was a large oil painted in chiaroscuro in 1761. We unfortunately lack the painting, but we do have several drawings for it, as well as an etching (fig. 10) based on the drawings and, possibly, on the painting. Based on an ancient Roman painting of Roma, this *Britannia* again sits on a throne, like that portrayed by Natter, rather than on a globe. In her left hand is a *hasta*, but her right holds not a liberty cap but a figure of *Libertas*, holding the cap in one hand and a cornucopia in the other. This latter personification was based on the coin of Antoninus Pius mentioned above.

Libertas made her next appearance in the Hollis iconography in 1765, when Hollis, Cipriani, and Basire used a *Libertas* coin honoring Brutus to pay due homage to the Whig historian, Mrs. Catharine Macaulay (fig. 11).

Both the *Libertas* and *Britannia* of the book-binding stamps were used until 1764, when a fire broke out in the shop of the binder employed by Hollis and destroyed the binding tools. It is not

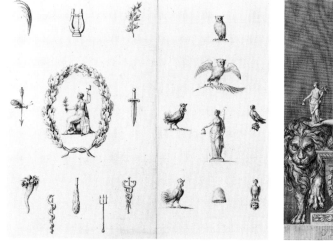

Fig. 9 a and b
John Baptist Cipriani
Designs for bookbinding tools for Thomas Hollis V. Wash drawings, 1759-1761. Houghton Library, Harvard University.

Fig. 10
John Baptist Cipriani
Etching after "O fair Britannia Hail." 1760. Houghton Library, Harvard University.

Fig. 11
James Basire
Engraving after a drawing by John Baptist Cipriani. 1767. Based on a coin of M. Junius Brutus. Houghton Library, Harvard University.

known precisely when the tools for the two goddesses were replaced, but it is certain from the Hollis diary that by 1767 he had received tools for these designs and fifteen others as replacements for the first tools designed by Cipriani. In the same year, 1767, the trident- and *pilleus*-bearing *Britannia* appeared in a portrait of Hollis by Cipriani. The goddess is in the lower right on the plinth of the obelisk bearing the Hollis bust (fig. 12).

By 1768 the *Britannia-Libertas* image was being used by artists other than Cipriani. In that year the young American painter Charles Willson Peale used the image, in standing form, in his allegorical portrait of Pitt. Paul Revere, in the same year, used a variant in his *Collidimur-Frangimur* emblem, to which he added a crown, seated *Britannia* on a throne, reverted to the penny's cartouche shield, and dropped the trident. Her companion, America, was a kind of seated *Libertas,* but with the *hasta* carrying the *pilleus.* No image resembling this is to be found in Hollis's source books for the symbolism of Liberty. Presumably the invention was Revere's own.

At an unknown date, unrecorded in the diaries, Cipriani designed, and Francesco Bartolozzi engraved, a large picture (fig. 13) which, even more clearly than the book-stamp design of 1759–1761, was derived from the sestertius of Antoninus Pius. In it there was a reversion to the Cipriani book-stamp design insofar as the olive branch attribute was included. But the globe on which Britannia sat was clearly emphasized—as in the Roman source—probably to underscore, as John Yonge Akerman wrote in 1844 of the original Roman coin, that "the figure seated on a globe doubtless typifies

the subjugated province [of Britain]."[1] The figure of *Britannia-Libertas,* beautifully drawn, is probably the most simple and handsome of all the Hollis designs. Although it may have been produced after Hollis's death, it is to be hoped that he was alive long enough to have had the pleasure of seeing it. The print was published in the Reverend John Disney's *Memoirs* of Thomas Brand-Hollis (Thomas V's major heir and executor) in 1808. But, as we shall see, it must have been first published some years before that.

There is among American coins a group which until now has not undergone the scrutiny of the iconographer. The earliest of these is a Massachusetts halfpenny, thought to be unique, and now in the numismatic collection at Evergreen House, Baltimore, Maryland (fig. 14). The coin is dated "1776" and traditionally is ascribed to Paul Revere. The reverse bears a triple-headed figure which may be related to those in the tradition discussed by Erwin Panofsky in his 1969 posthumously published study of Titian.[2] It is surrounded with the legend: "State of Massa ½ D." However, it is the obverse (fig. 14) that concerns us here.

The inscription running round the central figure of the obverse reads: "Goddess Liberty." Separated from the rest of the composition by a raised bar is the date "1776." Another similar coin cannot be located but was represented in a linecut on the title page of Sylvester S. Crosby's *Early Coins of America.* It differs from the above-mentioned coin largely in the use of the old Massachusetts symbol of the pine tree on the reverse side. In it the image of Liberty is surrounded by

Fig. 12
John Baptist Cipriani
Double Portrait of Thomas Hollis
Engraving, 1767.
Author's collection.

Fig. 13
F. Bartolozzi
Engraving after a design by John Baptist Cipriani of *Britannia-Libertas.* Date unknown. Houghton Library, Harvard University.

Fig. 14 a and b
Massachusetts half-penny
Design attributed to Paul Revere.
The Evergreen House Foundation,
The Johns Hopkins University.

the legend "Liberty and Virtue." It also is dated 1776.

The apparently unique strike of the coin at Evergreen House (fig. 14) shows a draped female figure seated exactly in reverse of the Hollis-Cipriani goddesses of the book stamps and the British penny design. The goddess now is perched rather perilously on the very edge of the globe—in this case clearly indicated as a globe of the earth. The *hasta* now is held in the right hand, but the left does not hold a branch of olive. Rather, a liberty cap hangs down from it, as in the Cipriani design of *Libertas* (fig. 8). The author of the halfpenny, whether Revere or someone else, combined the attributes of Cipriani's *Britannia* with his *Libertas* to produce a new image of the "Goddess Liberty." An additional innovation—for which I have found no precedent—is the small animal (dog?) at the feet of the goddess. So far as I have been able to discover, the two coins of 1776 are the third and fourth examples in American art of the use of the Hollis-Cipriani *Britannia-Libertas* image. On the first-mentioned coin of 1776 the shield of *Britannia* was dropped, as it was in "America in Distress" (a Revere political satire of 1775). On it *Britannia-Libertas* is shown with an oval shield marked with the English and Scots crosses and the *hasta* and *pilleus,* and is accompanied by the bow and arrow of the Indian maiden so often used to signify America—and so used by Revere in his *Obelisk* engraving of 1766. Were the American images mentioned above to be arranged in "evolutionary form," the sequence would run as follows:

1766
Obelisk [Brigham, Pl. 6][3] (fig. 15)
  a. *America:* Indian maiden with bow and arrows
  b. *Liberty:* Robed female with *hasta* and *pilleus,* winged in one form, unwinged in the other

1768
Frangimur-Collidimur [Brigham, Pl. 12] (fig. 16)
  a. *Britannia-Libertas: hasta* and *pilleus* "penny" *Britannia,* shield, no globe, but seated, crowned
  b. *America:* Seated, with *hasta* and falling *pilleus*

1774
Portraits of *John Hancock and Samuel Adams* [Brigham, Pls. 34 and 34a] (figs. 17 and 18)
  a. *Liberty: hasta* and *pilleus*
The Able Doctor [Brigham, Pl. 35] (fig. 19)
  a. *Britannia:* Oval shield and spear
  b. *America:* No attributes

1775
A Certain Cabinet Junto [Brigham, Pl. 44] (fig. 20)
  a. *Britannia-Libertas-America: hasta* and *pilleus,* bow and arrows
America in Distress [Brigham, Pl. 46] (fig. 21)
  a. *America-Libertas: hasta* and *pilleus;* bow, arrows, and feather bonnet

1776
Massachusetts halfpenny (fig. 14)
  a. *Goddess Liberty:* globe, *hasta,* and separate *pilleus* with a dog (?)
  b. *Liberty and Virtue: hasta* and separate *pilleus*

Fig. 15
Paul Revere
The Obelisk, details
Engraving, 1766.
The American Antiquarian Society.

Fig. 16
Paul Revere
Frangimur-Collidimur
Engraving from *Edes & Gill's Almanac* for 1769. The American Antiquarian Society.

Fig. 17
Paul Revere
The Hon.[ble] *John Hancock. Esq*[r].
Engraving for the *Royal American Magazine,* March 1774.
The American Antiquarian Society.

If the above sequence is correct, Revere used Hollis as a source of inspiration for his *Britannia* in 1768. In 1775 he produced a transitional figure in which the *Britannia-Libertas* has the attributes of *America* in addition. Thus the coins of 1776 (fig. 14) are the third and fourth examples of the allegorical figure of Liberty based on Hollis-Cipriani prototypes to be produced in the colony of Massachusetts.

The practice of using a figure of Liberty on the coins of the new states spread outside Massachusetts in the 1780s, before the Constitution was ratified. Examples from three other states have been found. In New York in 1787 a penny was struck with an obverse bearing the portrait of George II (figs. 22a and b). The reader will note that in this and the other state coins of the 1780s reproduced here, the portrait on the obverse is in all cases that of a king of England. Revere, in his print of 1775 (fig. 20) had clearly portrayed his subject as British America combined with Liberty. What is surprising is to find three states that, six to eight years respectively after the defeat of George III's army at Yorktown, were still striking coins bearing either his portrait or that of his grandfather, George II. We know that Jonathan Mayhew, Andrew Eliot, and many others in pre-Revolutionary America considered themselves just as British as their Whig friends "across the water."[4] A possible explanation of the persistence of the royal images after the Revolution is that in the period during which thirteen former colonies were being transformed into the thirteen states of the new nation, those who licensed the coinage still felt loyal to the "Protestant succession in the house of Hanover."[5] Whatever the explanation may be of the iconography of the obverse, the pennies of New York State (1787), Vermont (1788), and Connecticut (1789) all bore images of Liberty.

The New York State penny had a lady seated on a globe, like that on the Massachusetts halfpenny—clearly terrestrial (fig. 14). Her right hand held a branch (presumably of olive), her left the *hasta* and *pilleus*. Her shield was oval and bore what appear to be the crosses of Saints Andrew and George. But, although oval, the shield is bordered with asymmetrical forms that find their closest parallels in the shield of the British penny. With the exception of the border, the New York coin shows an extraordinary resemblance to the undated Cipriani design reproduced in figure 12—even to the position of the left arm and hand (completely different from that of the British penny). The legend on the reverse reads "VIRT. ET LIB.," presumably standing for "*Virtus et Libertas*" (courage and liberty).

The Vermont penny of 1788 bore a portrait of George III, and on the reverse, a seated lady (figs. 23a and b). But the seat on which she was perched was invisible, her *hasta* had no *pilleus,* and the shield was that of the English penny. Only the position of the left arm was reminiscent of the Cipriani print. She might well be nothing but a rough version of the penny *Britannia*. But she *is* identified by the accompanying legend: "INDE ET LIB," which probably stands for "INDE ET LIBERTAS" (and henceforth liberty)—although it is of course possible that the inventor mistakenly thought that there was a Latin word, such as "independentia," which stood for "independence." In any case, in the following year (1789) Connecticut issued a penny bearing George II's portrait on the obverse and a

M[r]. SAMUEL ADAMS.

The able Doctor, or America Swallowing the Bitter Draught.

A certain Cabinet Junto.

Fig. 18
Paul Revere
M[r]. Samuel Adams.
Engraving for the *Royal American Magazine,* April 1774.
The American Antiquarian Society.

Fig. 19
Paul Revere
The Able Doctor, or America Swallowing the Bitter Draught
Engraving for the *Royal American Magazine,* June 1774.
The American Antiquarian Society.

Fig. 20
Paul Revere
A Certain Cabinet Junto
Engraving for the *Royal American Magazine,* January 1775.
The American Antiquarian Society.

lady almost identical with Vermont's on the reverse (figs. 24a and b). The legend was the same as Vermont's on the reverse.

It is clear that three states in New England used an image of the penny *Britannia* (such as was used by Hollis on his early bindings) and verbally identified her with Liberty (Vermont and Connecticut) or, in the case of the Massachusetts half-penny of 1776, used a fusion of images of *Britannia* and *Libertas* (perhaps derived from the stamps designed by Cipriani). However, in the case of the New York State penny of 1787, the source would seem to have been the undated Cipriani-Bartolozzi engraving (fig. 13).

The Hollis image was accepted in Philadelphia as well as New England. In 1789 the third volume of the new review *The Columbian Magazine or Monthly Miscellany* was graced with an allegorical frontispiece showing the goddess of Liberty with the *pilleus,* seated before Apollo (fig. 25). The plate is inscribed:

America! with Peace and Freedom blest,
Pant for true Fame, and scorn inglorious rest:
Science invites; urg'd by the Voice divine,
Exert thy self, 'till every Art be thine.

Clearly, there has been a fusion of Liberty with "America." The "Explanation of the Frontispiece" explicitly explains most of the print's images:

The Genius of Foederate America is represented sitting under a palm-tree, the emblem of Peace. The tree is adorned with a wreath of laurel, entwining the badges of Liberty—the pole and cap. Around the Genius of America, are the symbols of Commerce, Science, Agriculture and Plenty.—The American Eagle affords

support to her arm; and, in this situation, she is supposed to be unconscious of her proximity to the temple of Fame, a view of which is represented in the back ground. Apollo, having heard the trumpet of the goddess, celebrating her praise, appears—and announces the honors to be conferred on her—At the same time, he points to the temple; and casts a splendour on the path leading to its portal.

While the meaning of the images is new, the fact that the visual images used belong ultimately to the Hollis *Libertas-Britannia* tradition is demonstrated by the union of the triad of seated Liberty, globe, and oval shield—now bearing not the crosses of Saint George and Saint Andrew but instead the seal of the United States, "invented" in Philadelphia in 1782.

We do not know who designed the 1789 engraving. It was not signed. But we can identify the artist who further reworked the Hollis image in 1790, when the *Columbian Magazine* (under the new title of *The Universal Asylum and Columbian Magazine*) was decorated with an engraved title page (fig. 26). The figure of seated America was shown in reverse, with the same oval shield decorated with the Seal and with the library globe, but there was no *pilleus*. This image is identified as a design by Charles Willson Peale, the same Whig artist who had done the Pitt portrait mentioned earlier, in the inscription on the print. A significant feature of the images accompanying America in this design is the addition, for the first time, of the painter's palette and brushes. There is reason to believe that some gentlemen of Philadelphia meditated on the two allegories of America from the *Columbian Magazine* and, like Hollis,

Fig. 21
Paul Revere
America in Distress
Engraving for the *Royal American Magazine*, March 1775.
The American Antiquarian Society.

Fig. 22 a and b
Designer unknown.
New York State penny
The Evergreen House Foundation,
The Johns Hopkins University.

Fig. 23 a and b
Designer unknown.
Vermont penny
The Evergreen House Foundation,
The Johns Hopkins University.

both further developed their source and commissioned an artist to execute it.

Dr. Robert C. Smith has shown that the Philadelphia artist Samuel Jennings had followed his fellow Pennsylvanians Benjamin West, Charles Willson Peale, and Henry Benbridge to London. By 1789 Jennings was exhibiting at the Royal Academy. In the year of the Peale engraving for *The Universal Asylum* of 1790 he conceived the idea of doing a painting for the new home of the Philadelphia Library Company, designed in 1789 by Dr. William Thornton, a native of the British West Indies. Jennings, presumably "urg'd by the Voice divine,"[6] offered to contribute, as he wrote, his "mite towards the Encouragement of Arts and Sciences," suggesting that he paint and present to the Library Company an allegory.[7] He suggested one of three topics: Clio, Calliope, or Minerva. The Library Company appointed a committee of five to respond to Jennings's offer. One, some, or all of the committee apparently had been reading *The Universal Asylum*. They wrote to Jennings on April 3, 1790, that of the three topics they preferred Minerva. But, they went on,

as a more general latitude has been so politely granted, they take the liberty of suggesting an Idea of Substituting the figure of Liberty (with her Cap and proper Insignia) displaying the arts by some of the most striking Symbols of Painting, Architecture, Mechanics, Astronomy & ca. whilst She appears in the attitude of placing on the top of a Pedestal, a pile of Books, lettered with, Agriculture, Commerce, Philosophy & Catalogue of Philadelphia Library. A Broken Chain under her feet, and in the distant back Ground a Groupe of Negroes sitting on the Earth, or in some attitude expressive of Ease & Joy.[8]

Thus the Library Company's committee brought slavery and its abolition literally into the picture.

In 1792 the finished painting was exhibited at the Royal Academy and dispatched to Philadelphia. To the general scheme of the committee, Jennings added some details. Like Peale in his picture of 1790, Jennings wrote that he had "represented Commerce by Shipping."[9] Like Peale, too, he had given his main figure the attributes of the library globe and the painter's palette. But unlike Peale's engraving, the Jennings painting has no oval shield, no Seal of the United States, yet there was a *pilleus*. Curiously enough, the subject is Liberty—but not American Liberty.

In his letter to the Library Company of 1792 Jennings pointed out that he had made a small copy of his painting (fig. 27), from which he intended to have a print made. This reduced version is today at Winterthur. In it, the seated Liberty is present, accompanied by the globe and *pilleus*. And with her is the third member of the Hollis triad—the oval shield with the crosses of Saints George and Andrew. *Libertas Americana* had recrossed the Atlantic and once again become *Britannia-Libertas*. In England she gained a new function as the presiding genius of emancipation. But the Hollis-Cipriani-Bartolozzi image remained in the United States as well, in the Library Company version, and bore witness to still another in the line of Hollis images. She no longer sits on a globe, but next to a globe, rationalized now as a terrestrial globe in a library. She holds books in her hand, and at her feet are spread symbols of the arts and sciences. The trident symbolizing military and naval power is gone. The olive branch of peace is also gone and

Fig. 24 a and b
Designer unknown.
Connecticut penny
The Evergreen House Foundation,
The Johns Hopkins University.

Fig. 25.
Anonymous artist
Engraving of America
From *The Columbian Magazine*.
Winterthur Museum Libraries.

Fig. 26
Charles Willson Peale
Engraved title page
From vol. 5 of *The Universal Asylum and Columbian Magazine*. Author's collection.

is replaced by the books of learning. What an appropriate monument to the symbolism invented by a man who inscribed a long quotation in a copy of Samuel Johnson's Hollis-financed pamphlet on the need for clothing French prisoners of war in 1760, taken from Milton's *Paradise Regained!* The passage (my italics) was taken from Book III, in which Milton has Christ tell Satan what true glory is:

They err who count it glorious to subdue
By conquest far and wide, to overrun
Large countries, and in field great battle win,
Great cities by assault. What do these worthies,
But rob and spoil, burn, slaughter, and enslave
Peaceable nations, neighboring or remote,
Made captive, yet deserving freedome more
Than those their conquerors, who leave behind
Nothing but ruin wheresoe'er they rove,
And all the flourishing works of peace destroy,
Then swell with pride, and must be titled Gods,
Great Benefactors of mankind, Deliverers,
Worshipped with temple, priest, and sacrifice;
One is the son of Jove, of Mars the other,
Till conqueror Death discover them scarce men,
Rolling in brutish vices, and deformed,
Violent or shameful death their due reward.
But if there be in glory aught of good,
It may by means far different be attained
Without ambition, war, or violence;
By deeds of peace, by wisdom eminent,
By patience, temperance.

How appropriate that Hollis's *Britannia* should be portrayed as victorious (to use one of his favorite mottoes) "BY DEEDS OF PEACE."

I should like to cite one last example of *Britannia-Libertas* as an example of the "Survivance des dieux antiques" (to borrow M. Jean Seznec's title).

It took Americans a long time to develop an image of America which was satisfactory. The "Indian Maiden" of Cesare Ripa's *Iconologia* was unpopular by the second half of the eighteenth century (appropriately, since—with her alligator—she referred to Spanish, not British, America). In his *A Certain Cabinet Junto* of 1775, Paul Revere made an America by fusing the bow-and-arrow attributes of the Indian maiden with the Hollis *Britannia-Libertas.* But from there on, that image became *Liberty,* not America. The states, with their atomistic antagonism to each other, were bound by Liberty but not by allegiance to the United States. Various efforts to symbolize union were made in the seal and coins of the new United States. They have been described above in their earlier phases. However, in Boston in 1804 a fresh attempt was made. That year John Coles published in Boston an engraving called "Emblem of the United States of America." It was engraved by Samuel Harris (fig. 28).

Harris was born in Boston on May 1, 1783. He was a precocious and brilliant young man whose family was unable to provide him with a college education. He was interested in linguistics, history, "antiquities," "natural history" (biology), and "natural philosophy" (roughly, the physical sciences),[10] and had a particular interest in astronomy. His parents apprenticed him to his uncle, the Boston engraver Samuel Hill, who did a considerable number of engravings, many of them charming, if crude, topographic works showing local scenes, made for the *Massachusetts Magazine.* The rest of Uncle Hill's works were portraits.

Between 1806 and 1807 Samuel Harris spent

Fig. 27
Samuel Jennings
Liberty Displaying the Arts and Sciences. Oil on canvas, 1792.
H. F. du Pont Winterthur Museum.

Fig. 28
Samuel Harris
Emblem of the United States of America. Engraving, 1804.
H. F. du Pont Winterthur Museum

part of his time developing his studies in linguistics. According to a biographical article published in 1812, his abilities brought him to the attention of certain interested persons, who made it possible for him to enter the junior class at Harvard in 1808. Before that, he had in 1806 and 1807 produced at least twelve quite skillful portraits in stipple for the *Polyanthos*—a magazine devoted to the fine arts, biography, and the stage, first published in Boston in 1806. As for Harris's career at Harvard, it was most successful: his knowledge of languages both classical and biblical was most impressive, and his efforts in his other fields of interest were apparently untiring. Like another brilliant young artist of his period, John Lewis Krimmel, Samuel Harris's career was cut short by drowning. He lost his life in the Charles River, at Cambridge, Massachusetts, on July 7, 1810.

Here, however, we are concerned with what is, so far as we know at present, Harris's earliest engraving. Unlike his later stipple portraits, the print made for Coles in 1804 was a line engraving. For a twenty-one-year-old whose only instructor had been the "folk" engraver Samuel Hill, the performance was extremely skillful. To represent the Union of the States, Harris used a form of the chain image that had been employed from at least 1776 by several engravers to symbolize the unity and equality of the new states. Amos Doolittle had in 1791 produced a version of this image in which each link in the chain was decorated with the seal and motto of one state. The chain surrounded a logical center consisting of the portrait of Washington. Whether because he was anti-Jeffersonian or because he wanted a more elaborately intellectualized center for union, Harris in 1804 chose to use his chain of states to enclose an elaborate allegory. The United States he personified as a classic female seated on a globe, an oval shield at her side, an olive branch in her right hand, her upraised left hand and arm supporting the *hasta*. Obviously, the source for the design is the Cipriani-Bartolozzi print of *Britannia-Libertas*. But Harris engraved her shield with the seal of the United States devised by Charles Thomson in 1782. The *pilleus* made way for the flag. The seventeen stars of the chain were echoed by the flag. The olive branches symbolic of the power of peace in the talons of the new imperial eagle were balanced by the olive branch extended by America. And near the goddess's feet, as in the paintings by Jennings, lie the symbols of music, painting, and literature, joined by Harris to agriculture, which is symbolized by the plow. In this engraving of 1804 a young man from Hollis's favorite American city used a Hollis-Cipriani symbol of *Britannia-Libertas* to symbolize an English-based culture which had begun to achieve, "by deeds of peace," the realization of the principles of that British constitution which Hollis loved so long and for which he had fought so hard.

Regional Preferences and Characteristics in American Decorative Arts: 1750-1800

by Charles F. Montgomery

When I began this essay my thought was to describe and attempt to explain groups of attributes found in decorative art objects that in recent years have been called regional characteristics and that are a matter of practical interest to students of American arts as a means of identifying where an object was made.

I began by seeking answers to such questions as the following:

Why does almost all Baltimore Federal furniture have inlays so alike that one can identify a Baltimore piece at a glance by the inlays?

Why is one able to recognize New York or Philadelphia Federal era chairs and tables by the legs?

Why do most Philadelphia Chippendale tripod-base tea tables and candlestands have a straight columnar shaft with a flattened ball turning at its base? Why do Philadelphia brass andirons display turnings similar to those of the tea tables and candlestands?

Why should carving on Philadelphia highboys and the ornament on iron firebacks cast in Pennsylvania and Virginia furnaces be so similar?

Why should most Philadelphia Queen Anne style chairs be constructed in the same way, and in a way different from that used in other American centers?

Why do virtually all New York silver tankards made between 1690 and 1750 have highly distinctive features—cocoon-shaped thumbpieces, cherub's-head handle terminals and foliated base-bands—that set them apart from tankards made in other American cities?

Why do a large proportion of Philadelphia,

Wilmington (Delaware), and Baltimore (Maryland) silver tea sets of the 1790s (167) feature pierced, fencelike galleries around their covers, when this ornamental device was not used elsewhere?

How does it happen that seven Rhode Island pewterers used only three kinds of porringer handles, and these were of a kind seldom used elsewhere and so distinctive as to merit the name "Rhode Island porringers"? (182)

In the course of investigation it became apparent that regional characteristics as defined by collectors, curators, and dealers were in large part the result of specialization and craft organization. It also became apparent that a larger issue was involved—the matter of the taste of the colonial American. That subject is too large to explore in more than a cursory manner here; however, in an effort to bring focus to my groping I began to ask other questions:

Why were so many porringers made in New England between 1730 and 1810, while only a few were made in New York and almost none produced in Philadelphia and the South?

Why was furniture of the bombé form made only in Massachusetts?

Why was furniture of the block-front form so popular in Boston; Salem, Massachusetts; Newport, Rhode Island; and Connecticut, but eschewed in New York, Philadelphia, and the South?

What is the explanation of the wide acceptance of the bonnet-top or scrolled-pediment highboy in Salem, Newport, rural New England, and Philadelphia when only a few were made in Boston and New York and almost none in the South?

Why was it so generally acceptable, even if on a limited scale?

Why was the windsor chair so widely accepted in America?

Finally, I asked, if a ship could sail in six or eight weeks from London to Boston or New York loaded with London fashions, why are some American-made objects twenty or thirty years behind English styles?

In a spirit of speculation I shall propose tentative answers to some of these questions. Some readers will find that the objects shown here seem to be very English in appearance; others will just as surely discern variations from English models in style, structure, and details of form and ornament. I shall suggest relationships among groups of furniture, silver, and pewter that I hope will stimulate readers to see these objects as totems of early America. In text and pictures I shall attempt to chart certain similarities and differences between various objects made *in* America. These regional differences are most clearly evident in furniture; they are sometimes evident in silver and pewter, but scarcely perceptible in American painting.

Today, scholars have come to see a special significance in the phenomenon of regional development. John Kirk, a furniture historian, has tentatively divided the eastern seaboard "into different regions that show genuine artistic cohesion" in terms of patterns of taste and style. He suggests that these "furniture regions" correspond to dialect regions revealed in the linguistic research of Hans Kurath. More specifically, Kirk believes that the varied styles and forms of early American chairs reflect "the strikingly different character of many different cultures that were to come to-

182
Porringer
Samuel Hamlin or Samuel E. Hamlin,
Providence, 1773-1810.
Yale University Art Gallery;
Mabel Brady Garvan Collection.

gether . . . to form the United States," and regional differences of style and practice in the decorative arts correspond to similar differences among the regions of England from which most of the early immigrants to the colonies came.[1] Although the study of regional styles and practices in English furniture design is just beginning, the existence of these differences is now recognized.

Whatever the specific regional ties between America and England may have been, the central fact remains that American colonists considered themselves Englishmen and from first settlement accepted English taste as their own. Prior to about 1740 the designs of the objects they used and cherished were based upon the designs of English architects, designers, and traditions. Further, as Professor Harris has pointed out in his essay here, the relationships between England and America remained exceptionally close even after the Revolution. Many advertisements, such as that of an immigrant upholsterer in Charleston who gave notice that he had "imported from England, trimmings of the general approved taste of that country and best suited for the furniture used in this," underscore the fact that Americans recognized London as their style center.[2]

Although they looked to London, Americans were insistent upon what they wanted in the way of imports. Placing an order for printed calicos in 1739, a New Yorker named Philip Livingston wrote Samuel Storke in London asking for "blew pencilled work'd Callico two Collours, All Large flowers." He admonished Storke to send no "Small Single flowers as you Sent me last year which I cant Sell," and advised him that other patterns "are not of ye Right Collours."[3] Indeed, these wishes were so confidently expressed that one can say with some degree of certainty that throughout the eighteenth century Americans increasingly exhibited a well-defined native taste.

From these circumstances, two questions emerge. The first is: what led the craftsmen of one region to give their works a distinctive set of tangible characteristics? The second, which I shall return to, is: what led the people of a particular region to express distinctive preferences? The most difficult element to ascertain is the extent to which those preferences influenced the artisan. Did these influences lead to distinguishing characteristics of objects? Hereafter, for the sake of clarity, the term "regional preferences" will refer to the expression of public attitudes and tastes; and "regional characteristics" to the specific contributions of the craftsmen.

Regional Characteristics

The inlays used on furniture made during the Federal era (1788–1825) are an example of a regional characteristic. So distinctive are the banding and eagles, shells, and other pictorial subjects used on furniture made in Baltimore and the surrounding countryside that their presence on a piece of furniture immediately suggests its place of origin. The same is true of inlays on furniture made in the Boston area. In either case, one can say with some assurance that a piece of furniture was made in Baltimore or in Boston.

The reason for this homogeneity is suggested by the inventory taken in 1800 of the estate of Thomas Barrett, a Baltimore inlaymaker, which discloses that fifteen Baltimore cabinetmakers were indebted to him. In Barrett's stock of unsold goods were 1,316 "shells for inlaying in furniture" and 76 yards of "band" or stringing.[4] The inference is clear that most, if not all, cabinetmakers in the Baltimore area bought their pictorial inlays and stringing from Thomas Barrett, and hence the frequency of similar inlaid designs in Baltimore furniture of the Federal period.

Barrett's accounting may also explain the presence of inlays of the Baltimore type on clock cases with movements made in the surrounding countryside by local clockmakers, as in Hagerstown, Maryland, and Manheim, Pennsylvania. If the cases, like the movements, were made locally, the inlays could easily have been purchased in Baltimore, the trading center for both Hagerstown and Manheim. According to this hypothesis, then, we can say that the expertise and taste of a single specialist in Baltimore accounts for a regional characteristic found not only in furniture made in Baltimore, but in cabinetwork made in adjacent areas.

Wherever there was a specialist such as Thomas Barrett at work there was a strong possibility that many craftsmen in the region would employ his talents. In a city with several cabinetmakers, for example, it would be routine for them to patronize the one or two turners for the "turned" legs that were commonly used on tables and much seating furniture after 1790. Sometimes one turner (a specialist) would so dominate the field in a region that he alone determined the shapes of legs on tables and chairs produced in "his" area.

Such specialization, the precursor of the in-dustrial age, also helps to explain why the columns of so many tripod-base tea tables made in Philadelphia exhibit the same contours—a pronounced, flattened-ball turning near the base of a straight shaft—contours widely recognized as a regional hallmark of tea tables made in this area (fig. 29). Just how many turners were producing "tea table columns" for cabinetmakers in that locale during the 1760s is not known, but at least one, Samuel Williams, left a record of his specialty. In 1767, Williams advertised that he had "Joiner's stuff as usual" and offered ready-made "mahogany and walnut tea table columns"—as well as "high and low post bedstead stuff"—to all joiners and others in town and country.[5]

As a specialist, the turner exerted an influence on crafts other than cabinetmaking, to which he was naturally tied by a common interest in woodworking. For the brazier, he made turned patterns of wood that—impressed in sand-filled flasks—determined the shape of brass castings that ultimately became candlesticks, andirons, and the like. Hence, it is perhaps no coincidence that andirons made in Philadelphia (fig. 30) occasionally have flattened ball-shaped brass finials reminiscent of the locally made tea-table columns.

The turner even helped the pewterer. Early in 1773, William, Daniel, and Nathaniel Proud, Providence chairmakers and turners, made wooden patterns for Samuel Hamlin, local pewterer and brazier. These patterns undoubtedly enabled Hamlin to make the set of pewterer's "moulds, of the newest and neatest fashions," that he advertised for sale a few months later.[6] Whether molds for the beautiful Rhode Island "flowered handle" pewter

Fig. 29
Column of tea table
Philadelphia, ca. 1765-1785.
Yale University Art Gallery;
bequest of Olive Louise Dann.

Fig. 30
Brass andirons
Philadelphia, ca. 1765-1785.
Mr. and Mrs. George M. Kaufman.

porringers (182) were among those Hamlin offered we shall probably never know. More important is the fact that one moldmaker could produce the means by which not only he himself but also all other pewterers in the neighborhood could make thousands of identical objects, which, in turn, can be recognized as a regional product. Hence we find all Rhode Island's post-Revolutionary pewterers making porringers with the same two or three kinds of handles and no other style.

The carver is another specialist whose "hallmark" is found not only in identical carving on the furniture of many different cabinetmakers but in designs for other crafts as well. The wooden patterns the carver made for the brazier determined the character of the brass castings that became the feet of andirons. In Philadelphia, these brass feet often look strikingly like the claw-and-ball feet of mahogany Chippendale style chairs made in the same city. We even find Philadelphia andirons with hairy paw feet, a kind of foot rarely found in America except on furniture made in Philadelphia.

The carver also made patterns for the iron founder, and the result is the expected one—in Philadelphia, for example, there are cast-iron designs similar in spirit to the carving found on Philadelphia furniture and on the woodwork of the city's finest houses. Indeed, bills exist from two Philadelphia carvers, Bernard and Jugiez, for carved wooden patterns for household firebacks to be cast at Isaac Zane's Virginia foundry.[7]

The work of the specialist is more readily apparent in ornament and details than in overall character. Furniture offers a good example of this distinction between the specific and the general.

Connoisseurs can often identify the origin of American Chippendale chairs, tables, and high chests by the way their feet are carved. But feet are only a single detail. It is much more difficult to account for the whole series of related elements that give the overall character to chairs made in Philadelphia, New York, or Boston. One is moved to speculate that the chairmakers in these cities worked according to a set of specific guidelines.

We know, for example, from newspaper advertisements that lumber dealers made a practice of selling boards precut to size for bedposts, chair backs, and other parts of furniture. It seems to follow that cabinetmakers bought such boards and supplied them to specialists who fashioned them according to patterns in their repertoire into furniture elements. Having been made ready, they could be easily and quickly assembled by the cabinetmaker when he needed them.

Thus it seems clear that the presence of craft specialists and a substantial trade in parts of objects, such as inlays, chair legs, chair backs, and so on, could and probably does account for many details of form and ornament that serve to identify the products of Boston, Newport, New York, Philadelphia, Baltimore, or Charleston. These cities were comparatively small in the eighteenth century, and the shops of silversmiths and cabinetmakers were usually clustered within a few streets of each other, those of the cabinetmakers often near the waterfront. Only a few craftsmen worked in each shop—a master and an apprentice or two, and sometimes one or more journeymen. To become a merchant was a goal of the craftsman. Buying and selling offered the greatest opportunity to make money and

Fig. 31
Silver tankard
Jacobus van der Spiegel,
New York, ca. 1690-1700.
Yale University Art Gallery;
gift of Spotswood D. Bowers and
Mr. and Mrs. Francis P. Garvan.

to rise in the social scale. Therefore silversmiths and pewterers sold, in addition to the goods they made, some wares imported from abroad. These articles, usually from England, where skilled labor was cheaper and more plentiful than in America, provided a regular supply of fashionable models that could be copied. This could account for the fact that some American-made silver and pewter objects are very like English examples, while there was less similarity in furniture, which was seldom imported.

The role of the silversmith was a special one. He catered to the desires of the wealthiest—the most status-conscious, and fashion-conscious—people in the society; his clientele would have been particularly interested in the latest London fashions. It seems almost axiomatic that the Ameri-can silversmith would attempt to duplicate, insofar as he was able, silver objects imported from London. However, this was not always true, as will be seen.

Strong Dutch and Huguenot influences, as well as English, are apparent in seventeenth- and early eighteenth-century New York silver. The subtleties of continental influences are particularly discernible in the teapots of Peter van Dyck and the sugar bowl of Simeon Soumain of the second quarter of the eighteenth century (138 and 139). Continental influences become less noticeable in objects made from about 1750, however.

New York tankards made between 1690 and 1750 are distinguished by the application of Dutch ornament to an English form (fig. 31), and certain Philadelphia area tea sets of the late eighteenth century (**167**) show strong regional characteristics

167
Tea service
Samuel Richards and Samuel Williamson, Philadelphia, 1797-1800. Private Collection.

that are very likely the result of the contributions of craft specialists. One or two silversmiths may have made the distinctive ornaments, two or more of which are found on virtually every New York tankard—a cocoon-shaped thumbpiece, a large cherub's-head handle-terminal, and a highly ornamental swag of fruit or a walking lion on the handle grip. The chased foliated bands found just above the base moldings may also have been the work of a specialist.

Pierced galleries are a regional hallmark of late eighteenth-century tea- and coffeepots and sugar bowls made in Philadelphia; Wilmington, Delaware; Baltimore; and Annapolis, Maryland (167). Banding for the galleries was probably made by a Philadelphia specialist in long strips and sold to silversmiths in the region.

Regional characteristics of this kind are not frequently found in American-made silver for a very good reason—each urban shop was a self-contained unit readily able to fashion objects to accord with English models to the extent the silversmith and his clients wished. However, there are many examples of early American silver that deviate from fashionable English usage. Often Americans were highly conservative and chose forms twenty or thirty years old and had them engraved in the latest fashion, or at another time (157; fig. 83) they chose a fashionable up-to-date form and had it embellished with old-style ornament.

The training received by artisans was also a factor in the development of the "local school" and regional cohesiveness. For example, between 1777 and 1823 there were at least 87 Baltimore shops producing cabinetwares, and the records for that time show that 237 apprentices were indentured. William Camp, who had the largest and one of the most stylish shops in town, took 53 young men as apprentices—probably one half of the men trained as Baltimore cabinetmakers between 1801 and 1822.[8] These figures suggest that the practices of that one shop could well have become the Baltimore idiom for the next generation.

The same situation probably prevailed in other cities and other crafts. There survives a remarkable group of mid-eighteenth-century needlework pictures (234) made by girls or women in the Boston area. The patterns and techniques of these pictures are so similar that there is little doubt that the makers were closely related in some way. And one can speculate with good reason that the makers had instruction from a woman such as Abigail Hiller, who advertised in 1754 that she would teach "Wax-Work, Transparent, Filligree, Feather-Work, Quill-Work, Japanning upon Glass, Embroidering, Tent Stitch, &c."[9]

Regional Preferences
As it has been made abundantly clear in this book, the prevailing taste in America was English and the style capital, London. The effect of this pervasive orientation upon the arts of early America is not easily determined, but in attempting to understand why some forms or particular expressions became popular while others were rejected, one phenomenon that occurs repeatedly should be noted: certain forms became popular in America after they had gone out of favor in England.

Such forms as the porringer and the tankard, made of silver and pewter in both England and

America, went out of fashion about 1740 or 1750 in England but continued to be made in some sections of America for another fifty years. In some cases—for example, the pewter porringer in New England—the form achieved vastly greater popularity in America than it had ever attained in England, yet the same pewter porringer seems never to have been popular in Philadelphia or the South. The relative acceptability of porringers and tankards in the various regional centers will be indicated in the chart near the end of this essay.

The experience and work of two non-English craftsmen, Johann Christoph Heyne and John Will, also demonstrate the impact of English taste in America. Both men were pewterers. Heyne came from Saxony in Germany to Bethlehem, Pennsylvania, in 1742, and Will came with his family from Nieuwied on the Rhine to New York a decade later. By 1757 Heyne had settled in Lancaster, Pennsylvania, where he made pewter for the surrounding countryside until about 1780. Much of his surviving pewter was made for the German congregations of the Lutheran churches of that region. His flagons with flaring bases, cherub's-head feet, and sharp spouts (199) are entirely in the German tradition, as are his tall standing cups with large knopped stems (200). Also German are his sharply tapering beakers and four surviving baroque style church candlesticks. In contrast, his domestic pewter made for the general public, such as small plates, flasks, and one known porringer, are in the English manner.

The story of the other German immigrant and his family is quite different. John Will arrived in 1752 in New York, where he made pewter until about 1774. His sons—Henry, Philip, and William— also pewterers, worked in New York, Albany, and Philadelphia. Among the many surviving pieces made by the Wills, only a few remind us of their German ancestry. They seem to have anglicized their wares from the very first, whereas Heyne made German forms throughout his career. Compare, for example, an American-style flagon (fig. 32), made by Henry Will by stacking one English-form tankard on top of another, with Heyne's flagon (199). One may guess that the Wills, seeking to please their customers, made pewter objects in accord with the taste of the predominant English population of Albany, New York, and Philadelphia. On the other hand, Heyne continued to make German forms for that part of his clientele which was German, the Lutheran congregations, and English pieces for the community at large, which was for the most part English.

But the tastes of the same ethnic groups were not necessarily uniform, and forms that were popular in one region met with complete rejection elsewhere, as we shall see in a review of furniture made for the storage of linen and clothing. In urban centers throughout the colonies the prevailing eighteenth-century practice was to store clothing in shallow sliding drawers six to ten inches deep. By mid-century, closets where clothing could be hung were being built in new houses. In rural households six-board chests, often painted red or grained in imitation of a finer wood and with lift-up tops in the seventeenth-century manner continued to be made throughout the eighteenth century.

The standard chest of drawers was four drawers high with straight front, but chests with serpentine

Fig. 32
Pewter flagon
Henry Will, New York, ca. 1765-1790.
Yale University Art Gallery;
Mabel Brady Garvan Collection.

and reverse serpentine fronts were popular. More ambitious forms were also fashioned. For example, about fifty surviving chests, chests-on-chests, and desk-and-bookcases with "kettle bases" of bulging contours (now called bombé; 102) are known which were made in Boston and Salem between 1755 and 1800. The number testifies to the popularity of the form in those cities. The prototype for Boston cabinetmakers may have been a mahogany English chest-on-chest (fig. 33) dating from about 1740, which according to tradition was owned by Charles Apthorp of Boston, who was called "the greatest and most noble merchant" in America at his death in 1758. The Apthorp connection would have given social status to the new form, which was similar in contour to tulip-shaped silver mugs and tankards. Ownership of bombé pieces is credited to Thomas Hutchinson, Governor of Massachusetts, Sir William Pepperell, and many of the richest merchants, including Edward Brinley, Apthorp, and, at the end of the Revolution, Elias Hasket Derby and Joseph Barrell.[10]

It seems strange that these baroque forms, which originated in the Italian cassone and were in turn modified by French designers and English cabinetmakers, found favor in colonial Massachusetts and nowhere else in America. Boston cabinetmakers were content to produce them in the image of an English model except for the substitution of a scrolled pediment for the pitch pediment usually found on English examples. But their magnificent and substantial qualities probably endeared them to Boston merchants, and in all likelihood their very Englishness enhanced their desirability. One can speculate that the undulating facade of curvilinear shape was also a factor in the acceptance of the bombé form. Another highly plastic furniture form, the "blockfront," was even more popular.

The blockfront had evolved in Boston during the 1730s (98). With three vertical panels—the outer two convex and the inner one concave—rising from the base molding through a succession of drawers on the facades of case pieces, the type is characterized by "richness, rationality, classic proportions, and an uncompromising symmetry. . . ."[11] In contrast to the bombé form, the blockfront was a Boston innovation without close English or European parallels; its precise source is unknown, though possible English precedents are rare Queen Anne style dressing glasses with blocked facades. Cabinetmakers in Boston and other nearby towns—Salem, Beverly, Newburyport, and Concord—seem to have adapted the idea found in these small-scale pieces to full-size chests of drawers, chests-on-chests, desks, desks and bookcases, high chests, and dressing tables in far more variety than was the case with bombé furniture. Although consistent references to the blockfront and bombé forms are lacking in account books or probate records, we can speculate that blockfronts were less expensive than comparable bombé forms. Whatever their cost, it is significant that for every bombé piece that survives there are perhaps ten or twenty examples of the blockfront; further, neither Rhode Island nor Connecticut cabinetmakers adopted the bombé form. The New Englander in search of rich, ornamental furniture appears to have found the native blockfront style more desirable than the bombé version fashioned so closely after an imported model.

About 1760, the blockfront form (100) as

Fig. 33
Bombé chest-on-chest
England, ca. 1740-1758.
Museum of Fine Arts, Boston;
gift of Albert Sack.
Believed to have been owned
originally by Charles Apthorp.

adopted by Quaker cabinetmakers in Newport, Rhode Island, enriched with great carved shells at the top of each panel and converted into a baroque tour de force, was the most original furniture form produced in eighteenth-century America. Made of the finest mahogany, blockfront furniture forms are substantial and massive in appearance. Inturning lines repeatedly lead the eye back within a closed composition typical of the Queen Anne style, of which the architectonic outline and the shell motif is also characteristic. In essence, the Rhode Island block-and-shell furniture was a restatement, really a new statement, of the Queen Anne style aesthetic at the height of the Chippendale era in America. From Rhode Island the form was disseminated to Connecticut, where it was often executed in a highly individualistic manner (101) in cherry with

ornamental scrolls suggestive of rococo frivolity and with other ornament that often deviates from the original restrained silhouettes and classical proportions of the Newport pieces. A few examples of blockfront furniture made in New York and the South are known, but the form found little acceptance there and only a few examples survive in comparison to a thousand or more New England examples.

Instead of using chests of drawers, the Pennsylvania Germans and rural New York Dutch stored their clothing and household linens in great wardrobes called *"shranks"* or *kas*, in which clothes could be hung on pegs. They were frequently painted, as were the large lidded chests (**118**) used by the Pennsylvania Germans. The latter, in which clothing was laid out flat, were a continuation of a

118
Painted chest
Berks County, Pennsylvania,
ca. 1780. The Metropolitan Museum
of Art; Rogers Fund, 1923.

seventeenth-century form, as were the lift-lid six-board chests, sometimes with one or two drawers, used throughout the eighteenth century by rural New Englanders.

Between 1720 and 1740, whenever more storage space was required, British and Americans alike used chests-on-chests with short feet or flat-topped high chests supported on tall legs fifteen to twenty-four inches high. The latter, today called highboys in America and chests on stand in England, went out of favor in England about 1740. Thereafter English tall chests were uniformly of the chest-on-chest variety. However, in America both the highboy and the chest-on-chest were in use from 1740 to 1800, and a comparison of their popularity and development in America raises interesting questions. The chest-on-chest proved to be acceptable and was made in every colonial center. In Boston and coastal Massachusetts, New York, and Charleston, it was the favored large-scale storage piece between 1760 and 1800, whereas the highboy (on tall legs) with matching dressing table (fig. 34) was the popular form in Salem and rural Massachusetts, Newport, and Philadelphia and its hinterlands. Usually costing upward of eight pounds in Massachusetts to as much as twenty or twenty-five pounds sterling in Pennsylvania, the highboy surely ranked with the richly furnished highpost bed as the ultimate status symbol in furniture. Just at the time when the flat-topped highboy went out of fashion in England, Americans added a scrolled pediment and made the form more imposing. The highboy with pediment qualifies as an American innovation; neither English prototypes nor published furniture designs are known for it. The basic idea of the scrolled pediment as it was applied to the design of the Philadelphia highboy (fig. 34) was surely derived from designs for chimneypieces (fig. 35) (fireplace room ends) in such English architectural pattern books as Abraham Swan's *The British Architect or the Builder's Treasury of Staircases* (London, 1745). Curiously, the pitch pediment, which was illustrated far more frequently in architectural pattern books and which was easier to make, seems to have had little appeal to Americans and was seldom used on highboys, though it is occasionally found on chests-on-chests.

In Philadelphia, an overlay of "modern" or rococo carving (shown in the same architecture pattern books as the designs for the pediment) similar to that found in the finest Philadelphia interiors was added under the pediment to give the highboy a fashionable look. The skirts of the finest Philadelphia highboys were also carved, as was the center drawer in the lower section. By the addition of pediment and up-to-date carving, an old form was updated. Such modernization was a common occurrence in American furniture of the 1750–1800 period. At the end of the century, in the neoclassical era, when old forms were retained they were thinned and lightened to conform to the new canons of design.

The formula for the New England highboy with pediment is essentially the same as for the Philadelphia type, except that the basic form underwent even less change from the New England Queen Anne style flat-top highboy. The proportions and mass of the New England pieces are lighter than in those from Philadelphia and, as is typical in New England, there is less ornament. As is clear

Fig. 34
Highboy and lowboy
Philadelphia, ca. 1765-1785.
Yale University Art Gallery;
Mabel Brady Garvan Collection.

Fig. 35
Abraham Swan
Plate L, The British Architect
(London, 1758). The plate is
dated 1745.

from figures 35 and 36, New England cabinet-makers also used architectural pattern books as sources for their designs. In rural New England the ornament was of the vernacular kind. Centers of attention—pinwheels, swastikas, and fans—catch light and sometimes give a sense of motion that replaces the whimsy and leafage of European-inspired rococo. Native woods like cherry or maple were often used, but in Salem and Charlestown, Massachusetts, and in Newport, mahogany was preferred.

In Boston the chest-on-chest rather than the highboy was the popular form, but it was often Americanized by giving it a blockfront facade. Case furniture in New York followed English models, the highboy being little favored there as compared to the chest-on-chest. Even more English in inter-pretation are the case pieces made in Charleston, South Carolina, where the chest-on-chest was popular and the highboy was not made at all. Indeed, some Charleston examples (109) were copied almost exactly from English designs. In summary, Boston, New York, and southern furniture made for the upper classes deviated less from English models than furniture made in Philadelphia and New England (outside of Boston).

It should be noted that clear-cut regional characteristics are found in the chairs produced in most regional centers, and it appears that the close-knit organization of cabinet- and chairmakers and their employment of specialists to fashion the legs and backs and to carve the ornament account in part for the close similarity of the chairs made in a given center. However, regional preferences are evident in the dispersion of windsor chairs, and this phenomenon is of such importance that its history must be sketched.

Windsor chairs based on English models were first made about 1740 in Philadelphia, where they soon became popular. Large numbers of them were exported to other regional centers in the North and South. Their broad acceptance quickly led to their manufacture in many places and thousands were made in the following two centuries.

A number of factors might account for the universal popularity of this form at a time when other furniture forms found varying degrees of acceptance in different regions. First, American windsor chairmakers lightened the relatively heavy and overengineered English windsor, and, by exploiting the different structural properties of native woods, were able to evolve a taut, springy armature, or cage, that was lightweight, strong, comfortable, and, when painted—green, blue, red, or black—exceptionally attractive (122).

A second feature of windsors that made them popular was their adaptability to prefabrication of parts. Chairmakers made hundreds of turned legs, stretchers, and steamed components in anticipation of later assembly, and this practice had the effect of reducing the amount of labor per component, thus drastically lowering the price of the completed chair.

This combination of factors—ingenious con-struction, comfort, color, and cheapness—seems to explain the phenomenal acceptance of the windsor, which was used everywhere by all classes. By 1800, these essentially "no-style" products lost their few regional attributes and became one of the first national expressions in furniture.

Fig. 36
Highboy
Connecticut, ca. 1760-1770.
Yale University Art Gallery;
Mabel Brady Garvan Collection.

Fig. 37
William Salmon, Jun.
Plate XXVI, Palladio Londinensis
(London, 1728).

Summary

The accompanying chart, showing estimates of quantities produced, suggests the regional preferences for the furniture forms, porringers, and tankards discussed above.[12] Study of the chart shows no consistent pattern of acceptance or rejection of English forms except in Charleston and the South. There, ready acceptance of English forms is apparent, although our information is limited to furniture. The English chest-on-chest, for example, was copied in Charleston (109) with little modification, and American style highboys and blockfronts were not used.

The chest-on-chest was made in every American regional center. However, its interpretation varied from the faithfully English version in Charleston to a slightly modified form in New York, to the highly modified forms produced in Pennsylvania, Connecticut, Rhode Island, and Massachusetts.

The bombé case piece, another English form, was made in Boston and Salem in comparatively limited numbers. Its acceptance may have been restricted to rich anglophiles.

The highboy, a survival in America after it went out of style in England about 1740, was very popular after that time in Philadelphia, Newport, and in all of New England except Boston. This American form found little favor in New York and was seldom made in the South.

The porringer, an eating and drinking vessel produced prior to 1740 in both England and America, went out of fashion in England about 1740.[13] After that time silver porringers became still more popular in Boston. Some were made in New York, but almost none were produced in Philadelphia or the South. Inexpensive pewter porringers followed the same pattern: they were very popular in New England; some were made and used in New York, but they were very little used in Philadelphia. Some of a special form with "tab handles" were made in Chester County and Lancaster, Pennsylvania, but the form was little used in the South.

Tankards also went out of fashion in England, soon after 1750, after a century of popularity. In America, silver tankards, which had been made since the 1670s, continued to be made in large numbers for church use and for the wealthy in Boston, Newport, New York, and Philadelphia. Many pewter tankards were produced for the less affluent in New York and Philadelphia. Limited numbers were also made in Connecticut.

Several patterns of American acceptance or usage seem to emerge for the period from 1740 to 1800. 1) In only a few instances, as with the bombé form in Boston and the chest-on-chest in Charleston, were English models clearly acceptable or followed in America. 2) Some old forms, such as the tankard, porringer, and highboy, became very popular in America after they had gone out of fashion in England. 3) Old forms were frequently modernized or made fashionable with new ornament, as happened with the Philadelphia highboy (fig. 34). 4) Old forms were sometimes modernized but ornamented with traditional or vernacular ornament that seems to capture the spirit of new, stylish ornament, as in some highboys made in New England (112).

These phenomena occur not only in the country

Patterns of Regional Production	Boston Region		Newport and Connecticut Region		New York Region		Philadelphia Region		The South: Charleston Region	
	City	Salem & Country	City	Country	City	Country	City	Country	City	Country
Bombé Case Pieces	some	some	none	none	none	none	none	none	none	none
Blockfront Case Pieces	many	some	many	some	few	none	none	none	none	none
Chest-on-chest	some	some	some	some	many	few	some	some	many	?
Highboy	few	many	some	many	few	few	many	some	none	few
Windsor Chair	many	many	many	many	many	many	many	many	some	some
Porringer (silver)	many	none	many	none	few	none	none	none	none	none
Porringer (pewter)	many	none	many	many	some	some	none	some	none	none
Tankard (silver)	many	none	many	none	many	some	many	none	none	none
Tankard (pewter)	few	none	few	few	many	some	many	none	none	none

but in the major American style centers, which were in constant and direct contact with England. Ships sailed from England to American ports in six to eight weeks, bringing fashionable silver, textiles, looking glasses, and some furniture. Despite this regular influx of English wares, some American silver and furniture was regularly produced that was twenty or thirty years behind English modes. It is true that not all imported goods were of the latest fashion; colonial Americans often complained about the old goods "palmed off" on them, but there was clearly a market for and an acceptance by some Americans of new styles as soon as they were available to the middle class in England. On the other hand, if one examines hardware catalogues sent out by English hardware firms between 1760 and 1800 one finds illustrated, for example, "teardrop" brass pulls for early eighteenth-century style furniture offered along with Queen Anne and Chippendale and even neoclassical style brasses. Obviously there continued to be a demand for old-fashioned hardware for a long time.

Clearly this was not a homogenous society. Some Americans, probably a minority, wanted up-to-date English styles but many others appear to have preferred traditional forms and to have been conservative in their taste. As early as the 1740s there was some reluctance to accept English furniture fashions unless they were modified. In the 1750s and 1760s many Americans began to assert their independence by adopting the highboy and the blockfront as their own and by continuing to use porringers and tankards. Probably the taste of these Americans influenced and was influenced by the inertia of American craftsmen. Colonial crafts-men were inherently conservative in their attitudes toward design and the adoption of new skills. It is true that in urban centers American craftsmen were challenged by immigrant craftsmen "late from London." But American craftsmen were slow to change, and there was little reason for their changing when their clientele was willing to accept the traditional form or modified versions of it. Further, the craftsman group appeared to be a tight little inbred society with intermarriage the norm and with craft knowledge passed on from father to son and from master to apprentice.[14]

The creation of regional characteristics as a result of the handcraft system continued after the adoption of the neoclassical style toward the end of the century. However, the phenomenon of regional preferences, so intimately related to consumer attitudes, tastes, predilections, and mores, appears to have undergone substantial change. No longer did old ideas linger in American hybrid forms such as the highboy and the blockfront, the updated porringer or the tankard.

The transition from Queen Anne style furniture or silver or pewter to the Chippendale style had been a comparatively easy but slow process. The two styles, Queen Anne and Chippendale, lasted for almost seventy years—from about 1730 to the 1790s. During the whole of that time gradual changes were being made, a step forward and a step backward, as styles slowly moved from the William and Mary to Queen Anne and eventually from Queen Anne to Chippendale. But the new neoclassical style introduced to America in the 1780s represented one of the most profound stylistic watersheds after 1700, perhaps even since the founding of the colonies. The break was sharp, the changes great, and the transformation from the Chippendale era to the neoclassical was made in a remarkably short space of six or eight

Probably the greatest force in effecting this rapid stylistic transformation was the supposed parallel between the United States and the Roman republic. Americans who related Washington to Cincinnatus and themselves to Roman citizens were eager to accept styles that were reputedly based on those of classical antiquity. Following the adoption of the federal Constitution, nationalistic fever ran high. Orators cried for an American style. A wave of neoclassicism swept away the forms of the baroque and rococo tradition and the range of regional preferences was diminished, yet the new styles in the decorative arts came from England and were more English than any for the previous forty years.

Although few of the new forms were far removed from English models, the same evolutionary process in effect earlier in the eighteenth century produced some forms in the Federal era that can only be called American. These included sofas in the Chippendale form but with lightened mass and modern neoclassical carving by the gifted Salem, Massachusetts, carver, Samuel McIntire; tabernacle looking glasses produced in New York and elsewhere in the 1780s and 1790s with frames thinned and with composition ornament of a new style, with leaves and flowers gilded and strung on wires instead of the earlier carved wood leafage; and lolling chairs with higher backs, lighter and more vertical silhouettes, and thin tapered or turned legs (132). Regional characteristics that were

the result of specialists' work continued in inlays, turnings, and other ornamental details used on city furniture. Regional preferences continued to be expressed for certain forms and materials, as in New England, where the lolling chair and furniture of reddish Honduras mahogany with contrasting veneers of light-colored figured birch or satinwood were the vogue (127). New Yorkers preferred furniture of very dark mahogany and with carving instead of inlay. The American eagle was a popular inlay, along with classical motifs, and the likeness of Washington scenes of naval victories regularly appeared in paintings on looking glasses.

As one studies these cultural expressions—whether in furniture, silver, or pewter—one senses that cultural patterns were probably not consciously conceived, yet each time an artisan or artist modified an English model, his deviation, though it was not an overt act of refusal, was nevertheless a step toward independence. These steps varied from craft to craft and region to region along the Atlantic seaboard. It is apparent that, haltingly but discernibly, American craftsmen were moving toward independence in the decorative arts. The divergence from the English norm seems to have been greatest prior to 1785. Later, during the Federal period, Americans felt the need for a new American style, and they embraced the neoclassical mode as their own. Sometime after 1800, they seem to have achieved a sense of national identity and to have become ready to participate as equals in the Atlantic community; they were then prepared to accept English and European styles made known by many publications and brought to America by European craftsmen during the nineteenth century.

A Display
of American Art

Paintings, Drawings and Watercolors

The principal current of painting in the English-speaking American colonies can be said to have begun effectively with the arrival of the artist John Smibert from England at the beginning of 1729. Although there had been considerable earlier activity in the functional arts (architecture, furniture, silver), the development of painting, except for a flurry of portraiture by anonymous limners in the Boston area around 1670, remained desultory until the 1730s.

Smibert, a London portrait painter, came to America with Dean, later Bishop, Berkeley to teach art and architecture in a projected college in Bermuda. While Berkeley's party waited in vain at Newport, Rhode Island, for funds for the college, Smibert went on to Boston in May 1729. The following year he exhibited his recent American

1
John Smibert
Nathaniel Byfield
Oil on canvas, 1730.
The Metropolitan Museum of Art;
bequest of Charles Allen Munn, 1924.

portraits, as well as plaster casts of antique sculpture and copies of old master paintings acquired or painted in Italy years earlier while on the Grand Tour. Among the paintings exhibited was a portrait of *Nathaniel Byfield* (1), the first judge of the Court of the Vice-Admiralty, who played an active role in Massachusetts political affairs and was described by contemporaries as dictatorial, overbearing, ambitious, and revengeful, although in his likeness at seventy-seven he appears more benign. The Reverend Mather Byles of Boston published a poetic encomium "To Mr. Smibert on the Sight of His Pictures," specifically noting that in the exhibition "Fixt strong in thought there Byfield's Lines appear."[1]

Viewed within the total context of English art, Smibert's American paintings are not exceptional. But in America, where images of any kind were rare, his paintings had a significant impact. Smibert painted over 225 portraits in America, but after 1740 physical infirmities curtailed his output, and by 1747 he had ceased painting.

Smibert was the most gifted and most influential of a number of European artists who settled permanently in America during the early years of the eighteenth century. Others include Justus Engelhardt Kühn (Germany), Jeremiah Theüs (Switzerland), Gustavus Hesselius (Sweden), and Peter Pelham (England). These artists were instrumental in the transmission of European artistic style, generally late baroque in character, to the colonies. Since nothing stylistic seems to have been absorbed by American artists from the indigenous Amerind population, American painting developed as a provincial branch of European art, although not without its own character.

Pre-Smibert painting in English America had begun in the seventeenth century in a flat, provincial style, as in *Mrs. Elizabeth Freake and Baby Mary* (fig. 38), a mixture of medieval and mannerist elements derived from English sixteenth-century painting. Whether because of an aesthetic preference for that style or because of the technical shortcomings of local artists, American painting tended to remain persistently two-dimensional. Indeed, even in Smibert's paintings, the forms became less substantial and the space less convincing during his years in America, either because the memory of his London manner had gradually dimmed or as an accommodation to local tastes. The alteration in Smibert's style can be compared with the change in the work of Hans Holbein the Younger when he moved from the Continent to England two centuries earlier. In fact, the parallel between these two artists similarly transplanted to provincial and stylistically insular places points up the valid generality that the entire relationship between painting in America and England, viewed from either side, is not unlike the relationship between painting in England and on the Continent, with similar attitudes of inferiority and a compulsion to seek national identity and recognition.

While Smibert's star was fading during the 1740s, the career of Robert Feke was ascending. Little is known about Feke's life. He was born in Oyster Bay, Long Island, New York, and received his first major commission at Boston in 1741, a group portrait of *Isaac Royall and Family* (fig. 39) modeled on Smibert's *The Bermuda Group: Dean George Berkeley and His Entourage* of 1729 (fig. 40). Feke's mature style, with its tasteful color relationships, clarity of composition, and increasing firmness in drawing, is well displayed in his portrait of *William Bowdoin* (2), a prominent Boston merchant described as having "his full share of Pride, Wealth and Ill-Nature."

Feke was the first major American artist to combine European stylistic influence—in this instance, conveyed by Smibert and English mezzotints—with the flat local manner so as to achieve a new, identifiably American, style. It subsequently emerged in the work of other American-born and -trained artists—for example, John Green-

Fig. 38
Anonymous artist
Mrs. Elizabeth Freake and Baby Mary. Oil on canvas, probably 1674. Worcester Art Museum.

Fig. 39
Robert Feke
Isaac Royall and Family
Oil on canvas, 1741. Harvard University Portrait Collection.

Fig. 40
John Smibert
The Bermuda Group: Dean George Berkeley and His Entourage
Oil on canvas, 1729. Yale University Art Gallery; gift of Isaac Lothrop of Plymouth, Massachusetts, 1808.

2
Robert Feke
William Bowdoin
Oil on canvas, 1748. Bowdoin
College Museum of Art; bequest
of Mrs. Sarah Bowdoin Dearborn.

wood, John Hesselius, Benjamin West, and John Singleton Copley—and sets them apart from such European-trained artists working in America as Smibert, Theüs, John Wollaston, or Joseph Blackburn. The paintings of the native artists retain the local characteristic of two-dimensionality, with emphasis on line and the pattern of color areas, and less concern for the three-dimensional representation of solid forms in space. This two-dimensionality is a result, in part at least, of the American artists' lack of opportunity to study old masters or even the best modern paintings at first hand, or to work in academies under the guidance of experienced teachers. Another characteristic of paint-

ings by American-born artists is strong, sometimes abrupt, contrasts of light and shadow, reflecting the fact that the artists acquired much of their sense of art through prints, especially black and white mezzotint engravings.

The careers of Smibert and Feke, who represent the two primary elements that converged to make an American art—of European style and native talent—terminated almost precisely at mid-century. Smibert died in 1751, and Feke vanished in 1750 into the same obscurity from which he had emerged a decade earlier. According to family tradition, he left for the West Indies.

A young Boston artist, John

Greenwood, was clearly influenced by Feke and painted portraits in a similarly planar and even more crisply linear, almost metallic, style, as in the portrait of *Mrs. Henry Bromfield* (fig. 41). Greenwood was active in Boston from 1745 until 1752, when, for unexplained reasons, he departed for Surinam (Dutch Guiana). There he painted *Sea Captains Carousing in Surinam* (3), one of the most engaging exceptions to the rule that American colonial painting consisted largely of portraits. The figures, some caught in acts of indiscretion, have traditionally been identified as mariners from Newport. The rowdy tavern scene, very different from Greenwood's portraits, may have been de-

3
John Greenwood
Sea Captains Carousing in Surinam
Oil on bed ticking, ca. 1752-1758.
The St. Louis Art Museum.

Fig. 41
John Greenwood
Mrs. Henry Bromfield
Oil on canvas, ca. 1749-1750.
Museum of Fine Arts, Boston;
Emily L. Ainsley Fund.

rived from a still unidentified Hogarth-like engraving. By 1758 Greenwood was in Amsterdam, where he engraved prints after old master paintings. Then, in 1762, he moved to London, exhibited occasionally at the Society of Artists, and subsequently ran a successful art auction house for thirty years.

There was a momentary lull in painting activity in Boston at mid-century following the death of Smibert, the disappearance of Feke, and the departure of Greenwood. By default, the best painter may have been Joseph Badger, a self-trained artist born in neighboring Charlestown. Badger was by profession a glazier and house and sign painter. His unsophisticated portraits, such as *Mrs. John Edwards* (4), wife of a Boston silversmith, lack the stylishness of Feke's work, even though the composition, as with so many American portraits, is derived from an English print source. Nevertheless, Badger's pictures have the provincial charm of folk art and a haunting appeal that derives from the muted colors and obscure backgrounds. Even the leathery likeness of *Mrs. Edwards*, wooden and solemn, is strangely magnetic in its literalness.

Most of Badger's known work dates from the latter part of his life. He had probably been eclipsed earlier by Feke in the 1740s, and undoubtedly yet again when Joseph Blackburn, a skillful and dexterous English painter, arrived in Boston in 1755. Over forty-five signed and dated examples of Blackburn's American work survive. His technical facility, especially in the depiction of fabrics, suggests that he may have worked as a drapery painter in London before coming to America. He was popular in the colonies, having painted—from 1754 to 1763, in Newport, Boston, and Portsmouth, New Hampshire—such members of the social, moneyed, and political aristocracy as *Susan Apthorp* (5), daughter of a wealthy Boston merchant. A major factor contributing to his success, in addition to the panache of his brushwork, was his introduction of the new rococo style, with its lighter, more high-keyed palette and animated compositions. After his first few years in America,

4
Joseph Badger
Mrs. John Edwards
Oil on canvas, ca. 1750-1760.
Museum of Fine Arts, Boston; gift
of Dr. Charles Wendell Townsend.

5
Joseph Blackburn
Susan Apthorp
Oil on canvas, 1757. Museum of
Fine Arts, Boston; gift of Mr. and
Mrs. J. Templeman Coolidge.

however, Blackburn encountered increasing competition from the extraordinarily talented young Boston artist John Singleton Copley. It was perhaps for this reason that Blackburn returned to England in 1763, where he continued to paint as late as 1778.

A number of European-trained artists (Charles Bridges and John Wollaston, for example) were attracted to the southern colonies by the lure of portrait commissions from wealthy plantation owners. Jeremiah Theüs, a Swiss, arrived in Charleston, South Carolina, about 1735. He painted there for almost forty years. In 1749 he advertised in the *South Carolina Gazette* that he painted, in addition to portraits, "landskips of all sizes, Crests and Coats of Arms for Coaches or Chaises." Four years later he gave notice "to all young Gentlemen and Ladies inclinable to be taught in the Art of drawing that an Evening school for that Purpose will be opened."[2] Theüs's portrait of *Elizabeth Rothmaler* (6), daughter of a Charleston merchant, combines

6
Jeremiah Theüs
Elizabeth Rothmaler
Oil on canvas, 1757.
The Brooklyn Museum; Carll H. DeSilver Fund.

effective brushwork and lively colors to produce a likeness of alluring freshness.

One of the most remarkable careers in the history of American art is that of Benjamin West. Born into a Quaker family in Swarthmore, Pennsylvania, the son of a tavernkeeper, West (as will be discussed later) became a founding member of the Royal Academy in London, Historical Painter to King George III, and the successor to Sir Joshua Reynolds as president of the Royal Academy, a post he held for almost three decades. As an adolescent West displayed a precocious talent for art, and received some instruction from an English

artist resident in Philadelphia, William Williams. His stiff little miniature *Self-Portrait* (7) of 1756, painted at the age of eighteen as a love token for a young lady in Philadelphia, suggests the influence of itinerant English portraitists, especially John Wollaston, who painted in the middle colonies in the 1750s. This influence is particularly evident in West's portrait of *Thomas Mifflin* (8), with its ambitious composition, muted background, and the young man's full jowls and almond-shaped eyes, which seem mannerisms of style rather than physical attributes. In later years Mifflin was painted by Copley, Charles Willson Peale, and

John Trumbull. He played a significant political and military role during the years of American independence, serving as delegate to the first Continental Congress (1774-1775), aide-de-camp to George Washington, major general in the Continental army, and the first governor of Pennsylvania (1790-1799).

The long careers of Benjamin West and John Singleton Copley followed parallel paths and, at critical junctures, impinged upon each other. Copley was born in the same year as West, 1738, and in similarly modest circumstances, as the son of a Boston tobacconist. He was also strongly influenced by

7
Benjamin West
Self-Portrait
Watercolor on ivory, 1756. Yale
University Art Gallery; the Lelia A.
and John Hill Morgan Collection.

English-trained artists, notably Smibert and his own stepfather, the engraver Peter Pelham, whom his widowed mother married when Copley was ten. Both West and Copley were deeply influenced by books on art theory by Du Fresnoy, De Piles, Richardson, and others. Also, living in the American colonies, where old master paintings were known only at second hand through engravings and copies, the two young artists derived an imprecise but strong sense of the importance of art from books. Both

8
Benjamin West
Thomas Mifflin
Oil on canvas, ca. 1758-1759. The Historical Society of Pennsylvania.

Copley and West aspired from their early years to pursue what the books declared to be the loftiest branch of art: history painting. Plate IX (9) of Copley's *Book of Anatomical Drawings*, a compilation of drawings and texts copied from several European anatomy books, indicates his youthful seriousness of purpose. The study of anatomy was basic to artistic training in European art academies, and as there was no such academy in Boston, Copley attempted to teach himself anatomy from the limited sources at hand.

Copley began to paint professionally in 1753, at the age of fifteen. His early style was an unpolished amalgam of influences from Smibert, Feke, Greenwood, Peter Pelham, and English prints. When Blackburn arrived in Boston in 1755, Copley's limitations, like Badger's, were exposed. For Copley this was an opportunity to learn, so that his paintings of the mid-1750s reflect the pronounced influence of Blackburn.

Like West, Copley tried his hand at miniature painting early in his career, both in watercolor on ivory and, in the case of the unusually large miniature portrait of *The Reverend Samuel Fayerweather* (10), in oil on copper. Fayerweather, rector of the Episcopal church at Kingston, Rhode Island, is repre-sented in his Oxford cap and hood, and black ministerial robe. The miniature has a simple unmarked spiral gadrooned silver frame that may be the work of Nathaniel Hurd, or of Paul Revere whose account book records that he supplied gold and silver miniature frames to Copley. The portrait itself is unusual for a miniature, given the vigorous brushwork that characterizes Copley's style after he had begun to move away from the influence of Blackburn.

Copley's masterpiece in this somewhat rough early manner is his portrait of *Epes Sargent* (11). Bold impasto helps to underscore the strength and vitality of the elderly

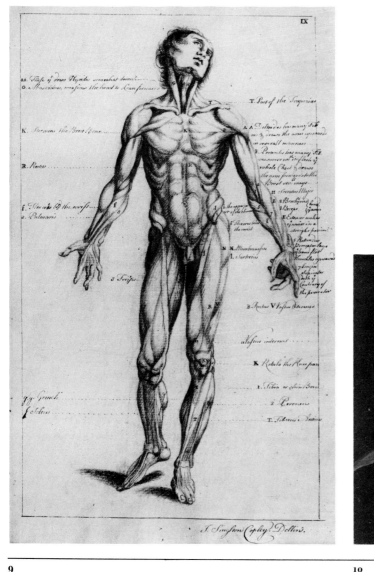

9
John Singleton Copley
Book of Anatomical Drawings, Pl. IX
Ink and red crayon on white paper,
1756. The British Museum.

10
John Singleton Copley
The Reverend Samuel Fayerweather
Oil on copper, ca. 1758.
Yale University Art Gallery;
Mabel Brady Garvan Collection.

Sargent, justice of the peace for Essex County, representative to the General Assembly, and proprietor of nearly half the land of Gloucester, Massachusetts, in 1750. The composition and color are reminiscent of earlier colonial portraits, especially those of Feke, but Copley makes novel use of the spare composition to concentrate the viewer's attention on Sargent's strong hand and weathered face.

By the mid-1760s, Blackburn having returned to England, Copley was unrivaled as the leading painter in New England, and indeed in the American colonies. But since Copley apparently wanted to know how his art compared with the work of contemporaries on the other side of the Atlantic, he sent a portrait of his half-brother *Henry Pelham (Boy with a Squirrel)* (fig. 42, p. 80), to London for exhibition at the Society of Artists in the spring of 1766. The painting won praise from both Joshua Reynolds and Benjamin West, who urged Copley to come to Europe to perfect his art. Copley, however, was re-

11
John Singleton Copley
Epes Sargent
Oil on canvas, 1759-1761.
National Gallery of Art; gift of the Avalon Foundation, 1959.

12
John Singleton Copley
Mrs. Thomas Boylston
Oil on canvas, 1766. Harvard
University Portrait Collection;
bequest of Ward N. Boylston, 1828.

luctant to abandon his successful career in Boston, but he did continue to send pictures to London.

Throughout the 1760s Copley's portraits were in great demand, for portraiture was the one artistic genre that accorded with the values of pragmatic American society. Established Protestantism in English America frowned upon painted religious images; there was no established state to seek glorification of its virtues through history painting; there was no art-collecting aristocracy. But portraits met a practical need, recording likenesses that often were sent to loved ones far away. At least in part because of this custom, the demand in America was for accurate, rather than flattering, likenesses. For example, Copley cautioned an English engraver who was making a plate after one of his portraits: "I shall . . . depend on Your perticular care in the preservation of the likeness that being a main part of the excellency of a portrait in the oppinion of our New England Conoseurs."[3]

Copley was a master of realistic portraiture, as is evident in his striking portrait of *Mrs. Thomas Boylston* (**12**). He sensitively delineated the different textures of the fabrics as well as the likeness of the sitter. His colors, deliciously tasteful, are restrained so as to enhance but not compete with the subject. Yet the full measure of Copley's skill in portraiture lay in his ability not only to depict external reality, but to capture the larger reality of the sitter within the context of his or her role as a functioning member of society. He achieved this sense of social context especially well in the glorious portraits of *Mr. and Mrs. Isaac Smith* (**13**, **14**; see discussion pages 34–35).

Another aspect of Copley's virtuosity was evident in his masterly pastel portraits, which are the most sophisticated drawings made in America before the Revolution. Copley himself was proud of his success in pastel; he wrote to West in London requesting that "when you write next time you will be more explicit on the article of Crayons and why You dis[ap]prove the use of them, for I think my best portraits done in that way."[4]

Although Copley began to make pastels in 1758, his most effective use of the medium is found in later portraits such as *Mrs. Joseph Barrell* (**15**). The second wife of a well-to-do merchant of Charlestown, Massachusetts, Mrs. Barrell wears a blue dress with a pink rosebud at the bodice, and a pink sack trimmed with ermine. Posed against an abstract tonal background in which the figure appears in strong relief, the style compares to Copley's of this period in its rich shadows, strong modeling, and informal pose. Copley's watercolor-on-ivory miniature *Self-Portrait* (**16**), based on a pastel (Winterthur Museum), was executed two years earlier in 1769, the year of Copley's marriage to Susanna Clark. It marks the period when Copley's

16
John Singleton Copley
Self-Portrait
Watercolor on ivory, 1769.
Mrs. H. Gordon Sweet;
on loan to the Yale University
Art Gallery.

15
John Singleton Copley
Mrs. Joseph Barrell
Pastel on paper mounted on linen,
ca. 1771. Museum of Fine Arts,
Boston; gift of Benjamin Joy.

American career crested. With a family to support and a handsome estate on Beacon Hill, Copley became increasingly dependent upon a steady flow of portrait commissions. Unfortunately, with the intensifying political crisis at this time, Americans had other things on their minds than having their portraits painted, and Copley found himself getting fewer commissions. He therefore in 1771 took up a long-standing invitation to visit New York, where he did a flourishing business for six months.

Several good portrait painters were also working in New York about this time—John Mare, Thomas McIlworth, Abraham Delanoy, and John Durand, among others—but none was in Copley's class as an artist. John Durand's appealing portrait of *Richard Crossfield* (**17**) is representative of this New York school. Details concerning Durand's career are sketchy, but he is known to have been active in Connecticut, New York, and Virginia; newspaper advertisements indicate that he opened a drawing school in New York in 1767, and the following year he solicited, apparently without success, commissions for history paintings. He did a number of portraits in Virginia in 1770, then again in 1781-1782, at which time he disappeared. As for Durand's portrait style, it was stiff and rigorously

17
John Durand
Richard Crossfield
Oil on canvas, ca. 1769 or ca. 1772.
The Metropolitan Museum of Art;
gift of Edgar William and Bernice
Chrysler Garbisch, 1969.

Fig. 42
John Singleton Copley
Henry Pelham (The Boy with a
Squirrel). Oil on canvas, 1765.
Private collection (Photo:
Museum of Fine Arts, Boston).

planar, with color areas crisply marked off from each other. The composition of *Richard Crossfield* suggests that Durand was aware of more sophisticated artistic ideas, most likely through mezzotints. However, the wooden pose, the lack of convincing articulation of the limbs, and the insubstantiality of the forms attest to his circumscribed training, the common handicap of all the native colonial American artists.

Although there was no art academy to train artists in America, Copley was able to get some long-range instruction from England. When his *Boy with a Squirrel* (fig. 42) was exhibited at the Society of Artists in London in 1766, Benjamin West, who had arrived in London himself only three years earlier, wrote to Copley that on the basis of his own experience of the limitations under which an artist had to work in America, he was certain that Copley would appreciate a professional critique. He then proceeded to give one, noting that Copley's picture was too "liney," the edges of depicted objects were too sharp, the forms did not partake of the roundedness that characterizes solid objects in the real world. What West was referring to, of course, was the two-dimensional or flat quality, the emphasis on line, color, and pattern that marked the work of virtually all native American artists. West's thoughtful gesture in writing to Copley typified the relationship he maintained with young American artists throughout his life. Generous and hospitable by nature, although also ambitious and possessed of an unerring instinct for the main chance, West habitually gave advice and instruction in his own studio to young American artists when they came to England. Copley, through his exchange of letters with West, was in effect a correspondence-course pupil in what has come to be known, largely because of Matthew Pratt's depiction of it, as West's "American school."

Matthew Pratt, born in Philadelphia and apprenticed to his uncle James Claypoole, was active as a portrait painter in his native city from 1758 until, in 1764, he accompanied West's fiancée, Elizabeth Shewell, to London, where he stayed on to attend the wedding and to study with West. After two and a half years in West's studio and a brief period of painting portraits in Bristol, Pratt returned to Philadelphia, where, except for a visit to New York in the early 1770s, he painted portraits until his death. Pratt's *The American School* (**18**) was exhibited at the Society of Artists in 1766, the same year as Copley's *Boy with a Squirrel* (fig. 42). Although the identity of several of the figures is uncertain, West is the figure standing at the left, and Pratt himself is probably the pupil seated next to him.

18
Matthew Pratt
The American School
Oil on canvas, 1765.
The Metropolitan Museum of Art;
gift of Samuel P. Avery, 1897.

Benjamin West had been in London only slightly more than two years when Pratt painted *The American School*. He had left Philadelphia in 1760 for Italy, where he spent the next three years studying the old masters and the works of classical antiquity. In 1765, the year in which *The American School* was painted, West was introduced to Dr. Robert Drummond, Archbishop of York, who commissioned him to paint *Agrippina Landing at Brundisium with the Ashes of Germanicus* (**19**), based on the account in the *Annals* of Tacitus (see above, page 36). Compositionally, West used a traditional stagelike setting, with the primary action highlit in the center and figures in the wings framing the action. The clear demarcation of receding planes and the dramatic expressiveness of the supporting figures reveals a debt to French seventeenth-century classicism. But the subdued palette, the procession resembling a monochromatic antique frieze, the use of specific and correct classical sources for figures and setting, the static composition, and the moralizing intent of the subject constitute an early effective statement of neoclassicism, anticipating the work of Jacques Louis David in France.

West began *Agrippina* in 1766. When it was finished in 1768, it was shown by Archbishop Drummond to King George III, who was so favorably impressed he commissioned West to paint another picture from Roman history, *The Departure of Regulus* (fig. 43). West's best-known painting, however,

Fig. 43
Benjamin West
The Departure of Regulus
Oil on canvas, ca. 1767.
Her Majesty the Queen.

19
Benjamin West
Agrippina Landing at Brundisium with the Ashes of Germanicus
Oil on canvas, 1768.
Yale University Art Gallery; gift of Louis M. Rabinowitz.

is *The Death of General Wolfe* (**20**; see above, page 36), which depicts the death of General James Wolfe on the Plains of Abraham at the moment of his dramatic victory over the French at Quebec in 1759. While it was not unusual to paint a scene from modern rather than ancient history, the accepted mode of representation was to clothe the figures in classical garb. When West departed from the convention, depicting the soldiers in contemporary uniforms, Sir Joshua Reynolds, president of the Royal Academy, warned him against this departure; West is recorded to have replied:

The event intended to be commemorated took place on the 13th of September, 1758, in a region of the world unknown to the Greeks and Romans, and at a period of time when no such nation, nor heroes in their costume, any longer existed. . . . The same truth that guides the pen of the historian should govern the pencil of the artist. I consider myself as undertaking to tell this great event to the eye of the world; but if, instead of the facts of the transaction, I represent classical fictions, how shall I be understood by posterity?[5]

Thus West made his didactic point that heroic deeds were as possible for modern man as for the ancients. George III declined an opportunity to buy the first version of *The Death of Wolfe* (National Gallery of Canada, Ottawa), sharing Reynolds's belief that modern dress made the significance of a scene too restricted to a particular time and place, rather than universal. When the picture was acclaimed at

20
Benjamin West
The Death of General Wolfe
Oil on canvas, 1771.
Her Majesty The Queen.

the Royal Academy exhibition in 1771, the king realized his error and commissioned the replica (20).

The Artist's Family (21), probably painted in 1772 or 1773, depicts West and his family in a tranquil domestic scene at a happy moment. West had just been appointed Historical Painter to the King (1772). He stands at the right, palette in hand, gazing at his wife and newborn son, Benjamin, Jr. His elder son, Raphael Lamar West, leans on his mother's chair. The painting also records a visit from West's Quaker father, John West, and half-brother Thomas, whose stiff poses and sober clothes contrast with the elegant dress of the other figures. This family portrait hung in West's studio throughout his life and was well known to visitors and students.

Throughout his career West made numerous drawings, mostly compositional studies for large pictures but landscape and figure studies as well. He modeled his early

21
Benjamin West
The Artist's Family
Oil on canvas, ca. 1772-1773.
Collection of Mr. and Mrs. Paul
Mellon.

drawing style on the baroque masters of the seventeenth century, whereas later he absorbed stylistic elements from the British painter John Hamilton Mortimer and from John Henry Fuseli. His wash drawing of 1783, *The Three Sisters* (22), either inspired by a literary source or simply a study for a group portrait, is composed of characteristically short, choppy, angular lines, and reveals West's concern with expressive attitude.

During the years when West consolidated his position as a history painter in London, Copley, despite West's repeated urging to come to Europe, remained in America painting portraits. When the political situation worsened in Boston—especially after the Boston Tea Party, of which Copley's in-laws were the victims—and portrait commissions fell off sharply, Copley decided to take West's advice and visit Europe. After a brief stay in London and more than a year of

22
Benjamin West
The Three Sisters
Pen and india ink wash drawing
on paper, 1783. The Nelson Gallery–
Atkins Museum; Nelson Fund.

travel and study in Italy, he returned to London, where in October 1775, he was united with his family, which had left America after the outbreak of hostilities at Lexington and Concord. Copley continued to paint portraits to support them, but he, like West, preferred to paint history pictures. His first important historical commission came from Brook Watson, a prosperous merchant, later Lord Mayor of London.

Copley's *Watson and the Shark* (fig. 44), painted and exhibited at the Royal Academy in 1778 where it caused a minor sensation, records a horrible scene from Watson's youth, when, while swimming in Havana harbor, he had been attacked by a shark and lost his right foot. The superb *Head of a Negro* (23) has been known for over a century as a sketch for *Watson*. Indeed it may have been intended as a sketch for the painting, but the animated, almost gay expression on the face of the black sailor bears little resemblance to the final picture.

23
John Singleton Copley
Head of a Negro
Oil on canvas, 1777-1783.
The Detroit Institute of Arts;
Gibbs-Williams Fund.

Fig. 44
John Singleton Copley
Watson and the Shark
Oil on canvas, 1778.
National Gallery of Art;
Ferdinand Lammot Belin Fund.

Copley's attraction to the style of Rubens is readily apparent in the color and facile handling of pigment in *Head of a Negro*. This Rubenesque quality reflects the growing competition between West, the leading history painter of the day, and Copley, the already mature artist with sufficient self-confidence and ambition to at least equal West or surpass him and achieve status with the old masters. In an echo of the seventeenth-century battle of the Poussinistes and Rubenistes, Copley set out to play the part of Rubens in counterpoint to West's classical affinity for Poussin.

In the following year, Copley was elected to full membership in the Royal Academy, and *Watson* was followed by several large paintings representing events from recent British political and military history. The first of these, *The Death of the Earl of Chatham* (**24**), commemorates an event that occurred in the House of Lords on April 7, 1778, when William Pitt, Earl of Chatham, suffered a stroke while

24
John Singleton Copley
The Death of the Earl of Chatham
Oil on canvas, 1779-1781.
The Trustees of the Tate Gallery.

participating in a debate on the war in America. During the two years while he worked on the large picture (1779-1780), Copley made numerous drawings and oil sketches to develop the composition. *Study for the Central Group* (25), for example, reveals his concern with the pose and placement of the figures, as well as with the effects of light and shadow. Moreover, West's *Death of Wolfe*, which initiated a revolution in history painting, was taken a step farther by Copley in *The Death of Chatham*. Not only was the event more recent in time and local in place, but Copley sought to elevate the commemorative nature of history painting by injecting the authenticity of group portraiture. *Study for Lord Mansfield* (26), one of many life studies Copley drew for the large picture in addition to his compositional studies, is scaled for transfer onto the canvas. Mansfield, a lifelong opponent of Chatham and his poli-

26
John Singleton Copley
Study for Lord Mansfield for
"The Death of the Earl of Chatham"
Black and white chalk on gray paper,
1779-1780. The Boston Athenaeum.

cies, is the one figure in the painting who remains seated on the occasion of Chatham's distress, an act of indifference noted pointedly in contemporary newspaper accounts of the painting.

Finished and exhibited privately in the spring of 1781, *The Death of the Earl of Chatham* was popular. Twenty thousand people paid one shilling each to see it during a six-week period. Indeed, it was this picture, together with *The Death of Major Peirson* (fig. 45), completed in 1784, that gained Copley recognition as a leading English history painter.

It is noteworthy that the two leading English history painters in the second half of the eighteenth century, West and Copley, were colonial Americans. When Copley and West went to Europe, they took with them, in addition to a firm resolve to pursue history painting, practical experience as portrait painters who produced realistic likenesses to suit the taste of their colonial patrons. Thus their subsequent innovations in history painting in England were invariably in the direction of greater realism: West's introduction of "real" Roman sculpture and architecture into such paintings with Roman subjects as *Agrippina*; his treatment of a modern historical scene in modern dress in *The Death of Wolfe*; Copley's use in *Watson and the Shark* of accurate background details of Havana taken from prints and maps; and his incorporation of real portraits into local and contemporary historical scenes to make them as real as possible, as in *The Death of Chatham*. Paradoxically, their influence found fertile ground not so much in America or England as in France, especially in David's realistic classicism (*The Death of Socrates, The Oath of the Horatii, The Oath of Brutus*) and modernism (*The Death of Marat*), and in his use of real settings and portraits (*The Oath of the Tennis Court*). Inasmuch as the colonial background of Copley and West af-

Fig. 45
John Singleton Copley
The Death of Major Peirson
Oil on canvas, 1782-1784.
The Tate Gallery.

25
John Singleton Copley
Study for the Central Group for
"The Death of the Earl of Chatham"
Black and white chalk on gray-blue
paper, 1779. The British Museum.

fected both their choice of history painting as a profession and the persistent growth toward greater realism in their art, it may be claimed that their innovations in history painting stand as one of the earliest direct American return contributions to the cultural life of Europe.

Looking back now to the colonies, we find that a small group of portrait painters flourished in Newport, Rhode Island, before the Revolution. One of these was Samuel King, who early in his career painted a remarkable portrait of *Ezra Stiles* (**27**), pastor of the Second Congregational Church of Newport and later president of Yale College. Stiles, who in 1770 had officiated at King's marriage to Amy Vernon, daughter of an influential Newport merchant and silversmith, was one of the most learned men of eighteenth-century New England. On the bookshelves behind him in the portrait are volumes labeled "NEWTON/PRIN.," "PLATO," "LIVY," "DV HALDE'S/HIST. OF/CHINA," a volume of the Talmud, and selections from such Puritan divines as Hooker, Mather, Chauncey, and Cotton. On the column at left is "one Circle and one Trajectory around a solar point, as an emblem of the Newtonian or Pythagorean System of the Sun & Planets & Comets." Above, on the wall, hangs "an Emblem of the Universe or intellectual World." The symbols suggest the wide-ranging interests of Stiles, who presumably set the emblematic program for the artist to follow. On the completion of the portrait, he wrote with prideful satisfaction in his literary *Diary*, "These Emblems are more descriptive of my Mind, than the Effigies of my Face."[6]

Many colonial American artists, Copley excepted, found that patronage, even for portraits, was insufficient to provide a livelihood, and that they were obliged to engage in other trades or activities. Some, like Smibert, sold art supplies and engravings; some, like Theüs, painted coach panels and tavern signs; others, like Peter Pelham, taught drawing; still others, like Badger, even did house painting and glazing. King himself pursued house and carriage painting, engraving, and frame and instrument making in addition to portraiture.

The most versatile of all the

27
Samuel King
Ezra Stiles
Oil on canvas, 1770-1771.
Yale University Art Gallery;
bequest of Dr. Charles Jenkins
Foote, B.A. 1883, M.A. 1890.

artists active during the period was Charles Willson Peale. Born in Maryland in 1741, Peale was a saddler's apprentice until his majority. An inquisitive pragmatist with immense confidence in his own abilities, Peale as a young man saw the work of an itinerant artist and decided that he could do better. He studied briefly with John Hesselius in Annapolis in 1763, visited Copley in Boston in 1765, and worked with West in London from 1767 to 1769. After his return, Peale became quite active in Annapolis, the flourishing colonial capital of Maryland. In 1773 he began his portrait of *William Buckland* (**28**), architect of one of the finest of the stately

Georgian houses in Annapolis, the Hammond-Harwood House, designed that same year for the lawyer Matthias Hammond. Peale represents Buckland as a working architect, with architectural books and drawing instruments on the table, and plans for the Hammond-Harwood House spread out before him. The model in the background suggests the classical tradition that provided the source for his designs. When Buckland died the following year, Peale stopped working on the painting and did not finish it until 1787.

Peale subsequently settled in Philadelphia, where he was an ardent Whig, an officer in the Con-

tinental army until 1778, and an active figure in local politics. In January 1779 the Supreme Executive Council of Pennsylvania commissioned him to paint an official portrait of *George Washington at the Battle of Princeton*. The portrait (Pennsylvania Academy of the Fine Arts) instantly generated praise and orders for some two dozen replicas (**29**). A metaphor of American nationalism and confidence, the painting commemorated Washington's victories over British forces at Trenton and Princeton, New Jersey, in the winter of 1776-1777. The American battle flag unfurls above rumpled Hessian standards taken at Trenton, and in

28
Charles Willson Peale
William Buckland
Oil on canvas, 1773-1787.
Yale University Art Gallery;
Mabel Brady Garvan Collection.

the background, American soldiers lead off British prisoners within view of the college buildings at Princeton. The portrait recalls Jefferson's description of Washington as "easy, erect, and noble." The monumental, full-length format is appropriate for a state portrait, but the pose is informal. In the version here (**29**) Peale painted out the blue ribbon across Washington's breast, following a change in the military uniform code in June 1780.

Washington sat for his friend Peale on seven different occasions, but it was this official portrait in particular that heightened Peale's reputation and brought him com-

29
Charles Willson Peale
George Washington at the Battle of Princeton. Oil on canvas, 1780-1781. Yale University Art Gallery; gift of the Maitland Fuller Griggs Fund and Mrs. Henry B. Loomis, in memory of Henry Bradford Loomis, B.A. 1875.

30
Charles Willson Peale
Walter Stewart
Oil on canvas, 1781.
Private collection.

missions from many other military figures. One of these was from *Walter Stewart* (**30**), a radical young Irishman who had emigrated to America upon his majority in 1776 to receive a commission as captain of the Third Pennsylvania Battalion. Jaunty, capable, and renowned for bravery, he advanced rapidly. Congress within the year awarded him a sword of honor and in 1777 promoted him to colonel ("The boy colonel," scoffed his detractors) in charge of the Thirteenth and Third Regiments of the Pennsylvania Line. Peale's portrait of Walter Stewart in military uniform, completed in the spring of 1781, includes the congressional sword and, in the background, the encampment of Stewart's regiments. The hand-

some, dashing officer is shown full length on a small canvas normally used for three-quarter-length portraits.

When Stewart was married in April 1781 to Deborah McClenachan, daughter of a well-to-do Irish merchant of Philadelphia, he commissioned Peale to execute a portrait of his bride (**31**). In this picture, finished in 1782, Peale captured the soft beauty of the eighteen-year-old girl and evoked a sense of her social station and style of life through the gracious ease of the pose and the carefully rendered details. On her right wrist Mrs. Stewart wears Peale's documented miniature portrait of her husband (location unknown).

Peale, who was also a prolific and

accomplished miniature painter, in 1781 did a miniature of *George Walton* (**32**), a member of the Continental Congress meeting in Philadelphia. Of lowly origins, Walton had educated himself in law and had become a fiery statesman, signer of the Declaration of Independence, and later governor and chief justice of Georgia. The intimate appeal of Peale's portrait of *Walton* is enhanced by the softness of the contours and gray-blue palette, the effective shading of the face and textiles, and the delicate details of hair, eyes, and lace.

In later years Peale increasingly turned his attention to art instruction, natural history, science, and technology. He established the first American museum, in

31
Charles Willson Peale
Mrs. Walter Stewart
Oil on canvas, 1781-1782.
Private collection.

32
Charles Willson Peale
George Walton
Watercolor on ivory, 1781.
Yale University Art Gallery;
Mabel Brady Garvan Collection.

Philadelphia, on the second floor of Independence Hall, where he displayed his portraits of American statesmen and military heroes as well as stuffed birds and the skeleton of a mastodon. He was also active in the establishment of one of the first American academies of art (the Pennsylvania Academy of the Fine Arts, the oldest American academy still in existence). And he sired a dynasty of painters predestined for their careers with such given names as Rembrandt, Raphaelle, Angelica Kauffmann, and Titian Ramsay.

Other American artists sought the same success that Peale had achieved in painting the leaders of the new nation. Joseph Wright studied in London during the late 1770s with West and John Hoppner. When Richard Oswald, the British peace negotiator, began to confer with

Benjamin Franklin in Paris in April 1782, he commissioned Wright to paint a portrait of the American scientist-philosopher-diplomat (**33**). Since Franklin would not endure lengthy sittings. Wright modeled his portrait on the 1778 pastel by the French artist Duplessis (fig. 46). He brought his own rendering up to date, however, by depicting Franklin in the red coat he wore during the negotiations and by an unsparing portrayal of Franklin's deeply furrowed face and the shadowy concavity above his upper lip caused by the loss of teeth. Before Franklin returned to America late in 1782, Wright completed four additional versions of the portrait for British patrons.

Unlike Peale, West, or Copley, John Trumbull was well born; he was also precocious, snobbish,

and irascible. Trumbull graduated from Harvard College in 1773. In 1775 he joined the Continental army in Boston, serving briefly as aide-de-camp to General Washington and then as adjutant under General Horatio Gates. In 1777 he quit the army, returned to his home in Lebanon, Connecticut, and "resumed his pencil." It was at this time that he began the double portrait of his parents (**34**), which he described as a "group, size of life, on a half length cloth reversed [on its side]; my father dressed in a blue damask night gown."[7] The artist's father, Jonathan Trumbull, Harvard graduate and merchant, served as governor of Connecticut throughout the Revolutionary period, 1769-83. In 1735 he had married Faith Robinson, a descendant of the Reverend John Robin-

33
Joseph Wright
Benjamin Franklin
Oil on canvas, 1782.
Benjamin Franklin Collection,
Yale University Library; gift of

William Smith Mason, PH.B. 1888,
M.A. (hon.) 1924.

Fig. 46
Joseph Silfrede Duplessis
Benjamin Franklin
Pastel, 1778.
New York Public Library; Astor,
Lenox and Tilden Foundations.

son, who had led the Pilgrims to Holland before they emigrated to America in 1620. The likenesses of the Yankee couple are rough-hewn and disarmingly candid. Trumbull presumably had completed the painting by June 1778, when he returned to Boston and rented the former studio of John Smibert.

Young Trumbull was greatly influenced by Copley, whom he had met in Boston in 1772. His double portrait shows similarities—in the setting, the reflection of objects on the polished table, and the treatment of two seated figures—to Copley's *Mr. and Mr. Thomas Mifflin* (fig. 47) painted in Boston in

the summer of 1773, and on which Trumbull may have observed Copley at work. His portrait is also similar to Copley's *Nicholas Boylston* of 1773 (fig. 48), which he had seen in the "philosophical chamber" at Harvard; the pose of Trumbull's father is the same, in reverse, as Nicholas Boylston's.

34
John Trumbull
Governor Jonathan Trumbull and Mrs. Jonathan (Faith Robinson) Trumbull. Oil on canvas, 1777-1778. The Connecticut Historical Society.

Fig. 47
John Singleton Copley
Mr. and Mrs. Thomas Mifflin
Oil on canvas, 1773. The Historical Society of Pennsylvania.

Fig. 48
John Singleton Copley
Nicholas Boylston
Oil on canvas, 1767. Harvard University Portrait Collection.

Determined to become a painter despite his father's protestations that he "pursue one of the learned professions," Trumbull journeyed to London in 1780 and began to study with Benjamin West. Soon, however, Trumbull, a former officer in the Continental army, was imprisoned in London in reprisal for the execution of Major André as a spy in New York. Freed in 1781,

he went back to Connecticut, but at the end of the war returned to West's studio. During this second European sojourn, from 1784 to 1789, Trumbull perceived that the increased realism of West and Copley had moved history painting in significant new directions. When he also understood that neither of these artists, both permanent residents in England, could treat a most

significant aspect of contemporary history, the American Revolution, he resolved to devote his own career to representing the events and "eminent men" of the War of Independence.

Trumbull began the first in a projected series of scenes of "national history," *The Death of General Warren at the Battle of Bunker's Hill, 17 June 1775* (35), in London

35
John Trumbull
The Death of General Warren at the Battle of Bunker's Hill, 17 June 1775
Oil on canvas, 1786.
Yale University Art Gallery.

in 1784. He had in fact viewed the battle on June 17, although from a considerable distance. The composition of the central death group, the Negro servant, the fleeing figures at the right, and the diagonals of smoke and banners echo Copley's much-applauded *The Death of Major Peirson*, exhibited the same year.

Three months after finishing *The Death of Warren*, in March 1786, Trumbull completed the second painting of the proposed series, *The Death of General Montgomery in the Attack on Quebec, 31 December 1775* (36), which conveys the sudden shock of the explosion that killed Montgomery and two aides as they led the American assault on Quebec. Trumbull patterned the poses, the slumping central figure, the Indian, and the tripartite composition on West's *Death of General Wolfe*, but, as in *The Death of Warren*, his own spontaneous brushwork and brilliant palette help to convery the dramatic excitement of the battle.

Trumbull hoped to realize a fortune from the sale of engravings made after these paintings, whose small format was specifically in-

36
John Trumbull
The Death of General Montgomery in the Attack on Quebec, 31 December 1775. Oil on canvas, 1786.
Yale University Art Gallery.

tended to accommodate engravers. The prints, however, were not popular in the United States, perhaps because they seemed to celebrate British victories.

In 1786, 1787, and 1789, Trumbull journeyed to France and became acquainted with many artists, including Mme. Vigée-le-Brun and Jacques Louis David. The influence of the latter's *Oath of the Horatii* can be detected in the three figures with upraised muskets on the left in *The Death of Montgomery*. The sensuous back view of a *Reclining Female Nude* (37) was drawn in Paris from life, probably in 1789, but perhaps during a later visit, in 1794-1795 or 1796. The drawing is enhanced by subtleties of modeling and form, linear rhythms, and the effect of light and color, but suffers somewhat from misapprehensions of foreshortening and anatomy.

When Trumbull returned to America in 1789, he spent five years traveling up and down the eastern seaboard making sketches for use in his American history paintings.

37
John Trumbull
Reclining Female Nude, Back View
Charcoal and white chalk on blue paper, probably 1789.
Yale University Art Gallery; gift of the Associates in Fine Arts.

In New York in 1790 he drew the likeness of *Hopothle Mico*, the Talasee King of the Creeks (**38**). With wiry strokes, he suggested the opulence of the military coat, medals, beads, and feathered headdress. And in a rare display of his ability to penetrate character, he conveyed the wistfulness and fortitude of the chieftain through the sensitive modeling of the face.

The sketch of *Major William Lithgow* (**39**) further demonstrates the fluency of Trumbull's fully developed linear style. Executed in pencil on a heavy laid paper card, the drawing served as a study for the likeness of Major Lithgow as an officer of the Eleventh Massachusetts Regiment in Trumbull's *Surrender of General Burgoyne at Saratoga, New York, 16 October 1777* (fig. 50). On the verso of the card, the artist made notations of subject, date, and colors: "Maj. Lithgow / Blue & White / Black Stock / Boston 10th July [?] '91."

In the course of his travels, between 1790 and 1793, Trum-

38
John Trumbull
Hopothle Mico
Pencil on paper, 1790.
Fordham University Library.

39
John Trumbull
Major William Lithgow
Pencil on paper mounted on card,
1791. Yale University Art Gallery;
gift of Mrs. Winchester Bennett.

bull completed over sixty miniature portrait studies in oil on mahogany panels. These miniatures are among the most successful productions of his career, unparalleled in their realism, spontaneity, and coloristic brilliance. Trumbull, who had lost the use of his left eye in a childhood accident, was at his best when painting on a small scale. He painted five miniatures of women in his family (40); these included portraits of his deceased mother, derived from a painting of 1779; his beloved cousin Harriet Wadsworth of Hartford, Connecticut, painted from memory in 1793, three months after her death; and his beautiful young niece, Faith Trumbull, who later married Daniel Wadsworth, founder of the Wadsworth Athe-

40
John Trumbull
Five miniatures framed together
Oil on mahogany panels.
Yale University Art Gallery.

Harriet Wadsworth, 1793
Faith Trumbull, 1791
Mrs. Jonathan Trumbull, 1793
Catherine Wadsworth, 1792
Julia Seymour, 1792

neum in Hartford.

Most of Trumbull's miniatures were undertaken as preparatory studies for the series of American history paintings in which historical accuracy was essential. The oil sketches of Ebenezer Stevens, Wil-liam Hull, John Brooks, and Thomas Seymour (41) provided likenesses for *The Surrender of Burgoyne* (fig. 50). Here Trumbull converts them from civilians of the 1790s into officers of the Con-tinental army in 1777, with sober expressions appropriate to the historical occasion.

Since Trumbull could not obtain life portraits of all who figured in the scenes he chose to paint, he took pains to procure likenesses from other sources if possible. For

41a
John Trumbull
Thomas Youngs Seymour
Oil on mahogany panel, 1793.
Yale University Art Gallery.

example, he took his portrait of Major General Nathaniel Greene, who had died in 1786, "from the only original picture remaining,"[8] C. W. Peale's 1783 portrait (fig. 49).

In 1791, when he made the life portrait of Henry Laurens (42) in Charleston, South Carolina, Trumbull was planning a painting of the Treaty of Paris. Although he

never carried out the idea, he also took the likenesses of four other commissioners (42) who had concluded the peace of 1783. He had included earlier a life portrait of

Fig. 49
Charles Willson Peale
Nathaniel Greene
Oil on canvas, 1783.
Independence National Historical
Park Collection, Philadelphia.

41
John Trumbull
Five miniatures framed together
Oil on mahogany panels.
Yale University Art Gallery.

Nathaniel Greene, 1792
William Hull, 1790
Ebenezer Stevens, 1790
Thomas Youngs Seymour, 1793
(illustrated in color)
John Brooks, 1790

John Adams in *The Declaration of Independence, Philadelphia, 4 July 1776* (fig. 51), painted in London in 1787, and in later years painted three full-size portraits of the second president. Trumbull's portrait of John Jay, coauthor of *The Federalist* and the first chief justice of the United States, is, however, less successful than his Adams. When in 1794 Trumbull accompanied Jay to London on a mission to resolve disputes between Great Britain and America, he decided to stay on until 1804 as a commissioner empowered

42
John Trumbull
Five miniatures framed together
Oil on mahogany panels.
Yale University Art Gallery.

Henry Laurens, 1791
John Jay, 1793
John Adams, 1793
George Hammond, 1793
William Temple Franklin, 1790

Fig. 50
John Trumbull
The Surrender of General Burgoyne at Saratoga, New York, 16 October 1777. Oil on canvas, ca. 1816. Yale University Art Gallery.

Fig. 51
John Trumbull
The Declaration of Independence, Philadelphia, 4 July 1776
Oil on canvas, 1786-1819/20. Yale University Art Gallery.

by Jay's treaty to judge cases of maritime law, an obligation that diverted his attention from art for a decade and proved detrimental to his career.

In addition to his painting, Trumbull began, during the early 1790s, to study architecture. His elevation and plan of a large house (43) typifies the clarity and precision of the inventive designs of symmetrically ordered buildings that he executed in Lebanon, Connecticut. However, though he was a friend of the architects Charles Bulfinch, Ithiel Town, and Alexander Jackson Davis, all of whom received important commissions, Trumbull never did realize his ambition to design government buildings.

In 1816 he finally settled in New York, where, increasingly pompous, intransigent, and querulous, he served as the unpopular president of the American Academy of Fine Arts. Between 1817 and 1824 he completed life-size replicas of four of his "national history" paintings, commissioned by Congress; they now hang in the rotunda of the Capitol in Washington, D.C. These large canvases are less successful than Trumbull's early small history sketches, in which he first applied the innovations in history painting of his expatriate countrymen West and Copley to American subjects, implanting their achievements within the artistic tradition of the new nation.

When Trumbull went to London in 1780 to study with Benjamin West, he was welcomed by and shared a studio room with West's senior pupil and assistant, Gilbert Stuart. Stuart was born in 1755 in the rural town of North Kingstown, Rhode Island, where his Scottish-born father operated a snuff mill. The mill failed in 1761, and Stuart's family moved to Newport, the colonial capital of Rhode Island. As a young boy, Stuart was apprenticed, first in Newport and later in Edinburgh, to an itinerant Scottish portrait painter, Cosmo Alexander, whose linear style is reflected in Stuart's few early portraits painted at Newport between 1773 and 1775. The double portrait of *Francis Malbone and His Brother Saunders* (fig. 52) is characteristic. The tight outlines and limited control of the medium in Stuart's early paintings stand in contrast to the easy fluidity of his developed style.

In 1777, two years after Stuart left America for England, he entered the London studio of Benjamin West, where he studied painting and assisted until 1782, and where, gradually, his raw style was transformed. *The Skater* (44), a portrait of his Scottish friend William Grant of Congalton, was exhibited at the Royal Academy in 1782, the year Stuart left West's studio to strike off

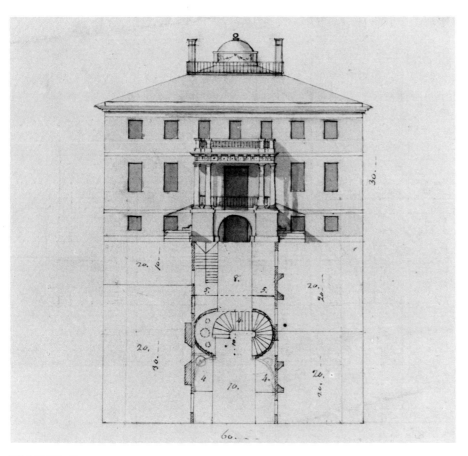

43
John Trumbull
Elevation and Plan of a Residence
Pencil, pen and ink, and ink wash
on blue paper, 1790-1794. Yale
University Art Gallery; gift
of the Associates in Fine Arts.

Fig. 52
Gilbert Stuart
*Francis Malbone and His Brother
Saunders*. Oil on canvas, ca. 1773-
1775. Private collection (Photo:
Frick Art Reference Library).

44
Gilbert Stuart
The Skater (Portrait of William
Grant). Oil on canvas, 1782.
National Gallery of Art; Andrew W.
Mellon Collection, 1950.

on his own. *The Skater*'s gliding pose suggests gracefulness, and Stuart reinforces the effect of motion by the slight forward lean of the figure and the crossing of the legs as the subject's skates push against the ice, leaving a faint line traced on the cold, hard surface. In the distant background rise the

towers of Westminster Abbey. This first full-length portrait by Stuart, daring in conception and brilliantly painted, achieved well-deserved critical success. In 1878, when *The Skater* was next exhibited at the Royal Academy, it was attributed to Thomas Gainsborough until its correct authorship was rediscovered.

The unfinished *Portrait of the Artist* (45), thought to have been painted by Stuart in London for his wife, Charlotte Coates, about the time of their marriage in 1786, demonstrates Stuart's facility for capturing a likeness with a minimum of effort. It also illustrates his technique: in working up a paint-

45
Gilbert Stuart
Portrait of the Artist
Oil on canvas, ca. 1786.
The Metropolitan Museum of Art;
Fletcher Fund, 1926.

ing, he did the preliminary drawing broadly with a brush to distinguish masses of light and shadow, rather than meticulously with chalk or pencil.

Success led to a profusion of portrait commissions in London, but it also tempted Stuart to immoderation. A lavish entertainer and witty raconteur, he soon lapsed into extravagance. By 1787 accumulated debt forced him to leave London for Dublin and a fresh start, but the same sequence of success, dissipation, and this time debtor's prison followed.

In 1793, after six years in Dublin, Stuart returned to America, where he seems to have controlled his personal weaknesses and worked successfully and contentedly until his death in 1828. He painted the leaders of the new Republic and is, of course, best known for his numerous portraits of George Washington (figs. 53-55). Yet prolific as he was, Stuart was able to avoid repeti-

Fig. 53
Gilbert Stuart
George Washington
(The "Vaughan" Portrait)
Oil on canvas, 1795.
National Gallery of Art;
Andrew W. Mellon Collection.

Fig. 54
Gilbert Stuart
George Washington
(The "Athenaeum" Portrait)
Oil on canvas, 1796. Museum of
Fine Arts, Boston; deposited by
the Boston Athenaeum, 1876.

Fig. 55
Gilbert Stuart
George Washington
(The "Lansdowne" Portrait)
Oil on canvas, 1796. The Pennsylvania Academy of Fine Arts.

tive mannerisms. *Mrs. Richard Yates* (46), painted in New York City shortly after he returned to America, is strikingly original. The portrait captures the instant, almost as a photograph might, when the sitter, intent at her work and interrupted, looks up from her sewing. The dexterity of her fingers, holding the thread taut, and the outward glance of her dark eyes convey a sense of quickness and vitality. The half-length seated figure is turned to the left, a device Stuart adopted to conceal the fact that Mrs. Yates was cross-eyed, and the neutral background serves as a foil to the luminous color and flickering highlights that enliven her costume.

Stuart's decorative elegance reached its peak in the portraits of the newlyweds *Josef de Jaudenes y Nebot* (48) and his wife *Mathilda Stoughton de Jaudenes* (47), painted

46
Gilbert Stuart
Mrs. Richard Yates
Oil on canvas, 1793/94.
National Gallery of Art;
Andrew W. Mellon Collection, 1940.

in New York City in 1794. Don Josef, born in Spain in 1764, was Spanish chargé d'affaires in Philadelphia. His wife, merely sixteen years old, was the daughter of John Stoughton, the Spanish consul in Boston. The young couple lived on a grand scale in Philadelphia until 1796, when Don Josef, disappointed at not being appointed Spanish minister to the United States, returned with his wife to his ancestral vineyards in Majorca.

The *de Jaudenes* portraits, in their overt references to wealth, are perhaps Stuart's most aristocratic likenesses. The splendor of Don Josef's richly embroidered garments and lacy jabot, enhanced by the sword that hangs at his side, is suggestive of an Old World courtier. His finery is surpassed only by that of his wife, a celebrated Boston beauty, who wears a floral-patterned dress, laces, glittering jewelry, and a crownlike feathered headdress.

While Gilbert Stuart represents the professional portrait tradition in America at its highest and most sophisticated level, another group of artists, primarily self-trained and many of them itinerant, was working contemporaneously in America, generally in small towns and rural communities for the expanded middle classes of the new Republic. Their work, at its best, is especially notable for its forthrightness, spontaneity, and decorative qualities.

47
Gilbert Stuart
Matilda Stoughton de Jaudenes
Oil on canvas, 1794.
The Metropolitan Museum of Art;
Rogers Fund, 1907.

48
Gilbert Stuart
Josef de Jaudenes y Nebot
Oil on canvas, 1794.
The Metropolitan Museum of Art;
Rogers Fund, 1907.

Ralph Earl, born in 1751 in Worcester County, Massachusetts, and self-trained, was one of the leading practitioners in the folk or rural tradition. His portrait of *Roger Sherman* (49), traditionally dated circa 1775, when Earl was living in New Haven, Connecticut, is the only known portrait by Earl painted before his departure for England after the war broke out. Roger Sherman, a Connecticut shoemaker, surveyor, and lawyer, was one of only two men who signed all three of the important documents of the Revolutionary era—the Declaration of Independence, the Articles of Confederation, and the Federal Constitution. Earl captured in Sherman's portrait a spirit that Americans like to think of as rugged Yankee individualism and determination. The sense of Sherman's character is reinforced by the spare, painted windsor armchair. While the portrait is awkward in drawing and perspective (the floor/wall lines behind the sitter do not converge), it has an appealing directness. It is also not without compositional

guile: the wedge of lace popping out of the waistcoat directs the eye to the head; the bow of the sitter's arms echoes vertically the horizontal movement of the arms of the chair; and the sitter's legs form one base of a triangle offsetting the flare of chair legs to the right.

Earl was a staunch Loyalist. Although he drew some of the first scenes of the war at Concord and Lexington, engraved by his fellow New Havener Amos Doolittle, his sympathies were Tory, and he left America for England in 1778 and did not return until 1785. During those seven years he was moderately active as a portrait painter in England, basing himself for the most part in Bristol, a center for American Loyalists.

Earl's portrait of *Major General Frederic Wilhelm Augustus, Baron von Steuben* (50), technically advanced in comparison with *Roger Sherman*, was painted following the artist's return to America. Baron von Steuben, a German by birth, came to America in 1777 after serving in the Seven Years' War

(1756-1763) in the army of Frederick the Great. When he offered his services to the Continental Congress, he was appointed inspector-general of the American army. As such, he played an important role in training the raw American troops. Earl has depicted von Steuben in the blue and buff uniform of the Continental army, with the two stars of a major general on his epaulettes. His uniform is decorated with the badge and medallion of the Prussian Order of Fidelity and the insignia of the American Society of the Cincinnati pinned to his lapel. His right hand rests on the hilt of a silver dress-sword (now in the collection of the Yale University Art Gallery) presented to him by Congress. The influence on Earl's painting style of his years in England is evident in the more sophisticated handling of the figure and the broader brushwork of the landscape background.

Landscape painting, which was to become a major mode of American artistic expression in the nineteenth century, was infrequent in the

49
Ralph Earl
Roger Sherman
Oil on canvas, ca. 1775. Yale
University Art Gallery; gift of Roger
Sherman White, B.A. 1899, LL.B. 1902.
(Color, p. 167.)

50
Ralph Earl
*Major General Frederic Wilhelm
Augustus, Baron von Steuben*
Oil on canvas, ca. 1786.
Yale University Art Gallery; gift

of Mrs. Paul Moore in memory of
her nephew Howard Melville Hanna,
Jr., B.S. 1931.

eighteenth. But a number of Earl's full-length portraits of the 1790s have effective topographical landscape backgrounds, and even his representations of people in interior settings often have a rolling landscape seen through an open window.

In fact, Earl occasionally ventured into pure topographical landscape (*Looking East from Denny Hill*, fig. 56). A characteristic landscape provides the setting for the double portrait of *Mrs. William Moseley and Her Son Charles* (**51**),

which contains the elements common to Earl's full-length portraits of the last decade of the century: the figures standing on a sunlit rise in the foreground, trees flanking the view of a wooded point of land at the bend of a winding river in the

51
Ralph Earl
Mrs. William Moseley and Her Son
Oil on canvas, 1791. Yale University Art Gallery; bequest of Mrs. Katherine Rankin Wolcott Verplanck.

Fig. 56
Ralph Earl
Looking East from Denny Hill
Oil on canvas, ca. 1797/98.
Worcester Art Museum.

middle distance, and a townscape on the horizon. Mrs. Moseley, the daughter of Oliver Wolcott of Litchfield, a signer of the Declaration of Independence and later governor of Connecticut, married William Moseley, a Hartford lawyer, in 1785. When this portrait was executed in 1791, the Moseleys lived in Hartford, the town that appears in the distance.

The identity of the artist who painted the portraits of *Dr. Hezekiah Beardsley* (52) and his wife, *Mrs. Hezekiah* [Elizabeth Davis] *Beardsley* (53), is unknown. An itinerant who painted portraits in Connecticut and Massachusetts from 1780 to 1800, the so-called Beards-

ley Limner must have worked in New Haven, where these portraits were painted, about 1788-1790. The Beardsley portraits seem a provincial Connecticut echo of the portrait conventions established by Copley in, for example, the portraits of *Mr. and Mrs. Isaac Smith* (13, 14). The Beardsley portraits are conceived as a pair, with the same furniture in each picture—an olive green windsor armchair and a simple board table, stained red, in front of a draped window. Hezekiah Beardsley would seem to have been copying into his "Extracts" notebook lines from Gibbon's *History of the Decline and Fall of the Roman Empire*. His wife, wearing his

miniature portrait around her neck, holds a flower (identical to those growing in the garden beyond) and an open book entitled *Reflections*. A basket of apples and pears on the table next to her may symbolize her own and the land's plenitude, while the intent gaze of the dog seated at her feet seems to symbolize domestic tranquility and fidelity.

The portrait of *Emma Van Name* (54), like the Beardsley portraits the work of an anonymous artist, prefigures the extensive proliferation of folk art in the United States in the nineteenth century. The still pose and patternized representation of a child with such accouterments as a piece of fruit or a coral-and-bells

52
"The Beardsley Limner"
Dr. Hezekiah Beardsley
Oil on canvas, ca. 1788-1790.
Yale University Art Gallery;
gift of Gwendolen Jones Giddings.

53
"The Beardsley Limner"
Mrs. Hezekiah Beardsley
Oil on canvas, ca. 1788-1790.
Yale University Art Gallery;
gift of Gwendolen Jones Giddings.

rattle restates a much earlier convention, going back beyond similar Hudson Valley paintings of the second quarter of the eighteenth century, as well as Boston paintings of the third quarter of the seven-

teenth century, to English, Dutch, and Flemish prototypes of the sixteenth and early seventeenth centuries. Apart from its formal qualities, the portrait entrances us both by the curious and even mys-

terious relationship between the possessive child and the giant glass goblet filled with strawberries, and by the pervading sense of love and subtle humor.

One active portrait painter,

54
Anonymous artist
Emma Van Name
Oil on canvas, ca. 1795.
Whitney Museum of American Art; gift of Edgar William and Bernice Chrysler Garbisch.

William Jennys, worked in and around New Milford, Connecticut, in the 1790s, in New York City in 1797-1798, and throughout much of New England, including Massachusetts and Vermont, from 1800 to 1805. Not only is nothing known of his training or apprenticeship, but his work is often confused with that of Richard Jennys, who worked in the same area in a similar style. The portrait of *Nathaniel Lamson* (55), however, painted in Stratford, Connecticut, about 1795, descended in a family that also had two signed and dated portraits by William Jennys, and displays many of this painter's mannerisms: an oriental cast of the eyes, a reluctance to depict hands, and a limited palette. Jennys portrayed most sitters within a painted oval spandrel, but Lamson is shown against a full dark brown monochromatic background, against which the sitter's olive green coat, bright blue-green dotted waistcoat, long white ruffle,

55
William Jennys
Nathaniel Lamson
Oil on canvas, ca. 1795.
Mary Allis.

56
Winthrop Chandler
View of a River with Trees and Figures
Oil on wood panel, ca. 1779.
Mr. and Mrs. Bertram K. Little.

and black bow tie appear in brilliant and startling contrast.

Winthrop Chandler was another member of the remarkable school of Connecticut country painters that flourished in the last quarter of the eighteenth century. Born in Woodstock, Connecticut, the son of a surveyor-farmer, Chandler, by tradition, is thought to have studied portrait painting in Boston during the 1760s. A versatile artist, best known for portraits such as *Captain Samuel Chandler* (fig. 57), he also did gilding, carving, illustrating, and drafting, as well as house and landscape painting. *View of a River with Trees and Figures* (56) is an over-mantle panel from the parlor of the Ebenezer Waters's house in Sutton, Massachusetts, circa 1779. Chandler painted scenes such as this in and around northeastern Connecticut for his family and neighbors. Crowded with figures, animals, birds, and brightly colored detailed renderings of

Fig. 57
Winthrop Chandler
Captain Samuel Chandler
Oil on canvas, ca. 1780.
National Gallery of Art; gift of Edgar William and Bernice Chrysler Garbisch.

rural architecture, they seem more decorative in intent than realistic.

The career of James Peale, to turn again to the mainstream, has long been overshadowed by that of his older brother, Charles Willson Peale. Having served as a studio assistant and helped with the full-length *Washington* commissions (see above, p. 92), James Peale's early work is derivative from and often even confused with that of his brother. A case in point is *The Ramsay-Polk Family* (57), painted about 1793 and sometimes attributed to the elder Peale, although probably the work of James. Mrs. Charles Peale Polk (Ruth Ellison), the wife of James's nephew, a portrait painter, is seated on a white windsor settee. Behind

57
James Peale
The Ramsay-Polk Family
Oil on canvas, ca. 1793.
Private collection.

her are the second Mrs. Nathaniel Ramsay, formerly Miss Heath, and her sister. (Nathaniel Ramsay had served as an officer in the same battalion with James Peale during the Revolution and had been married to James's older sister, Margaret Jane, until her death in 1788.) *The Ramsay-Polk Family* is in the tradition of the English conversation pieces of Devis and Zoffany. The background setting depicts Nathaniel Ramsay's shad and herring fishery sheds at Carpenter's Point on the eastern shore of Maryland, a favorite retreat for members of the Peale family, and although the poses are rigid and the treatment of costume linear and dry, Peale's light-color harmonies of blue, rose, and pink make for a pleasing result.

In addition to his portraits, conversation pieces, historical and classical compositions, and landscapes, James Peale painted miniatures and still lifes. He learned the art of painting in miniature from Charles Willson Peale, and, as with the early portraits in oil, many of his miniatures before the 1790s are difficult to distinguish from those of his brother. In 1786 the older Peale "left off painting in miniature"9 to allow James a free hand in that area. In the 1795 portrait of his nephew, *Rembrandt Peale* (**58**), James had finally arrived at a style of his own. His technique is looser than in his earlier miniatures. Breaking away from a monochromatic background, he used interlaced hatchings to represent the tonal variety of sky and clouds, and the rendering of the curve of the lips into a pursed smile is a mannerism that remained constant throughout his career.

Rembrandt Peale, Charles Willson's second son, who was only seventeen when his uncle painted this miniature likeness, would also have a distinguished career as an artist. He too became president of the American Academy of Fine Arts in New York, and he was a founder in 1826 of the National Academy of Design and cofounder, with his brother Raphaelle, of the Peale Museum in Baltimore.

Miniature painting flourished in America during the last quarter of the eighteenth century. John Ramage, who studied at the Dublin School of Artists in 1763, was established as a goldsmith and miniaturist in Boston by 1775. An ardent Tory, Ramage served in His Majesty's forces at Boston, but after a short stay in Halifax, Nova Scotia, settled in New York and resigned his commission. From 1777 until 1794, when he moved to Montreal, Ramage was the leading miniaturist in New York. His *Anthony Rutgers* (**59**), a merchant of New York and Curaçao, is elegantly dressed, wearing a dark green coat, a brown and white striped waistcoat, and a white lace frill. The lively *Rutgers* portrait, highly finished and fresh in color, is painted in line technique with a long stroke. Ramage's miniatures are always small, never exceeding two inches, and are often in gold frames skillfully chased by the artist himself.

58
James Peale
Rembrandt Peale
Watercolor on ivory, 1795.
Yale University Art Gallery;
gift of Mrs. John Hill Morgan.

59
John Ramage
Anthony Rutgers
Watercolor on ivory, ca. 1780-1790.
Yale University Art Gallery;
gift of Mrs. John Hill Morgan.

Another British artist who settled in New York was Archibald Robertson. He and his two artist brothers, Alexander and Andrew, were the sons of an architect from Aberdeen, Scotland. After studying at the Royal Academy in London, Archibald emigrated to America in 1791 and set up in New York as a miniaturist. With his brother Alexander, who joined him the following year, Robertson established the Columbian Academy of Painting.

In addition to miniatures, Robertson drew a large number of landscapes and city views in pen and ink or watercolor from about 1795 until his retirement in 1821. Along with William Birch (1755-1834) and his son Thomas Birch (1779-1851) of Philadelphia, Robertson was instrumental in introducing the English topographical watercolor tradition to America. His *New York from Long Island* (**60**) renders the city's skyline as it appeared about 1795. A large tree defines the foreground, framing Washington's headquarters, smaller houses and ships in the middle ground, and a panorama in the distance. The illusion of depth is reinforced by dark washes and hatching lines in the foreground, contrasted with thinner, more transparent washes and less detail in the distant sun-drenched city view.

Still-life paintings were rare in America before the last decade of the century, but the catalogue of the first public, professional American art exhibition in 1795 at the short-lived Columbianum Academy in Philadelphia suggests that still

60
Archibald Robertson
New York from Long Island
Ink and color wash on paper,
ca. 1794-1796. Columbia University;
gift of J. Pierpont Morgan.

life had by then become widely practiced. Both Copley and Charles Willson Peale are recorded as the authors of pure still lifes, none of which survived. The real founder of the genre in America, and one of the greatest of America's still-life painters, was Charles Willson Peale's son Raphaelle.

Among Raphaelle Peale's earliest known works is the India ink and pen drawing *A Deception* (**61**), presumably executed in Philadelphia in 1802. This drawing stands close to the beginning of the popular trompe l'oeil tradition in America. Peale reproduced paper, type, and script so accurately that the viewer may at first think that he sees a real rack of clippings and invitations. The stylistic source for

61
Raphaelle Peale
A Deception
Pencil and ink on paper, 1802.
Private collection.

this picture probably lies among the many trompe l'oeil engravings and watercolors made by Dutch, French, and English artists during the eighteenth century.

Even more often than trompe l'oeil, Raphaelle Peale practiced "normal" tabletop still life. A fine example of his mature work is the *Still Life with Celery and Wine* (**62**) of 1816. Like his earlier paintings, this work depicts fruit in a basket along with raisins, a stalk of celery, and a half-filled decanter on the table. It combines a neoclassical sense of compositional clarity with a more romantic naturalism, and delights in its gentle color relationships of yellows, browns, and greens, in the texture of the fruit, and in the homely, unposed objects themselves.

Quite different is the consciously composed and supremely elegant neoclassical *Still Life with Fruit* (**63**) by the Bostonian John Johnston —also a portraitist and pastelist, but far less well known than Peale. What Johnston created was a formal interpretation that emphasizes the purity of each object's shape and color. Indeed, the white background, rather Spanish in flavor, was unique in American still life at the time. In its clarity and formality, Johnston's painting relates to American neoclassical furniture and silver, and despite superficial similarities, it stands in contrast to

62
Raphaelle Peale
Still Life with Celery and Wine
Oil on wood panel, 1816.
Munson-Williams-Proctor Institute.

Peale's *Still Life with Celery and Wine*, which, although it adheres to the neoclassical style, looks ahead to nineteenth-century naturalism.

Pure neoclassicism appeared much more slowly and tentatively in American painting than in the functional arts. Its important early manifestation in the work of Benjamin West (for example, *Agrippina*, 19) did not develop much further in England, where the revolutionary implications of neoclassicism, so obvious in the subject matter of paintings, dictated a more conservative line of development. The place where neoclassical painting matured was France, and it was from France that fully developed neoclassicism entered American painting. The leading exponent of the French tradition of neoclassicism in American art was John Vanderlyn. Grandson of a Hudson Valley limner and house painter, Pieter Vanderlyn, John was born in Kingston, New York, in 1775. At seventeen he worked for Thomas Barrow, proprietor of a color shop, printseller, and framer, in New York City. There he enrolled in the drawing class at Archibald and Alexander Robertson's Columbian Academy of Painting. Subsequently, Vanderlyn copied portraits by Gilbert Stuart in New York, and during part of 1795 and 1796 he worked as Stuart's assistant in Philadelphia. In 1796, under the patron-

63
John Johnston
Still Life with Fruit
Oil on wood panel, 1810.
The St. Louis Art Museum.

age of Aaron Burr, he traveled to Paris, where he worked in the studio of François André Vincent at the Ecole des Beaux-Arts.

Vanderlyn executed the chalk drawing of *Mrs. Edward Church and Child* (64) in France in 1799. Against a black background, the soft, sculptural character of the figures is constructed with varied intensities in the stippling of the black and white chalk.

Vanderlyn's reputation is largely based on a group of history paintings, which received greater recognition in Europe than in America. The earliest of these, the *Death of*

Jane McCrea (65), was painted in Paris in 1804 and depicts the tragic death of Jane McCrea in July 1777 at the hands of two Mohawk Indians. The incident occurred while the American woman was being guided through the lines by the Indians to a reunion with her English husband-to-be, a lieutenant in Burgoyne's army. The Revolutionary press seized on the event as propaganda against the British. Thus Jane McCrea, the personification of innocence, became a symbol of American suffering under British aggression. This romantic tragedy resulted in popular Revolu-

tionary ballads, poems, and painted and engraved depictions. Vanderlyn specifically illustrated the scene, including the English lieutenant in the distance, as it had been described by Joel Barlow in his epic poem on the founding of America, the *Columbiad*:

With calculating pause and demon
  grin
They seize her hands and thro' her
  face divine
Drive the descending axe; the shriek
  she sent
Attain'd her lover's ear; he thither
  bent
With all the speed his wearied limbs
  could yield. . . .[10]

64
John Vanderlyn
Mrs. Edward Church and Child
Crayon on paper, 1799. The Metropolitan Museum of Art; bequest of Ella Church Strobell, 1917.

65
John Vanderlyn
Death of Jane McCrea
Oil on canvas, 1804.
Wadsworth Atheneum;
purchased by subscription.

Clearly, the three central figures, expressed in high relief like a classical metope, show the direct influence of antique sculpture.

Vanderlyn's monumental history painting, *Marius amidst the Ruins of Carthage* (**66**), was painted in Rome in 1807. Exhibited at the Paris Salon in 1808, the work was awarded a Gold Medal. The subject of Marius, a defeated and exiled Roman general, was derived from Plutarch's *Lives*. The figure of Marius himself Vanderlyn adapted from ancient sculpture, perhaps from the Ludovici Ares. The ruins of Carthage in the background of the painting are adapted from the Parthenon and the Claudian aqueduct. The melancholy mood of the painting invites the viewer to reflect, along with the brooding Marius, on the mutability of life. As Vanderlyn wrote, "I thought the man and the position combined, was capable of showing in two great instances the instability of human grandeur—a city in ruins and a fallen general. I endeavoured to express in the countenance of Marius the bitterness of disappointed ambitions mixed with the meditation of revenge."[11] Circumstantial evidence suggests that *Marius* was intended to make reference to Vanderlyn's patron, Aaron Burr, the fallen American vice-president. In its shift from the objective depiction of a particular scene, as in West's *Death of Wolfe* or Vanderlyn's own *Death of Jane McCrea*, to a composition that centers on the subjective state of mind of the figure represented, the picture demands the empathetic involvement of the viewer and thus, despite its formal classicism, reflects the new influence of romanticism.

Washington Allston, the first major American romantic artist, once

66
John Vanderlyn
Marius amidst the Ruins of Carthage. Oil on canvas, 1807.
The Fine Arts Museums of San Francisco.

said of his friend, the miniature painter Edward Greene Malbone, that "he had the happy talent among his many excellencies of elevating the character without impairing the likeness."[12] Malbone's miniature of *Allston* (**67**), painted before 1801, sustains this opinion. The portrait is marked by clear fresh colors, meticulous brushwork, the delicate shading which subtly models the head, and an acute sense of the sitter's character. Benjamin West commented: "I have seldom seen a miniature that pleased me more."[13]

Malbone was born in Newport, Rhode Island. Gifted, determined, and largely self-trained, he painted his first portraits in Providence in 1794. Malbone met Allston during his youth, and the two artists became friends. In 1801, after a few months with Allston in England, Malbone returned to America and became an itinerant miniaturist, visiting New York, Philadelphia, Charleston, and other cities. In 1807, not yet thirty, he died of tuberculosis. Despite his abbreviated career, Malbone painted over seven hundred miniatures.

Washington Allston was born into a wealthy and prominent family in Charleston, South Carolina. He graduated from Harvard in 1800, and, firm in his intention to be an artist despite objections from his family, went to England with Malbone. During his three years in London, Allston studied with Benjamin West and was much impressed by West's protoromantic *Death on a Pale Horse* (fig. 58), as well as by the works of Henry Fuseli. In 1803, joined by John Vanderlyn, he traveled through Holland and Belgium to Paris, where he studied paintings by Titian, Tintoretto, and Veronese in the Louvre. The following year Allston went on to Rome, where he became friends with the British poet Samuel Taylor Coleridge, who had a profound effect on the impressionable young artist. As Allston later wrote, "To no other man whom I have known do I owe so much intellectually, as to Mr. Coleridge."[14] One tangible result of their companionship in Rome was Allston's unfinished portrait of *Coleridge* (**68**), the completion of which was prevented by the poet's abrupt departure for England.

Primarily a painter of landscapes, history pictures, and moody "fancy" pieces, Allston seldom painted portraits, and then usually only personal friends and relations. His lyrical likeness of Coleridge, illuminated by a shaft of light, exhibits the influence of the portraits by Titian that Allston had seen at the Louvre. A mysterious charm, in part evoked through the use of cool tones and broad brushwork, reinforces the emotional vigor of the image.

It was during the second half of the eighteenth century that American art came of age. Throughout the first part of the century American artists were most often transplanted Europeans. Such talented local artists as Robert Feke were the exception. After mid-century, American-born artists were more common, and many of them went to Europe to study. Although

67
Edward Greene Malbone,
Washington Allston
Watercolor on ivory, prior to 1801.
Museum of Fine Arts, Boston;
Otis Norcross Fund.

Fig. 58
Benjamin West
Sketch for "Death on the Pale Horse"
Oil on canvas, 1802. Philadelphia
Museum of Art; given by Theodora
Kimball Hubbard in memory of
Edwin Fiske Kimball.

a few like Copley and West remained in England, the majority returned to America once the War of Independence had ended.

During the early years of the new Republic, American art became infused with a sense of national purpose. With independence achieved, it was felt that if America were to be a great nation it must have a flourishing cultural life, including a significant national school of art. American art would reflect the quality of American life. The private academies for art instruction of the Robertsons in New York and C. W. Peale in Philadelphia—direct precursors of institutionalized academies of art established in those cities in the first years of the nineteenth century —were founded, in part, in response to that sense of national need. From the end of the eighteenth century until the Civil War, the quest for national identity was a dominant motivating force in American art. Stuart, Trumbull, and Peale, their artistic skills expanded by study abroad, recorded the likenesses and activities of military heroes and the founding fathers. During the nineteenth century, artists like William Sidney Mount and George Caleb Bingham would turn to American subject matter in popular genre pictures, while Thomas Cole and the Hudson River artists would explore the landscape. This change reflected to some extent an increasing interest in American themes for their own sake, but also an attempt to find popular subjects that would develop the broad public support and patronage needed in a democratic society. Although America's artistic links with Europe remained strong in the nineteenth century, American art moved away from reliance on European stylistic and thematic models in pursuit of a cultural independence that would match the political independence that had now been won.

68
Washington Allston
Samuel T. Coleridge
Oil on canvas, 1806.
The Fogg Art Museum, Harvard
University; loan of the
Washington Allston Trust.

Prints

Prints were the principal form of pictorial imagery available to the majority of colonial Americans, and prior to the advent of easier means of mass communication, they served to inform people about the monuments and events of the world. Throughout the eighteenth century most prints circulating in America were imported from England and the Continent. As has been seen, such engravings played a significant role in the education of the American artist. European engravings of the highest quality, such as ". . . Mr. Garrick, Actor . . . The Twelve Months; Four Seasons . . . The Rake's and Harlots Progress; The idle and industrious apprentice; Beautiful Prospects, colored and without,"[1] were sold in American print shops and adorned the halls and staircases of colonial houses. American prints—that is, prints engraved, printed and published by either native artists or foreign-born artists working in this country—seemed to have served a more practical purpose. Local, and later national, motives demanded that the American printmaker supply his patron with engravings that

would be useful: they might be maps, trade cards, and bookplates; serve as propaganda, as, for example, caricatures of political events; encourage piety and love of country with portraits of venerable divines or patriots; or inspire local or national pride by way of city and landscape views.

Like other early American art forms, printmaking closely followed English models and methods. The mezzotint, recognized by its dark, velvety tones and richly modulated highlights, had originated in England in the late seventeenth century and was particularly popular for the reproduction of portraits both there and in America. Peter Pelham, who emigrated to America in 1727, had been apprenticed in London to John Simon, one of the city's leading engravers, and had produced more than twenty-five high-quality mezzotint portraits before his departure for America. In Boston in 1728 Pelham made a mezzotint of *Cotton Mather* (**69**), a noted clergyman and influential scientific and religious scholar, whose *Magnalia Christi Americana: or the Ecclesiastical History of New England* *from Its First Planting* (1702) is an important contribution to seventeenth-century religious thought. To assure himself of a profitable venture, Pelham first solicited subscribers for the print.

Possibly without realizing it, Pelham was on firm ground in his choice of subject for this first mezzotint produced in America. The tradition of making images of divines was well established in the colonies, for America's first print,

attributed to John Foster, a printer-printmaker in Boston, and dated about 1670, is a woodcut of Cotton Mather's grandfather, *Richard Mather* (fig. 59), also a clergyman.

Because he needed a likeness upon which to base his mezzotint, Pelham himself painted the portrait of Cotton Mather (American Antiquarian Society, Worcester, Massachusetts) as well as portraits of five other New England divines. However, many of the fourteen mezzo-

tints he produced in Boston before his death in 1751 were engraved after works of two prominent local painters, John Smibert and John Greenwood.

During the colonial period, engravers in Boston led the way in the development of the art of printmaking. Yet, however brilliant the highlights and rich the velvety blacks of Pelham's mezzotints, the demand was not sufficient to provide him a living from engraving alone.

Fig. 59
John Foster
Richard Mather
Woodcut (first state), ca. 1670.
Harvard College Library.

69
Peter Pelham
Cotton Mather
Mezzotint (only known state), 1728.
Yale University Art Gallery;
Mabel Brady Garvan Collection.

His dance and concert assemblies and his music and writing lessons were necessary supplements to his livelihood. Such versatility was the rule for the American artist. Thomas Johnston, another Boston engraver, also advertised himself as a japanner of furniture, coach and sign painter, church singer, publisher of singing-books, and builder of organs.

Johnston's 1759 line engraving of *Quebec, The Capital of New-France* (**70**), is one of a group of patriotic prints resulting from the outbreak of the French and Indian Wars in the 1750s. Unlike his earlier *Battle of Lake George* (fig. 60), printed in 1755, Johnston's *Quebec* is not taken from a first-hand account of the siege. Only a slight hint of the intense struggle is apparent in the smoke billowing from a single ship in the center

foreground. This is not surprising, since *Quebec* is based on an inset on a map by Nicolas de Fer, *La France Occidentale dans l'Amérique Septentrionale*, published in Paris in 1718.

The first state of *Quebec* was issued in August of 1759 while the city was under fire. A second state, published in October of the same year, differs only in the addition of a marginal description of the

70
Thomas Johnston
Quebec, The Capital of New-France
Line engraving (first state). 1759.
Yale University Art Gallery;
Mabel Brady Garvan Collection.

French surrender on September 17. Both the engraver and the publisher-printseller, Stephen Whiting, recognized the potential rewards from a second printing while colonists were rejoicing over the final defeat of the French and the beginning of British dominance.

Among the thirty engravings signed by or attributed to Johnston is the *Bookplate of William P. Smith* (**71**). Like some other prod-

ucts from his shop, it demonstrates more skill than originality. Closely patterned after contemporary English models, this bookplate is in the style conventionally known as "Jacobean," a style characterized by regular outline, strict symmetrical repetition of ornament, and a heavy, carved quality of decorative motif. Bookplates in this style often combine such elements as the fish-scale pattern framing the shield,

the scallop shell at its base, and the conspicuous helmet and crest shown in the Johnston example.

The use of heraldic labels to designate book ownership dates back to the fifteenth century and was maintained in the eighteenth by most gentlemen to signify not only possession but also an appreciation of the volumes in their libraries. In the South it was common practice to order bookplates

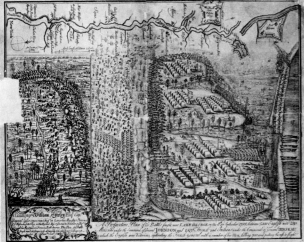

Fig. 60
Thomas Johnston
A Prospective Plan of the Battle fought near Lake George on the 8th of September 1755
Line engraving (first state), 1755.

Yale University Art Gallery;
Mabel Brady Garvan Collection.

71
Thomas Johnston
Bookplate of William P. Smith
Line engraving, ca. 1730-1740.
Yale University Art Gallery;
Mabel Brady Garvan Collection.

from England, whereas in northern cities, with more facilities for engraving and printing, commissions to design and produce bookplates went to local engravers.

The mixture of pride in ownership and pretension to literary accomplishment was pleasing to the American merchant, whose status as a gentleman was more easily established through expenditure than heredity. Consequently,

the names of some of the colonies' wealthiest merchants appear on bookplates made by native craftsmen. John Greenwood's recollection that one of his jobs as an apprentice to Thomas Johnston was the engraving of bookplates indicates that they were a common item in that shop.

Engraving was not only the province of the specialist or the craftsman-entrepreneur such as

Johnston, but it was also an integral part of the silversmith's craft. The silversmith's ability to design and execute armorial devices on silver objects was readily adapted to the engraving of copperplates for tradecards, currency, broadsides, and bookplates. The two renowned silversmiths Nathaniel Hurd and Paul Revere were among the most prolific printmakers in New England. Eleven bookplates have been

Fig. 61
John Singleton Copley
Nathaniel Hurd
Oil on canvas, ca. 1765.
The Cleveland Museum of Art; gift of the John Huntington Art and Polytechnic Trust.

72
Nathaniel Hurd
Bookplate of Thomas Child
Line engraving (one of two states), ca. 1765-1770. Bookplate collection, Yale University Library.

73
Nathaniel Hurd
Bookplate of Francis Dana
Line engraving (only known state), ca. 1770-1775. Bookplate Collection, Yale University Library.

74
Nathaniel Hurd
Danforth Bookplate
Line engraving (only known state), ca. 1770-1775. Bookplate Collection, Yale University Library.

attributed to Revere, and Hurd engraved plates for more than fifty different families. John Singleton Copley's portraits of them (figs. 61 and 62) attest to the importance of engraving as an attribute of their craft: Revere is portrayed holding a finished teapot, with engraving tools scattered about the table, while Hurd's occupation is indicated by design books, one of them J. Guillim's *Display of Heraldry,*

resting near his arm.

Guillim's book was an important source for Nathaniel Hurd's armorial engraving. Motifs from this book are found on silver objects produced in his shop and on twenty-eight of his known bookplates, including the *Bookplate of Thomas Child* (**72**). Although some of Hurd's bookplates are in the "Jacobean" and "Ribbon and wreath" styles, most of them can be

classified as "Chippendale." In English as well as in American bookplates, this style is characterized by an irregular cartouche, sprays of flowers and foliage, and S- and C-scrolls, and an emphasis on asymmetry (**73** and **74**). Hurd designed only three or four styles of mantling, which he used to frame different coats of arms. Like Hurd, Revere seems to have standardized the mantling encircling the arms

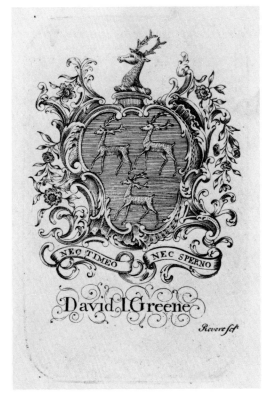

75
Paul Revere
Bookplate of David Greene
Line engraving (one of four known states), ca. 1760-1770. Bookplate Collection, Yale University Library.

Fig. 62
John Singleton Copley
Paul Revere
Oil on canvas, 1768-1770.
Museum of Fine Arts, Boston.

he engraved (**75-78**); only two types can be found on his eleven surviving bookplates, whereas the cartouches engraved on his silver vary greatly according to the formal requirements of each piece. The engraving of bookplates was, after all, a subsidiary art in the silversmith's shop. Made more as emblems of ownership than as works of art, bookplates were executed with skill and exhibited with pride, but they were esteemed for their adherence to convention, not their originality.

Pictorial prints, easily and quickly produced as well as inexpensive, were the major visual medium of revolutionary propaganda. Paul Revere's best-known engraving, *The Bloody Massacre* (**79**), was first issued soon after the tragic encounter between British soldiers and so-called "innocent" Bostonians on March 5, 1770. Depictions of this event were extremely popular: Revere, Henry Pelham—from whom Revere plagiarized this scene—and Jonathan Mulliken of Newburyport, as well as an anonymous English engraver, found it profitable to print and sell copies of the scene. Two states of Revere's *The Bloody Massacre* are known: the first, a unique impression, called the "eight o'clock state," and the more common and accurate "ten o'clock state," shown here.

Surely the most ambitious political print prior to the Revolution is Charles Willson Peale's mezzotint, *Mr. Pitt* (**80**). Painted, engraved, and published in London while Peale was working with Benjamin West from 1767 to 1769, *Mr. Pitt* was the artist's first engraving, his only known attempt in historical painting or engraving in the Grand Manner, and a financial failure. Nevertheless, two states were issued; this, the second state, differs from the first only in the addition of the names "Sidney" and "Hamden [sic]" engraved on the bust-length figures decorating the altar front.

Mr. Pitt is full of both explicit and implicit meaning, much of which was explained in an accompanying broadside, "A Description

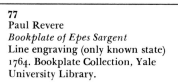

76
Paul Revere
Bookplate of Andrew Oliver
Line engraving (only known state),
ca. 1760-1770. Bookplate Collection, Yale University Library.

77
Paul Revere
Bookplate of Epes Sargent
Line engraving (only known state)
1764. Bookplate Collection, Yale University Library.

78
Paul Revere
Bookplate of Isaiah Thomas
Line engraving (only known state)
ca. 1765-1770. Bookplate Collection, Yale University Library.

of the Picture and Mezzotinto OF MR. PITT."[2] William Pitt, leader of the radical Whigs and venerated by colonials because of his opposition to certain policies of George III, such as the Stamp Act, is represented "in a Consular Habit, speaking in Defense of the Claims of the American Colonies, on the Principles of the British Constitution." Peale, in identifying Pitt with Brutus, presents the theme of the justifiable execution of regal tyrants. "With MAGNA CHARTA in one Hand," Pitt points "to the Statue of British *Liberty*, trampling under Foot the Petition of the Congress at New-York." "*Liberty*" stands on a pedestal decorated with an American Indian, who "in an *erect* posture . . . listens to the Orator, and has a

79
Paul Revere
The Bloody Massacre
Line engraving, colored (second state), 1770. Yale University Art Gallery; John Hill Morgan Collection.

Bow in his Hand, and a Dog by his Side, to shew the natural *Faithfulness and Firmness of* America." The treatment of the Indian, a stern and uncompromising figure, is more hostile than earlier depictions, reflecting the increasing tensions between the colonies and the mother country. The altar and flame signify "that the Cause of Liberty is sacred" and it is defended by "the Heads of Sidney and Hampden," both heroes of the radical Whigs and whose theories guided the Whigs in the civil war against Charles I and the revolution of 1688 against James I. Further reference to the English civil war, which at this time was a symbol of justifiable revolt against tyrannical monarchy, is found in the background showing the Banqueting Hall at Whitehall, where King Charles I was led to his execution and where "the Liberty of the British People" was secured. Peale's print, along with scores of other political engravings produced in both England and the colonies, serves to document the protests of Englishmen over threats to their right to liberty.

Their independence won, the colonists were no longer Englishmen; they were Americans, and for this new citizenship they demanded images of their own leaders and patriots. The story of the painter's response, especially in the work of Peale, John Trumbull, and Gilbert Stuart, has already been told. And the American printmaker, always quick to see an opportunity, gave the people what they wanted.

Among the nearly nine hundred distinct prints and their more than six hundred different states recording the likeness of George Washington is Amos Doolittle's *A Display of the United States of America* (**81**). Today, it is difficult

80
Charles Willson Peale
Mr. Pitt
Mezzotint (second state), 1768.
Yale University Art Gallery;
Mabel Brady Garvan Collection.

to imagine the intensity of feeling this man evoked. Indicative of the esteem paid to so many of the new nation's leaders is the brief account by the Marquise de La Tour du Pin of her journey between Albany and Boston in 1794. She noted that one of her hosts:

At the close of the meal . . . rose, and baring his head, solemnly pronounced these words: "We are about to drink to the health of our well-loved President." One could not at that time find a cabin, no matter how secluded, where the expression of love for the great Washington did not terminate each repast.[3]

In Doolittle's print Washington is represented as commander-in-chief in a bust-length portrait, probably taken from the etched profile by Joseph Wright. He is surrounded by a chain of fourteen circles: besides the seal of the United States, encircled in red at the top, each link bears the name and seal of the original thirteen states, the number of senators and representatives, and its population.

Following his apprenticeship to a silversmith, Doolittle was active as an engraver in New Haven, Connecticut, from 1775 until his death in 1832. His early and very

large stipple and line engraving, *A Display of the United States* (**81**), was first issued in 1788, and was reworked five times: the second state in 1790, two in 1791, one in 1794, and one in 1796. That shown here, the fourth state, was issued in 1794 and differs from the second state in the addition of the arms of Vermont and a blank shield under the statistics of the territories. Having found an incredibly successful format and business venture, Doolittle published *A New Display*, featuring John Adams, in 1799 (fig. 63), now with sixteen states. He did so again in 1803 with a

81
Amos Doolittle
A Display of the United States of America. Stipple and line engraving, colored (fifth state), 1794. Yale University Art Gallery; gift of C. Sanford Bull, B.A. 1893.

Fig. 63
Amos Doolittle
A New Display of the United States of America
Line engraving, 1799. Yale University Art Gallery; gift of C. Sanford Bull, B.A. 1893.

portrait of Jefferson.[4]

Edward Savage was one of the most prolific engravers of notable personages during the 1790s. Born in Princeton, Massachusetts, Savage was trained as a goldsmith until he began to paint watercolor miniatures and oil portraits in the style of Copley about 1785. It was fitting that his first major portrait was one of George Washington and other members of the first family (Harvard University) which was commissioned in 1789. After two years of study in London, where he produced engravings in stipple and mezzotint, Savage returned to America and settled in Philadelphia from 1795 to 1801. All of Savage's engravings published in America were executed during this short period, in which John Wesley Jarvis and David Edwin served as assistants in his shop. Although it is signed by Savage, there is considerable controversy as to the authorship of his most famous print, *The Washington Family* (fig. 64), because the brilliant handling of the difficult technique of stipple engraving seems beyond his capabilities.[5]

Philadelphia was the political and intellectual capital of the country during these years, and Savage took advantage of the plethora of salable faces. His mezzotint portraits of Thomas Jefferson and Benjamin Rush (82 and 83) are simple bust-length compositions, designed from Savage's own oils, which he exhibited at his Colum-

Fig. 64
Edward Savage
The Washington Family
Stipple, colored, 1798.
Yale University Art Gallery;
Mabel Brady Garvan Collection.

82
Edward Savage
Thomas Jefferson
Mezzotint (second state), 1800.
Yale University Art Gallery;
Mabel Brady Garvan Collection.

83
Edward Savage
Benjamin Rush
Mezzotint (only known state), 1800.
Yale University Art Gallery;
Mabel Brady Garvan Colection.

bian Gallery on Chestnut Street until he left Philadelphia in 1801 to move to New York and later to Boston. Jefferson, the leading political theorist in America, was vice-president and soon to be elected president when the print was published in 1800. This second state, with Jefferson's name added in open block capitals below the publication line, is particularly rare. The engraved portrait of Rush was also published in 1800, when Rush was treasurer of the Mint

of the United States. Although he is best known as a patriot and signer of the Declaration of Independence, he was also a distinguished physician and author; his *Medical Inquiries and Observations Upon the Diseases of the Mind* (1812) was the first systematic treatment of the subject in America.

Savage's *David Rittenhouse* (84), after a replica of Charles Willson Peale's portrait of 1791 (original at American Philosophical Society, Philadelphia), is a much more com-

plex composition than the previous two examples. Rittenhouse is seated at a table on which books and a telescope rest to indicate his dedication to science and astronomy. He had built the first orrery in America (University of Pennsylvania, Philadelphia) and had succeeded Benjamin Franklin as president of the American Philosophical Society in 1791. When this mezzotint was published in 1796, the year of the subject's death, Rittenhouse was the leading scientist in the country.

DAVID RITTENHOUSE, L. L. D. F. R. S.

President of the American Philosophical Society.

84
Edward Savage
David Rittenhouse
Mezzotint (only known state), 1796.
Yale University Art Gallery;
Mabel Brady Garvan Collection.

Nothing was more effective than election or death in increasing the sale of portrait engravings. When Alexander Hamilton was killed by Aaron Burr in a duel, William Rollinson was prepared to take advantage of the opportunity. Rollinson had come to New York from England in 1788—one of his first jobs had been the chasing of silver for Washington's inaugural suit. After 1791 he had worked almost exclusively as an engraver, producing bookplates, trade cards and certificates, banknotes, portraits, maps and views, in line, stipple, and aquatint techniques until his death in 1842. *Hamilton* was ready for sale less than two months after the tragic incident, and it was issued twice; the first state (**85**) announces Archibald Robertson of the Columbian Academy of Painting as copublisher, from whose portrait the design was engraved.

Rollinson's *Hamilton* is the artist's tour de force in portrait engravings in the quality of the stipple engraving, even though it suffers from the awkward articulation of the body and poor perspective. The subject is shown in half-length, with military hat and sword, books, papers, and seals representing his activities during the Revolution and the early years of the new republic. Hamilton served as aide-de-camp and personal secretary for Washington during the war, wrote at least two-thirds of the *Federalist* papers in support of the notification of the Constitution, was appointed the first secretary of the treasury, and, as a leading Federalist, he was a major voice of conservatism in government.

The most common method of printmaking in America, as well as in Europe, throughout the eighteenth century was line engraving. Mezzotint, stipple (a dot technique quicker but less consistent than mezzotint), and aquatint (an etching technique especially suited to reproducing tones), all became popular techniques during the century and provided new methods to suit the commercial printmaker's needs for portraits and views. The woodcut, a technique practiced in Europe since the fifteenth century and in this country since the seventeenth, was frequently used for book and periodical illustrations and occasionally for broadsides. *A Front View of Yale-College, and the College Chapel, New Haven* (**86**), a woodcut published by Daniel Bowen of New Haven in 1786, is the forerunner of the modern college catalogue, complete with a history of the school and lists of its

85
William Rollinson
Alexander Hamilton
Stipple (first state), 1804.
Yale University Art Gallery;
Mabel Brady Garvan Collection.

courses of study. Founded in 1701 to equip young men for service "in Church and Civil State," the Collegiate School moved from Saybrook to New Haven and was renamed for its benefactor, Elihu Yale, in 1718. The second Yale College hall was built in 1750, "being 100 feet long, and 40 feet wide, three stories high, containing 32 chambers and 64 studies convenient for the reception of 100 students." The College Chapel, "50 feet by 40, with a steeple 125 feet high," was built in 1761 and housed a library of 2500 volumes. It has long been thought that the bewigged figure in cap and gown about to enter the Chapel is Ezra Stiles, president of Yale from 1778 until 1795 (see 27). Surely the once brilliant and still bright coloring of the buildings and caricaturelike figures animating the foreground made this print an attractive advertisement for prospective students.

Americans were proud not only

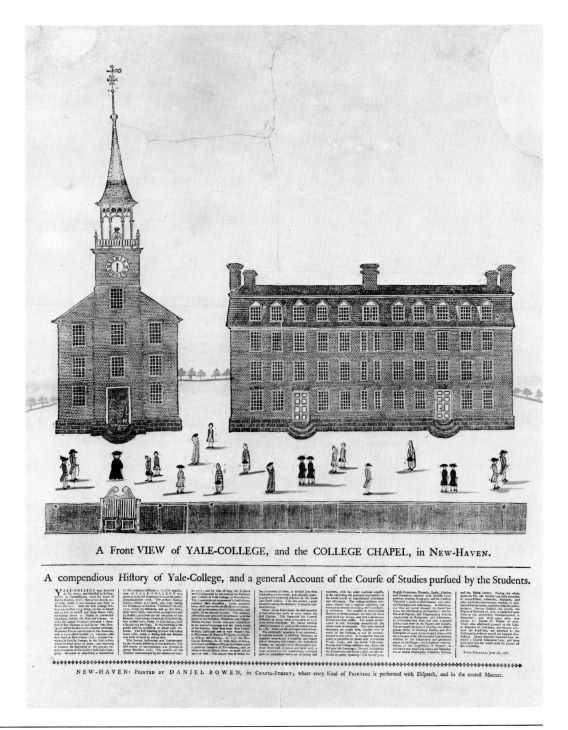

86
Anonymous artist
*A Front View of Yale-College,
and the College Chapel, New-Haven*
Woodcut (only known state), 1786.
Yale University Art Gallery; gift
of Jesse Lathrop Moss, B.A. 1869.

of their leaders and educational institutions, but also of their commercial success and flourishing cities. Such pride was the stimulus for William Birch when he first conceived his edition of "about 25 or 30 of the principal Buildings and Views" of Philadelphia. Birch published his twenty-seven line engravings, in addition to a title page, frontispiece, and printed page of introduction, as *The City of Philadelphia, in the State of Pennsylvania North America; as it appeared in the Year 1800*. He made most of the engravings after watercolor sketches, probably prepared by his son Thomas. Three editions were published, one in 1800, one in 1804, and the last in 1827-1828; the subscription book (Historical Society of Pennsylvania, Philadelphia) noted 156 first edition

purchasers, including Thomas Jefferson, Gilbert Stuart, and Thomas Mifflin (see 82, 45, 8).

As in his book of English town and country scenes entitled *Délices de la Grande Bretagne*, published three years before he emigrated to America from London in 1794, Birch had a specific point of view: he wanted to portray not only the architectural advancements of the city, but the people and their activities as well. *Back of the State House, Philadelphia* (87) depicts Independence Hall, which was the Pennsylvania state house as well as the seat of Congress and the United States Supreme Court until 1800. Like virtually all in Birch's volume, it presents a scene with reference to the city's origins, its present conditions, and its future prosperity. *Preparation for War to*

defend Commerce (**88**) is an early industrial genre scene representing the construction of the frigate *Philadelphia* at the busy Southwark shipyard. The *Philadelphia* was a source of pride and provided a sense of security; carrying thirty-six guns, it had been specially designed to have more firepower and greater speed than European ships as Americans strengthened their defenses during the quasiwar with France (1798-1801). The attractive composition, with the diagonal of the scaffolding dominating the scene, and the pleasing coloring combine to make *Preparation for War* the most desirable of Birch's *Views*.

Like painting and the other arts in America after the Revolution, printmaking was used to further a sense of national purpose. Indeed, Birch's glorification of Philadelphia

BACK of the STATE HOUSE, PHILADELPHIA.

87
William Russell Birch
Back of the State House, Philadelphia. Line engraving, colored (first state), 1799.
Yale University Art Gallery; Mabel Brady Garvan Collection.

in his introduction to *Philadelphia Views* paralleled the pride of achievement voiced by many about the country as a whole.

The ground on which it stands, was, less than a century ago, in a state of wild nature, covered with wood, and inhabited by Indians. It has, in this short time, been raised, as it were, by magic power, to the eminence of an opulent city, famous for its trade and commerce, crowded in its port, with vessels of its own producing, and visited by others from all parts of the world. . . . This Work will stand as a memorial of its progress for the first century. . . .[6]

Faith in the potential progress and mission of the new republic is the message of John Boqueta de Woiseri's *A View of New Orleans taken from the Plantation of Marigny* (**89**, ill. p. 22). In the

Philadelphia General Advertiser of February 21, 1804, he announced the publication of this view and its companion "Plan of New Orleans."[7] Very little is known of Boqueta de Woiseri except that he executed views in watercolor and aquatint of most of America's major cities, including Philadelphia, New York, Boston, Charleston, Baltimore, and Richmond. Celebrating the recent purchase of the Louisiana Territory from France in October, 1803, Boqueta de Woiseri's aquatint, which is printed partially in color, seems prophetic—on the starred banner held by an American eagle is written "UNDER MY WINGS EVERY THING PROSPERS."

From part-time engravers who were primarily printers, school-teachers, silversmiths, or painters there evolved in the beginning of

the nineteenth century highly skilled professionals capable of handling the complex techniques of aquatint and color printing, which succeeded line or mezzotint engraving in popularity. And their works, especially engravings like Birch's *Philadelphia Views*, allowed Europeans to be introduced to the wonders of the New World. Although few American prints produced in the second half of the eighteenth century display great innovation or startling quality, they nevertheless provided Americans with images that were useful and at times elevating. Produced in large quantities, they broadcast common ideas and sentiments to all levels of society and, in this respect, they were the most popular and influential art form in eighteenth-century America.

Preparation for WAR to defend Commerce.

The Swedish Church Southwark with the building of the FRIGATE PHILADELPHIA.

88
William Russell Birch
Preparation for War to Defend Commerce. Line engraving, colored (only known state), 1800.
The Athenaeum of Philadelphia; gift of Mrs. Charles Fearon, 1952.

Furniture

American furniture as a medium represents a strong statement of indigenous craft practice and design. As pattern books and immigrating craftsmen from England transmitted each successive wave of stylistic influence, their effects were tempered by interaction with a vigorous existing shop practice here. Yet—and this is most significant—furniture was not only made but also owned by all social classes, in both city and country; it is, therefore, perhaps the most sensitive barometer of the vision and values of the entire society.

Furniture gains additional significance because of the nature of the colonial society in which it was used; America was more uniformly middle-class, in reality and in identity, than any country the world had seen before, more so than the seventeenth-century Netherlands, certainly more so than eighteenth-century England. And,

in this middle-class society, furniture was the most universal art form. Furniture shared important basic qualities with the architectural styles from which it derived—design, materials, scale, and surface effects—however, furniture had the advantage of costing less. It therefore provided the means through which the population at large could experience new ideas, principles, and techniques as they became available. Furniture was that part of the personal environment with which the majority of people were physically and psychologically intimate, that part of an individual's real property through which he could most naturally express his identity.

Sometime late in the third decade of the eighteenth century, furniture-makers in the American colonies began to respond to the impulses of a new style, now commonly referred to as Queen Anne, which

90
Upholstered settee
Philadelphia, ca. 1740.
The Metropolitan Museum of Art;
Rogers Fund, 1925.

had been introduced into England during the Queen's reign (1702-1714). In this new mode walnut continued to be the fashionable wood. Palladian classicism influenced the design of case furniture, which was conceived architecturally in proportion and detail.[1] Mass was articulated by curved outlines in seating furniture and the limited range of ornament featured naturalistic shells, volutes, and C-scrolls. Every American cabinetmaking center adopted the style, but in Philadelphia (which entered an era of renewed growth about 1730) chairmakers produced exceptional designs embodying the serpentine "line of beauty," which the English artist William Hogarth, in his *Analysis of Beauty* (1753), described as a dominant compositional element of the arts of the era.

In the walnut settee illustrated (**90**), a unique American example of the form, the debt of Philadelphia chairmaking to English and, especially, Irish chair design is readily apparent. In particular, the trifid foot and beading on the knee follow Irish practices, and the settee's undulating top rail and large upholstered surfaces create a richer, more baroque effect than is usual in most American furniture.

According to tradition, James Logan, William Penn's secretary, is thought to have owned the settee at his Germantown house, "Stenton," but the 1752 inventory of his estate falls to support the tradition. The piece descended in the Smith family of Philadelphia, possibly from Logan's daughter Hannah, who married John Smith of Burlington, New Jersey, in 1748. A "settee covered with damask £9.10.0" was listed in Smith's inventory of 1771 and may indeed be this very example.[2] The evaluation is exceptionally high, and the Logans and Smiths, prominent Philadelphia Quakers, had the means to own such a piece of furniture.

Rich stuffs used for upholstered furniture, window curtains, and festooned, four-post beds added immeasurably to the color and luxury of domestic interiors of well-to-do eighteenth-century Americans. The high backs, enclosing wings, and soft surfaces of easy chairs offered protection from drafts, and inviting, cushioned comfort, especially when upholstered with needlework, wool moreens, or damasks. Like the settee, the easy chair (**91**) is also an outstanding example of the Philadelphia chairmaking school. Its C-scrolls on the arms uncurl from the cone-shaped armrests and supports in a manner reminiscent of strapwork in a baroque-style cartouche. As in the best chairs of the type, the stump rear legs are bowed and visually thrust the massive form upward. Well-formed cabriole legs and claw-and-ball feet,

91
Easy chair
Philadelphia, 1740-1750.
Private collection.

rounded corners on the seat frame, and skillfully carved scallop shells on the knees are also hallmarks of the Philadelphia school.

In the best American Queen Anne style furniture, the form becomes the ornament and is the dominant aspect of the whole. In this regard, the Queen Anne style walnut armchair (92) is a paramount example of the Philadelphia school. Curves, volutes, and shells echo throughout this tall-backed, sculpturesque form; the sensuously modeled lines demonstrate the great skill of the chairmaker, who, with his eye and a drawknife, could shape sawn pieces of wood into a subtle and fluid conception.

Although English furniture scholars date chairs in this mode to about 1710-1720, in America their introduction may not have occurred until after 1730. Compared with the English examples, the American chairs have leaner outlines and a sparing use of veneer and carving. Sometimes the splats and less frequently the seat rails of these American chairs are veneered, but in general Philadelphia chairmakers usually confined their carved ornamentation to scallop shells, scrolls, and occasional leafage on the knees, eschewing the more abundant foliate carving and rich veneers typical of English models.

The side chair (93) is a slightly later representative of the Philadelphia Queen Anne style chair, and its additional ornamental detail attracts the eye more readily to surface than to plastic form. A shell emphasizes the indented front of the seat rail; leaf carving spills over the

92
Armchair
Philadelphia, 1730-1750.
Mr. Peter W. Eliot.

tops of the knees, and wavy lines frame the shell on the crest. Made from native cherry, this chair exhibits typical regional characteristics as they developed in Philadelphia chairmaking shops. To achieve the maximum curvilinear form, the seat, for example, is constructed with thick boards mortised and tenoned together, to which the tops of the front legs are doweled and the molded lip for the slip seat is fastened. This structural method was not used in the other colonies, except occasionally in Connecticut.

Elsewhere, as on the New York chair illustrated (94), the tops of the front legs were mortised and tenoned directly to the seat rails, a method of construction which produced a compass seat of more languid outline.

Eight chairs made for a member of the Apthorp family are outstanding examples of eighteenth-century New York furniture. According to tradition, the exceptional chair shown here (94) belonged to the Boston merchant Charles Apthorp and his wife, Grizzell Eastwicke, although it is also possible that it

came into the family from their son Charles Ward Apthorp, who lived in New York. The broad seat, the large scrolled knee brackets, the squared rear feet, and the undercut shell with floral streamers are all features closely related to English and European prototypes. The outlines of the Apthorp chair are more massive than those of the Philadelphia chairs, in part because the stretchers are retained. The delicate undercutting on the shell and the fiery walnut veneer on the splat are exceptionally fine features.

93
Side chair
Philadelphia, 1740-1750.
Mrs. Alfred Elliott Bissell.

94
Side chair
New York, 1730-1750.
Benjamin Ginsburg.

In response to the need for new household forms which followed the introduction of tea from the Orient, cabinetmakers were called upon to make tea tables for the home. The preferred form in New England was a rectangular table, with a molded edge to prevent precious china and silver tea vessels from sliding off. An outstanding example (95) of this classic form, its ends fitted with additional slides for candles, is illustrated here. Linear elegance epitomizes New England Queen Anne style cabinetwork, and it is achieved here through the clarity of the line defining the serpentine edges of the skirt and the attenuated cabriole legs.

The Connecticut tea table (96), a more simplified, pared down, maple version, exemplifies the manner in which form became the primary element of design in American Queen Anne furniture, especially in that produced in rural areas. Here the main structural line rises in a continuous curve through the slender legs to an ogee arch in the skirt. The generous rectangular top with its molded edge acts as a foil to the open, curvilinear design of the base. Some prosperous household in the Saybrook-Lyme area of coastal Connecticut, where the table was found in the early years of the twentieth century, probably used it for serving tea or breakfast.

A similar uninterrupted fluid line modulates the verticality of the legs and the horizontality of the skirt on a dressing table made in Newport, Rhode Island (97). The curves swing into one another with a continuous flow, and both frame and echo the central ornamental feature, a stylized scallop shell. Popular throughout the eighteenth century from New Hampshire to Maryland, dressing tables were designed to match high chests or highboys, as storage forms for use in the bedroom. On the basis of the signature of Christopher Townsend (1748) on a high chest and a documented dressing table (1746) by Job Townsend, this example can be

95
Tea table
New England, 1740-1760.
Mr. and Mrs. Stanley Stone.

96
Tea table
Saybrook-Lyme area, Connecticut,
1740-1780. Wadsworth Atheneum;
gift of Mrs. Augustus C. Downing.

tentatively attributed to the workshop of the two brothers, who were founders of the Newport furnituremaking school.[3] Newport was a wealthy, populous, cosmopolitan center of international and coastal trade, with ninety-odd cabinetshops serving local and distant markets.

The Townsend family in succeeding generations, along with another Newport cabinetmaking family, the Goddards, are most notable for their exceptional contribution to the development of "blockfront" furniture, a major innovation of New England cabinetmakers. The term derives from the manner in which the facades of desks, chests,

97
Dressing table
Newport, 1740-1770.
Mrs. Thomas M. Cole.

bureau tables, and other case pieces were contoured with two raised, vertical panels, each flanking a central, recessed panel. Although the exact source of this New England form has not been established, small-scale blocking was used in the colonies in the early eighteenth century on the drawers of desk interiors and English dressing glasses. Blockfront furniture was being made in Boston by the 1730s (the earliest documented example was signed and dated by Job Coit in 1738), in Newport by the middle of the century, in Connecticut by the 1760s, and it continued to be popular in New England until at least 1800.

One of the several blockfront forms produced in Boston is a round-blocked dressing table (**98**). Unlike the preceding Newport table (**97**), whose lines flow out, away from the form, this Boston example has a compact and self-contained composition, in which the arc of the round blocking is repeated in the scalloped outlines of the skirt, in the contours of the facade, and in the edge of the overhanging top. This interplay and repetition of curves give stature and cohesion to this diminutive table, an exceptional example of the possibilities inherent in blockfront design.

In both Massachusetts and Rhode Island the blockfront form was adapted to another type of dressing table: the traditional English bureau table, which is a chest of drawers with a double-pedestal base, a central recess, and a long top drawer. In fact, the components of this particular form, with their receding and projecting arrangement, readily lent themselves to being treated with blockfront orna-

mentation. Concave and convex shells crowning the blocked panels are the distinguishing glory of the best Newport blockfront furniture, and the Newport bureau table illustrated (**99**), the shells and additional details, such as the continuation of the block-and-scroll motif down into the feet, contribute to the opulence and vitality of the composition. A dozen such block-and-shell tables are known today—all associated with the workshops of the Townsend and Goddard families of Newport.[4]

The most spectacular example of Newport blockfront furniture is a desk and bookcase (**100**) that stands eight feet high, made for the wealthy Providence merchant John Brown. Outlined by architectural details in dark mahogany, the lighter-colored mahogany facade is composed with careful attention

98
Blockfront dressing table
Boston, 1730-1750.
The Dietrich Brothers Americana
Corporation.

99
Blockfront bureau table
Newport, 1760-1790.
The Metropolitan Museum of Art;
gift of Mrs. Russell Sage, 1909.

to the sculptural and compositional elements. Divided into two sections—desk and bookcase—whose blocking is crowned by shells with curving rays, the whole is supported on ogee bracket feet, and completed by a scrolled pediment enclosing a pair of fielded panels. Its height and verticality are emphasized by spiral finials on fluted urns. The architectural basis of its design was suitable and complementary to the classically inspired interiors of the time. Few objects speak more pointedly of the wealth and dignity

100
Blockfront desk and bookcase
Newport, 1765-1785.
Yale University Art Gallery;
Mabel Brady Garvan Collection.

of the patrons or of the design capacities of the makers.

The cherry chest-on-chest made in Connecticut (**101**) is a visual translation and fanciful elaboration of the Newport design formula, with its large two-tiered façade rising in three blocked panels, finished with shells, and contained by flanking twisted columns. It also incorporates a wealth of eccentric ornamental detail, such as the arching terminal bands under the shells, the frondlike, central finial support, and the pinwheel rosettes. The multiplicity and rhythmic

enrichment of detail is characteristic of much of the best rural American furniture and is rarely encountered on urban wares like the Newport blockfront pieces. Samuel Loomis (1748-1814) of Colchester, Connecticut, may have made this chest-on-chest, judging by its similarities to the documented chest-on-chest-on-frame by him at the Wadsworth Atheneum.[5] In the eastern area of Connecticut where Loomis worked, adjacent to the Rhode Island border, there flourished a school of cabinetmaking that rendered the Newport idiom in its own

fanciful manner.

In Massachusetts, where the blockfront form was interpreted more modestly than it was in either Newport or Connecticut, the monumental expressions of the cabinetmaker's craft were bombé case pieces—that is, case pieces whose sides swell outward in elongated, serpentine curves above the base molding. Richly ornamented with gilding, architectural detailing, surface carving, and bold outlines, the bombé desk and bookcase (**102**) by George Bright was made for Samuel Barrett, brother-in-law of

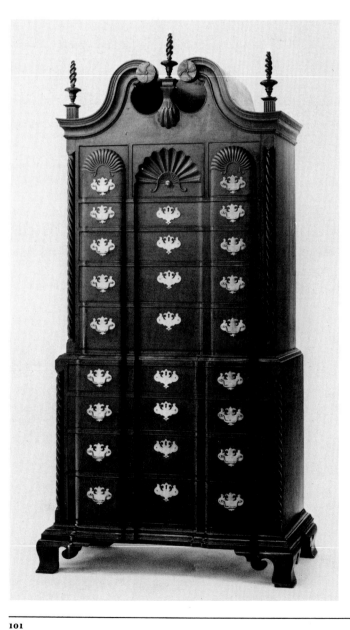

101
Chest-on-chest
Colchester, Connecticut, area,
1780-1805. The Connecticut
Historical Society, Hartford;
gift of Elinor B. Ingersoll.

the painter John Singleton Copley. The foliate carving on the short cabriole legs, the ogee outlines of the mirror frames, and the floral pendants on the swan's-neck pediment are expressions of the rococo aesthetic—although the overall form of the desk, with its swelled section close to the ground, corresponds more closely to baroque taste. This arrangement of weight and mass can be compared to the Queen Anne style silver teapots of Peter Van Dyck (137 and 138), rather than to rococo style hollow-ware, such as the double-bellied teakettle on stand

by Joseph Richardson (146). Unlike the blockfront form, an American innovation, the bombé adheres to English design; imported English bombé pieces, such as the chest-on-chest owned by the Boston merchant Charles Apthorp (fig. 33), may have served as models for American cabinetmakers. The bombé was made in America only in Massachu-

102
Bombé desk and bookcase
George Bright, Boston, 1770-1792.
Museum of Fine Arts, Boston;
bequest of Miss Charlotte Hazen.

setts, a situation which may reflect the inherent conservatism of both artisan and patron in that area.

The publication in 1754 of Thomas Chippendale's pattern book, *The Gentleman & Cabinet-Maker's Director*, made readily available to the American cabinet-maker a new style and a new aesthetic. This book included furniture fashions current in London, as well as new designs by Chippendale. Although the Chippendale style is sometimes equated with rococo, it is important to recognize that it primarily represents an overlay of new ornament on English forms, forms defined by Palladian principles and classical ideals of structure. Case pieces were modeled on architectual forms like those used for fireplace overmantles, doorcases and win-dows. Classical moldings were employed, and classical proportions were followed. Indeed, the first eight plates in Chippendale's book are of the five orders—Tuscan, Doric, Ionic, Corinthian, and Composite. The highly ornamental designs he showed thereafter reveal three stylistic influences—the delicate, naturalistic ornament of the modern, or French, rococo taste, the exotic motifs of Chinese origin, and that peculiar and perpetual favorite of English culture, Gothic ornament. While Chippendale's *Director* may have been the most important English pattern book for mid-eighteenth-century American cabinetmakers, it was not the only one. Pattern books, which made designs for furniture easily available, were a new phenomenon, and books such as Matthias Lock's *New Book of Ornaments* (1752), Thomas Johnson's *New Book of Ornaments* (1760) and *One Hundred and Fifty New Designs* (1761), Ince and Mayhew's *Universal System of Household Furniture* (1760), and Robert Manwaring's *Cabinet and Chair-Maker's Real Friend and Companion* (1765) must also have served to inform American craftsmen of the latest London fashions.

Chippendale's *Director* had its most notable influence in America in Philadelphia. Few examples of American furniture show such a close parallel to designs illustrated in Chippendale's book as a chair (**103**) whose back design combines two patterns in the *Director's* Plate IX (fig. 65). The chair is like one of a set made for the Fisher

103
Side chair
Philadelphia, 1755-1785.
Private collection.

Fig. 65
Designs for a chair backs
Thomas Chippendale, *The Gentleman and Cabinet-Maker's Director*
(London, 1762), pl. IX.

family of Wakefield, Pennsylvania, by Thomas Affleck, one of Philadelphia's most prominent cabinetmakers.[6] Affleck had his own copy of "Shippendale's Designs," and other Philadelphia cabinetmakers probably had access to the *Director* through one of the city's three library companies, whose membership rolls included most of the city's finest furnituremakers of the time.

On this Philadelphia chair, the intertwining lines flow smoothly from the crest rail into the splat and successfully capture the sense of airiness and unity conveyed by Chippendale's designs. At the same time, the chair is also representative of the alterations Chippendale's designs underwent at the hands of American craftsmen. Cabriole legs, with claw-and-ball feet of the

George II era, have been retained even though they appear in Chippendale's *Director* only in a tea caddy, and had been superseded in London high fashion by the scroll foot. Chippendale's instructions concerning the upholstering of the seat over the rail have been disregarded in favor of a slip seat. Other changes include the narrower proportions of the seat, a thinner, more nearly vertical silhouette with outflaring stiles, and stump rear legs. The result is an American chair of light, lean, yet sturdy appearance.

Chippendale foresaw that less skillful cabinetmakers might have to simplify his designs, and advised that "if any of the small Ornaments should be thought superfluous, they may be left out, without spoil-

ing the Design." The modifications effected in another Chippendale chair (104) are of a more fundamental nature. The paired S-scrolls of the splat, embracing a cord and tassel, are only vaguely reminiscent of a design for a chair in the center of Plate XIIII of Chippendale's *Director* (fig. 66), and the stop-fluting of the stiles introduces new architectural overtones. Coupled with the symmetrical shells on the crest and the front seat rail—carry-overs from the preceding era—these stylistically conservative and moderated features point to the preferences of Philadelphia merchants, who sought elegance with restraint, and to the ability of Philadelphia chairmakers to satisfy these demands.

Although Philadelphia Chip-

Fig. 66
Designs for a chair backs
Thomas Chippendale, *The Gentleman and Cabinet-Maker's Director*
(London, 1762), pl. XIIII.

104
Side chair
Philadelphia, 1760-1780.
Department of State,
Diplomatic Reception Rooms; gift of Mr. and Mrs. George M. Kaufman.

pendale chairs sometimes reflect the influence of the *Director*, chairs made in Boston rarely exhibit a close reliance on this English pattern book. Boston chairs are ornamented with shallower, more abstract carving than contemporary Philadelphia examples, and even retain turned stretchers. The Massachusetts chair in this series (**105**) is similar to others branded "M. MacKay," presumably for Mungo MacKay, a Boston resident.[7] Its block-and-spindle stretchers, wide seat, squarish back, and ample proportions are all characteristic of the school. The thinness of the splat, legs, seat rails, and stiles, as well as the raking side claws on the feet, rectilinearity of its parts, and

the delicate crispness of the carving —all further identify it as a Massachusetts chair.

While Philadelphia and Boston chairmakers looked abroad for inspiration and guidance in the design of chairs, Connecticut artisans were content to look to the cities of America. Eliphalet Chapin, born and probably apprenticed in Enfield, Connecticut, worked for five years in Philadelphia before returning to his native state as a fashionable cabinetmaker. His cherry chair (**106**), smaller in scale and simpler in ornamentation than comparable urban examples, is constructed in the Philadelphia manner, with "through tenons" on the side seat rails, quarter-round corner

blocks with vertical grain, stump rear legs, and arched lower edges of the seat rails. The splat design shows evidence of both Philadelphia and Massachusetts models. Chapin's chair, though lacking in ornamental carving, makes a virtue of plainness. Uniform surfaces created by the dense cherry wood intensify the sculptural contrast of solids and voids already enhanced by the outflaring back and delicately wrought cabriole legs.

Chapin adapted an urban ideal to a rural reality and created an appealing individual aesthetic. Even more highly individualized than Chapin's chairs, however, are the productions of the Dunlap family of New Hampshire. Located

105
Side chair
Massachusetts, possibly Boston,
ca. 1765. The Metropolitan Museum
of Art; Rogers Fund, 1944.

106
Side chair
Attributed to Eliphalet Chapin,
East Windsor, Connecticut, ca. 1780.
Yale University Art Gallery;
Mabel Brady Garvan Collection.

far from Boston, the nearest large city, and lacking an apprenticeship to a craftsman acquainted with the urban high-fashion design vocabulary, John and Samuel Dunlap combined new ideas and elements of old styles that had lingered on in their isolated New Hampshire community. The chair seen here (**107**), attributed to Major John Dunlap,[8] thus incorporates the verticality and the separation between the base of the splat and the seat rail reminiscent of William and Mary style banister-back chairs, with a pierced Queen Anne style splat, and Chippendale style fluted Marlborough legs and "ears" (crest rail terminals). This mixture of elements from three styles would

strike a discordant note were the elements not subservient to an extroverted, decorative impulse that demands another standard of evaluation. In its original state, with deep blue paint and a bright needlework seat, this chair would have lent any rural home the colorful cheer characteristic of virtually all folk art.

Although there was a widespread vogue for chairs with pierced splats soon after the middle of the eighteenth century in America, not all these chairs displayed the fragile delicacy of the rococo. In Newport a preference for more plastic, more baroque forms persisted, as is suggested by the corner chair (**108**) from a pair owned by the

eighteenth-century Providence merchant John Brown. Made of very heavy mahogany that shows the variation between the dark color of heartwood and the lighter color of sapwood, the chair gives one a sense of presence, mass, and strength. Undulating curves are echoed in the arm supports and in the line of the front seat rails, whose depth of contour is unusual. The two splats, interlaced with wide bands of strapwork, complement the muscular quality of the rest of the chair.

Whereas in Boston, Philadelphia, and other urban centers in America, English models were transformed and pieces were recognizably different from their English

107
Side chair
Attributed to Major John Dunlap,
Goffstown or Bedford, New
Hampshire, 1770-1790.
The Metropolitan Museum of Art.
gift of Mrs. J. Insley Blair, 1943.

108
Corner chair
Newport, ca. 1760.
Mr. Peter W. Eliot.

protoypes, this was decidedly not true in Charleston, South Carolina. There, the almost literal adaptation of English design in high-style furniture reflected that city's closer social and artistic ties to London. In construction, proportion, and ornamental features, the mahogany chest-on-chest (109) attributed to Thomas Elfe reveals the London training of its maker (he emigrated about 1745) and his continuing acquaintance with London fashions (the form itself, the chest-on-chest, was a London preference). Ogee bracket feet support a three-drawer lower section and an eight-drawer upper chest, which is enclosed by fluted chamfered corners. The cornice is embellished by a curvilinear fretwork band and an arching scroll pediment terminating in carved rosettes. The two-dimensional fretwork is at once varied, delicate, and restrained in its flat symmetry.

A highly original combination of the old and new is characteristic of the wares produced by Philadelphia cabinetmakers, particularly of high chests such as the example known because of its carved bust as the "Pompadour" highboy (110). Derived from the English chest-on-frame, which was displaced by mid-century in England by the chest-on-chest, the Philadelphia high chest is basically an architectural, carefully proportioned, classical form with pediment and ornament derived from architectural pattern books—all overlaid with foliate, or figurative, or rocaille ornament. The carving displays a sense of lightness, whimsy, asymmetry, and instability. The concentration of these rococo elements at the vertical extremes of the blond-colored ma-hogany case creates a sense of vitality and movement within a basically static form. Indeed, it was primarily the unidentified carver—through his use of a rich and various vocabulary of fretwork, bas-relief, vines, and free-standing figurative sculpture—who gave this piece its rococo character and monumental stature. Since the urn finials were copied from examples in Chippendale's *Director* (fig. 68), and the scene of fighting swans and spouting dragon on the carved lower drawer is clearly derived from Thomas Johnson's *A New Book of Ornaments* (1762) (fig. 67), this nameless carver no doubt chose many of his other designs from pattern books. The conjunction in mid-eighteenth-century Philadelphia of skilled carvers (such as Hercules Courtenay and Bernard and Jugiez) and in-

109
Chest-on-chest
Attributed to Thomas Elfe,
Charleston, South Carolina, ca. 1770.
Colonial Williamsburg Foundation.

Fig. 67
Design for a Chimney-piece tablet
Thomas Johnson, *A New Book of Ornaments by Thos Johnson, Carver...*
(London, 1762), pl. 5.
The Victoria and Albert Museum.

Fig. 68
Design for a library bookcase
Thomas Chippendale, *The Gentleman and Cabinet-Maker's Director,* pl. XCII.

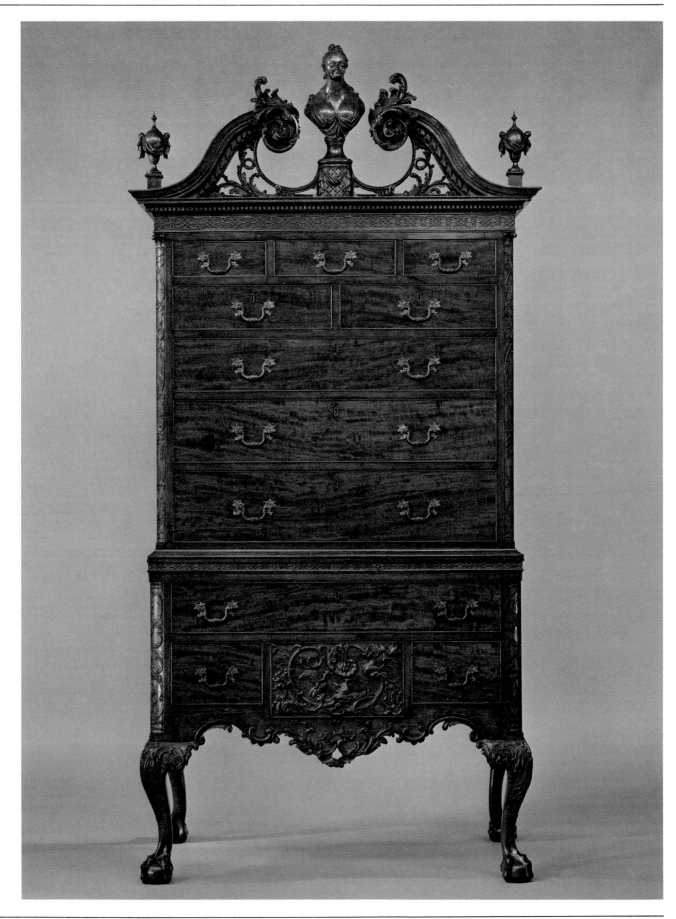

110
High chest
Philadelphia, ca. 1770.
The Metropolitan Museum of Art;
Kennedy Fund, 1918.

ventive cabinetmakers (such as Thomas Affleck and Benjamin Randolph) produced an interpretation of the rococo that was distinctly American.

Splendor and luxury, qualities usually associated with the rococo style, are much in evidence in the tables created for the social rituals of the affluent. In Philadelphia, the economic capital of the colonies, the round tea table, such as **111**, with its elaborately carved tripod base, ornamented column, revolving "birdcage," and delicately edged top—was an ostentatious piece of furniture that served as the focal point of the ceremony of tea drinking. Single slabs of "curl'd" mahogany were often edged, as in this piece, by a crisp, "scollop'd" ogee molding, which was not only a

decorative feature but, as with the Queen Anne tea table, also a guard against accident. These tea tables, like the Philadelphia high chest, were the work of craft specialists—highly proficient carvers and turners—who used their skills to the utmost. A flattened ball is the central feature of the pillar, and a quartet of vase-shaped colonettes support the wooden plates of the "birdcage," which allows the top of the table to tip and turn.

The spirit of the rococo, with its emphasis on interpenetrating ornament and lightness in form, sometimes was absorbed and interpreted in rural America with inventive and original motifs that captured the essence of the academic style. The Connecticut high chest (**112**) stands in the same relation to the

Philadelphia high chest as much of Connecticut painting does to urban painting. For example, the illusion of overlap and of spatial depth in the foliate scrolls on the Pompadour high chest pediment—as well as in the portrait of *Mrs. Isaac Smith* by Copley (14; illustrated p.35)—is entirely absent in the Connecticut high chest. Instead, the craftsman emphasized form and clarity of line in the serpentine curves of the legs, skirt, and pediment. The surface ornamentation—two gyrating swastikas—convey a sense of swirling motion in harmony with the rococo spirit.

Eighteenth-century Connecticut, though it prospered as an agrarian society, lacked a major urban center. The arts that flourished in the colony's seaports and market

111
Tea table
Philadelphia, 1760-1775.
The Metropolitan Museum of Art;
Rogers Fund, 1925.

towns tended to reflect its character as a crossroads of native culture. Owing to the migration of craftsmen and the importation of urban wares, the influences of Boston, Newport, New York, and Philadelphia were far stronger than any direct suggestion of style from abroad. Translated into cherry, the preferred Connecticut cabinet wood, furniture of high-style origin was adapted to the tastes of a prosperous gentry and to the abilities and tools of nonspecialized but versatile cabinetmakers.

112
High chest
Connecticut, ca. 1780.
Greenfield Village and The Henry
Ford Museum.

In rural New Hampshire, the dynamics of wealth, creative interest, and a curiously free ability to recombine elements from high-style precedents combined to produce masterpieces of American design. A New Hampshire chest-on-chest-on-frame (**113**) represents a very different trend in rural craftsmanship from that of the Connecticut high chest (**112**). A compendium of varied moldings, shells, scoring, scrolls and plumes, forming a sort of fancy headdress, echoes and balances an equally extravagant

113
Chest-on-chest-on-frame
Attributed to the Dunlap school
of cabinetmakers, New Hampshire,
1790-1795. The Currier Gallery
of Art.

base composed of squat cabriole legs with spurlike responds, radiating fans, and conjoined S-scrolls. Soaring between these dark, complex areas of intense decoration, the fiery curly maple drawer fronts, carefully chosen to alternate to the left and right as they ascend, lend a strong, barely disciplined rhythm to an area otherwise devoid of formal decorative devices. Because of stylistic similarities to five other inscribed pieces, this example is attributed to the New Hampshire cabinetmaking school founded by Major John Dunlap and Lieutenant Samuel Dunlap.[9] An urban cabinetmaker would have objected most strongly to precisely the strongest design characteristics of this piece and the Dunlap chair (107): their

verticality and lack of Palladian unity; yet it is these qualities which give much rural furniture its compelling allure.

The gaming or card table, with sunken wells for counters, square corners for candles, and convenient fold-out, fold-away construction, was a furniture form that became increasingly popular in the Chippendale era. Made in the major urban centers, it varies considerably in the regional interpretations. The example from Massachusetts (114) exhibits the sharp, lean lines preferred on furniture from that colony. The center of this square-cornered table is magnificently ornamented with a needlework panel on whose crimson ground cards and counters depict a game in

progress around a medallion of brightly wrought flowers. The table is supported by four cabriole legs with low-relief carving on the knees and terminating in superb claw-and-ball feet, strongly rendered in the classic, Massachusetts form. The daughters of William Samuel Johnson, first president of Columbia University (then known as King's College), are credited with the embroidery of the top and of the table's accompanying pole screen (115), whose panel is worked in tent stitch.

A pole screen or firescreen was described by Thomas Sheraton as "a piece of furniture to shelter the face or legs from the fire."[10] However, this one, a premier example of the Chippendale era, serves as

114
Card table
Massachusetts, 1760-1780.
Mr. and Mrs. Stanley Stone.

115
Pole screen
Massachusetts, 1760-1780.
Mr. and Mrs. Stanley Stone.

stand and frame as well for the colorful still-life picture, which is at least thirty or forty years earlier than most American still-life paintings in oil or water color. This Massachusetts firescreen, supported on cabriole legs, which spring from the floor with energy and grace, has a neatly carved baluster, finial, and rat-claw feet. The unusual threaded shaft permits the height of the screen to be easily adjusted.

The rectilinearity of the Massachusetts table contrasts with the curves of the New York form (**116**). More than twenty-five examples of these serpentine card tables have descended in prominent New York and New Jersey families.[11] The glory of the table shown here is the sweeping serpentine line of the top linking the square, projecting corners. The skirt assumes that shape emphasized along the edge by rich gadrooning that conveys a sense of movement flowing into the cabriole legs. Their form is peculiar to New York—ample yet not ungainly, resting on large, square-topped claw-and-ball feet. Asymmetrical carving of C-scrolls and suspended leafage graces the knees and completes the statement of flamboyant, rococo elegance. This table also exhibits specific features of its formal group: a drawer concealed by the gate and a fifth, swing-leg to support the open top.

Another outstanding example of New York Chippendale style furniture is the upholstered stool (**117**). Although it is a small object, its well-formed cabriole legs with claw-and-ball feet, together with the clear definition of its oval top by the rich mahogany seat rails, give the same sense of masculine strength and bold outline as is conveyed by the New York card table. The low-relief carving on the knees and the wedge of crosshatching are less rococo in spirit than the asymmetrical leafage of the gaming table, but the carving is of a type that

116
Card table
New York, 1765-1785.
Yale University Art Gallery;
Mabel Brady Garvan Collection.

117
Stool
New York, 1760-1780.
Mr. and Mrs. Stanley Stone.

persisted in New York for fifty years. Stools, especially ones finished in the elegant and rich manner of this example, are rare survivals in American eighteenth-century furniture.

Although furnituremakers in many rural areas did not reflect high-style modes in their furniture, some created notably original forms. By the last quarter of the eighteenth century, a distinctive school of decorated furniture emerged in the soil-rich counties to the west of Philadelphia, where German immigrants from the Rhine Valley and nearby Switzerland had been settled since the 1740s. In their close, religion-centered communities, Old World standards and customs remained virtually unchanged, despite some absorption of English influences. The chests produced in *Schreinerei*, or joiners' shops, were of an ancient, lift-top form—constructed in the continental manner of dovetailing boards at the corners, as opposed to the panel-and-frame construction of the English joiner. These chests were further set apart from English furniture types by intricately painted designs composed of floral and figural motifs closely related to the Germanic *Fraktur*, or manuscript illumination.

On the example of this type shown (**118**), certain features reveal the interaction of both Germanic and English cultures: the horsemen are no longer knights or courtiers, but rather English cavalry officers; the unicorns are direct copies of that fabled creature depicted in the British royal coat of arms (fig. 69); and imported English brasses decorate the drawer fronts. Thus symbols from Anglo-American culture were adopted by German craftsmen and then combined with traditional German working methods and ornamental forms to create a distinctly Pennsylvanian furniture form.

118
Painted chest
Berks County, Pennsylvania,
ca. 1780. The Metropolitan Museum
of Art; Rogers Fund, 1923.
(Color, p. 59.)

Fig. 69
British royal coat of arms

Windsor chairs, common seats of an unacademic sort, were universal in both city and country in eighteenth-century America. These painted wooden plank-bottom chairs could be used both in and out of doors. Because they were relatively impervious to weather and wetness, they were ideal for the garden or the hall, and their resistance to staining made them suitable even for the dining room. They were thus found in the most fashionable of houses, in the humblest of dwellings, and in public buildings (members of the Continental Congress sat on windsor chairs in Independence Hall).

The mystery of their name has fascinated furniture historians for generations, but as yet no satisfactory explanation has been found for its origin. The form was appar-ently introduced into America from England, where it was known from the 1720s; and from the 1740s, American chairmakers set about developing their own particular interpretations. A virtual industry in windsor chairmaking began in Philadelphia, whence the chairs were exported in large numbers to other American ports. Through the copying of imported examples and the emigration of craftsmen from Philadelphia, windsor chairmaking was established throughout America.

The skills of the turning-and-chairmaking branches of the furniture industry were fundamental in the production of windsor chairs. Beautifully turned maple legs and arm supports mark the best examples, as do thick seats, made of easily worked soft wood, usually tulip-poplar or white pine, modeled and contoured with drawknives or spokeshaves. Thin spindles, which formed the backs and the bent crest and arm rails, were generally made from oak or hickory —strong woods that become pliable with the application of heat and moisture. Because of the variety of woods used in their construction, windsor chairs were usually painted, green for the most part, but red, black, yellow, and other colors were used as well.

Because of the rapid production of their component parts, windsor chairs were easy to assemble in volume. The Connecticut chair-maker Ebenezer Tracy had 6400 "chair rounds" and 277 "chair bottoms" in his estate inventory when he died in 1803, an amount that suggests the quantities of parts that were being turned out in the

119
Windsor armchair
Philadelphia or New York, 1760-1780.
Colonial Williamsburg Foundation.

eighteenth century.[12] In its way, the windsor chair clearly prefigured the mass production of chairs in nineteenth-century factories.

Because of the role exports played in their early history, windsor chairs are often difficult to assign to regional areas—a problem exemplified by (119). This early green low-back armchair has a straight-edged seat front, cylindrical turnings at the base of its legs, and pointed bulb feet, features often associated with early Philadelphia windsors. However, the underside of the seat bears the brand "PVR"— for Philip Van Rensselaer of Cherry Hill, Albany, New York—and the same elements are also found on the chair in the portrait of Connecticut-born Roger Sherman by Ralph Earl (49). Both examples may have been exported from Philadelphia, but this type was made elsewhere

49
Ralph Earl
Roger Sherman
Oil on canvas, ca. 1775.
Yale University Art Gallery;
gift of Roger Sherman White,
B.A. 1899, LL.B. 1902.

as well. Another early example of the form, whose turnings relate to those in 119, is the black comb-back child's high chair (120), whose parts are not so massive as those of 119, but whose wide straddle and scroll-carved ears mark

it as a fine early product of the Philadelphia school.

Elliptical seats, boldly peaked at the front, snaking arms, and scroll-eared crest rails characterize another type of high-backed windsor chair (121). The type may have origi-

nated in Massachusetts, for such chairs are found on the islands of Nantucket and Martha's Vineyard, where, in the eighteenth century, this chair was owned by Captain Obadiah Pease. The vigorous outlines of its parts and the boldness of

120
Windsor high chair
Philadelphia, 1755-1775.
Yale University Art Gallery;
Mabel Brady Garvan Collection.

its turning are qualities it shares with both preceding examples.

A different interpretation of the windsor form is represented by the continuous bow-back armchair branded by Ebenezer Tracy (122). Lighter, with exaggeratedly tapering legs and knife-sharp edges in its saddled seat, it exemplifies the attributes of late eighteenth-century American windsors. Indeed, the continuous bow-back, whose line sweeps from the top of the spindles through the arms, is the most graceful type of windsor chair, pushing the material to its limits to create a neat and lightweight seat.

The year 1788, when the federal Constitution was adopted in America, was marked by the publication in England of two epochal works:

121
Windsor armchair
Massachusetts, 1780-1800.
Yale University Art Gallery;
Mabel Brady Garvan Collection.

122
Windsor armchair
Ebenezer Tracy, Lisbon,
Connecticut, 1785-1795.
Yale University Art Gallery;
Mabel Brady Garvan Collection.

123
Chest-on-chest
William Lemon, carving by Samuel
McIntire, Salem, Massachusetts, 1796.
Museum of Fine Arts, Boston;
M. and M. Karolik Collection.

The Cabinet-Maker and Upholsterer's Guide by George Hepplewhite, and *The Cabinet-Maker's London Book of Prices, and Designs of Cabinet Work*. These two books influenced American cabinetmaking and played a central role in ushering in a new era of style, the neoclassical. In America, this new style is now widely designated as Federal, because its duration parallels the "Federal" period in the nation's political history. The term has also won favor as a substitute for the traditional names conferred upon English neoclassical furniture (Adam, Hepplewhite, and Sheraton), which are not meaningful in characterizing American work. The elegant plainness, rectilinearity, and geometric character of Federal furniture appealed to many republican Americans who were conscious of their ideological ties to classical Rome. Case pieces, in particular, provided an opportunity for designers to embody those philosophical ideals through the decorations that had allegorical implications.

The chest-on-chest (**123**) made in 1796 for Elizabeth Derby of Salem, Massachusetts, is an eloquent expression of the ideals and expectations of Americans for their new nation. The repeated carved images of abundance and fertility (baskets of fruits, flower vases, cornucopias,

bunches of grapes, garlanded putti) are presided over by a figure bearing the attributes—virtue (wreath), truth (golden sun), and power (pike)—associated with the new America. Thus the new republic is presented as a harbinger of wealth and prosperity—an iconographic program reflecting the personal experience of the Derbys. This family amassed a great fortune in international trade, made possible by the new economic atmosphere of free enterprise brought about by national independence. Samuel McIntire's bill of October 22, 1796, to Elizabeth Derby—for "Carving Base Mouldings & Brackets for a Case Drawers made by Mr. Lemon at 39 . . . to Carving Freeze, Roses &c for the top at 24 [shillings]"—is the basis for attributing the carving to McIntire, master carver, architect, and designer of Salem. Although the figure on the chest is not mentioned in the bill, it, too, is believed to be his creation.[13]

Despite its iconographic embellishments and neoclassical style carving, the Derby chest retains several rococo elements (ogee bracket feet, carved rocaille motifs) and is therefore stylistically transitional. Its combination of old and new ornamentation reflects not so much the state of American design in 1796 as the form of an almost identical chest made five years

earlier for the Derbys—and now in the Garvan Collection at Yale University (fig. 70). That chest also features a serpentine front lower case, bracket feet, an upper case flanked by supporting columns, and a broken, pitched pediment with a similar carved figure. A Phrygian cap (or *pilleus*, symbol of liberty) on the figure's pike (*hasta*) is an allusion to the freedom of the newly established nation.

Other meaningful associations rest in the abstract geometry of neoclassical design, as explained by Thomas Sheraton in his *Drawing-Book* of 1793: "Time alters fashions and frequently obliterates the works of art and ingenuity; but that which is founded on Geometry and real Science, will remain unalterable."[14] His remark implies a concern with permanence shared by the American statesman Gouverneur Morris, who advised George Washington in 1790: "I think it of very great importance to fix the taste of our country properly, and I think your example will go very far in that respect. It is therefore my wish that everything about you should be *substantially good and majestically plain, made to endure*"[15]—ideas in accord with the rational-minded, truth-seeking intellectual movement called the Enlightenment.

Few American forms demonstrate

Fig. 70
Chest-on-chest
Stephen Badlam, Lower Dorchester Mills, Massachusetts, with carved figures by John and Simeon Skillin, Boston, 1791. Yale University Art Gallery; Mabel Brady Garvan Collection.

so great a reliance on geometrical organization as do the dozen or so surviving gentlemen's secretaries made in Salem about 1790-1810. In the example illustrated (124), the oval motif, always framed within rectangles, is used repeatedly on the veneered surfaces. As with many other Federal pieces, the rectilinear elements that are visible on the outside usually correspond to the interior structure and define the functional spaces. The structure is thus brought to the surface and not only acts as an organizing device

124
Gentleman's secretary and bookcase
Salem, Massachusetts, 1800-1810.
The Metropolitan Museum of Art;
purchase, by exchange.

but also determines the general appearance of the secretary. Salem cabinetmakers regularly made furniture for export, shipping it as "venture cargo": that is, as consignments to ship captains, who sold the wares wherever the opportunity arose, and used the proceeds to buy goods for the cabinetmakers to sell. It is not surprising, therefore, that a similar secretary, labeled by the Salem cabinetmaker Nehemiah Adams (now at the Winterthur Museum in Delaware), was discovered about forty years ago in Capetown, South Africa, where its first owner purchased it.[16]

In the years following the Revolution, both Salem and Baltimore became established as active ports, competing with the older cities on the East Coast. Both also became cabinetmaking centers, producing furniture that rivaled the quality of that made in Philadelphia or New York. In this period of growth and prosperity, Salem nurtured the talent of the designer and carver Samuel McIntire, who was patronized by prominent Salem merchants. McIntire was the architect of their houses, the decorator of their interiors, and the embellisher of their furniture. When he died in 1811, the Salem diarist William Bentley noted: "By attention he soon gained a superiority to all of his occupation. . . . In sculpture he had no rival in New England."[17] Typical of the quality of his carving are the basket of fruit, urn with acanthus leaves, rose swags, and garlands of grapes—all executed with the utmost delicacy—on a shield-back chair (125) traditionally ascribed to the hand of McIntire. This chair, once owned by Elias Hasket Derby, is closely related to a design in Plate VIII of Hepplewhite's *Guide* (1788) (fig. 71).

Feathery streamers of leaves and flowers, exotic ostrich plumes, and touches of gilt on a white ground give another Derby family piece, a painted, oval-back chair (126), the "rich and splendid appearance" that Hepplewhite associated with japanned or painted furniture.[18] It is one of some twenty surviving pieces of furniture associated with the Derby family. Closely modeled upon English precedents, this chair may have been one of the set of "24 Oval Back Chairs, Stuff'd Seats, covered with Hair Cloth, 2 Rows Brass Nails at 34/ (each, totalling) 40: 16: 0" for which Elias Hasket Derby was billed by Joseph Anthony & Co. of Phila-

Fig. 71
Design for a chair back
George Hepplewhite, *The Cabinet-Maker's and Upholsterer's Guide* (London, 1788), pl. 2.

125
Side chair
Carving attributed to Samuel McIntire, Salem, Massachusetts, ca. 1795. Museum of Fine Arts, Boston; M. and M. Karolik Collection.

126
Painted chair
Philadelphia or Salem, ca. 1796. Museum of Fine Arts, Boston; M. and M. Karolik Collection.

delphia on December 13, 1796.[19]

On a visit to Boston in 1782, the Marquis de Chastelleux noted that the "inhabitants of Boston are fond of high play," referring to games that help to account for the large number of Federal style card tables in existence today.[20] Particularly striking examples of the form were made in Boston and Salem, where cabinetmakers favored the contrasts of light and dark made possible by veneering and inlay work. Often effects of that type were enhanced by the beauty of such native woods as bird's-eye maple and figured birch. In the oval and rectangular areas defined by these woods, a coloristic effect was accomplished without paint. On the example illustrated (**127**), that subdued use of color combines with a subtle curvature of the top and a reeding of the legs to produce a restrained vivacity characteristic of the finest American furniture in this style.

Innovations in design are not as common in American furniture of the Federal period as in that of preceding decades, but a few forms were made with no known English prototypes. Consider, for example, the tambour desks produced in New England and probably first made by John and Thomas Seymour of Boston. Unlike the writing desk illustrated in Plate 50 of Sheraton's *Drawing-Book* and the majority of English desks, the Seymour desks feature two or more drawers—a modification that does not make for greater comfort for a person sitting at the desk, but that efficiently increases storage space. A superb desk of this kind (**128**) is closely related to a labeled example by John and Thomas Seymour in the Winterthur Museum.[21] Among its distinctive features are the curly maple used for the tambours, the delicacy of the inlay, the ivory-bound keyholes, the Bilston-enamel drawer pulls ornamented with painted figures to represent the seasons, the

127
Card table
Boston or Salem, ca. 1800.
Mr. and Mrs. George M. Kaufman.

mahogany sides of the small drawers, and the blue paint on the interior of the cabinet.

Many desks of this type (costing $20 to $100), were apparently sold, ready-made, at Seymour's Boston Furniture Warehouse. According to an 1805 advertisement, the warehouse had on hand "the largest assortment of furniture ever offered for sale in the Commonwealth by retail for exportation."[22] The advertisement also reflects the changing character of the furniture industry—that is, the making of furniture in anticipation of sale, rather than on commission. Following the labor strikes of 1794-1796 in Philadelphia and of 1802 in New York, the wage scale for journeymen was regulated by contract-price books modeled after *The Cabinet-Maker's London Book of Prices of 1788*. The price books specified

128
Tambour desk
Attributed to John and Thomas Seymour, Boston, 1795-1805.
Mr. and Mrs. George M. Kaufman.

piecework rates to be paid for fashioning pieces of furniture of stipulated size and detail.

The rare ebony armchair (**129**) made by Ephraim Haines of Philadelphia for the banker Stephen Girard was part of a set which included a sofa, ten side chairs, two armchairs, four stools, and two frames for marble slabs. The set, as such, confirms the new developments in manufacturing. Surviving bills establish that Haines designed, joined, and polished the finished pieces, but that he subcontracted all the other work. The ebony as well as the upholstery fabric was obtained by Girard himself through an agent in France. Barney Schumo received £7:15:7 1/2 for all the turning; John R. Morris was paid $76.50 for carving the ornamentation; George Breidenhart upholstered the furniture at the cost of $93.86; and Robert Pullen was paid $29.56 for "Plated beading" for the sofa and chairs. For the entire set, Haines received $525—with one armchair costing $31.[23] Although American furnituremakers rarely used ebony, Girard was a French immigrant, and his choice of materials for this set reflects the prized status of this wood in the French cabinetmaking tradition.

In the Federal period the various furnituremaking operations were developed into specialized occupations. One was the manufacture of inlays, stringing, and banding. In all large American cities, cabinetmakers purchased the characteristic ornaments of the Federal period— paterae, eagles, fans, and so on— from local inlay makers or importers of English goods. The role of the inlay maker, as wholesale supplier to many shops in a city, was undoubtedly responsible for the similarity of the inlays used in an area. This is true, for example, of the corner quarter-fans popular in New York (133), and of the characteristic patterned stringing favored by

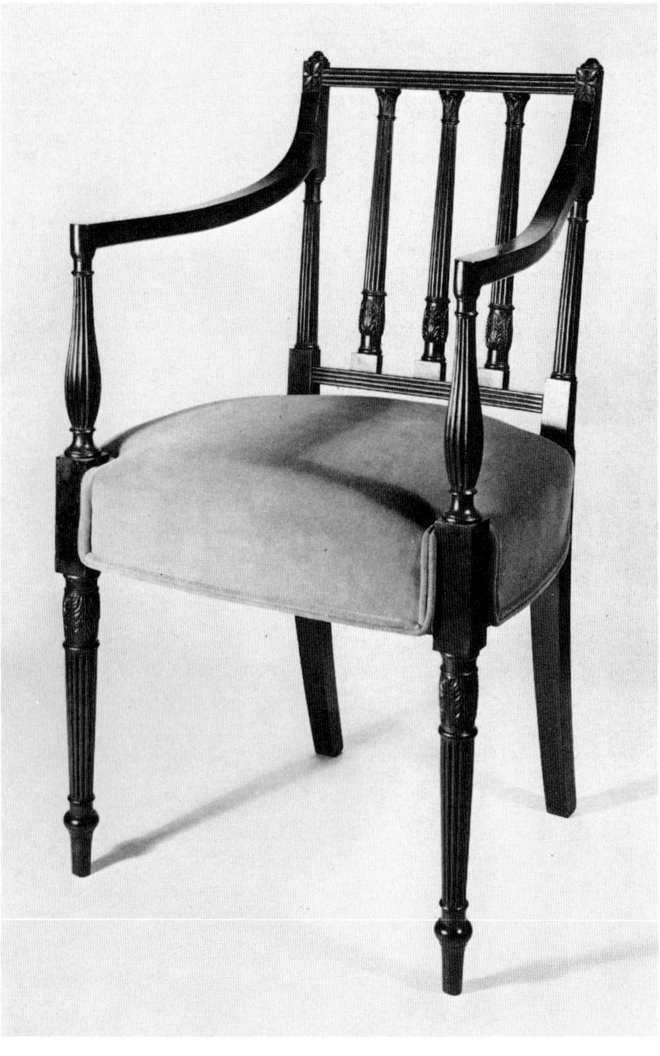

129
Armchair
Ephraim Haines, Philadelphia,
1806-1807. Girard College; estate
of Stephen Girard, deceased.

131
Candlestand
Connecticut, ca. 1805.
Mr. and Mrs. Christopher Ireland
Granger.

Boston cabinetmakers.

Baltimore style pendant husks, so distinctive as to constitute a regional characteristic, appear on the fine Maryland sofa (**130**), one of the most beautiful forms made in the Federal period—the cabriole sofa. Sofas of that distinctive shape, with an arching mahogany-outlined back that sweeps forward into continuous arms, are the "cabriole sofas" referred to in price books and pattern books of the late eighteenth and early nineteenth centuries.[24] A half-upholstered seat rail, and S-curved rear legs are also characteristics found on other Baltimore sofas. On the sofa illustrated, the simplicity of the exposed wooden members contrasts with the richness of the fabric, visually confining it within sharp boundaries, just as the richly figured veneers are held within crisp geometrical shapes in much Federal furniture. The piece thus synthesizes comfort, restraint, and elegance according to Sheraton's formula: "The grandeur introduced into the drawing room is not to be considered as the ostentatious parade of its proprietor, but the respect he pays to the rank of his visitants."[25]

In rural areas, where there was no easy access to an inlay maker, cabinetmakers produced their own ornaments, such as the eagle with shield motif that distinguishes a Connecticut candlestand (**131**). Although not as refined as urban inlay, the results were often highly successful, as the soaring bird on this oval stand testifies. Its wings spread in ascending flight, the eagle bears a striped shield, which echoes the graceful reeding of the candlestand's base. A symbol of patriotism, the eagle was universally known throughout the country and appeared as an ornament on all manner of things as an expression of the pride Americans felt in their new nation.

Typical of an American, and par-

130
Sofa
Baltimore, Maryland, 1790-1800.
Mr. and Mrs. Edward A. Kilroy, Jr.

ticularly a New England, approach to comfortable seating in the Federal era were the lolling, or "Martha Washington," chairs (**132**), survivals of the upholstered-back, open-arm chair form of the Chippendale era (see the chair in Copley's portrait of Mrs. Isaac Smith,

page 35). Such chairs went out of fashion in London with the advent of neoclassicism. In the United States they were modified with features of the new style (simpler and thinner arms, tapered legs, and veneered ornament) and became a distinctively American form.

During the neoclassical period, much specialized furniture designed to meet multiple needs was pioneered abroad. Among the new forms were the sideboard, the lady's desk, and the sewing stand. The New York sideboard (**133**) illustrates the type of modification and simpli-

132
Lolling chair
New England, probably Portsmouth, New Hampshire, 1800-1810.
The Metropolitan Museum of Art; gift of Mrs. Russell Sage, 1909.

fication that English designs underwent in the hands of an American maker. The emphasis on geometry and on the brilliance of the mahogany veneer, the subtle combination of pictorial and abstract inlays, the accents of the blue and white English enamel hardware, and the

finesse of the tapering legs aligned with the contour of the case help to make this one of the most refined of surviving American sideboards. Though long attributed to Matthew Egerton of New Brunswick, New Jersey, on the basis of its similarity to his labeled work,[26] its history

of ownership in the Weeks family of Oyster Bay, Long Island, suggests that it may have instead originated in New York, the nearby center of the regional style to which Egerton's work is closely related.

American designs for sewing stands—objects defined by Shera-

133
Sideboard
New York, ca. 1790.
Museum of Fine Arts, Boston;
M. and M. Karolik Collection.

ton's *Cabinet Dictionary* as pouch tables "used by the ladies to work at, in which bag they deposit their fancy needlework"—were also modifications of their English prototypes. New England examples are for the most part square with canted corners, while those from Philadelphia almost invariably have astragal ends or are of kidney shape. The illustrated example (**134**), attributed to the shop of John and Thomas Seymour, is representative of the finest New England type with characteristics similar to those of the Boston card table (**127**)—contrasting light and dark veneers, serpentine top, and reeded legs that form ovolo corners. Sewing tables,

delicate, feminine, and somewhat frivolous in function and appearance, were expensive items, made only for people of wealth. Like the Gilbert Stuart portrait of *Mrs. Richard Yates* (**46**), they bear witness to the ritualization of sewing as an accepted social grace.

In that time there came together in Roxbury, Massachusetts (on the outskirts of Boston), a remarkable group of craft specialists; clockmakers, cabinetmakers and carvers, painters on glass, gilders, and looking glass makers worked together to produce clocks and furniture of distinction. First among this group was Simon Willard, brother of Benjamin and Aaron, all clock-

makers. Inventor, innovator, and one of the remarkable craftsmen of his time, he made tall clocks and timepieces (clocks without striking mechanisms) and showed evidence of his interest in the natural sciences by making instruments that related mean and solar time, as well as orreries to chart the movements of the solar system. In 1802 he patented the movement for a comparatively inexpensive timepiece now known as the banjo clock (**135**). For this new movement a new case was conceived with a square box for the pendulum and circular housing for the movement and dial. Often an eagle surmounted the whole.

Although Simon Willard (for a

134
Work table
Attributed to John and Thomas Seymour, Boston, ca. 1800-1810.
Mr. and Mrs. Eric M. Wunsch.

fee) allowed some of his favorite former apprentices to use the inscription, "S. Willard's patent," several features of this clock, such as the T-bridge method of hanging the pendulum and the movement itself, suggest that it was made in the master's "Clock Manufactury." The unique blue dial and the colorful decoration in red, blue, and gold on the white background of the glass door and throat panels support the view that this is one of Willard's presentation clocks made for a wedding or special occasion.

By 1805, the influence of the more imitative phase of neoclassicism—which had been popularized in France during the revolution and the Empire—had reached America. Furniture patterned directly after Greek and Roman models then became the fashion. Thomas Hope's *Household Furniture and Interior Decoration*, published in London in 1807, did much to popularize the style. His "klismos" chair designs, featuring continuous wooden members extending from top back rail to front seat rail probably influenced the Boston fancy-chairmaker Samuel Gragg, who at the time was experimenting with the use of bentwood. Gragg combined the painted features of the American fancy-chair tradition with technical advances and up-to-date styling to produce imaginative, delicate, and colorful luxury items that were among the outstanding innovations of their time. His surviving chairs, of which only three sets are known, well merit the adjective "elastic," a term used in the patent issued to Gragg on August 31, 1808.[27] In this example (**136**), the formation of the stile, side seat rail, and front leg from one piece of wood is nothing less than a virtuoso accomplishment. It exploits the design possibilities inherent in the use of bentwood and foreshadows, both from the point of view of technology and design, the internationally popular, massproduced, nineteenth-century furniture of Michael Thonet.

135
Patent timepiece or banjo clock
Simon Willard, Boston, ca. 1805.
Private collection.

136
Bentwood side chair
Samuel Gragg, Boston, 1808-1812.
Mr. and Mrs. Bertram K. Little.

Silver and Gold

For centuries, objects made of silver and gold have had a special significance in Western society. As precious metals, they have symbolic as well as intrinsic value. As decorative pieces, they have aesthetic and associational impact, suggesting in the mind of the beholder multiple levels of meaning. In religious rites and social rituals, the importance of the occasion is confirmed by the beauty, rarity, and cost of objects fashioned in these metals; in turn, the occasion endows the metals with symbolic importance. This symbolic process is most apparent in such works as the Admiralty Oar (143) and the Torah bells (153). But it is also evident in less ritualistic objects, such as coffeepots, teakettles, and even shoe buckles —all of which command greater attention and are given added social meaning precisely because they are made of silver and gold.

The supporting role played by such objects in religious and social contexts inevitably gives rise to a concern with style, manifest either in the deliberate retention of significant older forms or, more commonly, in "fashion consciousness." In early America, where painting and sculpture languished because of a widespread mistrust of the fine arts that was rooted in religious and social attitudes, the earliest manifestations of style consciousness occurred in silver. Objects made by silversmiths consistently exhibited the attributes of the formal modes—the Queen Anne, rococo, and neoclassical styles—before comparable attributes appeared in other decorative or fine arts.

In the transmission of style from London to the colonies, the silversmith was in the vanguard. As newspaper advertisements for silver vividly reveal, the newest fashions from the English capital were frequently brought to the attention of the buying public. The silversmith was kept abreast of the latest European trends through the importation of ready-to-market silver wares, which sold along with those he made in his own shop.

Fig. 72
Two-handled covered cup
John Coney, Boston, ca. 1718.
R.W. Norton Art Gallery,
Shreveport, Louisiana.

In his community, the silversmith held a prestigious position, not only because he provided merchandise that was at the height of fashion, but also because he was, de facto, the local banker. In a society that relied on precious-metal coins for commercial exchange, the transformation of silver and gold into household objects represented a means of saving with style. Moreover, because the objects could be readily identified with respect to owner and maker, they provided an extra measure of security against theft. Thus they constituted wealth, indicating the affluence and the taste of the owner, as well as demonstrated the ability of the silversmith to give the shape of fashion to raw material.

Silver pieces in the late baroque style known as Queen Anne probably began to appear in America about 1715, although the earliest datable example is a two-handled cup (fig. 72) purchased in 1718 from the Boston silversmith John Coney by Harvard students as a gift for their tutor, Henry Flynt. In this

137
Teapot
Peter Van Dyck, New York, 1715-1725.
Yale University Art Gallery;
Mabel Brady Garvan Collection.

new style, the heavily gadrooned, repoussé surfaces and compact massing of earlier baroque silver pieces were replaced by curved outlines and simple decoration. The plain surfaces of Queen Anne silver emphasized the beauty of the metal.

The evolution of the Queen Anne style in silver was influenced by the development of new forms of silver for serving tea, a drink that had been introduced in the mid-seventeenth century. Although merchants had originally imported china serving accessories from the Orient,[1] English silversmiths soon realized, as tea drinking gained popularity, that handsome profits were to be made in supplying a growing market. Teapots, sugar bowls, tea caddies, milk jugs, and sal-

vers thus became part of their repertoire. The plain and ascetic forms of Oriental models were soon blended with native baroque traditions, a combination that eventually evolved into the Queen Anne style.

The emphasis on smooth surfaces and curvilinear forms characteristic of this style is exemplified in American silver by a New York teapot (**137**) made by Peter Van Dyck, sometime between 1715 and 1725, for Johannes Van Brugh and his wife Margaretta Provoost, whose initials form the engraved cipher. Van Dyck, the son of Dutch immigrants, had been apprenticed to a French Huguenot master, Bartholomew Le Roux. One of the continental influences evident in his silver is the applied strapwork or

"cut-card" work that ornaments the cover of this teapot. Originated in France, "cut-card" decoration was brought to England by refugee Huguenot silversmiths. Craftsmen such as Le Roux, direct inheritors of that tradition, brought it to America, where they trained apprentices of diverse ancestry. Thus Peter Van Dyck was exposed to three design vocabularies—Dutch, English, and French—even though he resided in a remote corner of the British Empire. On his teapot, the "cut-card" decoration is discreetly applied in order to vary—but not to distort—the soft reflections produced by the smooth and continuous surface of the body. Significantly, that restraint, combined with an emphasis on clean, curvilinear shapes articulating empty space, pre-

Fig. 73
Teapot
J. Lamb and T. Tearle, London, 1718. The Victoria and Albert Museum, London.

figured by a few years the sculptural role played by the voids in Philadelphia Queen Anne chairs.

An octagonal teapot, also by Van Dyck (**138**), exhibits a different surface effect. The paneled division of the pear-shaped body and the resultant planes of reflected light may be regarded as a carry-over of the baroque style. But the plain surface and overall curvilinear design are constants of the Queen Anne aesthetic. Van Dyck's teapot— the only one of its kind surviving in America today—is an adaptation of a more common form that in the eighteenth century was called an "eight-square teapot."[2] The form, first produced in Holland, was later copied in France and England (fig.73). The chaste lines and sense of

138
Teapot
Peter Van Dyck, New York, 1720-1735.
Yale University Art Gallery;
Mabel Brady Garvan Collection.

verticality of Van Dyck's interpretation (138) establish it as one of the masterpieces of this international form.

No better expression of the Queen Anne style exists than the diminutive sugar bowl (139) made by Simeon Soumain for Henry and Elizabeth Cruger of New York about 1740. With the exception of the engraved ciphers, the bowl relies entirely on the shaping of the form for its aesthetic impact. Soumain adhered closely to Chinese covered bowls (fig. 74) as models for his design; but he also made some subtle, yet important, changes. The bowl body has a very slightly flared lip, and the top repeats the S-shaped rhythm of the bowl walls— features not found in the Oriental prototypes. In addition, Soumain organized his piece in a European manner: the overall height relates to the width in a ratio of 7:8, the classical sesquiseptimal proportion, whereas the top, when placed inside the lip, measures a quarter of the entire height. As a result, his composition,

Fig. 74
Chinese covered bowl
ca. 1719.
The Metropolitan Museum of Art;
Winfield Foundation gift fund,
1961.

139
Covered sugar bowl
Simeon Soumain, New York, 1738-
1745. Yale University Art Gallery;
Mabel Brady Garvan Collection.

although based on an Oriental form, achieved a quite different effect through his use of traditional principles of proportion.

Similar transformations of an Oriental model may be observed in the globular teapots favored in New England, such as one made in Boston by Jacob Hurd for Sir William Pepperell about 1740 (140). Although ceramic wine- and hot-water pots imported from China served as prototypes, the self-contained composition of the Oriental form was significantly altered by European craftsmen. For example, in Hurd's teapot, the gentle movement of the "duck's-neck" spout and the open curvature of the C-shaped handle reflect European modifications. Moreover, anticipating the free flow of rococo design, those elements move away from the object's center of mass, which is much higher on this New England example than it was on the two earlier New York teapots (137 and 138).

Another accessory for tea drinking produced by Hurd was the

140
Teapot
Jacob Hurd, Boston, 1735-1745.
Yale University Art Gallery;
Mabel Brady Garvan Collection.

salver. The three known examples by him are up-to-date variations of a form that had been in use at least since the mid-seventeenth century. The salver (141), which Hurd made for the Clarke family of Boston, is organized as an octagon, outlined by alternating concave and convex curves that are separated by linear elements. Within the molded border, Hurd engraved a band of diaper work, shells, and foliage that acts as a foil between the angular edge and the smooth surface of the tray, which is ornamented at the center with the arms of the Clarke family. This skillful incorporation of an engraved motif into the overall design is characteristic of Hurd's work. As for some elements of his engraving, particularly armorial devices, it is likely that he was inspired by such imported pattern books as J. Guillim's *Display of Heraldry* (London, 1724)—a copy of which is depicted in John Singleton Copley's portrait of Hurd's silversmith son Nathaniel (fig. 61), who probably inherited it from his father.[3]

Guns, cannons, swords, halberds, banners—the weapons of war—are incorporated into the large engraved cartouche on Jacob Hurd's recognized masterpiece, the monumental two-handled cup ordered by several Boston merchants for presentation to Captain Edward Tyng, who on the "24th of June 1744" took "ye First French Privateer on this Coast" (142). The cup honors naval prowess, valued in an age when New England fortunes in shipping were partly dependent upon the ability to defend one's goods against piracy—and were occasionally dependent upon the practice of piracy itself. In its design, the cup relies upon balanced proportioning for the organization of its handles, lid, finial, body, and base. Throughout, the serpentine elements outline smoothly flowing surfaces that display the natural beauty of the metal to great advantage—in much the same way as the Soumain sugar bowl (139), whose general shape is, by coincidence, echoed in the cartouche on the cup. As ritualistic presentation pieces, monumental cups like this were intended for prominent display and occasional use in drinking ceremonies. On the day this cup was presented to Edward Tyng, it was used to serve "bishop," a sweet drink made of wine, citrus juice, and sugar with mulled and spiced port.

141
Salver
Jacob Hurd, Boston, 1740-1750.
Yale University Art Gallery;
Mabel Brady Garvan Collection.

142
Two-handled covered cup
Jacob Hurd, Boston, 1744.
Yale University Art Gallery;
Mabel Brady Garvan Collection.

Even more ceremonial in implication is a mace in the form of an oar (**143**) made between 1740 and 1750 by Jacob Hurd. It was used by the Boston vice-admiralty court to serve as its symbol of office. Such oar-shaped maces were carried in procession upon the entrance of the president of the admiralty court and rested in a bracket before him as he presided. Charles Le Roux made one for the New York court, the only other known example in America. The oldest surviving oar-shaped mace made in England once belonged to the Cinque Ports and is thought to be of Elizabethan date.[4] Hurd's oar, although apparently a miniaturization of a functional device, actually incorporates the design principles of the Queen Anne style—a solution that distinguishes it from a representative oar mace made in England at an earlier date (fig. 75). Its simple, attenuated form is governed by sound proportions: the length of

the blade approximates the length of the handle and socket, while the length of the central shaft approximates their combined lengths.

Silver punch bowls also served as ceremonial objects. Introduced into England during the reign of Charles II, they were frequently awarded as trophies for horse races or given as pieces to commemorate historic occasions. The punch bowl (**144**) made in 1763 by the Boston silversmith William Homes for presentation to Thomas Dawes typifies the commemorative attributes of the form. As the engraved cartouche indicates, Dawes was honored by the field officers of his regiment for his services as adjutant, and on this bowl martial symbols, similar to those on the Tyng cup (**142**), celebrate his military accomplishments. The Dawes bowl is thus a link between past and present, an image of historical continuity, like the famous "Liberty

Bowl" in the Museum of Fine Arts, Boston. Made by Paul Revere in 1768, that bowl honors the ninety-two members of the Massachusetts House of Representatives who voted not to rescind a circular letter protesting the Townshend Acts. The vote, which resulted in the suspension of the House by the royal governor, was one in a series of protests leading to the Revolution. To this day, Revere's bowl remains an effective symbol of national identity.

Punch bowls, like two-handled cups, were the focal point of drinking ceremonies. The beverage itself had been introduced into Europe at approximately the same time as tea, but the strainer, a refined accouterment used in serving it, did not appear in America until the middle of the eighteenth century. Strainers often had two long handles that permitted them to rest on the edges of the punch bowl. Characteristically, the perforations

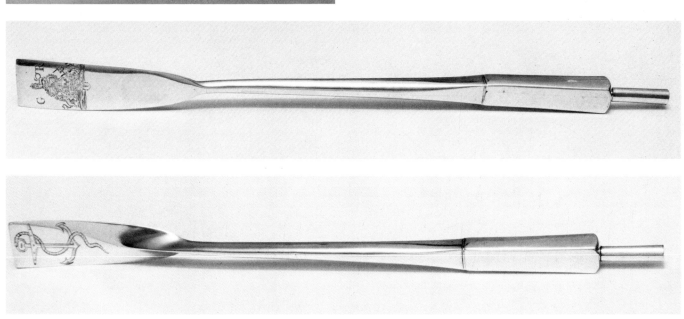

Fig. 75
Oar mace
Made for the Admiralty Court of Lostwithiel, England, 1670. The Worshipful Company of Goldsmiths, London.

143 a and **b**
Admiralty Oar
Jacob Hurd, Boston, ca. 1740.
Massachusetts Historical Society.

in the strainer were arranged in a decorative manner. In a unique example (145) made by Jonathan Clarke, a silversmith who worked in Providence and Newport, Rhode Island, the perforations spell out "Jabez Bowen Providence January 1765"—the name of the owner, his place of residence, and a significant date, a unique form of ornamentation. Intricate and delicate scrolls in the form of the letters S, C, and reversed C make up the openwork handles and produce a lively visual effect, modestly echoing the formal concerns of the rococo style.

When Jabez Bowen purchased his strainer, the rococo style in

144
Punch bowl
William Homes, Boston, 1763.
Museum of Fine Arts, Boston;
gift of Mrs. Ambrose Dawes in
memory of her husband.

145
Punch strainer
Jonathan Clarke, Providence, 1765.
Yale University Art Gallery;
Mabel Brady Garvan Collection.

silver had been fashionable in the colonies for almost twenty years. Among the earliest and most monumental American examples of the style is the teakettle on a stand (**146**) made by Joseph Richardson between 1745 and 1755 for the Philadelphia merchant Clement Plumstead (d. 1745), or for his widow, Mary (d. 1755). This teakettle belies any facile generalizations made about a time lag in the transmission of designs between England and the colonies. Indeed, form and ornament combine here to make a rather complete statement of the English rococo aesthetic. Shells, flowers, foliage, and animals are asymmetrically deployed about an inverted pear shape that reverses logical relationships of weight and creates an arresting appearance of instability.

The profusion of naturalistic ornament reflects the penetration of French ideas into English silver design, often through the work of Huguenot silversmiths. Paul de Lamerie, an immigrant Huguenot working in London, made such a teakettle (fig. 76) in 1744/45, for the wedding of David Franks and Margaret Evans of Philadelphia. The appearance of de Lamerie's elaborate piece in Philadelphia at that particular time undoubtedly attracted great notice.[5] Certainly, Richardson, an active silversmith who carried on a lively silver importing business, would probably have known about it. Richardson's teakettle thus appears to be a master craftsman's response to the challenge presented by exposure

to an imported object, the one by de Lamerie or some other piece like it. Yet in its application of ornment, it is restrained in comparison with the teakettle fashioned by de Lamerie. Richardson confined the rococo ornament within sharply bounded compartments that do not interpenetrate. This design runs counter to the spirit of the style as it was practiced in England and Europe, but it is characteristic of Philadelphia workmanship. So restrained an interpretation of rococo ornament may, to a certain degree, represent the sort of misunderstanding inherent in all imitation. But the process of imitation carries within it the seeds of innovation, and Richardson's conservative approach prefigures the restrained ornament in such original

147
Teapot
Gabriel Lewyn, Baltimore, 1760-1770.
Yale University Art Gallery;
John Marshall Phillips Collection.

designs as the high chests of drawers made by Philadelphia cabinet-makers between 1760 and 1785.

Greater ease in the handling of fluid, asymmetrical repoussé orna-ment is exhibited on the teapot made about 1770 by Gabriel Lewyn in Baltimore (147), a city that at that time was an artistic province of Philadelphia. Lewyn's proficiency is therefore surprising. Little is known about him except that he worked in Baltimore from 1768 to 1780 and belonged to the Evangelical High German Church

Fig. 76
Teakettle on stand
Paul de Lamerie, London, 1744-1745.
The Metropolitan Museum of Art;
gift of George D. Widener and
Eleanor W. Dixon (Mrs. Widener
Dixon), 1958.

146
Teakettle on stand
Joseph Richardson, Philadelphia,
1745-1755. Yale University Art
Gallery; Mabel Brady Garvan
Collection.

there. In this piece, his only known teapot and the outstanding example of his craftsmanship, he surpasses the work of Joseph Richardson in his understanding of the European rococo canon. Lewyn's integration of form and ornament—his ability to make the ornament appear as part of the form, not as an accretion—is in pointed contrast to Richardson's earlier teakettle.

Another master of the rococo style in America was the silversmith Myer Myers. Born to immigrant Dutch parents in 1723, Myers was one of the first artisans of Jewish ancestry to take advantage of the Act of 1726 by the New York colonial legislature that permitted Jews to practice the profession of their choice. Except for his prolonged stays in Connecticut and Philadelphia during the Revolutionary War, Myers lived and worked in New York, where he was prominent in his community and in

148
One of a pair of candlesticks
Myer Myers, New York, 1760-1775.
Yale University Art Gallery;
Mabel Brady Garvan Collection.

his craft. In 1770 he held office as president of Shearith Israel, the city's Sephardic congregation, and in 1783 he was chosen chairman of the New York Gold and Silversmiths Society. Attentive to London fashions, he made a variety of objects in the English rococo manner. His close adherence to English models is evident in the set of four candlesticks he made in 1759 for the wedding of Catherine Livingston in New York. One of a pair (**148**) is illustrated here. (The matching

pair is in the Metropolitan Museum of Art.) The faint cast outline of London hallmarks on another candlestick by Myers indicates that at times he used an English object as a pattern for the mold of his own product.

One of the most prominent silversmiths working in the rococo style was Paul Revere of Boston. In 1761, Revere made a rococo salver (**149**) for Lucretia Chandler at the time of her marriage. One of the earliest surviving rococo salvers in

America, it resembles in outline the scalloped tops of contemporary tea tables and stands. The nervous quality of its shape is characteristic of rococo design. Revere made four almost identical salvers with molded borders, and may have copied or used as a model an English example, such as the 1753 salver by William Peaston of London, now in the Victoria and Albert Museum (fig. 77).

A characteristic aspect of rococo taste was the opulent display of wealth, even in such small, elegant

149
Salver
Paul Revere, Boston, 1761.
Museum of Fine Arts, Boston; gift of Henry Davis Sleeper in memory of his mother, Maria Westcote Sleeper.

Fig. 77
Salver
William Peaston, London, 1753.
The Victoria and Albert Museum.

objects as snuff and scent boxes, shoe buckles, and buttons. The full vocabulary of rococo ornament is articulated on the surface of the small snuffbox (**150**) made by Joseph Richardson between 1750 and 1770. S-scrolls and C-scrolls, diapering, shells, flowers, and foliage, all worked on the surface, give the metal itself an irregular contour. English prototypes for such boxes were widely available in America—in fact, Richardson himself imported chased snuffboxes in 1759 and 1760.[6] In Philadelphia, similar decoration appeared on carved woodwork and furniture, and it is even possible that Richardson obtained the pattern for his repoussé work from a professional woodcarver.

Among the variety of small items bought for personal enhancement is the coral with whistle and bells (**151**) made in gold by Daniel Christian Fueter of New York for Mary Livingston as a gift to her granddaughter, Mary Duane. The coral and bells was a toy, a teething object, a ward against illness (coral was traditionally believed to possess a protective medicinal value),[7] and a frivolous symbol of status. In 1761, William Ball, the Philadelphia merchant-silversmith, noted in his account book the arrival on March 2 of "18 Wissels and Bells," for which he paid "£34:16:0" and which were to be sold individually at "£2:15:0" chased or "£2:5:0" plain.[8] Although they were imported into America in quantity, "coral and bells" made in silver by American craftsmen are rare, and only four in gold are known,[9] including this one by Fueter, which is the most elaborate interpretation of the form.

The alternating motion of the gadrooned bands of Fueter's whistle with coral and bells, its profuse floral and rocaille orna-mentation, and its crowning putto reveal a feeling for rococo design that was not common in America. Its play of curve against curve and its overall sense of swirling movement are in the tradition of the great French designer and silversmith Juste-Aurèle Meissonier, whose work is exemplified in his design for a censer (fig. 78). Fueter undoubtedly became familiar with this tradition in Switzerland, where he was born in 1720. Trained in Bern, Fueter fled that city in 1749, after having been sentenced to death for conspiring to overthrow the aristocratic government of the province. He made his way to London, where he registered his mark at Goldsmiths' Hall in 1753 before coming to New York the following year. That Fueter maintained direct contact with continental fashion is suggested by his advertisement in 1769, which informed his New York customers

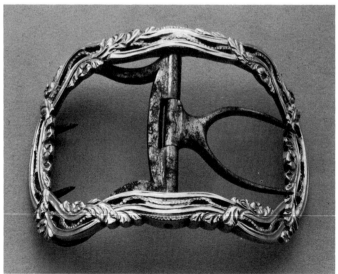

150
Snuffbox
Joseph Richardson, Philadelphia, 1750-1770. Yale University Art Gallery; Mabel Brady Garvan Collection.

152
Shoe buckle
Myer Myers, New York, 1760-1775. Yale University Art Gallery; Mabel Brady Garvan Collection.

"that Mr. John Anthony Beau, Chaiser, from Geneva, works with him."[10]

In the eighteenth century, gold buckles were among the most fashionable objects of personal adornment. The shoe buckle shown here (152), which was made by Myer Myers of New York, undoubtedly added to the splendor of its owner's costume. It was presented to Daniel McCormick—a director of the Bank of New York in 1786 and alderman of the East Ward in 1791—by Robert Arcdeckne. Although Myers conceived of his composition symmetrically, the form of the buckle is defined by the ornament, thus making this small object one of the fullest expressions of rococo

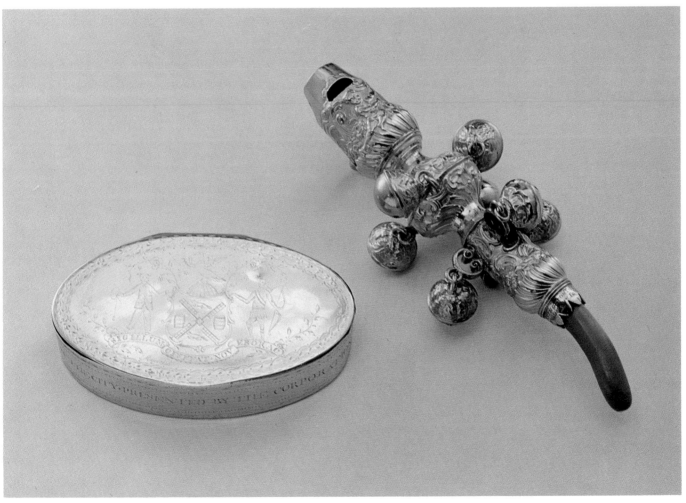

162

151
Coral and bells
Daniel Christian Fueter, New York, 1760-1770. Yale University Art Gallery; gift of Mrs. Francis P. Garvan, James R. Graham, Walter M. Jeffords, and Mrs. Paul Moore.

Fig. 78
Design for a censer
Juste-Aurèle Meissonier, ca. 1735.
Oeuvre de Juste-Aurèle Meissonier (Paris, 1800), pl. 32.

sensibility in America.

Myer Myers infused his work with an up-to-date rococo spirit even when carrying out commissions for such traditional pieces as Torah bells, or *rimonim*, for the synagogues in Newport, New York, and Philadelphia. Torah bells were placed atop the two rollers bearing the Torah scroll. The six pairs of bells he made are today the most famous of eighteenth-century American religious objects. Four of the pairs, one of which was made for Congregation Mikveh Israel in Philadelphia about 1772 (fig. 79), feature three tiers and the elaborate rococo chasing and ajouré work for which Myers is known. This three-tier design closely follows English precedents—a pair made by Gabriel Sleath of London in 1718 for the Sephardic Congregation at Barbados (fig. 80) is surely a prototype. In his design, however, Myers did not use the pyramidal arrangement of the annular tiers seen in the Sleath bells; instead, he placed the largest tier in the center and thus created a more fluent rococo effect, reminiscent of the inverted-pear form of many contemporary tea- and coffeepots. In another pair of Torah bells made for Congregation Mikveh Israel (153), Myers employed not the three-tiered shape but the traditional rounded form that is more in keeping with the name of these bells, for *rimonim* is the Hebrew word for pomegranates. This pair has bold, swirled gadrooning similar to that of the "coral and bells" (151) made by Daniel Christian Fueter of New York. In echoing the shape of the pomegranate in these rounded Torah bells, Myer restates the traditional association of fruitfulness and life with the words of the Torah. A Hebrew name for the Torah rollers, *ez hayyim*, "tree of life," also reflects this association, as does the profuse floral ornamentation in Myers' three-tier examples.[11]

Just as Myer Myers introduced new elements into his designs but retained traditional forms for the

153
Torah bells
Myer Myers, New York, 1772.
Kahal Kadash Mikveh Israel in
the City of Philadelphia.

Fig. 79
Torah bells
Gabriel Sleath, London, 1719.
Bevis Marks Synagogue, London.

Fig. 80
Torah bells
Myer Myers, New York, ca. 1765.
Kahal Kadosh Mikveh Israel in
the City of Philadelphia.

Jewish faith, John Coburn did the same for the Protestant faith in a Communion dish (154) he made for presentation to the Brattle Street Church in Boston by Thomas Hancock in 1764. The traditional element is the symbolic cherub's head on the rim—a baroque ornament, precedents for which can be found in engraved New York tankards and published heraldry motifs made a half century earlier (figs. 81 and 82). Two new elements are introduced in the dish: the rococo-style engraving of the Hancock family arms and the narrow brim instead of the earlier broad brim. This same combination of new and old appears in the other five dishes in the set—two by Coburn and three by Samuel Minott. Torah bells and Communion dishes, each in their own way, suggest that their designers exercised stylistic choices which were in keeping with the unspoken need for continuity in ritual.

154
Communion dish
John Coburn, Boston, 1764.
Museum of Fine Arts, Boston;
gift of the Benevolent Fraternity
of Churches.

Fig. 81
Engraved tankard top
Peter Van Dyck, New York, N.Y.
ca. 1705-1715. Yale University Art
Gallery; Mabel Brady Garvan
Collection.

Fig. 82
*Coat of arms with three cherubs'
heads.* John Guillim, *A Display of
Heraldry* (London, 1724), sect. III,
p. 83.

In colonial America, the marriage of new forms with old ornamentation or of new ornamentation with old forms is not uncommon in objects made for domestic use. For instance, the chocolate pot made by Zachariah Brigden about 1760 (155) restates a favored Queen Anne formula for this form, but the arms of Ebenezer Storer on its body are engraved in the rococo manner. Its plain, tapering, cylindrical body and scrolled handle and spout are strikingly similar to those of a pot made twenty to thirty years earlier by Charles Le Roux of New York (now in the Garvan Collection, Yale University).

Another old form with new ornament is the American silver porringer with "keyhole handle," so called because the outermost pierced opening on the handle resembles the opening in a lock escutcheon. The example shown here (156) was made by Paul Revere, Sr., father of the patriot. The intertwining S-curves and C-scrolls of the keyhole handle, which was introduced about 1740, anticipated the pierced back of the Chippendale chair and may well have been in the vanguard of rococo ornament in America. However, the bowl with bellied sides, outflaring lip, and boss in its bottom had been in use for at least fifty years by the makers of both silver and pewter porringers. The porringer, a vessel used for both eating and drinking, was made in rather greater numbers in America than in England prior

155
Chocolate pot
Zachariah Brigden, Boston, ca. 1755.
Museum of Fine Arts, Boston;
gift of the Misses Rose and
Elizabeth Townsend.

156
Porringer
Paul Revere, Sr., Boston, 1740-1750.
Yale University Art Gallery; gift
of the daughter of William Inglis
Morse, Mrs. Frederick W. Hilles.

to 1740, when its production almost ceased in England. From that time until about 1810 great numbers of porringers were produced in New England, especially of pewter in Rhode Island and Connecticut. A small number of porringers was made in New York but virtually none were made in Philadelphia. Soon after 1800 silver porringers went completely out of fashion and pewter porringers followed in a few years.

The silver tankard made by Paul Revere for Thomas Greene in 1762 (157) offers another example of the persistence of a form in America. Straight-sided, dome-topped tankards such as this one had been popular in New England since about 1730 and continued to be produced until at least 1786.[12]

Elsewhere during that period, the bulbous tulip shape had been introduced, and especially in Philadelphia, it was favored for tankards. Even in Boston, a few tankards of this form apparently were produced. One of these is a tulip-shaped tankard made by Revere about 1760 (now at the Rhode Island School of Design, Providence). It attests to the fact that he used the form on occasion, but it also suggests that clients in the Boston area preferred the straight-sided shape. One of the most elegant of American tulip-shaped tankards is the example made by the New York silversmith Ephraim Brasher (158). Sturdily poised on an ample, round foot, its traditional form is imbued with rococo grace by the spirited outline of the double scroll, the richness of

the Sands family arms, the steep profiles of the domed top, and its nervous lip. Romance surrounds its history. It is probably the tankard reported in *The New York Packet and the American Advertiser* of April 5, 1781, to have been stolen at Fishkill, New York, from Comfort Sands.

In contrast, Paul Revere's tankard (157) adheres to an older formula, although it does exhibit up-to-date ornamental elements— a finely engraved cartouche displaying the asymmetry characteristic of the rococo era, and a spiral finial echoing those found on Massachusetts case furniture of the Chippendale period. Revere's skillful assembly of these elements makes this tankard an authoritative interpretation of its kind.

157
Tankard
Paul Revere, Boston, 1762.
Yale University Art Gallery;
Mabel Brady Garvan Collection.

158
Tankard
Ephraim Brasher, New York, 1765-
1780. Mr. and Mrs. James H. Halpin.

In the 1780s, Philadelphia was the most important city in America. Its preoccupation with style was only one aspect of the active exchange of ideas and merchandise with Europe that made it the capital of colonial fashion, long before it became the capital of the Federal union in 1790. Among Philadelphians, Samuel Powel was one of the most worldly: he had met royalty, conversed with Voltaire, and been granted an audience by the Pope. Active in civic affairs, he was a man of means with a grand house in the most fashionable part of the city. Regarding his hospitality, John Adams wrote in 1787: "Dined at Mr. Powel's . . . a most sinful feast again! Everything which could delight the eye or allure the taste; curds and creams, jellies, sweetmeats of various sorts, twenty sorts of tarts, fools, trifles, floating islands, whipped sillibub etc., etc."[13]

It is little wonder that Powel should own extraordinary table silver, the quality of which is exemplified by a fluted dish (159), one of a pair. Made by Joseph Richardson, Jr., the dishes were used for serving vegetables or fruit. Only the more sophisticated American silversmiths, including Myer Myers and Daniel Christian Fueter, produced dishes of this type, which followed the general pattern of contemporary Irish and English models.

In England during the 1760s and 1770s classical, geometrically regular forms were beginning to replace the graceful irregularities of the rococo style. In time, Americans followed the English examples. In 1774 Richard Humphreys, the Philadelphia silversmith, produced what appears to be the first neoclassical work made in the colonies: a symmetrical tea urn with a square base and with rectangular handles (fig. 83). It was the forerunner of a style that was to dominate American silver after the American Revolution. The general appearance of this urn is similar to the ceramic interpretations of antiquity being produced by Josiah Wedgwood in England. It is significant, however, that the engraved inscription and cartouche of this classically inspired urn were still executed in the rococo manner. Perhaps James Smither, who engraved it, was as yet unacquainted with neoclassical patterns, or his clients still preferred the more familiar style. Humphreys' urn—presented by the first Continental Congress to its secretary, Charles Thomson—marks the start of a flourishing iconographic association of America with republican Rome. This association was to become increasingly intentional, especially after the adoption of the Federal Constitution in 1788 and during the presidency of George Washington, who was often compared with Cincinnatus, the Roman patriot who laid down his plow to defend his country.

The adoption of the neoclassical style in America, heralded by the Humphreys urn in 1774, was retarded by the Revolutionary War, which severely curtailed the production of luxury goods at home and blocked the importation of fashions directly from London. The silver that was made during the war years tended to be conservative, retaining rococo forms and ornamentation. For example, a

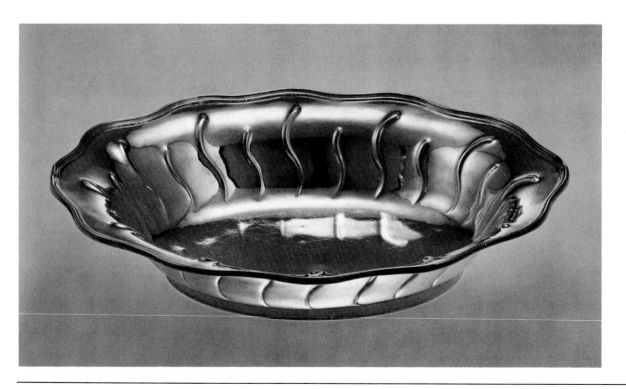

159
Dish
Joseph Richardson, Jr., Philadelphia,
ca. 1775. Philadelphia Museum
of Art; McIlhenny Fund, 1956.

double-bellied coffeepot was made by Paul Revere for Paul Dudley Sargent in 1781 (**160**). Coffeepots in this rococo form had been imported into America nearly twenty years earlier, as an advertisement in the *Pennsylvania Journal* of December 15, 1763, clearly states: "just imported in the last vessels from London . . . chased and plain double and single belly'd coffee-pots."[14] Such pots soon became a standard item in the American silversmith's repertory. The remarkable fact is that this rococo form continued to be produced until the 1790s. Examples made by Joseph and Nathaniel Richardson of Philadelphia date from the late 1780s, and a similar pot by Revere was charged to Dr. John Warren in 1791.[15]

A pronounced verticality of body and base, and an absence of chased and repoussé ornament on the surface are characteristic of the American interpretation of the double-bellied coffeepot. The Sargent coffeepot shares these qualities of simplicity and verticality, while also illustrating Revere's own interpretation of this frequently produced item. Over a period of nearly two decades, identical cast spouts appear regularly on his coffeepots[16] as do the gadrooned

Fig. 83
Urn
Richard Humphreys,
Philadelphia, 1774.
Private collection.

160
Coffeepot
Paul Revere, Boston, 1781.
Museum of Fine Arts, Boston;
gift of Mrs. Nathaniel Thayer.

bands at the base of the splayed foot and at the lip of the top.

Even the wealthiest of patrons sometimes favored forms that were no longer fashionable. In 1797, Salem's millionaire merchant, Elias Hasket Derby, purchased a large oval waiter (**161**). Made by Paul Revere, it is not unlike another tray (fig. 84) made nearly sixty years earlier in England by Henry Herbert.[17] The outline of each tray is defined by segments forming a scalloped edge, ornamented with cast decoration. In keeping with the concerns of the neoclassical style, however, Revere has varied the sizes of the segments according to strict geometric rules.

On the Revere tray, the central medallion, hanging from a bowknot and engraved with the Derby cipher, repeats the oval shape of the tray. This association of oval and bowknot is reminiscent of the designs on the back of a number of neoclassical chairs purchased by Derby about 1796 (126), and a similar combination of old and new design elements can be found on other furniture purchased by the Derbys slightly earlier. The relative cost of furniture and silver is also

Fig. 84
Tray
Made for the Kingston-upon-Thames Corporation by Henry Herbert, London, 1738. The Worshipful Company of Goldsmiths, London.

161
Waiter
Paul Revere, Boston, 1797.
Yale University Art Gallery;
Mabel Brady Garvan Collection.

suggested by Derby purchases. A double chest (fig. 70) which Derby bought in 1791 from Stephen Badlam for £26:17:6, may be compared to the £27:14:10 charged by Paul Revere for this "Silver Waiter."[18]

A self-conscious articulation of neoclassical principles of ornament and design—geometrical regularity, restraint, and intellectual abstraction—characterizes the decoration of the gold freedom box (**162**) made by Samuel Johnson and engraved by Peter Maverick. An early example of the many official presentation pieces made in this style, it was presented to Baron Federic von Steuben by the Common Council of New York for his part in freeing the city from British occupation in 1784. It is among the first known American objects to display bright-cut engraving, a type of ornamentation much favored in the late eighteenth and early nineteenth centuries and associated with the neoclassical style. With tightly spaced incisions and lines, bright-cut engraving has the effect, like inlay, of varying the surface while remaining two-dimensional.

From 1693 on, gold and silver boxes enclosing the city seal and granting the recipient the "freedom of this corporation" had been made in New York. During the eighteenth century, the Common Council records disclose that twenty-five such pieces were commissioned—three in silver and twenty-two in gold. In the Johnson boxes, the city seal includes the American eagle, which replaced the royal crown as a crest in 1783. As a new symbol of nationhood, the eagle often decorates objects produced during the Federal period. In sum, iconography rather than decoration, abstraction rather than sensuous appeal, was affecting the look of objects.

162
Freedom box
Samuel Johnson, New York, 1784.
Yale University Art Gallery;
Mabel Brady Garvan Collection.
(Color, p. 197.)

After the Revolution, the newly formed American government sought to establish peaceful relationships with the Indians, who had for the most part sided with the British during the war. In 1789, Congress voted money for the purpose of negotiating with the Indian tribes. In that same year the first presidential medal was produced for distribution to Indians as a token of friendship. The practice of offering medals to the Indians had a long history in America, having begun with the colonists and their regional governments in the early days of settlement. Typical of the medals made just prior to the Revolution is one (**163**a and b) that was part of a set of six presented to the chiefs of the Six Nations by Sir William Johnson in 1766. Made by Daniel Christian Fueter, these round medals, which were struck, show an Indian and a settler sharing a peace pipe under the motto "HAPPY WHILE UNITED"

163 a and **b**
Indian peace medal
Daniel Christian Fueter, New York, 1766. American Numismatic Society.

164 a and **b**
Indian peace medal
Joseph Richardson, Jr., Philadelphia, 1793. Chicago Historical Society; Gunther Collection.

on one side and a portrait of George III on the other side.

In contrast, the medals of the early Federal period (1789-1795) showed President Washington and an eagle, and proclaimed a goal of the new nation in the words "E PLURIBUS UNUM." Instead of being round, the new medals were oval; they were cut from sheets of silver and engraved with designs instead of being struck. One example (**164**), made in 1793, is identified as the work of Joseph Richardson, Jr., by his "JR" mark. Richardson and other Philadelphia silversmiths made a variety of objects for use as Indian trade silver, including armbands such as the one shown here (**165**). In the two years from June 10, 1796, to June 4, 1798, a total of over 4,400 pieces of silver were charged to Tench Francis of Philadelphia, Purveyor of Public Supplies—most of them in the form of brooches, gorgets, hair pipes, ear bobs, and armbands.[19]

165
Indian armband
Joseph Richardson, Jr., Philadelphia, 1792-1796. Yale University Art Gallery; Mabel Brady Garvan Collection.

In domestic silver of the Federal era, the conceptual character of the neoclassical style is expressed through the use of geometrical forms and classically inspired ornament. The cake basket (**166**) made by Simeon Bayley of New York City, in its elongated shape, angular outline, and double band of precisely regulated leaves and scrolls, reflects the ordered design of the neoclassical style. The two-dimensional quality of the engraving and pierced ornamentation correspond with the low-relief, abstract carving found on chair backs of the Federal era. At one end of the basket's interior, the initials of Edward and Mary (Elsworth) Dunscombe are engraved within an oval framed by swags of drapery and streamers. So lavish a basket stands as evidence of the increasing affluence of post-Revolutionary New York, fast becoming America's foremost city.

In the affluence of the Federal period, silver characteristically expressed the paradox of postwar design: dependent independence. New feelings of pride in American workmanship and enthusiasm for the possibilities of free trade were coupled with an eager return to English models. In 1789, for example, a Philadelphia silversmith advertised: "TEA SETS AND SIDEBOARDS OF PLATE not inferior in workmanship to any from Europe . . ."[20] At this time, 108 silversmiths were working in Philadelphia—approximately double the number who worked there prior to the Revolution.

It had now become fashionable for Americans to order silver in

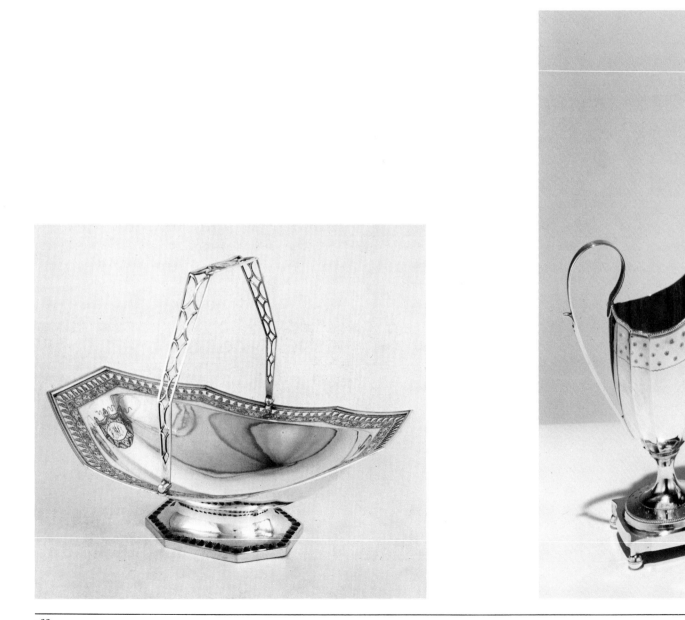

166
Cake basket
Simeon Bayley, New York, 1790-1795. Museum of the City of New York; gift of George Elsworth Dunscombe.

larger quantities than ever before. The matched tea service, for example, was deemed as necessary to the fashionable hostess in America as it was in England. Some services included as many as nineteen silver pieces.[21] Four pieces from one set (**167**) and a pair of tongs from another (**168**; ill. p. 55), all made by Philadelphia silversmiths Samuel Richards and Samuel Williamson, are shown here. The trend to increase the size of a silver order indicates a change both in economics and fashion. During this period the silversmith's shop expanded as the silversmith's art made the transition from handcraft to industrial venture. By 1807 Williamson (his partnership with Richards dissolved around 1800) employed at least six craftsmen. By 1810, his staff had increased to twelve men and he was engaged in marketing ready-to-sell silverware in the coastal trade, shipping merchandise to Virginia, Louisiana, and the West Indies.[23]

Philadelphia tea sets of the Federal period were classical in ornament, form, and proportion. The bodies of coffeepots, teapots, and sugar bowls were urn-shaped. Cream pitchers were fashioned in the form of inverted helmets. Pierced galleries placed at vessel rims created a delicate play of void and solid. The wide bands of "Gothick" fluting on the Richards and Williamson set were also common to most Philadelphia silver of the time. Other ornament, such as the bright-cut stars on the Richards and Williamson tea set, is more unusual. It seems to have

167
Tea service
Samuel Richards and Samuel
Williamson, Philadelphia, 1797-
1800. Private Collection.
(Color, p. 55.)

been derived from English models, such as the tea sets from the shop of the London silversmith Hester Bateman.

In Federalist Boston similar trends in taste and craft operation were evolving. For instance, Paul Revere was actively engaged in expanding the activities of his shop and in increasing the prestige of his craft. By the start of the nineteenth century he had become a craftsman-entrepreneur, directing his ball-and-cannon foundry and his copper-rolling mills. He helped found the Massachusetts Charitable Mechanic Association and served as its first president. His coffee urn (**169**) made

169
Coffee urn
Paul Revere, Boston, 1793.
Museum of Fine Arts, Boston;
gift of Henry Davis Sleeper
in memory of his mother, Maria
Westcote Sleeper, by exchange.

171
Sugar basket
Paul Revere, Boston, ca. 1798.
Museum of Fine Arts, Boston;
Helen and Alice Colburn Fund.

for Burrell Carnes in 1793 reflects the fashion of creating larger, more impressive tea and coffee services. Its platform supporting a fluted urn of attenuated profile conveys the refined elegance of the neoclassical style. To achieve this fashionable fluted form in other vessels Revere exploited technology, using single sheets of rolled silver, instead of raising the form from a solid ingot, for such forms as the teapot (170) he made in 1796. Teapots like these exemplify his outstanding work in silver during the Federal period. Their elliptical, columnate form epitomizes classical taste, as do his sugar baskets (171) made to ac-

170
Teapot
Paul Revere, Boston, 1796.
Museum of Fine Arts, Boston;
Pauline Revere Thayer Collection.

company urn-shaped coffeepots and helmet-shaped pitchers.

Paul Revere, one of the central figures in the history of American silver, is remembered for many of his creations. But perhaps none are more innovative than his "Revere pitchers." Twelve survive, some bearing dates from 1802 to 1806. One of them is shown (**172**). This pitcher was made for Samuel Gilbert, a printer and the secretary of the Massachusetts Charitable Mechanic Association, whose vigorous attack on the problem of delinquent membership prompted the association in 1806 to vote to present him with the piece of plate "of the value of thirty dollars . . . for his services and extra services."

Revere found the model for these pitchers in inexpensive English pitchers (fig. 85) made of creamware and decorated with transfer prints. Imported from Liverpool, these ceramic objects found wide popularity in America in the early years of the nineteenth century. Silver "Revere pitchers" have continued to be produced ever since and are highly popular in America today. In adapting an already accepted shape from ceramics to silver, Revere took notice of the excellence of a mass-marketed design, exalted it and asserted its importance. As an entrepreneur-craftsman he undoubtedly realized that, henceforth, the needs and purchasing power of a larger public—not the patronage of a few wealthy individuals—would become an increasingly important factor in the evolution of forms in silver and other decorative arts.

Fig. 85
Creamware pitcher
Liverpool, England, ca. 1800.
Yale University Art Gallery;
Mabel Brady Garvan Collection.

172
Pitcher
Paul Revere, Boston, 1802-1806.
*The Paul Revere Life Insurance
Company.*

Pewter

The widespread use and long period of popularity of pewter in America was clearly set forth soon after 1800 by Thomas Danforth Boardman in his autobiography: "From the Landing of the Pilgrims to the Peace of the revolution Most all, if not all [people] used pewter plaits and platters, cups, and porringers imorted from London . . . [or] made up [here] of the old worn out [pewter]. This was done in Boston, New York, Providence, Taunton and other places."[1] Indeed, when Boardman, a member of the pewter-making Danforth family in Connecticut and one of the most successful practitioners of the craft, wrote these words, the craft was more than one hundred and fifty years old. As early as 1635 Richard Graves had set up shop in Salem, Massachusetts, to rework old pewter, and by 1640 three pewterers were practicing the craft in Boston. All were English-trained.

The forms of the earliest known American pewter, which probably dates from the late 1600s, approximate English models, as do the few other extant American pieces made before 1750. British pewterers set the standard for quality, but beginning in the 1760s American pewterers advertised that they made "the best pewter" (and stressed "ready money given for old pewter or exhanged for new"). John Skinner of Boston offered "Hammer'd plates the same as London . . . with all other sorts of Pewter Ware usually made in New England . . . at the very lowest Rate for Cash or Old Pewter." Indeed, after 1750, regional preferences are evident in the products created in the shops of Boston; Providence and Newport, Rhode Island; Norwich, Hartford, and Middletown, Connecticut; New York City; and Philadelphia. In the 1770s and 1780s many American innovations were made. It appears that American pewterers were not always satisfied to follow English models, and distinctive American forms appeared.

Inasmuch as many pewterers were braiziers as well, they were capable of making their own molds.[2] And it was in the making of molds that the creative energy of the pewterer found opportunity for ex-

173
Deep dish
Samuel Danforth, Hartford, Connecticut, 1795-1816.
Yale University Art Gallery;
Mabel Brady Garvan Collection.

pression; for molds, in which the molten alloy was cast, determined the shape of each part and, in turn, the whole of each vessel. The pewterer's molds, like the print-maker's copperplate, established the character of the multiplied image.

On occasion the ingenious pewterer used castings for more than one purpose. Johann Christoph Heyne, for example, employed a six-inch plate for the bottom of his flagons (198), and Samuel Danforth used a six-inch basin as a foot for his flagons (203) and stood his baptismal basins upon half a basin (202). For his extended-base teapots, Danforth employed a casting of the upper section, instead of the conventional Queen Anne style base, as the foot.

There appear to have been strong regional preferences for particular forms. New Englanders usually drank from pint and quart mugs, whereas New Yorkers preferred covered tankards, many of which have flat tops. Philadelphians bought both mugs and tankards in large numbers, often pear-shaped, but only one Philadelphia flat-lidded tankard has been found to date. Large numbers of New England porringers survive, as do a few from New York. Only one Philadelphia example is known. Con-necticut pewterers, on the other hand, were partial to eleven- and thirteen-inch deep dishes at a time when pewterers in other areas were making flat dishes in both the same and larger sizes. The largest dishes known are the sixteen-and-a-half-inch deep dishes made by the Bassetts and Henry Will in New York, and a nineteen-inch flat dish by Simon Edgell of Philadelphia.

That the pewterer had a voice in the choice of forms is suggested by the fact that Connecticut-trained men continued to make eleven- and thirteen-inch (**173**) deep dishes when they migrated from Connecticut to New York, North Carolina, and Georgia, although other American pewterers eschewed dishes of those sizes. On the other hand, what would seem to have really influenced John Will, the German émigré who came with his family from Nieuwied on the Rhine to New York about 1752, was his English clientele, with the result that his pewter appears to have been completely anglicized. Thus with some few exceptions, his work and that of his illustrious pewter-making sons, Henry, William, and Philip, is in the English manner. In contrast, most of the pewter forms of Johann Christoph Heyne, made for Lutheran churches in German communities, remained Germanic in form until the very end of his career. His pewter made for the general public, however, became anglicized.

Although the American pewterer was free from Old World guild supervision and domination, he followed traditional practices, marking his flatware with a full-name touch (the maker's mark) and frequently identifying his locale with an appropriate Boston, New York, or Philadelphia stamp. As in England, an initial stamp was used by the maker to mark hollow-ware such as mugs, tankards, porringers, and smaller objects. Positive identification of initial stamps is possible when they are found with other identified touches, as on a plate (**174**) made by John Will.

Prior to the American Revolution colonial American pewterers, following English custom, used such touches as a lion in an oval or gateway (**175**), a rose and crown (**176**), a fully rigged ship, and pseudo-hallmarks reminiscent of English silver marks. Once the country gained its independence, most Americans adopted new marks featuring an American eagle (**177**), sometimes with a shield on its breast, or grasping in its talons a pole with a Liberty cap. Other stamps were "Federal Constitution" and "Liberty and Peace," which

174
Initial and other identifying marks
From a plate by John Will, New York, 1752-1774. Yale University Art Gallery; Mabel Brady Garvan Collection.

175
Rampant lion in oval mark
From a plate by Thomas Danforth II, Middletown, Conn., 1755-1782. Yale University Art Gallery; Mabel Brady Garvan Collection.

176
Rose and crown mark
From a footwarmer by Henry Will, New York and Albany, 1761-1793. Yale University Art Gallery; Mabel Brady Garvan Collection.

177
American eagle mark
From a plate by Parks Boyd, Philadelphia, 1795-1819. Yale University Art Gallery; Mabel Brady Garvan Collection.

are found, along with an American eagle, on the handles of some pewter spoons (**178**) made by George Coldwell in the 1790s in New York City. On other spoons (**179**) Coldwell stamped "Peace and Amity" beneath a liberty cap on a pole flanked by American flags.

Spoons and buttons were made by the millions in America, where all pewterers, most tinkers, and many peddlers and householders owned brass molds for making those easily cast and much needed objects. In an era when table knives and forks were the exception rather than the rule, probably every household had pewter spoons and plates. The designs of new pewter spoon molds paralleled those of silver spoons, but molds continued in use for a long time, with the result that many spoons were old-fashioned.

Although not as numerous as spoons and plates, a great many American pewter porringers have survived. Today they are generally used only as dishes for children or

178
Spoon
George Coldwell, New York, 1787-1811. The Metropolitan Museum of Art; Rogers Fund, 1963.

179
Spoon
George Coldwell, New York, 1787-1811. The Metropolitan Museum of Art; gift of Mrs. Blair in memory of her husband J. Insley Blair, 1941.

180
Porringer
Thomas D. Boardman, Hartford, Connecticut 1805-1820.
Yale University Art Gallery;
Mabel Brady Garvan Collection.

bowls for candy, but in the past they served primarily as vessels for drinking, eating, and probably dipping. While records indicate that porringers were imported in substantial numbers prior to 1750, almost all of those that have survived in America were American-made. Some following English patterns have crown, dolphin, and geometric handles. All of these continued to be made after the Revolution, and even the distinctly English crown handle type (**180**) continued in use until the 1820s. Beginning in the 1770s may new

American handle designs were introduced. Among the most beautiful are two types called "plain handle" (**181**) and "flowered handle" (**182**), which were made in Rhode Island. These names appear in the 1801 inventory of David Melville, a Newport pewterer who may have designed the "plain handle" for Newport's numerous Quakers. The serpentine outline of the plain handle echoes the circles of the bowl, which are repeated in the boss at the bottom of the porringer.

"Flowered handle"—a highly appropriate name—was the most

popular of all American porringer styles, with its lively interlaced handle strongly reminiscent of Chippendale chairbacks. As explained above (p. 54), this handle may have been the 1773 innovation of Samuel Hamlin, a pewterer from Providence, who later was to serve as lieutenant in the Continental army.

Most porringers in their day were described as "bellied," referring to the shape of their bulging bowls. Others, which were called "flat," may have been the basin porringers (that is, small basins ranging from

181
Porringer
Attributed to Thomas Melville,
Newport, 1793-1796.
Yale University Art Gallery;
Mabel Brady Garvan Collection.

182
Porringer
Samuel Hamlin or Samuel E. Hamlin,
Providence, 1773-1810.
Yale University Art Gallery;
Mabel Brady Garvan Collection.

two to six inches in diameter, with added porringer handles) made by many pewterers, chief among them the Richard Lees, father and son. The elder Lee wandered through much of New England peddling their pewter wares, brass dippers, and skimmers before settling in Springfield, Vermont, in 1802. Gifted and inventive, the Lees created several highly distinctive porringers, the majority of which are very small (**183**) and hold only half a gill. These may have been toys, although it is more likely that they served as "dram cups," measures for drinks or medicine. The "RL" and fleur-de-lis stamped on the handle serves both as an ornament and as identification of the maker. Unfortunately, we do not know whether it stood for the elder Richard Lee or the younger.

The rarity of one type of American drinking vessel, the nursing or "sucking" bottle, is not hard to understand. Although seemingly unsanitary, they were made by several American pewterers, among them being Frederick Bassett of New York City and the Boardmans of Connecticut, who had branch outlets in New York and Philadelphia. Said to have been called "mamas" by the Pennsylvania Germans, the forms of some are curvaceous and ample, as is the bottle illustrated here (**184**).

Mugs and pots for drinking all manner of liquids were made in half-gill, gill, half-pint, pint, and quart capacities in Connecticut, and

183
Porringer
Richard Lee, Sr. or Jr.,
Springfield, Vermont, 1788-1820.
Private collection.

184
Nursing bottle
Unknown maker, Pennsylvania,
1750-1800. Yale University Art
Gallery; Mabel Brady Garvan
Collection.

in pint and quart sizes in every other pewtering center in America. The three largest sized mugs usually followed English prototypes and had hollow handles. Barrel-shaped mugs, which are distinctively American, were produced first by Parks Boyd and later by Robert Palethorpe, Jr., both working in Philadelphia. Typical of the normal American quart mug made after 1725 is that by Samuel Hamlin of Providence (185). Based upon English models, it has a tapering body, larger at the bottom than at the top; a molded base; and a hollow S-shaped handle ending in a bud-shaped terminal. Occasionally, as on this one, such mugs had encircling fillets about the barrel.

New England mugs of a unique and American form were advertised by the Boston pewterer John Skinner as "very neat canns." One such mug (186) made by Nathaniel Austin of Boston and Charlestown, Massachusetts, illustrates their distinctive features, a solid strap handle (in this case, with "N. Austin" cast as an ornament on the handle tip), a shell-like thumb grip near the top of the strap handle, and sharply tapering body, usually with a fillet near the top. In all probability an as yet unknown brazier fashioned the molds for all the New England pewterers who had made mugs of this kind—John Skinner, Robert Bonynge, Nathaniel Austin, and Richard Lees, Gershom Jones, and possibly the Melvilles of Rhode Island.

185
Quart mug
Samuel Hamlin or Samuel E. Hamlin, Providence, 1794-1810.
Yale University Art Gallery; gift of Mrs. James C. Greenway.

186
Quart mug
Nathaniel Austin, Charlestown, Massachusetts, 1763-1807.
Yale University Art Gallery; Mabel Brady Garvan Collection.

Tankards, which are mug-shaped drinking vessels with hinged covers, are comparatively rare, for they were probably not made in large numbers except in New York. Despite the Dutch backgrounds of a large part of the population, the tankards made there were based on English silver prototypes, presumably because tankards did not exist in Holland. Those with flat-topped covers, which were made in England soon after 1650 and which went out of style around 1700, were superseded successively by straight-sided vessels with domed covers (circa 1690), pear-shaped forms (circa 1730), and taller and thinner straight-sided vessels (circa 1760). American pewter tankard styles evolved in somewhat the same manner, although the old styles were never dropped for the new ones until 1800, when tankards went almost completely out of fashion. For example, the standard late seventeenth-century version (**187**), which had a flat cover, an overhanging lip, and a broad stocky barrel with an S-shaped handle terminating in a fishtail, was made by John Bassett in New York City after 1720 and possibly as late as 1761. However, the form continued to be produced after John's death by his son Frederick until the end of the century. Both men also made later style tankards like the large two-quart example (**188**) by John Bassett. On it a domed cover replaces the flat top, the overhanging lip is eliminated, and a fillet has been added on the lower part of the barrel. Four members of the Bassett family, beginning with Francis, John's cousin, made pewter in New York City during the eighteenth century in competition with several

187
Quart tankard
John Bassett, New York, 1720-61.
Helen and Harvey Muehlenbeck.

188
Three-and-one-half-pint tankard
John Bassett, New York, 1720-61.
Yale University Art Gallery;
Mabel Brady Garvan Collection.

other father and son groups, such as Joseph Leddell, Sr. and Jr., William and Cornelius Bradford, Peter and William Kirby, and the German immigrants John Will and his sons, Henry, Philip, and William.

Henry Will worked both in New York City and Albany, Philip in New York and Philadelphia, but William, after presumably learning his craft from his brother Henry, moved to Philadelphia about 1764 and had an outstanding career as a public servant as well as a pewterer. He was three times elected high sheriff of the city and county of Philadelphia, and during the Revolution served not only as captain, lieutenant colonel, and colonel in the Continental army, but also at one time as its storekeeper at Lancaster. With Charles Willson Peale and four others, Will was a Commissioner of Personal Effects and Forfeited Estates of Traitors. In 1785 he was elected, along with Robert Morris, financeer of the Revolution, as representative from Philadelphia to the General Assembly of Pennsylvania. His reputation today, however, rests upon more than two hundred pieces of pewter, in a wide variety of forms, which show an acute sensitivity to shape and proportion as well as a sense of style keener than that of any other American pewterer. William Will's pear-shaped tankards (189) exemplify the curvilinear lines of the fully developed Queen Anne style and his straight-sided tankards (190) are similar to the silver tankards of the 1760s and 1770s.

Few pewter teapots survive made by American pewterers, with the exception of those made by William Will. His earliest pieces are globu-

189
Quart tankard
William Will, Philadelphia, 1764-1798. Yale University Art Gallery; Mabel Brady Garvan Collection.

190
Quart tankard
William Will, Philadelphia, 1764-1798. Yale University Art Gallery; Mabel Brady Garvan Collection.

lar, tightly curved pint and quart sizes, with S-shaped spouts, high-domed covers, and ball-shaped pewter finials, and occasionally cabriole legs and claw-and-ball feet (**191**). To this basic form, Will, about 1785 or 1790, added ornamental beading around the cover and to the finial, which he flattened to a disc (**192**). His latest teapots (**193**) are drum-shaped and in the neo-classical style. These pots with

191
Teapot
William Will, Philadelphia, 1764-1785. Dr. and Mrs. Robert Mallory III.

straight spouts, like his coffeepots, are ornamented with several rows of beading and are close counterparts to the silver teapots produced by the Philadelphia silversmiths Joseph and Nathaniel Richardson. As companion pieces to his teapots, Will made cream pitchers in at least two styles—the globular Queen Anne, with cabriole legs and shell feet, and the rococo, with double-bellied bodies and reverse C-scroll

192
Teapot
William Will, Philadelphia,
1788-1798. Charles V. Swain.

193
Teapot
William Will, Philadelphia,
1785-1798. Dr. and Mrs. Robert
Mallory III.

handles (**194**). The later pitchers match Will's double-bellied sugar bowls (**195**) but have neoclassical beaded ornament and probably date after 1785.

Although the only known surviving American or English pewter coffeepots are a half-dozen splendid urn-shaped pieces made by William Will of Philadelphia, there is ample proof that coffeepots were made by two other eighteenth-century American pewterers: four sizes of them were listed in the inventory of Thomas Byles taken in 1770, and

coffeepot molds were listed in John Andrew Brunstrom's inventory of 1793. Will's 1799 inventory included twelve coffeepots at $2.00 each, far more expensive than the quart mugs at 67 cents each and teapots at 80 cents each. Half-gallon measures were $1.67 in the same listing. At the end of the eighteenth century, when other pewterers looked backward and continued the designs of earlier masters, only William Will in America was ready to accept the challenge of neoclassical design. With his

drum-shaped teapots he succeeded admirably, as he did in some of his urn-shaped communion flagons.[3] Will was also equal to the challenge offered by the coffeepot (**196**), which poses the problem of juxtaposing a wooden handle of irregular shape and a metal spout on a symmetrical form. Not only did he achieve a pleasing balance of handle and spout, he executed a series of dramatic contrasts between concave and convex elements in the main body and achieved a unified whole. The owner's cipher is en-

194
Creamer
William Will, Philadelphia,
1785-1798. Charles V. Swain.

195
Covered sugar bowl
Attributed to William Will,
Philadelphia, 1764-1798.
Charles V. Swain.

196
Coffeepot
William Will, Philadelphia
1785-1798. Dr. and Mrs. Robert
Mallory III.

closed within an engraved circlet.

A two-handled cup of large size (**197**) with gadrooned base and ornament is one of the most ambitious surviving forms by an early American pewterer. Bearing a maker's mark "R.B.," it is similar in shape to cups made by Boston silversmiths in the early eighteenth century for the service of communion in New England churches or for drinking caudle or posset in homes.[4] This cup may have been used for either purpose after 1731, when Robert Bonynge, to whom it is attributed, began to work in Boston. It may be like those made earlier in the "caudle cup mould" that was included among the tools of Thomas Burroughs, Sr., who soon after 1684 moved from Boston to New York City, where he died in 1703. Later two-handled cups by William Will of Philadelphia and

197
Two-handled cup
Attributed to Robert Bonynge,
Boston, 1731-1763. Dr. and Mrs.
Melvyn D. Wolf.

the Boardmans of Connecticut lack the tension and integration of the Bonynge cup with its interacting bands of gadrooning on the body and beading on the handles.

Two-handled and standing silver cups were often used in New England churches before 1725, but after that time, beakers became the norm. In similar manner Boston's design-conscious "R.B." probably began to make sleek and smoothly flaring five-inch beakers (**198**) after making his gadrooned cups.[5] In turn, those beakers appear to have inspired the making of large numbers of beakers of similar size and shape between about 1770 and 1835 by several of Connecticut's pewtering Danforths and Boardmans.

Typical of some twenty known flagons made by the Lancaster, Pennsylvania, pewterer Johann Christoph Heyne for Pennsylvania

198
Beaker
Robert Bonynge, Boston, 1731-1763.
Yale University Art Gallery;
gift of Mary E. Dwight to
Sterling Memorial Library.

churches, mostly of Lutheran denomination, is one inscribed "The Peters Kirche/in Mt. Joy Town Ship/von John Dirr/1771" (**199**). Germanic in form with its flaring base, cherub's-head feet, and sharp spout, this flagon is an instance of a German craftsman's continuing to make objects in German style in America. This seems to have happened only when there was a receptive clientele—as indeed there was in the self-contained Pennsylvania German communities. There the German lan-

200
Standing cup with cover
Johann Christoph Heyne, Lancaster,
Pennsylvania, 1756-1780. Yale
University Art Gallery; Mabel
Brady Garvan Collection.

guage was the basis of the spoken word for more than two hundred years. Still owned by St. Peter's Church are a six-inch plate and a standing cup made by Heyne and a tankard made by the German-born William Will.

Equally Germanic in form, and as impressive as his flagons, are covered church cups made by Heyne (200). With large knopped stem to insure a firm grip by priest or communicant, with echoing curves on bases and cover and horizontal bands that determine

199
Flagon
Johann Christoph Heyne, Lancaster, Pennsylvania, 1771. Yale University Art Gallery; Mabel Brady Garvan Collection.

centers of attention, these cups are considered to be one of the finest designs in American pewter. More subtle (though less forceful) are the lines of the slightly later cup or chalice (**201**) made by Peter Young of Albany, New York. The tankards made by Young, who worked first in New York City and was probably trained there, deviate only slightly from the New York norm. However, his chalices and those of his follower Timothy Brigden have no exact parallels in Anglo-American pewter.

At the very end of the eighteenth century Samuel Danforth's Hartford, Connecticut, shop produced several innovative forms through the unorthodox use of castings. Danforth inverted part of a basin casting to serve as a foot for a handsome baptismal basin (**202**). In a similar way, he provided an impos-

201
Chalice
Peter Young, Albany, New York, 1775-1795. Dr. and Mrs. Robert Mallory III.

202
Baptismal basin
Samuel Danforth, Hartford, Connecticut, 1795-1816. Yale University Art Gallery; Mabel Brady Garvan Collection.

ing base to his flagons by adding a six-inch basin turned upside down. He heightened their ceremonial aspect by adding spires (203).

The making of pewter and britannia (a special grade of pewter) continued in the United States until about 1870, with the emphasis gradually shifting from plates, dishes, and drinking vessels to lamps, pitchers, and tea and coffee services. In order to survive, pewterers sought new markets in the growing cities and, via the peddler's cart, in the back country. From small shops of master and apprentice with perhaps a journeyman or two, the making of pewter grew to factory production with twenty to a hundred men employed. The metal grew thinner, harder, and shinier until, at the end, it was used as a base for silver plate and lost its identity.

203
Flagon
Samuel Danforth, Hartford,
Connecticut, 1795-1816.
Yale University Art Gallery;
Mabel Brady Garvan Collection.

Brass

Early in the seventeenth century, braziers set up shop in the British colonies of North America. Henry Shrimpton, who called himself brazier, was working in Boston as early as 1639, but the earliest known dated and identified American brazier's product was made almost a hundred years later. Three-legged bell-metal pots, variously marked "1730, L. Langworthy" and "L.L. Newport," were made by Lawrence Langworthy, who emigrated in 1730 from Ashburton in Devonshire, England, to Newport, Rhode Island, where he worked as a brazier and pewterer.

Colonial braziers, like pewterers, relied upon scrap metal for the raw material from which they fashioned objects, since there was little copper and no calamine (zinc ore) mined in America. Nevertheless, they made "all sorts of Brass Work"; James Byers of New York, for example, advertised in *The New York Gazette* of December 13, 1762, "Andirons, Tongs and Shovels, Fenders, Candlesticks, Buckles . . . Brasses for Mills, Brass Chambers for Pumps," and other wares. However, except for andirons, it is impossible to differentiate brass objects made in America from those produced in England, and it is for their andirons that early American

204
Pair of brass andirons
Possibly Rhode Island, 1740-1760.
Mr. and Mrs. Stanley Stone.

braziers are acclaimed.

Until well into the nineteenth century in America, a land of forests, the wood-burning fireplace supplied heat for the home. And even though Benjamin Franklin found the fireplace inefficient and invented the Franklin stove, and the Pennsylvania Germans found the five-plate stove more effective and prefer it to this day, the wood-burning fire remains a source of pleasure and stands as a symbol of domestic tranquility. For it the blacksmith forged firedogs and the brazier cast ornamental andirons in harmony with other household furnishings.

The earliest andirons attributed to American braziers have large "penny" feet with a low arched support and baluster-shaped shafts with ball tops. They are usually found in New England, most often in Rhode Island. Indeed, it is tempting to speculate that these distinctive brass andirons were made by Lawrence Langworthy or his son Southcote, who followed his father in the craft after the latter's death in 1739. On two pairs (one of them 204), the finest examples of the form, a Georgian urn and flame finial is used instead of the ball finial. These probably were made between 1725 and 1750 and are related in form to English andirons of that time.

With the adoption of the coal grate in England about 1750, the need for andirons in that country diminished and few new English styles appeared to serve as models for American braziers. They then began to design their own, and American andirons produced after 1750 deviate sharply from known English examples. Usually these new style andirons of the Chippendale period follow closely the design principles of American furniture.

The combination of classical form and rococo ornament of American highboys with ball-and-claw feet, fluted colonettes, scrolled pediments, and flame finials is duplicated in a group of American andirons exemplified by the outstanding pair shown here (205). The tapered and fluted columns, moldings, plinths, and proportions are based on the classical idiom; the ornamental parts—the flame, and double swirl finials—are rococo. On another type (206), the rococo ornament overlays the form as well, the spiraled vase-shaped shafts giving an overall sense of movement

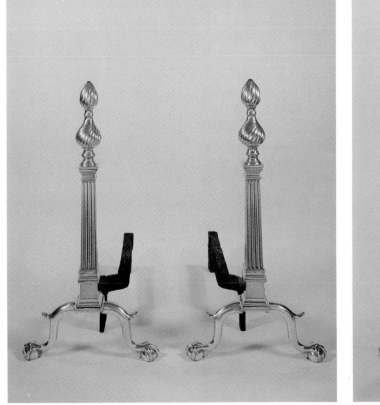

205
Pair of brass andirons
America, 1760-1785.
Mr. and Mrs. George M. Kaufman.

206
Pair of brass andirons
America, 1760-1780.
Yale University Art Gallery;
bequest of Olive Louise Dann.

seldom found in American arts.

The patterns for these andirons were produced by woodworkers who had learned the orders from English architectural pattern books and who adapted some of the ornamental designs set forth by them. Indeed, the andiron patternmakers were the turners and carvers who made the columns of tea tables and carved facades, legs, and feet of the furniture. So there was good reason for the similarity between furniture

and andirons (see p. 53).

Numerous advertisements in the 1760s and 1770s by Boston, New York, and Philadelphia braziers offered andirons of their own manufacture. The prominent Philadelphia brazier Daniel King called attention in 1767 to "a new and curious Set of Patterns for Brass Fire Dogs, neater and more to order than any yet made on the Continent."[1] Three years later, King billed John Cadwalader

for six pairs of andirons—for one pair with Corinthian columns he charged the princely sum of £25, the charge for a pair with "counter flutes" was £10, and £9 was the cost of a pair with plain flutes.[2] The prices are significant. Twenty-five pounds at that time was the price of the finest Philadelphia-made highboy with carved ornament, and ten pounds was the amount Thomas Affleck charged for a mahogany desk or sofa. In other words, to have

Fig. 86
*Brass andirons with engraved
eagle*
Probably Maryland, ca. 1800.
Mr. and Mrs. Stanley Stone.

warranted such prices brass andirons must have been highly prized, and they continue to be prized by connoisseurs today as among the finest and most distinguished of eighteenth-century American design.

The neoclassical andirons of the 1790s were the same in form as those of the Chippendale era, but the mass was lightened, the silhouette clarified, and the rococo flame finials often replaced by chaste urns. Although the columns were usually left plain and unfluted, some braziers substituted large-scale, oversized urns for the columns. As might be expected, the vocabulary of ornament conformed to neoclassical taste, with eagles, flags, paterae, and drapery engraved on the more ambitious examples (fig. 86).

Prior to 1790 few braziers marked their wares, but about one pair of andirons in ten made after that time bears their maker's stamp, such as those (**207**) by Richard Wittingham, who came from Birmingham, England, in 1791 to New York City, where he made some of the most beautiful pieces. Other well-known makers of that era include John Bailey of New York, John Clark, James Davis, and John Molineux of Boston, Barnabas Edmonds of Charlestown, Massachusetts, and Thomas Brooks of Philadelphia.

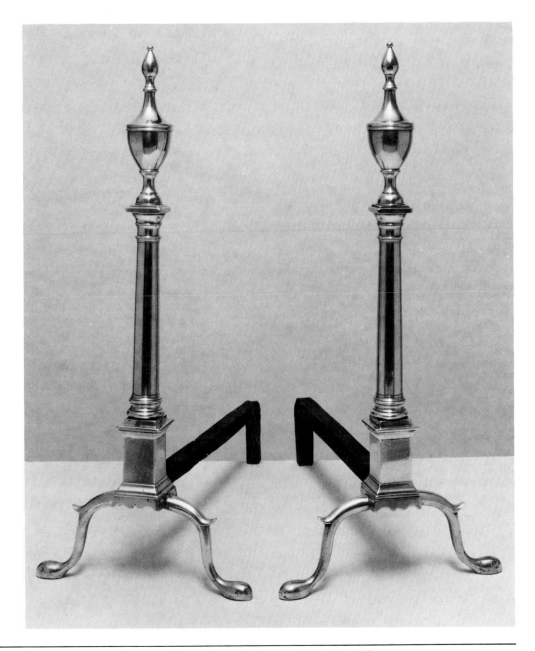

207
Pair of brass andirons
R. Wittingham, Sr., New York,
1795-1805. Mr. and Mrs. George
M. Kaufman.

Ceramics

Ceramic vessels were necessary in every colonial household for the daily preparation, storage, and serving of food and drink. From the time of first settlement, small potteries in America successfully produced utilitarian earthenware; almost all finer ceramics were imported from or via England. Scarcity and intransigence of skilled workmen, high capital expenditures for building kilns and obtaining raw materials, and the competition of English merchants, who could export large quantities of European and Oriental wares to the colonies at comparatively cheap prices, made the founding of large-scale enterprises for the production of fine ceramics in America nearly impossible. However, three attempts—by Bonnin and Morris in Philadelphia, John Bartlam in Charleston, South Carolina, and Gottfried Aust and Rudolf Christ at Salem, North Carolina—were made during the 1750-1800 period.[1] It is in the continuing craft tradition of small-scale production of earthenware and stoneware that the most characteristic American expressions in ceramics are found; the potters who worked at the many scattered kilns adhered closely to the English and Germanic folk traditions in which they had been trained. The strength of these traditions had two effects: sometimes potters would, with more than ordinary care, model a classic example of a traditional form or type of decoration; or, under the influence of newer fashions or individual whimsy, potters would evolve variations or new applications of form and technique that in time produced distinctive native products.

The most ambitious ceramics manufactory before the Revolution was the Philadelphia firm of Bonnin and Morris, which operated for only two years, from 1770 to 1772, and produced soft-paste porcelain dinner- and tea-ware decorated with underglaze blue painting and transfer-printed designs in the manner of the contemporary British factories —Bow, Liverpool, and Worcester.

Pickle stand or sweetmeat dish
Bonnin and Morris factory,
Philadelphia, 1770-1772,
soft-paste porcelain.
The National Museum of History and Technology (Smithsonian Institution); gift of the Barra Foundation.

Ornamented with floral and foliate motifs, shells, pierced work, and molded scroll decoration, the elegant designs show the same use of rococo decorations found in other arts produced in Philadelphia during the period. The prominent Wharton and Cadwalader families patronized the firm, and purchased pickle stands (**208**) and fruit baskets (**209**) like these shown here. A pickle stand (or sweetmeat dish), with random tiny scallop shells and corals clustered on its central shaft like a marine incrustation, and a fruit basket, with its delicately arched and looping bands and applied flowers, indicate the technical abilities of the Bonnin and Morris enterprise. Despite the high quality of its products, the porcelain manufactory experienced great difficulties; high labor costs forced its prices to be "greatly more than for European ware."[2] Josiah Wedgwood was unnecessarily fearful of competition when he wrote: ". . . the trade to our colonies we are apprehensive of loseing in a few years, as they have set on foot some Potworks there . . . [which] make us very uneasy for our trade and our Posterity."[3]

209 a and **b**
Fruit basket
Bonnin and Morris factory,
Philadelphia, 1770-1772,
soft-paste porcelain.
Mr. and Mrs. Richard Stiner.

West of Philadelphia, in the fertile Pennsylvania-German farm country of Montgomery, Lancaster, and Bucks counties, a very different ceramic tradition flourished. Based on traditional folk materials, forms, and techniques, rather than on elegant high-style precedents, the pottery of this area was rich and complex. In its use of varied decoration, a dish attributed to Henry Roudebuth of Montgomery County (**210**) demonstrates the striking effects the German potters were capable of producing. Upon a cream-colored slip ground stands a regal peacock arrayed in exotic plumage whose outline is echoed by the meandering stem of a blossoming tulip. The date "1793" and the maker's initials "HR" balance these predominant elements. The sgraffito, or scratched decoration, voids created by the removal of whole areas of slip, and random dabs of color create an interplay between the pure pattern of the surface and the representation of flower, fowl, and inscription. A shiny lead-based transparent glaze covers the surface, making it impervious to liquids.

Some of the finest Pennsylvania-German pie dishes were decorated

210
Dish
Probably by Henry Roudebuth,
Montgomery County, Pa., 1793,
earthenware. The Metropolitan
Museum of Art; gift of
Mrs. Robert W. deForest.

with figural groups. Two pairs made by David Spinner (1738-1841) were probably made for display. On the pair "Deers Chase" (211 and 212), a mounted officer and lady gallop across one dish and defy its boundaries as the front of the lady's horse reappears on the second dish, following the hounds and their leaping quarry.

The picturesque finery of the military and their parade activities is evoked on two other dishes by David Spinner, one inscribed "Sholder Firelocke" (213) and the other depicting two musicians (214). The pairs of stiff but jaunty soldiers drill or march to the music of the fife and drum. Although Spinner and Roudebuth were virtual contemporaries, working in the same geographic area, their dishes present two different visions: Roudebuth's is overwhelmingly ornamental in its emphatically decorative elements; Spinner's is dependent upon narrative interest, though his two-dimensional figures are defined solely by line, rhythm, and color.

Many German and Swiss settlers came to Pennsylvania as members of religious communities. Notable

211
Dish
David Spinner, Bucks County, Pa., ca. 1800, earthenware.
Philadelphia Museum of Art; gift of John T. Morris.

212
Dish
David Spinner, Bucks County, Pa., ca. 1800, earthenware.
Philadelphia Museum of Art; gift of John T. Morris.

among these sectarian groups were the Moravians from south-central Germany, an industrious and talented people who practiced many crafts. In the 1760s one of their congregations moved from the parent settlement at Bethlehem, Pennsylvania, to Bathabara and later to Salem in piedmont North Carolina, where their potters began production of lead-glazed earthenware to supply their own needs and those of the surrounding countryside. So great was the demand for their wares that at the opening of the kiln on June 15, 1761, it was recorded that "people gathered from 50 and 60 miles away to buy pottery, but many came in vain, as the supply was exhausted by noon."4

Stamped on the back "FR" (probably for Friedrich Rothrock of Friedberg, a village south of Salem), the slip-decorated dish (**215**) is a stunning representative of the Moravian earthenwares. Lush leafage and exuberant flowers are painted in bright red and green slip on a light yellow ground, with a masterful control unmatched on

213
Dish
David Spinner, Bucks County, Pa.,
ca. 1800, earthenware.
Philadelphia Museum of Art;
gift of John T. Morris.

214
Dish
David Spinner, Bucks County, Pa.,
ca. 1800, earthenware.
Philadelphia Museum of Art;
gift of John T. Morris.

any other American pottery. A wave-and-dot border in red and chocolate brown adds a vibrant, abstract element at the edge, emphasizing the circular shape of the dish and effectively setting off the floral decoration from the surrounding space. The interplay of luminous, harmonic coloring with solid, heavy drawing lends this dish an otherworldly beauty that belies its lowly origins.

215
Dish
Friedrich Rothrock, Southern Wachovia, North Carolina, ca. 1795, earthenware. Old Salem, Inc.

A very different feeling is projected by a diminutive five-inch-high New England jug (216). Its narrow-based earthenware form glistens with a coat of brown, almost black, "Albany" slip, which acts as a foil for a swiftly brushed floral spray almost Oriental in its spontaneity. A painted meander and incised lines encircle the tapering shoulder. The strap handle's highly arched profile, reminiscent of the handles on neoclassical silver helmet-shaped pitchers, is in keeping with the jug's date of manufacture. It was made about 1798 by Abel Wadsworth at the potworks of Captain John Norton (1758-1827) of Bennington, Vermont, for presentation to Ominidia Armstrong, who was then aged ten. This finely proportioned jug stands at the beginning of the Bennington pottery trade in New England.

216
Jug
Abel Wadsworth, Captain John Norton pottery works, Bennington, Vermont, 1793-1798, earthenware. Bennington Museum, Inc.

Although they are not as gaily colored or intricately decorated as the ceramics of the Pennsylvania Germans or Moravians, red earthenwares with trailed-slip decoration have an unambiguous appeal. Like the oblong dish shown here (**217**), these wares often have brick-red surfaces deftly ornamented with splotches of copper oxide green, manganese purple, or iron oxide black and varied groupings of parallel meandering white slip bands. Round or oblong dishes, plates, and trenchers, shaped over a wooden or clay "bat" or form and given a protective coggled edge with a wooden roller, were extensively made after about 1790 all along the Atlantic seaboard; this example was probably made in Connecticut or eastern Massachusetts, perhaps on Cape Cod, between 1800 and 1820.[5]

217
Dish
New England, possibly Connecticut, late 18th or early 19th century, earthenware with slip decoration. The Society for the Preservation of New England Antiquities; gift of William Sumner Appleton.

Stoneware, made of clay containing silica and kaolin and fired at a higher temperature than earthenware, was first made in America early in the eighteenth century. Hard, thick-walled, inert, nonporous, and therefore ideal for salting, pickling, and storing acidic foodstuffs, stoneware became the dominant ceramic for utility vessels and containers in the years following the Revolution. Among the earliest and finest examples is a wide-mouthed jar with sturdy hand grips and ample, gently serpentine outlines (**218**). The New York City potters who made this jar between 1790 and 1810 were expert at decorating the gray, salt-glazed bodies of their wares with carefully incised figures filled in with brilliant blue cobalt oxide glaze. Here, in an exceedingly rare example decorated on two sides, a large, loose-limbed lion strides across one side, while on the other a sinuous flower, with radiating petals, soar-

218 a and **b**
Jar
New York ca. 1800, stoneware.
Mr. and Mrs. John Paul
Remensnyder.

ing leaves overlapping the stem, and a spiky shoot, seems to cling to the swelling surface.

Unlike earthenware, stoneware tended to be responsive to fashionable design, and with the introduction of neoclassical taste in the final decades of the eighteenth century, high-shouldered vessels with long tapering sides and narrow bases, patterned after antique Mediterranean forms, began to appear. Another jar from the New York City potteries (219) displays this contour as well as unusual two-color decoration. Broad, dark blue leaves sway on either side of an undulating, pale blue-green vine, creating a relaxed rhythm perfectly in accord with the delicate borders and decorative bands so often found on decorative arts of the Federal era. The restraint and poise of these early stonewares continued to influence the design of many American ceramic forms far into the nineteenth century.

219
Jar
New York, 1775-1800, stoneware.
Yale University Art Gallery;
gift of Mr. and Mrs. Charles F.
Montgomery.

Glass

Three glass manufactories of major importance were established in America during the eighteenth century. All were founded by German immigrants, who recruited and hired German glassblowers. The dependence of the colonies and the later United States on English window glass and bottles was the major stimulus for these entrepreneurs, who hoped to compete successfully for the New World market.

Casper Wistar (1694-1752), a German immigrant from Wald-Hilspach and a Philadelphia button manufacturer, founded a glass factory near Alloway Creek in Salem County, New Jersey, in 1739, with four German glassblowers he had recruited in Europe. After Wistar's death in 1752, his son Richard continued in the business until 1780, when poor health and disruption of markets by the Revolution forced him to

220
Candlestick
Attributed to the glassworks of Caspar Wistar, Wistarburg, Salem County, New Jersey, 1740-1780.
The Corning Museum of Glass.

dissolve the firm.[1]

The Wistar factory produced mostly window and bottle glass. In addition to these standard products, the workers made offhand pieces in the Germanic tradition of free-blown, tooled glassmaking. At present, two candlesticks, several electrical tubes of the sort made popular by Benjamin Franklin, and a number of whimsy pieces are attributed to the Wistar factory on the basis of family ownership, analysis, and various documentary sources. After the factory's closing in 1780, the workmen departed for New England, New York, and the Ohio River Valley, disseminating their style, known as the "South Jersey" tradition, over a wide area of the United States. A simple candlestick shown here (220) is related in style to two examples attributed to Wistar. The domical foot, simple shaft decorated with knopped handgrips, and deep socket

with flat flange are all elements derived from Germanic traditions of the seventeenth and early eighteenth centuries but are here simplified into a rigorously functional, closed form. Elimination of transitional elements and lack of finish make the stick appear smaller and contribute to a sense of the spontaneous shaping of fluid, molten glass by the glassblower's tools. A similar simplification of forms and lack of interest in concealing the evidence of toolmarks are also characteristic of many popular and folk arts.

The main products of eighteenth-century glasshouses were window glass (generally aquamarine in color and bottles—round-bellied, square, or straight-sided—made of olive-green or black glass with many impurities. Glassblowers often had the privilege of fashioning molten glass left over at the end of the workday into utilitarian objects for

personal use. Exploiting the heaviness and irregularity of the glass in their offhand pieces, they produced forms of surprising monumentality and sureness of line.

One jug (221) was made by expanding the neck of a squat bottle form. The thick-walled, globular body, enlivened by striations and bubbles, rises through a smooth throat to a plain lip, tracing an ogee curve of great vigor—a line echoed and reinforced by the heavy applied handle. Even simpler and more forceful is a jar (222) of classic profile, with an extremely active line that rises swiftly to a sharply rounded shoulder and flaring neck, checked by a neatly rolled rim. The glassblower's control of his material, gained through repetition of a limited repertoire of shapes, lends restrained integrity to what might easily have turned out to be a leaden, clumsy form.

Henry William Stiegel (1729-

221
Jug
Eastern United States, 1790-1810.
The Corning Museum of Glass.

222
Jar
Eastern United States, 1790-1810.
The Corning Museum of Glass.

1785) was the second major figure in American glassmaking. He was born in Cologne, Germany, and emigrated to Pennsylvania, was the proprietor of an iron furnace in Elizabeth, Lancaster County, when he built the first of his glass factories there in 1763. After 1765 he built a second and a third factory in nearby Manheim—an establishment that continued in operation until 1774, when it closed because of over-extended finances. At the height of its productive capacity, however, the factories employed some 130 men, including both English and German glassblowers.

No documented examples of glass from Stiegel's factories survive, but extensive newspaper advertisements indicate that Stiegel intended his works to rival both sophisticated British tableware and continental folk forms of enameled glass. Eighteenth-century American glass closely resembling either British imitations of Venetian diamond-patterned tableware or enamel-decorated glass is thus referred to as "Stiegel type," with the under-standing that it was not necessarily made in Stiegel's factories, but rather belongs to the tradition established by his workmen.

In contrast to the offhand pieces of the South Jersey tradition, Stiegel type ware is deliberately stylish and elegant in line, surface, and finish. Flasks (223,224), most of which were amethyst-colored and stopped with a cork, were employed as pocket bottles for gin and whisky. Their somewhat unstable, flattened ovoid bodies terminate in sharply pinched-in throats; and spark-

223-228
Two flasks, sugar bowl, pitcher, and two salts
Attributed to the glasshouse of Henry William Stiegel, Manheim, Pennsylvania, 1769-1774; larger flask (224) also possibly Ohio, 1770-1810. Yale University Art Gallery; Mabel Brady Garvan Collection.

ling surface patterns were achieved by molding the gather of glass before expanding it into its final form.

Even more characteristic of Stiegel type tablewares are covered sugar bowls, creamers, and footed salts (**225-228** and **229**). Molded and expanded diamond surface patterns, in brilliant cobalt-blue, amethyst, or clear lead glass, reflect the love of the rococo period for seemingly precious materials and nervous surface decoration, while vase-shaped or double ogee bodies,

perched on small applied feet, and (in the blue sugar bowl) swirl-ribbed finials directly reflect silver and ceramic forms in their instability and interaction with space. Such tableware was much in demand among prosperous, fashion-conscious segments of the English-speaking population.

German workmen at Manheim made enamel-decorated forms for sale to the large German population of Pennsylvania. The "We two will be true" tumbler (**230**) exemplifies the characteristics of these

wares: generously applied areas of strongly contrasting colors, which suggest a set repertoire of foliate and decorative motifs, articulated by abbreviated black lines. Of particular interest is the dove perched on a sprouting heart, a folk symbol of love. The perfunctory, though competent, execution of this tumbler and the facile manipulation of folk symbols suggest that it represents a commercialization of the original folk idiom, perilously close to what would today be called "kitsch."

229
Covered bowl
Attributed to the glasshouse of
Henry William Stiegel, Manheim,
Pennsylvania, 1772-1774.
The Corning Museum of Glass.

230
Enameled tumbler
Attributed to the glasshouse of
Henry William Stiegel, Manheim,
Pennsylvania, 1772-1774.
The Corning Museum of Glass.

John Frederick Amelung (d. 1798) came to Maryland from Bremen, Germany, in 1784 with sixty-eight workmen; in the following year he built a glass factory at New Bremen, Maryland, near Frederick. Like its predecessors, the factory suffered throughout its existence from competition with imported goods and was finally forced to close in 1795.

A number of authenticated examples made at the Amelung factory survive, among which are engraved presentation pieces. These include "pokals" (covered goblets), covered sugar bowls, goblets, tumblers, case bottles, decanters, and wineglasses, and confirm the productive range and high quality of the glass made at New Bremen.

As in the Wistar and Stiegel factories, Amelung's workmen brought a tradition of blown and engraved glass to many other American factories founded in the early nineteenth century, particularly to those in Pittsburgh, Pennsylvania, where a sophisticated school of engraved glass arose in the 1800–1810 era.

A monumental pokal, or goblet (231), one of a pair, exemplifies the smoky, crystalline glass, large in size and scale, as well as the deeply cut, delicate engraving found on Amelung presentation pieces. Standing securely on a flattened domical foot, an inverted ogee baluster capped with a ring supports a deep, high-sided bowl with wheel-cut floral sprays and

cartouche. Originally the goblet may have been covered by a set-in domical lid (now lost), with an ogee finial similar to the stem baluster. The compelling combination of baroque forms and rococo engraving indicates the traditional nature of this vessel, based on German precedents a century old.

Glass made in factories established after the demise of the three great eighteenth-century houses of Wistar, Stiegel, and Amelung was directly dependent on their personnel; as a consequence, glass design after 1800 was extremely conservative. Some forms continued virtually unchanged, while others reflected a fusion of the English and Germanic traditions. A large green bowl (232) illustrates the

231
Goblet
Glass manufactory of John Frederick Amelung, New Bremen, Maryland, 1793. The Corning Museum of Glass.

232
Bowl
Attributed to Baltzer Kramer, overseer, the New Geneva Glass Works, New Geneva, Pa., 1798-1807 The Corning Museum of Glass.

survival of older traditions as a result of the movement of workmen from the three factories. The bowl's probable maker, Baltzer Kramer, had previously worked in both the Stiegel and Amelung factories before overseeing the New Geneva Glass Works, built in western Pennsylvania in 1798. Molded in a twenty-rib mold and expanded, the bowl is made of nonlead window or bottle glass, and possesses not only architectural strength in its molded foot and outfolded rim, but a body of great amplitude and nearly hemispherical lines.

Among the most beautiful examples of Anglo-Germanic glass is a pair of candlesticks (233) that were free-blown and tooled in an American factory between 1800 and 1820. Long shafts, composed of two elegant ogee balusters on either side of a triple ring, rest on circular applied feet and support swirl-ribbed overlays, tall sockets, and flanges. The exceptionally pure, nonlead glass lends a refined smoothness and luminosity to the forms; the candlesticks are a victory of the glassblower over his difficult medium. Dependent both on the English design tradition and on the skilled labor of Germanic workmen, these sticks are among the first American masterpieces in glass.

233
Pair of candlesticks
Probably southern New Jersey,
1800-1820. The Metropolitan
Museum of Art; Rogers Fund, 1935

Textiles

In 1777 a young Philadelphia girl was advised by her mother that "needlework is a most important branch of female education," and indeed, instructors such as Bridget Suckling of Boston were readily available to teach young ladies "plain Work, Dresden, Point (or Lace) Work for Child Bed Linnen, Crosstitch, Tentstitch, and all other kinds of needlework."[1] Needlework was one of the few avenues of self-expression available to women in the eighteenth century, and thus the most important artistic statements made by American women of this time were a result of their working of native and imported materials into embroidered pictures, bed hangings, coverlets, and quilts.

One of an extensive group of pictures, valances, chair seats, and petticoat borders with similar themes and motifs, "The Fishing Lady" (234) derives its name from the lady so occupied in the center of the picture. She and her male companion are flanked by two other couples; the foreground is filled with birds, dogs, ducks, deer, and flowers; and buildings dot the tree-covered hills in the background. While the maker's sense of perspective may not be "worthy of Claude Lorraine,"[2] the final composition is a delight. Traditionally attributed to Eunice Bourne of Barnstable, Massachusetts, this mid-eighteenth-century picture derives from an English tradition of pictorial embroidery that was strongest in the late seventeenth century. Such a richly colored set as "The Fishing Lady" may reflect the mature maker's youthful training in a Boston school, where she would have been exposed to many design sources, including engravings and illustrated books, under the guidance of an instructor.[3]

In the same Massachusetts coastal tradition is the set of crewel embroidered bed hangings made about 1745 by Mary Bulman (b. 1715) of York, Maine (235).

234
Embroidered picture,
"The Fishing Lady" Possibly by Eunice Bourne,
Barnstable, Massachusetts, ca. 1750.
Museum of Fine Arts, Boston;
Seth Kettell Sweetser Fund.

This unique complete surviving set was begun by Mrs. Bulman after her husband's death at the Battle of Louisburg, Nova Scotia. The verses on the valances, from Isaac Watts's "Meditations in a Grove,"[4] are testimony to her feelings of sadness and loss.

Beds were often the single most expensive item of household furniture, and their costly hangings were an accurate barometer of a family's economic standing and social aspirations. Embroidered crewelwork bed hangings, although less lavish than imported silk hangings, were nevertheless made by women with "sufficient means to afford some leisure."[5] Trailing vines with large multicolored flowers and leaves flow gracefully over

235
Bed hangings
Mary Bulman, York, Maine, ca. 1745.
Old Gaol Museum, York, Maine.

the curtains and coverlet; much open background space, a characteristic of American crewel hangings, acts as a foil to focus attention on the precisely worked ornament. Mrs. Bulman may have purchased her designs and materials from a Boston source; in fact, similarities between details in the hangings (such as the small trees in the valances and the birds in the headcloth) and the "Fishing Lady" group suggest a common source.[6] Her stylized flowers are also closely related to the patterns found on Boston silver of the period.[7]

While most crewel embroidery was done in New England, a few examples of crewelwork done in Pennsylvania and New York have survived. The coverlet (**236**), made

235
Bed hangings (detail)
Mary Bulman, York, Maine, ca. 1745.
Old Gaol Museum, York, Maine.

by Clarissa Stokradt (or Stokraad) Deyo of Kingston, New York, in the second quarter of the eighteenth century, is one of a small group of related coverlets produced by Hudson Valley women with Dutch backgrounds. Each of the over two hundred naturalistic elements in this coverlet is different. Four large green leaves jut diagonally from a central floral motif surrounded by concentric rectangles composed of serried rows of multicolored leaves, flowers, and grapes connected by a thin line. In contrast to New England work, little space is left unadorned. The abundant nervous and irregular ornament set within a largely symmetrical framework produces a bold, shimmering effect.

A bright blue background of

236
Coverlet
Clarissa Stokradt (or Stokraad)
Deyo, Kingston, N.Y., 1728-1748.
Colonial Williamsburg Foundation.

glazed calamanco, a kind of woolen fabric, immediately catches the eye in a quilted coverlet probably made in New York or New England about 1770 (237). Its embroidered vines and floral motifs are scattered over the surface in an apparently random fashion, and a strip of rose glazed calamanco frames the composition.

Another form of coverlet is the bed rug, most popular in the Connecticut Valley. A heavy and warm outermost covering, it was sewn with running stitches on a wool backing and was made entirely from materials prepared in the home. Their designs seem to be simplified versions of the elaborate floral patterns of eighteenth-century Indian palampores (which

238
Bed rug
Philena McCall, Lebanon, Conn., 1802. Wadsworth Atheneum.

were in turn a product of English and European influence), although other design sources have been suggested.[8] The example shown here (238), both initialed and dated, was made by Philena McCall (1783-1822) of rural Lebanon, Connecticut, in her twentieth year. Similar to other rugs made in or near Lebanon, Philena's is dominated by a plant with five carnationlike flowers, and bordered with other flowers encircled by a reticular leaf design. Bold in mass and color, this rug exemplifies the simple strength of the country tradition.

Textiles were the most important product of English manufacturing in the second half of the eighteenth century. Americans imported great quantities of woolens, linens,

237
Coverlet
New York or New England, ca. 1770.
Colonial Williamsburg Foundation.

cottons, and silks and, following English customs, used them as clothing, upholstery, and drapery. Worn fragments of these valuable English materials were frequently utilized by needlewomen in creating their own handsome appliquéd coverlets and quilts. Ladies of the Byrd and Harrison families who lived in the Westover and Berkeley plantations along the James River in Virginia appliquéd flowers painstakingly cut from English chintz onto a fine muslin ground in the late-eighteenth-century example seen here (**239**). These flowers, enclosed in a geometric framework made up of strips of calico, symmetrically surround the central motif of a flowering vine rising

luxuriously from a rolling turf. Included within the central diamond-shaped section is a lively chipmunk with real personality; pineapples, a symbol of hospitality particularly meaningful in the gracious and wealthy Virginia society, are also featured.

Restrictive mercantile laws prevented Americans from developing their own textile industry before the Revolution, and after a hiatus during the war years, trade in textiles from England to America resumed with its former vigor along the old lines of communication and credit. Indeed, in 1784 Lord Sheffield observed that printed textiles were still "one of the most considerable articles imported

into the American states" from England.[9] Even a decade later, American textile production was largely limited to "fabrics of the simple but most important and necessary kinds."[10]

Despite this predominant reliance on English goods, the late eighteenth century also saw the first steps taken in the development of the textile industry that was to play such a significant role in nineteenth-century America. Among the pioneers in this movement was John Hewson, one of the first Americans to manufacture quality printed textiles.[11] Trained in England, Hewson emigrated to Philadelphia in 1773 and operated a printworks there from 1774 to 1810,

239
Coverlet
Members of the Byrd and Harrison families of Westover and Berkeley plantations, Charles City County, Virginia, ca. 1770.

Valentine Museum, Richmond; gift of Susan McGuire Ellett.

producing goods closely related to English chintzes of the late 1780s and 1790s.[12] Some ten examples of his work are known, including the center square used in an appliqué coverlet made in the early nineteenth century and now attributed to an unidentified "E.C." (240). In superb condition, this square contains Hewson's characteristic urn of flowers surrounded by birds and butterflies. The quiltmaker added a band of quilted featherwork to the square, and enclosed it within borders of floral prints alternating with areas of intertwining stuffed work. The whole design, while retaining much of the movement and rhythm of the earlier style, achieves a regularity and simplicity characteristic of the neoclassical period.

240
Coverlet
Printed by John Hewson, Philadelphia, and probably quilted by unidentified "E.C.", ca. 1774-1809. The St. Louis Art Museum; gift of Miss Mildred Petrie.

Catalogue

Notes

The Making of an American Culture

1
Quoted in *Pennsylvania Magazine of History and Biography*, 19 (1895): 531–532.

Style in American Art 1750–1800

1
See Grose Evans, *Benjamin West and the Taste of His Times* (Carbondale, Illinois, 1959), p. 5 and plates 1, 2.

2
Ibid., p. 100.

3
Bernard Bailyn, "Political Experience and Enlightenment Ideas in Eighteenth-Century America," *American Historical Review* (January, 1962), p. 339.

4
Wendell Garrett, "John Adams and the Limited Role of the Fine Arts," *Winterthur Portfolio*, I, 243–244.

The Metamorphoses of Britannia

1
John Yonge Akerman, *Coins of the Romans Relating to Britain Described and Illustrated* (London, 1844), p. 32.

2
Erwin Panofsky, "Reflections on Time," *Problems in Titian Mostly Iconographic* (New York, 1969), pp. 88–108.

3
Clarence S. Brigham, *Paul Revere's Engravings* (New York, 1969).

4
A common eighteenth-century phrase applied to the Pretender, here used to denote Great Britain.

5
A phrase used quite often by Hollis to stress his loyalty to George III and the British constitution—so long as the monarch observed the constitution.

6
The reference is to the inscription quoted above in connection with figure 19.

7
R. C. Smith, quoting from a letter written by Jennings to his father, January 12, 1790. "Liberty Displaying the Arts and Sciences," *Winterthur Portfolio*, II (Winterthur, Del., 1965), 88.

8
Minutes of the Proceedings of the Library Company of Philadelphia, III, 206.

9
Ibid., p. 92.

10
Polyanthos, N. S. 1 (February, 1812): 3–15.

Regional Characteristics and Preferences in American Decorative Arts: 1750–1800

1
John T. Kirk, *American Chairs: Queen Anne and Chippendale* (New York, 1972), pp. 195–198.

2
Advertisement of T. Bradford in the

Charleston Evening Gazette, February 22, 1786, in Alfred Coxe Prime, compiler, *The Arts and Crafts in Philadelphia, Maryland, and South Carolina 1786–1800* (The Walpole Society, 1932), p. 217.

3
Quoted in Florence M. Montgomery, *Printed Textiles: English and American Cottons and Linens 1700–1850* (New York, 1970), p. 41.

4
Quoted in Charles F. Montgomery, *American Furniture: The Federal Period* (New York, 1966), p. 13.

5
Pennsylvania Chronicle, September 9, 1767, as printed in Alfred Coxe Prime, compiler, *The Arts and Crafts in Philadelphia, Maryland, and South Carolina 1721–1785* (Walpole Society, 1929), pp. 185–186.

6
Connecticut Courant, November 23, 1773, as quoted in Charles F. Montgomery, *A History of American Pewter* (New York, 1973), p. 33.

7
Charles F. Hummel, *Winterthur Newsletter*, vol. 5, no. 9 (November 27, 1959), p. 1.

8
John Henry Hill, "The Furniture Craftsman in Baltimore, 1783–1823" (unpublished master's thesis, University of Delaware, 1967), pp. 45–46.

9
Boston Gazette, June 11, 1754, as printed in George Francis Dow, compiler, *The Arts and Crafts in New England 1704–1775* (Topsfield, Mass., 1927), p. 288.

10
Gilbert T. Vincent, "The Bombé Furniture of Boston," in Walter Muir Whitehill, Jonathan Fairbanks, and Brock Jobe, editors, *Boston Furniture of the Eighteenth Century* (Boston, 1974), p. 150 and *passim*.

11
Margaretta Markle Lovell, "Boston Blockfront Furniture," in Whitehill, Fairbanks, and Jobe, *Boston Furniture of the Eighteenth Century*, p. 78.

12
The quantification implied in the chart is based on rough estimates of the number of survivals observed by the author in many museums, private collections, dealers' shops, and publications, over the course of forty years. It is true that these estimates may not bear an exact relationship to the numbers originally produced. However, as the numbers of survivals range from fifty ("few" in the chart) to more than a thousand ("many") of a form and the case pieces under consideration are of comparable attractiveness and importance, it seems reasonable to suppose that the ratio between the number originally produced and the number surviving is reasonably constant for a given form, whether it was made in Philadelphia, New York, or New England.

13
Although pewter porringers and tankards continued to be made in Bristol, England, by Robert Bush, Bush and Perkins, and others after 1740, the writer believes they were chiefly made for export to America.

14
Whereas painters and sculptors traveled to Italy and England for training and from one part of the American colonies to another to execute commissions, most native artisans served their apprenticeships and often worked all their lives in one community without traveling elsewhere.

15
Although only forms in the Chippendale mode were listed in the "Prices of Cabinet and Chair Work," a Philadelphia manuscript inscribed "Binjamin Lehman" and dated January, 1786, the 1794 *Philadelphia Cabinet and Chair-Makers Book of Prices* (journeymens' piecework rates) lists only objects in the new neoclassical style. Significantly, "A table of Prices for Cabinetwork in Hartford, Connecticut," published in 1792, gives no indication of the adoption of the new style; only old forms were listed. Yet the advertisement of the Hartford cabinetmaking firm of Kneeland and Adams in the same year included some furniture in the neoclassical style, and a set of shield-back chairs is well documented as having been made by them in 1795.

28
(detail)

Paintings, Drawings, and Watercolors

1
Mather Byles, "To Mr. Smibert on the Sight of His Pictures," *Daily Courant* (London, April 14, 1730), in Henry Wilder Foote, *John Smibert, Painter* (Cambridge, Mass., 1950), pp. 54–55.

2
Alfred Coxe Prime, *The Arts and Crafts in Philadelphia, Maryland and South Carolina*, The Walpole Society (1929), I, 10–11.

3
In Guernsey Jones, ed., *Letters and Papers of John Singleton Copley and Henry Pelham, 1739–1776*, Massachusetts Historical Society Collections, vol. 71 (New York, 1970), p. 31.

4
Ibid., p. 51.

5
In John Galt, *The Life, Studies and Works of Benjamin West, Esq., President of the Royal Academy of London* (London, 1820), II, 48.

6
In Franklin Bowditch Dexter, ed., *The Literary Diary of Ezra Stiles* (New York, 1901), I, 132–133.

7
Sizer, ed., *Autobiography of Trumbull*, pp. 44, 55 [no. 33 in "Account of Paintings" under Lebanon].

8
For the quotation, see inscriptions in catalogue entry for no. 41.

9
Quoted in Charles Coleman Sellers, *The Artist of the Revolution: The Early Life of Charles Willson Peale* (Hebron, Conn., 1939), pp. 252–253.

10
In Samuel Y. Edgerton, Jr., "The Murder of Jane McCrea: The Tragedy of an American 'Tableau d'histoire,' " *Art Bulletin*, 47, no. 4 (1965), 485–486.

11
Quoted in Kenneth C. Lindsay, *The Works of John Vanderlyn* (Binghamton, N.Y., 1970), p. 71.

12
In William Dunlap, *A History of the Rise and Progress of the Arts of Design in the United States* (New York, 1969), II, 16.

13
In Ruel Pardee Tolman, "Malbone, the American Miniature Painter," *Art Quarterly* 2, no. 2 (1939), 123.

14
In Dunlap, *A History of the Rise and Progress of the Arts of Design*, II, 167.

Prints

1
William Hogarth's engravings after his own series of paintings, *The Rake's and Harlot's Progress* and *The Idle and Industrious Apprentice*, were popular in Europe as well as in England and the colonies. That colonials demanded their merchants to have these images on hand illustrates their desire to be fashionable and discerning, and today these engravings rank high in critical estimations of eighteenth-century printmaking. The advertisement is for Nathaniel Warner's shop in Boston in 1757. For this and other printsellers' advertisements see George Francis Dow, *The Arts and Crafts in New England 1704–1775* (1927; reprint ed., Topsfield, Mass.: Wayside Press), pp. 36–37.

2
The broadside is quoted in Frank H. Sommer, "Thomas Hollis and the Arts of Dissent," *Prints in and of America to 1850* (Charlottesville, Va., 1970), pp. 148–151. For a more detailed treatment of the various levels of meaning in this print, see the bibliography in the catalogue entry for no. 80.

3
Quoted in Halsey and Cornelius, *The American Wing*, pp. 238n–239n.

4
The author has not seen the Doolittle print of Jefferson. For his reference to it see the Reverend William A. Beardsley, "An Old New Haven Engraver and his Work: Amos Doolittle," *Papers of the New Haven Colony Historical Society*, 8 (1914): 144.

5
Concerning this controversy see Harold Dickson, "The Case Against Savage," *American Collector*, 14, no. 12 (1946), pp. 6–7, 17.

6
Quoted in Martin P. Snyder, "William Birch: His Philadelphia Views," *PMHB*, 73, no. 3 (1949), p. 298.

7
Quoted in *American Printmaking*, p. 48.

34
(detail)

Furniture

1
The furniture designs were closely linked to architectural designs and often appear in architectural pattern books such as the cabinet on stand, or "Draw's," signed "Thos. Langley" and dated 1739, plate 155, *The City and Country Builders and Workman's Treasury of Designs*, by Batty Langley, 1740.

2
A copy of the inventory is in the object folder at the Metropolitan Museum of Art, New York.

3
For the Christopher Townsend high chest, see *The John Brown House Loan Exhibition of Rhode Island Furniture* (Providence, R.I., 1965), no. 57, pp. 86–87. For the Newport dressing table by Job Townsend, see Joseph Downs, "The Furniture of Goddard and Townsend," *Antiques*, 52, no. 6 (December, 1947), p. 427, fig. 1.

4
A signed example by Edmund Townsend is owned by the Museum of Fine Arts, Boston. See Edwin J. Hipkiss, *Eighteenth-Century American Arts: The M. and M. Karolik Collection* (Cambridge, Mass., 1950), no. 38, pp. 68–69. Another by Daniel Goddard was illustrated in *American Antiques from Israel Sack Collection*, II, 506–509.

5
Minor Myers, Jr., and Edgar deN. Mayhew, *New London County Furniture 1640–1840* (New London, Conn., 1974), no. 35.

6
William MacPherson Hornor, Jr., *Blue Book, Philadelphia Furniture* (Philadelphia, 1935), pp. 74, 91, pl. 115.

7
Decorative Arts Photographic Collection, The Henry Francis du Pont Winterthur Museum.

8
The Dunlaps and Their Furniture (Manchester, N. H., 1970), no. 78.

9
A chest-on-chest inscribed "William Houston" at the Henry Francis du Pont Winterthur Museum; a chest-on-chest-on-frame signed "John Dunlap/1784," whereabouts unknown; chest-on-chest twice painted with the initials "S. D.," anonymous collection; chest-on-chest inscribed "Salisbury" at Winterthur; chest-on-chest-on-frame with a mock promissory note signed by Hugh and Samuel Gregg, the Metropolitan Museum of Art, New York. For the attribution to Samuel Dunlap see, *The Dunlaps & Their Furniture* (Manchester, N. H., 1970), no. 1.

10
Thomas Sheraton, *The Cabinet Dictionary*.

11
Morrison H. Heckscher, "The New York Serpentine Card Table," *Antiques*, 103 (May 1973): 975.

12
"Connecticut Cabinetmakers Part II: Checklist up to 1820," *The Connecticut Historical Society Bulletin*, 33 (January, 1968): 25.

13
Fiske Kimball, "Furniture Carvings by Samuel McIntire," *Antiques*, 19 (March 1931): 210.

14
Thomas Sheraton, *The Cabinet-Maker and Upholsterer's Drawing-Book* (1802; reprint ed., New York: Praeger Publishers, 1970), frontispiece.

15
Wendell Garret, "Editorial," *Antiques*, 107 (May, 1975): 877.

16
Charles F. Montgomery, *American Furniture: The Federal Period* (New York, 1966), no. 181. Hereafter cited as Montgomery.

17
Fiske Kimball, "Samuel McIntire," *Samuel McIntire: A Bicentennial Symposium* (Salem, Mass., 1957), pp. 26–27.

18
Montgomery, no. 17.

19
Montgomery, p. 445.

20
Montgomery, p. 319.

21
Montgomery, no. 184.

22
Mabel M. Swan, "John Seymour & Son, Cabinetmakers," *Antiques*, 32 (October, 1937): 178.

23
Hornor, *Blue Book*, facsimile reproduction of Ephraim Haines's bill to Stephen Girard, p. 243.

24
Montgomery, no. 265.

25
Thomas Sheraton, *Cabinet Dictionary*, 2 vols. (1803; reprint ed., New York: Praeger Publishers, 1970), II, 218.

26
Hipkiss, *Eighteenth-Century American Arts: The M. and M. Karolik Collection*, no. 44, pp. 80–81.

27
Patricia E. Kane, "Samuel Gragg: His Bentwood Fancy Chairs," *Yale University Art Gallery Bulletin*, 33 (Autumn, 1971):27.

Silver

1
For an expanded discussion of the ritual of tea drinking see Rodris Roth, "Tea Drinking in 18th-Century American: Its Etiquette and Equipage," *Contributions from the Museum of History and Technology, United States National Museum Bulletin* (Washington, D.C.: Smithsonian Institution, 1969), no. 225, paper 14, 61–91.

2
Simeon Soumain advertised one as a lottery prize in 1727. *The New York Gazette*, April 3–10, 1727, see Rita Susswein Gottesman, *The Arts and Crafts in New York 1726–1776*, I (New York: New-York Historical Society, 1938), 61.

3
The elder Hurd seems to have referred to this book of armorial devices a number of times. Compare, for example, the arms of the merchant John Rowe on the 1740–1745 grace cup now at the Museum of Fine Arts, Boston (Buhler, *American Silver*, vol. I, no. 187), with Guillim, Sec. III, Chap. XIV, p. 166, arms of Rowe of

Lamerton; see also the Flynt arms on the 1738 teapot also at the Museum of Fine Arts (Buhler, *American Silver*, vol. 1, no. 182) and Guillim, Sec. III, p. 110; similarly Guillim's description of the arms of Sir John Fleet, Sec. III, Chap. XXII, p. 239, and Hurd's engraving of Thomas Fleet's coat of arms on a 1750 teapot also at the Museum of Fine Arts, Boston (Buhler, *American Silver*, vol. 1, no. 194). For a discussion of American silversmiths' practice of providing customers with arms from Guillim, see Martha Gandy Fales, "Heraldic and Emblematic Engravers of Colonial Boston," *Boston Prints and Printmakers 1670–1775, Publications of the Colonial Society of Massachusetts*, 46 (Boston, 1973): 210.

4
Charles Jackson, *An Illustrated History of Silver Plate* (London: Country Life and Batsford, 1911), II, 1046.

5
J. M. Dennis, "London Silver in a Colonial Household," *Bulletin of the Metropolitan Museum of Art*, N. S., 26 (December 1967): 174–179.

6
Fales, *Joseph Richardson*, p. 133.

7
A Full View of All the Diseases Incident to Children from their Birth to the Age of Fifteen (London, 1742), p. 76.

8
Berenice Ball, "Whistle with Coral and Bells," *Antiques*, 80 (December 1961): 555. She notes that "most of these particular sales were to other Philadelphia silversmiths, so the eventual customer's price was certainly higher."

9
Other known examples of coral and bells in gold are by: Henricus Boelen, New York, c. 1740 (Ginsburg & Levy, Inc.); George Ridout, New York, c. 1745 (collection of Mr. and Mrs. Ferdinand H. Davis, on loan to the Museum of the City of New York); and Nicholas Roosevelt, New York, c. 1760 (Metropolitan Museum of Art, New York).

10
New York Gazette and Weekly Mercury, July 31, 1769, quoted in Gottesman, *Arts and Crafts in New York*, pp. 42–43.

11
Guido Schoenberger, "The Ritual Silver Made by Myer Myers," *Publications of the American Jewish Historical Society*, 43 (1953): 1–9.

12
Dome tops occur in Boston tankards dating from about 1715-1720, such as those by John Edwards (Buhler and Hood, *American Silver*, vol. 1, no. 68) and John Dixwell (Buhler and Hood, *American Silver*, vol. 1, no. 79). Starting around 1730, the height of the dome top is accentuated by the addition of a finial, and tankards following this model were made until the mid 1780s. See, for example, the tankard made in 1786 by Benjamin Burt (now at the Museum of Fine Arts, Boston, M. and M. Karolik Collection, Buhler, *American Silver*, vol. 2, no. 307.).

13
Quoted in H. D. Eberlein, *The Colonial Homes of Philadelphia* (Philadelphia: J. P. Lippincott, 1912), p. 55.

14
Reprinted by Alfred Coxe Prime in *The Arts & Crafts in Philadelphia, Maryland and South Carolina, 1721–1785* (1929; reprint ed., New York: Da Capo, 1969), p. 80.

15
A late example of this form by the Richardsons is now at the Yale University Art Gallery (Buhler and Hood, *American Silver*, vol. 2, no. 884). Revere's pot for John Warren is now at the Museum of Fine Arts, Boston (Buhler, *American Silver*, no. 388).

16
Examples of Revere coffeepots with identical spouts from this period include one at the Worcester Art Museum dated 1773 (Graham Hood, *American Silver* [New York: Praeger Publishers, 1971], fig. 148) and two at the Museum of Fine Arts, Boston: the Sargent pot illustrated here (1781) and the Warren pot mentioned above (1791).

17
The tray is dated 1738. It was made for the corporation of Kingston-upon-Thames. See Michael Clayton, *The Collector's Dictionary of the Silver and Gold of Great Britain and North America* (New York and Cleveland: World Publishing Co., 1971), p. 325.

18
The cost of the tray is recorded in Paul Revere's account books for 1797 and quoted in Buhler and Hood, *American Silver*, p. 198. The cost of the chest is recorded in bills from Stephen Badlam and John and Simeon Skillin; see Mabel M. Swan, "A Revised Estimate of McIntire," *Antiques*, 20 (December 1931): 340, 342.

19
Harold E. Gillingham, "Indian Trade Silver Ornaments made by Joseph Richardson, Jr.," *The Pennsylvania Magazine of History and Biography*, 67 (1943): 83–91.

20
Joseph Cooke in the *Federal Gazette*, January 21, 1789; reprinted in Prime, *Arts & Crafts in Philadelphia*, p. 102.

21
In her book *Early American Silver* (1970, paperback ed., rev., New York, 1973, p. 145), Martha Gandy Fales writes, "Joseph Richardson, Jr. . . . made dozens of silver services . . . which included a coffee pot, teapot, sugar dish, slop bowl, cream pot, a dozen teaspoons, and a dozen tablespoons." One such service, dated c. 1795, is now at the Henry Francis du Pont Winterthur Museum, Winterthur, Delaware.

22
For these figures and a discussion of Samuel Williamson's trade and shop prac-

tice, see Ellen Beasley, "Samuel Williamson, Philadelphia Silversmith, 1794–1813," unpublished master's thesis, University of Delaware, 1964.

Pewter

1
Dean A. Fales, Jr., "T. D. B. [Thomas Danforth Boardman] Tells All," *Pewter Collectors' Club of America Bulletin*, no. 46 (February 1962), p. 109. This article is based on an undated autobiographical account of the life and business career of Thomas Danforth Boardman in the Connecticut State Library, Hartford, Connecticut; business papers of Thomas Danforth Boardman.

2
As Pierre Auguste Salmon, a pewterer from Chartres, commented: "It is . . . the pewterer who makes his molds." See Salmon, *L'Art du potier d'étain* (Paris, 1788), p. 93.

3
For illustration, see Montgomery, *A History of American Pewter*, p. 81.

4
"Caudle" was defined as a warm drink of wine or ale with gruel, sugar, and spices, and "posset" as a beverage of hot milk curdled by ale or wine and seasoned with spices.

5
The legend "Dwight MDCCXXXX" is believed to have been inscribed at a later date.

Brass

1
Quoted in Henry J. Kauffman, *American Copper and Brass* (Camden, N.J., 1968), p. 151.

2
Nicholas B. Wainwright, *Colonial Grandeur in Philadelphia: The House and Furniture of General John Cadwalader* (Philadelphia, 1964), p. 38.

Ceramics

1
Although John Bartlam may first have instructed Gottfried Aust in the mystery of making Queens ware in 1771, William Ellis (who had worked at Hanley in England and later for Bartlam in South Carolina) spent five months in 1773-1774 helping Aust begin production of the Queens ware and of white salt-glazed stoneware.

2
Johann David Schoepf, *Travels in the Confederation: 1783–84*. Trans. and ed. Alfred J. Morrison (Philadelphia, 1911).

3
Ibid., p. 21, n. 36.

4
Quoted by John F. Bivins, Jr., "The Moravian Potters in North Carolina, 1756–1821," *Ceramics in America*, ed. Ian M. G. Quimby (Charlottesville, Va., 1973), p. 257.

5
Joseph Johnson Smith, *Regional Aspects of American Folk Pottery* (York, Pa.: The Historical Society of York County, 1974), pp. 16, 37–40.

Glass

1
On the Wistarburg glass factory, see Arlene Palmer, "The Wistarburg Glassworks of Colonial New Jersey" (unpublished master's thesis, University of Delaware, 1973).

Textiles

1
Esther Ames, *Nancy Shippen: Her Journal Book*, quoted in Mary Taylor Landon, and Susan Burrows Swan, *American Crewelwork* (New York, 1970), p. 18; *Boston Gazette*, no. 2 (July 1751), quoted in George Francis Dow, compiler, *The Arts and Crafts in New England, 1704–1775* (Topsfield, Mass., 1927), p. 274.

2
As noted by Harrison Gray Otis in 1829 in reference to another example of the "Fishing Lady" group; quoted in Nancy Graves Cabot, "The Fishing Lady and Boston Common," *Antiques*, 40, no. 1 (July 1941), p. 8.

3
See the 1738 newspaper advertisement of a Mrs. Condy of Boston quoted in Dow, *Arts and Crafts*, p. 274.

4
In his *Horae lyricae* (7th ed., 1737).

5
Ann Pollard Rowe, "Crewel Embroidered Bed Hangings in Old and New England," *Boston Museum Bulletin*, vol. 71, nos. 365 and 366 (1973), p. 104.

6
Ibid., p. 135.

7
This relationship is noted by Robert C. Smith in his "The Decorative Arts," in Louis B. Wright et al., *The Arts in America: The Colonial Period* (New York, 1966), pp. 321–322.

8
William L. Warren, "The New England Bed Rugg," in Wadsworth Atheneum, *Bed Ruggs/1722–1833* (Hartford, Conn., 1972), pp. 16–19.

9
Lord Sheffield, *Observations on the Commerce of the United States*, quoted in Florence Montgomery, *Printed Textiles* (New York, 1970), p. 85.

10
Tench Coxe, *A View of the United States of America*, quoted in Montgomery, *Printed Textiles*, p. 36.

11
Other early American efforts at textile manufacturing and printing are discussed in Montgomery, *Printed Textiles*, pp. 85–103.

12
Ibid., p. 97.

Suggestions for Further Reading

The literature concerning American art during the last half of the eighteenth century is extensive. Except for the relevant portions of such general histories as William H. Pierson, Jr., and Martha Davidson (eds.), *Arts of the United States* (New York, 1960), Louis B. Wright *et al.*, *The Arts in America: The Colonial Period* (New York, 1966), and Daniel M. Mendelowitz, *A History of American Art* (New York, 1970), there have been few attempts to cover all facets of the period. The following brief suggestions are intended to direct the reader to the basic and more reliable works in each area of the arts, but of necessity many useful and important works have been omitted. Additional and more detailed references can be found in the notes to this book and in the following bibliographies: Walter Muir Whitehill, Wendell D. Garrett, and Jane N. Garrett, *The Arts in Early American History: Needs and Opportunities for Study* (Chapel Hill, North Carolina, 1965), Charles F. Montgomery (compiler), *A List of Books and Articles for the Study of the Arts in Early America* (Winterthur, Delaware, 1970), and Frederick L. Rath, Jr., and Merrilyn Rogers O'Connell (compilers), *Guide to Historic Preservation, Historical Agencies, and Museum Practices: A Selective Bibliography* (Cooperstown, New York, 1970). The extensive bibliography in *Prints Pertaining to America in the Henry Francis du Pont Winterthur Museum* (Walpole Society, 1963) is the kind of specialized source needed in other areas. A major reference tool is the nine-volume printed edition of the card catalogue for *The Winterthur Museum Libraries Collection of Printed Books and Periodicals* (Wilmington, Delaware, 1974). These libraries were developed to foster the study of early American art, and the publication of their resources is a milestone in that endeavor.

Monographs dealing with various fields of American art during this period appear in the following journals, among others: *Antiques* (1922-), *The American Art Journal* (1969-) (see in particular the May 1975 issue devoted to "1776—How America Really Looked"), *American Art Review* (1973-), *The Art Quarterly* (1938-), and *Old-Time New England* (1910-). The journals, bulletins, and regular and occasional publications of museums such as The Metropolitan Museum of Art, the Museum of Fine Arts, Colonial Williamsburg, the Yale University Art Gallery, and especially the Henry Francis du Pont Winterthur Museum contain much valuable information.

An understanding of the developments in architecture from 1750 to 1800 is fundamental to the study of the decorative arts. The first and in some respects still the best modern survey of American architecture during this era is S. Fiske Kimball, *Domestic Architecture of the American Colonies and of the Early Republic* (New York, 1922). This well-researched and carefully considered work by one of America's leading art historians has been updated but not superseded by Hugh S. Morrison, *Early American Architecture, from the First Colonial Settlements to the National Period* (New York, 1952), and William H. Pierson, Jr., *American Buildings and Their Architects: The Colonial and Neo-Classical Styles* (Garden City, New York, 1970). Anthony N. B. Garvan widened the context of our understanding with his *Architecture and Town Planning in Colonial Connecticut* (New Haven, Connecticut, 1951), and Alan Gowans has imaginatively examined the relationships between architecture and furniture in *Images of American Living* (Philadelphia, 1964).

Much of research begins with, in the words of Sir Lewis B. Namier, "finding out who the guys were," and a number of admirable biographical dictionaries of American artists and craftsmen are available to assist in the initial spadework. Among these are Ethel Hall Bjerkoe, *The Cabinetmakers of America* (Garden City, New York, 1957), Stephen G. C. Ensko, *American Silversmiths and Their Marks*, vol. III (New York, 1948), Ledlie Irwin Laughlin, *Pewter in America: Its Makers and Their Marks*, 2 vols. (New York, 1940; revised edition, Barre, Massachusetts, 1970), George C. Groce and David H. Wallace, *The New-York Historical Society's Dictionary of Artists in America 1564-1860* (New Haven, Connecticut, 1957), Mantle Fielding, *American Engravers upon Copper and Steel* (Philadelphia, 1917), and the same author's *Dictionary of American Painters, Sculptors, and Engravers* (New York, 1926, revised edition 1965), David McNeely Stauffer, *American Engravers Upon Copper and Steel*, 2 vols. (New York, 1907), and *The Britannica Encyclopedia of American Art* (New York, 1973). Carl Bridenbaugh deals with the artisans of the seventeenth and eighteenth centuries in historical terms in *The Colonial Craftsman* (New York, 1950). George Francis Dow compiled contemporary Boston newspaper advertisements and notices pertaining to artists and craftsmen and published them as *The Arts and Crafts in New England, 1704-1775* (Topsfield, Massachusetts, 1927). Volumes similar in format and equally useful have been compiled by Rita Susswein Gottesman for New York, covering the years 1726 to 1804, Alfred Coxe Prime for Philadelphia, Maryland, and South Carolina (1721-1800), and James H. Craig for North Carolina (1699-1840).

The literature concerning American painting begins with the publication of William Dunlap's *History of the Arts of Design in the United States*, 2 vols. (New York, 1834, revised edition 1969). Edgar P. Richardson, *Painting in America: The Story of 450 years* (New York, 1956), is a standard introductory text that can be supplemented with the more colorful works of James Thomas Flexner, including *First Flowers of Our Wilderness* (Boston, 1947) and *The Light of Distant Skies, 1760-1835* (New York, 1954). Harry B. Wehle, *American Miniatures, 1730-1850* (Garden City, New York, 1927), is a thorough account of its speciality. Among the most distinguished of the many studies of American painters are Jules David Prown, *John Singleton Copley*, 2 vols. (Cambridge, Massachusetts, 1966), Charles Coleman Sellers, *Charles Willson Peale* (New York, 1969), Theodore Sizer (with the assistance of Caroline Rollins), *The Works of Colonel John Trumbull* (New Haven, Connecticut, 1967), and Irma B. Jaffe, *John Trumbull* (Boston, 1975). Ian M. G. Quimby (ed.), *American Painting to 1776: A Reappraisal* (Charlottesville, Virginia, 1971) contains reports on much recent investigation. *American Paintings in the Museum of Fine Arts, Boston*, 2 vols. (Greenwich, Connecticut, 1970), and Albert Ten Eyck Gardner and Stuart P. Feld, *American Painting: A Catalogue of the Collection of the Metropolitan Museum of Art*, volume I, *Painters Born by 1815* (New York, 1965), are two cornerstones in any

17
(detail)

library of early American painting. The publication of Theodore E. Stebbins, Jr., *A History of American Drawings and Watercolors* (New York, scheduled for 1976), will fill an existing gap in the literature. Also note the biographical works by Groce and Wallace and by Fielding previously cited.

An early and still valuable reference work is the catalogue of topographical views presented in I. N. Phelps Stokes and Daniel C. Haskell, *American Historical Prints* (New York, 1932). Wendy J. Shadwell, *American Printmaking: The First 150 Years* (New York, 1969), is a sound general survey, and Clarence S. Brigham, *Paul Revere's Engravings* (Worcester, Massachusetts, 1954), is a detailed look at the work of the most famous, if not necessarily the best, colonial printmaker. Current scholarship is presented in an excellent series of published conference reports, beginning with John D. Morse (ed.), *Prints in and of America to 1850* (Charlottesville, Virginia, 1970), followed by Walter Muir Whitehill and Sinclair Hitchings (eds.), *Boston Prints and Printmakers 1670-1775* (Boston, 1973), and to be continued next year with the results of a 1974 session held at Colonial Williamsburg. Also see *Prints Pertaining to America* . . . and the works by Fielding and Stauffer listed above.

E. Alfred Jones, *The Old Silver of American Churches* (Letchworth, England, 1913), of enduring value because of its

treatment of some two thousand documented examples, and Francis Hill Bigelow, *Historic Silver of the Colonies and Its Makers* (New York, 1917), are representative of the best in early silver scholarship. John Marshall Phillips, the leading authority of his generation and a pioneer in the teaching of decorative arts, contributed a short but significant survey entitled *American Silver* (New York, 1949). Two more recent general accounts are Graham Hood, *American Silver* (New York, 1971), which concentrates on stylistic development, and Martha Gandy Fales, *Early American Silver for the Cautious Collector* (New York, 1970, revised edition 1973), a more comprehensive book, which includes an annotated bibliography. Two works completed within the last five years have become basic to any study of American silver: *American Silver, Garvan and Other Collections in the Yale University Art Gallery* (New Haven, Connecticut, 1970) by Kathryn C. Buhler and Graham Hood, and *American Silver 1655-1825 in the Museum of Fine Arts, Boston* (Greenwich, Connecticut, 1972) by Mrs. Buhler. Mrs. Buhler has also provided a documented study of craft organization in her introductory essay to *Colonial Silversmiths, Masters & Apprentices* (Boston, 1956). Of the few monographs on individual American craftsmen, the recent study of *Joseph Richardson and Family, Philadelphia Silversmiths* (Middletown, Connecticut,

1974) by Mrs. Fales is outstanding. The Department of American Decorative Arts and Sculpture in the Museum of Fine Arts has produced an excellent exhibition catalogue covering *Paul Revere's Boston: 1735-1818* (Boston, 1975), which brings together much of Revere's work.

Helen Comstock, *American Furniture: Seventeenth, Eighteenth, and Nineteenth Century Styles* (New York, 1962), is still the most generally used introduction to the study of American furniture. Peter Ward-Jackson, in his *English Furniture Designs of the Eighteenth Century* (London, 1958), has provided an annotated selection of the printed sources that form the background to American cabinetmaking. Many of the masterpieces of the era are included in Joseph Downs, *American Furniture, Queen Anne and Chippendale Periods* (New York, 1952), and Charles Montgomery, *American Furniture, the Federal Period* (New York, 1966), both catalogues of the Winterthur collection, and Richard H. Randall, Jr., *American Furniture in the Museum of Fine Arts, Boston* (Boston, 1965). Patricia E. Kane, *Three Hundred Years of American Seating Furniture: Chairs and Beds from the Mabel Brady Garvan and Other Collections at Yale University* (Boston, 1976), illustrates many examples and gives extensive information on eighteenth-century chairs. Regional variations in furniture are explored by John Kirk in his beautifully illustrated *American*

54
(detail)

Chairs: Queen Anne and Chippendale (New York, 1972), and Dean A. Fales, Jr., *American Painted Furniture, 1660–1880* (New York, 1972), examines a delightful class of American furniture. The Winterthur Conference Report for 1969, *Country Cabinetwork and Simple City Furniture* (Charlottesville, Virginia, 1969), contains important essays by leading scholars, and Walter Muir Whitehill, Brock Jobe, and Jonathan Fairbanks (eds.), *Boston Furniture of the Eighteenth Century* (Boston, 1974), is the best regional study. Biographical information on cabinetmakers can be found in the dictionary by Bjerkoe mentioned above.

Charles F. Montgomery, *A History of American Pewter* (New York, 1973), deals with the social, economic, and technical aspects of the pewterer's craft, and as the catalogue of the Winterthur collection, provides a history of form as well. Still a standard reference is the monumental work by Ledlie Laughlin previously mentioned.

An introductory study of the techniques and products of the brass founder is given in Henry J. Kauffman, *American Copper and Brass* (Camden, New Jersey, 1968), and in the more specialized *Early American Andirons and Other Fireplace Equipment* (Nashville, Tennessee, 1974) by Kauffman and Quentin H. Bowers.

While quality ceramics were imported into eighteenth-century America from England, Europe, and China, numerous native potters produced many handsome examples of redware and stoneware, which are discussed in Lura Woodside Watkins, *Early New England Potters and Their Wares* (Cambridge, Massachusetts, 1950), and Donald Blake Webster, *Decorated Stoneware Pottery of North America* (Rutland, Vermont, 1971). Edwin Atlee Barber deals with the colorful sgraffito wares of Pennsylvania in his *Tulip Ware of the Pennsylvania-German Potters* (Philadelphia, 1903), and a more recent regional study is John Bivins, Jr., *The Moravian Potters in North Carolina* (Chapel Hill, North Carolina, 1972). The results of the Winterthur Conference for 1972 were published as *Ceramics in America* (Charlottesville, Virginia, 1973), and Graham Hood has meticulously handled the archaeological and documentary evidence concerning America's first and only major eighteenth-century porcelain factory in *Bonnin and Morris of Philadelphia* (Chapel Hill, North Carolina, 1972).

For many years the standard works on American glass have been Helen and George S. McKearin, *American Glass* (New York, 1941) and *Two Hundred Years of American Blown Glass* (Garden City, New York, 1950). While much new material has been provided in articles in *Antiques*, *The Journal of Glass Studies* (published since 1959 by the Corning Museum of Glass) and elsewhere, these two pioneering works remain unsurpassed.

The major contribution made by American women to the art of 1750–1800 was in the area of needlework, and a vast literature of wildly uneven quality complicates the study of these pictures, samplers, bed hangings, coverlets, and quilts. Among the most useful works on needlework are Ethel Stanwood Bolton and Eva Johnston Coe, *American Samplers* (Boston, 1921), Mary Taylor Landon and Susan Burrows Swan, *American Crewelwork* (New York, 1970), and the excellent recent article by Anne Pollard Rowe, "Crewel Embroidered Bed Hangings in Old and New England," *Boston Museum Bulletin*, 71 (1973). Abbott Lowell Cummings (compiler), *Bed Hangings* (Boston 1961), remains a standard work, and contains a helpful glossary of materials. Quilts are extensively treated in Patsy and Myron Orlofsky, *Quilts in America* (New York, 1974), which can be supplemented with the numerous illustrations in Carleton L. Safford and Robert Bishop, *America's Quilts and Coverlets* (New York, 1972). A 1972 exhibition at Wadsworth Atheneum produced a superb catalogue entitled *Bed Ruggs/1722–1833* (Hartford, Connecticut, 1972). The basic source for printed fabrics is Florence M. Montgomery, *Printed Textiles: English and American Cottons and Linens, 1750–1850* (New York, 1970), which also contains an essential chapter, "Furnishing in American Homes."

Short Title List and List of Abbreviations

Allen, *American Book-Plates*
Charles Dexter Allen, *American Book-Plates*, New York and London, 1895.

***American Church Silver* (1911)**
American Church Silver of the Seventeenth and Eighteenth Centuries, with a Few Pieces of Domestic Plate, Museum of Fine Arts, Boston, 1911.

American Printmaking
American Printmaking: The First 150 Years, Museum of Graphic Arts, New York, 1969.

***American Silver* (1960)**
American Silver and Art Treasures, The English-Speaking Unions of the United States and the British Commonwealth, London, 1960.

***American Silversmiths* (1906)**
American Silver, the Work of Seventeenth and Eighteenth Century Silversmiths, Museum of Fine Arts, Boston, 1906.

Barber, *Tulip Ware*
Edwin Atlee Barber, *Tulip Ware of the Pennsylvania-German Potters: An Historical Sketch of the Art of Slip-Decoration in the United States*, Philadelphia, 1903.

Boston Prints
Walter Muir Whitehill and Sinclair Hitchings, eds. *Boston Prints and Printmakers 1670-1775*, Boston, 1973.

Buhler, *American Silver*
Kathryn C. Buhler, *American Silver, 1655–1825, in the Museum of Fine Arts, Boston*, Boston, 1972.

Buhler and Hood, *American Silver*
Kathryn C. Buhler and Graham Hood, *American Silver: Garvan and Other Collections in the Yale University Art Gallery*, New Haven, Conn., and London, 1970.

***Colonial Silversmiths* (1956)**
Colonial Silversmiths, Masters and Apprentices, Museum of Fine Arts, Boston, Boston, 1956.

***Connecticut Furniture* (1967)**
Connecticut Furniture: Seventeenth and Eighteenth Centuries, Wadsworth Atheneum, Hartford, Conn., 1967.

***Copley* (1965–1966)**
John Singleton Copley, 1738–1815, National Gallery of Art, Washington, D.C., 1965.

Fales, *Joseph Richardson*
Martha Gandy Fales, *Joseph Richardson and Family, Philadelphia Silversmiths*, Middletown, Conn., 1974.

Gardner and Feld, *American Paintings*
Albert Ten Eyck Gardner and Stuart P. Feld, *American Paintings: A Catalogue of the Collection of the Metropolitan Museum of Art*, New York, 1965.

27
(detail)

Garvan Prints (1931)
Exhibition of Prints Relating to American History: Being a Part of the Prints Contained in the Mabel Brady Garvan Collection of American Arts and Crafts at Yale University, The Library of Congress, Washington, D. C., 1931.

Gilbert Stuart (1967)
Gilbert Stuart: Portraitist of the Young Republic, 1755–1828, National Gallery of Art, Washington, D.C., 1967.

Girl Scout Loan Exhibition (1929)
Loan Exhibition of Eighteenth and Nineteenth Century Furniture and Glass . . . For the Benefit of the National Council of Girl Scouts, Inc., American Art Galleries, New York, 1929.

Guilland, *Folk Pottery*
Harold F. Guilland, *Early American Folk Pottery,* Philadelphia, 1971.

Halsey and Cornelius, *The American Wing*
R. T. H. Halsey and Charles O. Cornelius, *A Handbook of the American Wing,* 6th rev. ed., New York, 1938.

Halsey and Tower, *Homes of Our Ancestors*
R. T. H. Halsey and Elizabeth Tower, *The Homes of Our Ancestors,* Garden City, N.Y., 1935.

Hipkiss, *Karolik Collection*
Edwin J. Hipkiss, *Eighteenth-Century American Arts: The M. and M. Karolik Collection,* Cambridge, Mass., 1950.

Hood, *American Pewter*
Graham Hood, *American Pewter: Garvan and Other Collections at Yale,* New Haven, Conn., 1965.

Jaffe, *Trumbull*
Irma B. Jaffe, *John Trumbull: Patriot-Artist of the American Revolution,* Boston, 1975.

John Trumbull (1956)
John Trumbull, Painter-Patriot, Wadsworth Atheneum, Hartford, Conn., 1956.

Jones, *Old Silver*
E. Alfred Jones, *Old Silver of Europe and America from Early Times to the Nineteenth Century,* Philadelphia, 1928.

Kirk, *Early American Furniture*
John T. Kirk, *Early American Furniture,* New York, 1970.

Laughlin, *Pewter in America*
Ledlie I. Laughlin, *Pewter in America: Its Makers and Their Marks,* Boston and Barre, Mass., 1940–1971, 3 vols.

McKearin and McKearin, *American Blown Glass*
Helen and George S. McKearin, *Two Hundred Years of American Blown Glass,* Garden City, N.Y., 1950.

Miniatures (1927)
Catalogue of an Exhibition of Miniatures Painted in America, 1720–1850, Metropolitan Museum of Art, New York, 1927.

Montgomery, *American Pewter*
Charles F. Montgomery, *A History of American Pewter,* New York, 1973.

Mount, *Gilbert Stuart*
Charles Merrill Mount, *Gilbert Stuart, A Biography,* New York, 1964.

Nutting, *Furniture Treasury*
Wallace Nutting, *Furniture Treasury,* Framingham, Mass., 1928.

Paintings by Trumbull and Morse (1935)
Paintings by John Trumbull and Samuel Finley Breese Morse, Yale University Gallery of Fine Arts, New Haven, Conn., 1935.

Park, *Gilbert Stuart*
Lawrence Park, *Gilbert Stuart, An Illustrated Descriptive List of His Works,* New York, 1926.

Parker and Wheeler, *Copley Portraits*
Barbara N. Parker and Anne B. Wheeler, *John Singleton Copley: American Portraits,* Boston, 1938.

Paul Revere's Boston (1975)
Paul Revere's Boston, 1735–1818, Museum of Fine Arts, Boston, 1975.

Philadelphia Silver (1956)
Philadelphia Silver, 1682–1800, Philadelphia Museum of Art, Philadelphia, 1956.

Prown, *Copley*
Jules David Prown, *John Singleton Copley,* Cambridge, Mass., 1966, 2 vols.

Safford and Bishop, *Quilts and Coverlets*
Carleton L. Safford and Robert Bishop, *America's Quilts and Coverlets,* New York, 1972.

Sellers, *Portraits and Miniatures by Peale*
Charles Coleman Sellers, *Portraits and Miniatures by Charles Willson Peale,* Philadelphia, 1952.

Silver by New York Makers (1937–1938)
Silver by New York Makers, Late Seventeenth Century to 1900, Museum of the City of New York, New York, 1937.

Sizer, *Works of Trumbull*
Theodore Sizer, *The Works of Colonel John Trumbull, Artist of the American Revolution,* New Haven, Conn., 1967.

Sizer, ed., *Autobiography of Trumbull*
Theodore Sizer, ed., *The Autobiography of Colonel John Trumbull, Patriot-Artist, 1756–1843,* New Haven, Conn., 1953.

Stauffer, *American Engravers*
David McNeely Stauffer, *American Engravers on Copper and Steel,* New York, 1907.

Stokes and Haskell, *American Historical Prints*
I. N. Phelps Stokes and Daniel C. Haskell, *American Historical Prints, Early Views of American Cities, etc.,* New York, 1932.

Abbreviations

AAFA	American Academy of Fine Arts, New York, N.Y.
AIC	Art Institute of Chicago, Chicago, Ill.
BAFA	*Bulletin of the Associates in Fine Arts at Yale University*
BM	Brooklyn Museum, Brooklyn, N.Y.
CHS	Connecticut Historical Society, Hartford, Conn.
DIA	Detroit Institute of Arts, Detroit, Mich.
ESU	English-Speaking Unions of the United States and the British Commonwealth, London, England
L.	See "Laughlin" in Short Titles list.
LC	Library of Congress, Washington, D.C.
MCNY	Museum of the City of New York, New York, N.Y.
MFA	Museum of Fine Arts, Boston, Mass.
MGA	Museum of Graphic Art, New York, N.Y.
MIA	Minneapolis Institute of the Arts, Minneapolis, Minn.
MMA	Metropolitan Museum of Art, New York, N.Y.
MMAB	*Metropolitan Museum of Art Bulletin*
NG	National Gallery of Art, Washington, D.C.
NPG	National Portrait Gallery, Washington, D.C.
PAFA	Pennsylvania Academy of the Fine Arts, Philadelphia, Pa.
PCCA	*Bulletin of the Pewter Collectors' Club of America*
PMA	Philadelphia Museum of Art, Philadelphia, Pa.
PMHB	*Pennsylvania Magazine of History and Biography*
RISD	Museum of Art at the Rhode Island School of Design, Providence, R.I.
VMFA	Virginia Museum of Fine Arts, Richmond, Va.
WA	Wadsworth Atheneum, Hartford, Conn.
WM	Whitney Museum of American Art, New York, N.Y.
YUAG	Yale University Art Gallery, New Haven, Conn.

Measurement Abbreviations

D.	Depth
DIAM.	Diameter
H.	Height
L.	Length
O.D.	Overall depth
O.H.	Overall height
O.L.	Overall length
O.W.	Overall width
S.H.	Seat height
W.	Width
WT.	Weight

Catalogue: Paintings, Drawings and Watercolors

1
John Smibert, 1688–1751
Nathaniel Byfield (1653–1733)
1730. Oil on canvas.
H. 30″ (76.2 cm); w. 25″ (63.5 cm).

Inscription: "Ætatis 78. 1730", lower left (age incorrect; possibly inscribed at a later date).
Replicas: See Henry Wilder Foote, *John Smibert, Painter* (Cambridge, Mass., 1950), p. 141.
Provenance: Sir William Pepperell, Kittery Point, Me.; the Sparhawk-Jarvis-Cutts family; Mrs. Mary C. King, Montclair, N.J. (1919); purchased by Charles Allen Munn (1919–1924).
Exhibitions: Newark Museum, N.J., *Early American Portraits* (1947), no. 28. YUAG, *The Smibert Tradition* (1949), no. 9. Baltimore Museum of Art, Md., *Man and His Years (Art and Aging)* (1954), no. 48.
Bibliography: Henry Wilder Foote, *John Smibert, Painter* (Cambridge, Mass., 1950), pp. 54ff., 140–141. Gardner and Feld, *American Paintings*, I, 2–3, illus. p. 2. John Smibert, *The Notebook of John Smibert. With Essays by Sir David Evans, John Kerslake, and Andrew Oliver* (Boston, 1969), pp. 88, 105.
Lender: The Metropolitan Museum of Art, New York, N.Y.; bequest of Charles Allen Munn, 1924. 24.109.87.

2
Robert Feke, ca. 1707–ca. 1752
William Bowdoin (1713–1773)
1748. Oil on canvas.
H. 50 1/4″ (140.3 cm); w. 40 1/4″ (114.9 cm).

Signature: "R F Pinx / 1748", lower left.
Provenance: William Bowdoin, Boston, Mass. (1748–1773); his daughter, Mrs. Sarah Bowdoin

Dearborn (1773–1826).
Exhibitions: MMA, *Colonial Portraits* (1911), no. 24, illus. facing p. 56. Newport Historical Society, *Rhode Island Tercentenary Retrospective Exhibition* (1936). BM, *Face of America* (1967–68), no. 2.
Bibliography: Henry Wilder Foote, *Robert Feke, Colonial Portrait Painter* (Cambridge, Mass., 1930), pp. 73, 129–130. Marvin S. Sadik, *Colonial and Federal Portraits at Bowdoin College*, Bowdoin College Museum of Art (Brunswick, Me., 1966), pp. 52–55, illus. p. 53. R. Peter Mooz, "The Art of Robert Feke" (Ph.D. diss., University of Pennsylvania, 1970).
Lender: Bowdoin College Museum of Art, Brunswick, Me.; bequest of Mrs. Sarah Bowdoin Dearborn. 1826.10.

3
John Greenwood, 1727–1792
Sea Captains Carousing in Surinam
Ca. 1752–1758. Oil on bed ticking.
H. 37 3/4″ (95.8 cm); w. 75 1/4″ (191 cm).

Signature: "J. Greenwood Pinxit 17—", lower left.
Provenance: Descended in the Jenckes family, Rhode Island; to Mary Jenckes Wild, Rhode Island (ca. 1820); Arthur Cushing, Providence, R.I. (1943); Richard Morrison, Boston, Mass. (until 1948).
Exhibitions: Addison Gallery of American Art, Andover, Mass., *John Greenwood in America, 1745–52* (1943), pp. 47, 71, fig. 37. AIC, *From Colony to Nation* (1949), no. 59, illus. p. 18. MFA, *The Rathbone Years: Masterpieces Acquired for The Museum of Fine Arts, Boston, 1955–1972, and for The St. Louis Art Museum, 1940–1955* (1972), no. 173, illus. p. 198. NPG, *In the Minds*

and Hearts of the People: Prologue to Revolution (1974) (not in catalogue).
Bibliography: Frank Weitenkampf, "John Greenwood: An American-Born Artist in 18th Century Europe, with a Checklist of His Etchings and Mezzotints," *Bulletin of the New York Public Library*, 31, no. 8 (1927), pp. 623–634. "An Eighteenth-Century Tavern 'Conversation Piece'," *Connoisseur*, 123, no. 512 (1949), pp. 113–114, illus. p. 113.
Lender: The St. Louis Art Museum, St. Louis, Mo. 256:48.

4
Joseph Badger, 1708–1765
Mrs. John Edwards (Abigail Fowle, 1679–1760)
Ca. 1750–1760. Oil on canvas.
H. 47″ (119.4 cm); w. 36″ (91.4 cm).

Provenance: Descendants of Mrs. John Edwards; her great-grandson, Thomas Carter Smith; his daughter, Frances Barnard Townsend; her son, Dr. Charles Wendell Townsend, Boston, (until 1924).
Exhibitions: RISD, *Old and New England* (1945), no. 8, illus. p. 15. AIC, *From Colony to Nation* (1949), no. 19. DIA, *Painting in America, The Story of 450 Years* (1957), no. 21.
Bibliography: Lawrence Park, "An Account of Joseph Badger, and a Descriptive List of His Work," *Massachusetts Historical Society Proceedings*, 51 (1918): 164. Frank W. Bayley, *Five Colonial Artists* (Boston, 1929), illus. p. 21 (misidentified as "Mrs. Jonathan Edwards, née Sarah Pierepont [sic]"). MFA, *American Paintings in the Museum of Fine Arts, Boston* (Boston, 1969), vol. I, no. 80; vol. II, fig. 13.
Lender: Museum of Fine Arts, Boston, Mass.; gift of Dr. Charles Wendell Townsend. 24.421.

5
Joseph Blackburn, active in
America, 1754–1763
Susan Apthorp (Mrs. Thomas
Bulfinch, 1734–1815)
1757. Oil on canvas.
H. 50″ (127 cm); w. 40″ (101.6 cm).

Signature: "I. Blackburn Pinxit
1757", left center.
Provenance: J. Templeman Cool-
idge, Jr., Boston, Mass. (1895–
1945).
Exhibitions: Copley Hall, Boston,
Mass., *Portraits of Women* (1895),
no. 25. Copley Society, Boston,
Mass., *Portraits by American
Painters before the Revolution*
(1922), no. 18. MFA, *One Hundred
Colonial Portraits* (1930), no. 7,
fig. 7. Colorado Springs Fine Arts
Center, *Likeness of America,
1680–1820* (1949), no. 8, illus. no. 6.
Bibliography: Lawrence Park,
*Joseph Blackburn, a Colonial
Portrait Painter* (Worcester,
Mass., 1923), no. 5, pp. 15–16.
Theodore Bolton and Harry L.
Binsse, "An American Artist of
Formula, Joseph Blackburn,"
Antiquarian, 15, no. 5 (1930),
p. 88. MFA, *American Paintings
in the Museum of Fine Arts,
Boston* (Boston, 1969), vol. I,
no. 196; vol. II, fig. 26.
Lender: Museum of Fine Arts,
Boston, Mass.; gift of Mr. and
Mrs. J. Templeman Coolidge.
45.517.

6
Jeremiah Theüs, 1719–1774
Elizabeth Rothmaler (Mrs. John
Waites, later Mrs. Paul Trapier;
dates unknown)
1757. Oil on canvas.
H. 29 7/8″ (75.9 cm); w. 25″ (63.5
cm).

Signature: "Jh Theus. [mono-
gram] 1757", lower left.

Provenance: Elizabeth Rothmaler,
Georgetown, S.C. (until her
death); her son, Thomas Waites
(until 1860); his daughter, Mrs.
Orlando Savage Rees; her son,
Francis Rees; youngest child of
Francis Rees (until 1923).
Exhibitions: Art Gallery, University of Minnesota, Minne-
apolis, Minn., *Survey of Colonial
and Provincial Painting* (1939),
no. 37, illus. p. 14. Baltimore Museum of Art, Md., *Age of Elegance: The Rococo and Its Effect*
(1959), no. 419. North Carolina
Museum of Art, Raleigh, *Carolina
Charter Tercentenary Exhibition*
(1963), no. 33, illus. p. 51. BM,
Face of America (1967–1968),
no. 6, fig. 13.
Bibliography: William Dunlap,
*A History of the Rise and Prog-
ress of the Arts of Design in the
United States* (New York, 1834;
reprint, New York, 1969), I, 31.
John Hill Morgan, "Notes on
Jeremiah Theüs and His Portrait
of Elizabeth Rothmaler," *Brook-
lyn Museum Quarterly*, 11, no. 2
(1924), pp. 47–54. Margaret
Simons Middleton, *Jeremiah
Theüs: Colonial Artist of Charles
Town* (Columbia, S.C., 1953),
p. 162, illus. p. 102.
Lender: The Brooklyn Museum,
Brooklyn, N.Y.; Carll H. DeSilver
Fund. 23.61.

7
Benjamin West, 1738–1820
Self-Portrait
1756. Watercolor on ivory (in
silver locket).
Oval: H. 2 1/2″ (6.5 cm);
w. 1 13/16″ (4.7 cm).

Inscription: "Benjⁿ West, / Aged
18 / Painted by himself / in the
Year 1756 / & presented to Miss
Steele / of Philadelphia", on
back of locket.

Provenance: Gift of the artist to
Elizabeth Steele (later Mrs. Wal-
lace), Philadelphia, Pa. (1756); her
daughter, Mrs. John Cook, Phila-
delphia, Pa.; her husband, John
Cook, Philadelphia, Pa.; sold
to the artist's nephew, Joseph
West (ca. 1850); his daughter,
Mrs. Edward Wilcox (1885);
Colonel Cornelius De W. Wilcox,
West Point, N.Y.; purchased by
Mrs. John Hill Morgan, Farming-
ton, Conn. (1924–1940).
Exhibitions: PAFA, *Sixth Annual
Exhibition* (1817), no. 87. MMA,
Miniatures (1927), p. 56. BM, *Five
Centuries of Miniature Painting*
(1936), no. 257.
Bibliography: Harry B. Wehle,
American Miniatures, 1730–1850
(New York, 1927), p. 16. William
Sawitzky, "The American Work
of Benjamin West," *PMHB*, 62,
no. 4 (1938), pp. 452–453, fig. 14.
Ann C. van Devanter, "Benjamin
West and His Self-Portraits,"
Antiques, 103, no. 4 (1973), pp.
764–765, fig. 1.
Lender: Yale University Art Gal-
lery; the Lelia A. and John Hill
Morgan Collection. 1940.529.

8
Benjamin West, 1738–1820
Thomas Mifflin (1744–1800)
Ca. 1758–1759. Oil on canvas.
H. 48 1/8″ (122.2 cm); w. 36 1/4″
(92 cm).

Provenance: Thomas Mifflin,
Philadelphia, Pa. (ca. 1758/59–
1800); his descendants; William
Mifflin, Philadelphia, Pa. (until
1910).
Exhibitions: PMA, *Benjamin
West, 1738–1820* (1938), no. 9,
fig. 9. Pennsylvania State Uni-
versity, State College, *Centennial
Exhibition* (1955), no. 4. BM,
Face of America (1967–1968),

no. 14, fig. 14. PAFA, *Philadelphia
Painting and Printing to 1776*
(1971), no. 33.
Bibliography: Theodore Bolton
and Harry L. Binsse, "Wollaston,
An Early Portrait Manufacturer,"
Antiquarian, 16, no. 6 (1931), pp.
50–52 (discussed as a Wollaston).
William Sawitzky, "The American
Work of Benjamin West," *PMHB*,
62, no. 4 (1938), pp. 443–445,
457–458, fig. 21. Nicholas Wainwright, *Paintings and Miniatures
at the Historical Society of Pennsylvania* (Philadelphia, 1974),
pp. 174–175, illus. p. 37.
Lender: The Historical Society of
Pennsylvania, Philadelphia, Pa.

9
John Singleton Copley, 1738–1815
*Book of Anatomical Drawings,
Plate* IX
1756. Ink and red crayon on
white paper.
H. 10 3/4″ (27.3 cm); w. 17 1/16″
(43.3 cm).

Provenance: John Singleton
Copley, Boston, Mass. (1756–1774),
and London (1774–1815); his
widow, Mrs. John Singleton
Copley, London (1815–1836); her
son, John Singleton Copley, Jr.,
The Rt. Hon. the Lord Lynd-
hurst, London (1836–1863);
probably sold at Lyndhurst
Library Sale (no. 676) at Christie,
Manson and Woods, London
(1864).
Exhibitions: NG, *Copley* (1965–
1966), no. 3.
Bibliography: Laurence Binyon,
*Catalogue of Drawings by British
Artists and Artists of Foreign
Origin Working in Great Britain,
Preserved in the Department of
Prints and Drawings in the
British Museum* (London, 1898–
1907), I, 247–248. Jules David
Prown, "An 'Anatomy Book' by

John Singleton Copley," *Art Quarterly*, 26, no. 1 (1963), pp. 31–46, fig. 14; *Copley*, I, 18–19, 235.
Lender: The British Museum, London.

10
John Singleton Copley, 1738–1815
The Reverend Samuel Fayerweather (1725–1781)
Ca. 1758. Oil on copper.
H. 3″ (7.6 cm); w. 2 1/2″ (6.4 cm).

Provenance: Descendants of Rev. Samuel Fayerweather; to Edward D. Harris, Cambridge, Mass., and Yonkers, N.Y. (1873–1915); Childs Gallery, Boston, Mass. (1948).
Exhibitions: MMA, *Four Centuries of Miniature Painting* (1950). MFA, *New England Miniatures, 1750–1850* (1957), no. 59, fig. 16. NG, *Copley* (1965–1966), no. 11, illus. p. 27.
Bibliography: Augustus Thorndike Perkins, *A Sketch of the Life and a List of the Works of John Singleton Copley* (Boston, 1873), pp. 53–54. Parker and Wheeler, *Copley Portraits*, p. 260. Prown, *Copley*, I, 30, 105, 156–57, 214, fig. 74.
Lender: Yale University Art Gallery; Mabel Brady Garvan Collection. 1948.69.

11
John Singleton Copley, 1738–1815
Epes Sargent (1690–1762)
1759–1761. Oil on canvas.
H. 49 7/8″ (126.7 cm); w. 40″ (101.8 cm).

Provenance: Descendants of Epes Sargent, Gloucester and Boston, Mass.; to Epes Sargent IV; the sitter's great-great-grandson, John James Dixwell, Boston, Mass. (1871–1876); his daughter, Mrs. George H. Clements, Boston,

Mass. and New York, N.Y. (1876–ca. 1930); her daughter, Mrs. Oswald Whitman Knauth, New York, N.Y. (ca. 1930–ca. 1940); her son, Arnold Whitman Knauth II, New York, N.Y., and Rockport, Mass. (ca. 1940–1958); Milch Gallery, New York, N.Y. (1958); Hirschl and Adler Gallery, New York, N.Y. (until 1959).
Exhibitions: World's Columbian Exhibition, Chicago, *American Retrospective Art* (1893), no. 203. MMA, *The Hudson Fulton Celebration Exhibition* (1909), vol. 2, no. 8, illus. facing p. 6. AIC, *From Colony to Nation* (1949), no. 29, illus. p. 34. NG, *Copley* (1965–1966), no. 14, illus. p. 30.
Bibliography: Charles Sprague Sargent and Emma Worcester Sargent, *Epes Sargent of Gloucester and His Descendants* (Boston, 1923). Parker and Wheeler, *Copley Portraits*, pp. 171–172, pl. 21. Prown, *Copley*, I, 33, 113, 190–191, 227–228, fig. 89.
Lender: National Gallery of Art, Washington, D.C.; gift of the Avalon Foundation, 1959.

12
John Singleton Copley, 1738–1815
Mrs. Thomas Boylston (Sarah Morecock, 1696–1774)
1766. Oil on canvas.
H. 50 5/8″ (128.6 cm); w. 40 1/4″ (102.3 cm).

Signature: "Jnᵒ S. Copley / pinx 1766", middle right.
Provenance: Mrs. Thomas Boylston, Boston, Mass. (1766–1774); her son, Thomas Boylston, Boston, Mass. (1774–1798); his nephew, Ward Nicholas Boylston, Princeton, Mass. (1798 until 1828).
Exhibitions: MFA, *John Singleton Copley, 1738–1815* (1938), no. 12. NG, *Copley* (1965–1966), no. 30, color pl. 4. Fogg Art Museum,

Cambridge, Mass., *American Art at Harvard* (1972), no. 7, illus.
Bibliography: Laura Huntsinger, *Harvard Portraits* (Cambridge, Mass., 1936), ed. Alan Burroughs, pp. 25–26. Parker and Wheeler, *Copley Portraits*, p. 47, pl. 69. Prown, *Copley*, I, 54, 104, 142–143, 210, fig. 178.
Lender: Harvard University Portrait Collection, Cambridge, Mass.; bequest of Ward N. Boylston, 1828. H 16.

13
John Singleton Copley, 1738–1815
Isaac Smith (1719–1787)
1769. Oil on canvas.
H. 49 1/4″ (125 cm); w. 39 1/2″ (100.4 cm).

Provenance: Isaac Smith, Boston, Mass. (1769–1787); probably his son, Isaac Smith, Boston (1873–1885); William Smith Carter, New York, N.Y. (1915); Theodore Parkman Carter, Paris, France (1938; on loan to the Metropolitan Museum of Art, New York, N.Y.); M. Knoedler and Co., Inc., New York, N.Y. (1940).
Exhibitions: MMA, *Colonial Portraits* (1911), no. 21. NG, *Copley* (1965–1966), no. 39, color pl. 7.
Bibliography: Frank Bayley, *The Life and Works of John Singleton Copley* (Boston, 1915), p. 229. Parker and Wheeler, *Copley Portraits* (Boston, 1938), pp. 183–184, pl. 96. Prown, *Copley*, I, 68–70, 114, 142–143, 182–183, 192–193, 229, fig. 255.
Lender: Yale University Art Gallery; gift of Maitland Fuller Griggs, B.A. 1896, L.H.D. 1938. 1941.73.

14
John Singleton Copley, 1738–1815
Mrs. Isaac Smith (Elizabeth

Storer, 1726–1786)
1769. Oil on canvas.
H. 50 1/8″ (127.3 cm); w. 40 1/8″ (101.9 cm).

Provenance: Same as its pendant, no. 13.
Exhibitions: MMA, *Colonial Portraits* (1911), no. 22. NG, *Copley* (1965–1966), no. 40, illus. p. 57.
Bibliography: Frank Bayley, *The Life and Works of John Singleton Copley* (Boston, 1915), p. 228. Parker and Wheeler, *Copley Portraits*, p. 184, pl. 97. Prown, *Copley*, I, 68–71, 114, 142–143, 182–183, 192–193, 229, fig. 256.
Lender: Yale University Art Gallery; gift of Maitland Fuller Griggs, B.A. 1896, L.H.D. 1938. 1941.74.

15
John Singleton Copley, 1738–1815
Mrs. Joseph Barrell (Hannah Fitch, 1753–1777)
Ca. 1771. Pastel on paper mounted on linen.
H. 23″ (58.4 cm); w. 17 1/4″ (43.8 cm).

Provenance: Descended in the family of Mrs. Benjamin Joy, the sitter's daughter, to Mrs. Charles Joy, Boston, Mass. (1915–1930); Benjamin Joy, Boston, Mass. (1939–1952).
Exhibitions: MFA, *One Hundred Colonial Portraits* (1930), no. 10, fig. 10. NG, *Copley* (1965–1966), no. 33, illus. p. 52.
Bibliography: Parker and Wheeler, *Copley Portraits*, p. 218. Prown, *Copley*, I, 66–68, 103, 162–163, 208, fig. 233. MFA, *American Paintings in the Museum of Fine Arts, Boston* (Boston, 1969), vol. I, no. 289; vol. II, fig. 75.
Lender: Museum of Fine Arts, Boston, Mass.; gift of Benjamin Joy. 52.1472.

16
John Singleton Copley, 1738–1815
Self-Portrait
1769. Watercolor on ivory.
Oval: H. 1 1/2″ (3.8 cm); w. 1 1/8″
(2.9 cm).

Signature: "JSC [monogram]
1769", lower right.
Provenance: John Singleton Copley, Boston, Mass. (1769–1774),
and London (1774–1815); Mrs.
Gardiner Greene, Boston, Mass.;
the artist's great-grandson, Rev.
John Singleton Copley Greene,
Sr., Boston, Mass. (1873); his
daughter, Mary Amory Copley
Greene, Boston, Mass.; her
nephew, Henry Copley Greene,
Cambridge, Mass. (1915–1957);
Katrine Rosalind Copley Greene,
New York, N.Y. (1966).
Exhibitions: MMA, *Miniatures*
(1927), p. 23 [illus.]. MFA, *John
Singleton Copley, 1738–1815*
(1938), no. 92, color illus. on
cover; *New England Miniatures,
1750–1850* (1957), no. 44, fig. 1 and
color fig. 12.
Bibliography: Harry Wehle and
Theodore Bolton, *American
Miniatures, 1730–1850* (New
York, 1927), pp. 24–25, pl. 9.
Parker and Wheeler, *Copley Portraits*, pp. 243–244, pl. 129. Prown,
Copley, I, 68, 105, 150–153, 212,
fig. 250.
Lender: Mr. and Mrs. H. Gordon
Sweet. On indefinite loan to the
Yale University Art Gallery.
2.6.1972.

17
John Durand, active 1766–1782
Richard Crossfield (dates unknown)
Ca. 1769 or ca. 1772. Oil on canvas.
H. 50 1/4″ (127.6 cm); w. 34 1/2″
(87.6 cm).

Provenance: Descendants of
Richard Crossfield; sold by the
family to an anonymous dealer
(1965); purchased by Edgar William and Bernice Chrysler Garbisch, New York, N.Y. (1966–
1969).
Exhibitions: Grand Palais, Paris,
*Peintures naïves américaines,
XVIIᵉ XIXᵉ siècles: Cent onze
tableaux de la Collection Edgar
William et Bernice Chrysler Garbisch* (1968), no. 13, illus. p. 29.
Bibliography: William Dunlap, *A
History of the Rise and Progress
of the Arts of Design in the
United States* (New York, 1834;
reprint, New York, 1969), I, 144–
145. Gardner and Feld, *American
Paintings*, I, 55–56. "Recent
Acquisitions," *Antiques*, 99, no. 3
(1971), illus. p. 344.
Lender: The Metropolitan Museum of Art, New York, N.Y.; gift
of Edgar William and Bernice
Chrysler Garbisch, 1969. 69.279.2.

18
Matthew Pratt, 1734–1805
The American School
1765. Oil on canvas.
H. 36″ (91.5 cm); w. 50 1/4″ (127.6
cm).

Signature: "M. Pratt / ad. 1765.",
lower left of painting on the easel.
Provenance: Matthew Pratt, New
York, N.Y. (1765–1805); descended
in artist's family; Mrs. Rosalie V.
Tiers Jackson (1888); purchased
by Samuel P. Avery, New York,
N.Y. (1896–1897).
Exhibitions: Society of Artists of
Great Britain, London, *Spring
Gardens Exhibition* (1766), no.
130. PAFA (1811), no. 105 (as
"School of West"); *Loan Exhibition of Historical Portraits* (1887–
1888), no. 459 (as "West's School
of Painters in London"). MMA,
*Retrospective Exhibition of
American Painting* (1896), no.
241; *Life in America* (1939), no.
18. PMA, *Benjamin West* (1938),
no. 63. Tate Gallery, London,
American Painting (1946),
no. 169.
Bibliography: William Sawitzky,
Matthew Pratt, 1734–1805 (New
York, 1942), pp. 10, 35–38, pl. 6.
Gardner and Feld, *American
Paintings*, I, 20–22, illus. p. 21.
Lender: The Metropolitan Museum of Art, New York, N.Y.;
gift of Samuel P. Avery, 1897.
1897.29.3.

19
Benjamin West, 1738–1820
Agrippina Landing at Brundisium with the Ashes of Germanicus
1768. Oil on canvas.
H. 64 1/2″ (163.8 cm); w. 94 1/2″
(230 cm).

Signature: "B. West Pinxit: 1768",
lower center.
Replicas: A small preliminary
sketch, dated 1766, is now in the
Philadelphia Museum of Art. For
other replicas, see article by
Staley cited below in Bibliography.
Provenance: Commissioned by
Dr. Robert Drummond, Archbishop of York, England (1768);
Silberman Galleries, New York,
N.Y. (1947); purchased by Louis
M. Rabinowitz, New York, N.Y.
(1947).
Exhibitions: High Museum of
Art, Atlanta, Ga. (1947). Columbus Gallery of Fine Arts, Ohio,
The Colonial Americas (1947),
no. 23. Cleveland Museum of Art,
Ohio, *Neo-Classicism: Style and
Motif* (1964), no. 76, [illus.].
Bibliography: Grose Evans, *Benjamin West and the Taste of His
Times* (Carbondale, Ill., 1959),
pp. 5, 21, 44, 50, pl. 1. Allen
Staley, "The Landing of Agrippina at Brundisium with the
Ashes of Germanicus," *Philadelphia Museum of Art Bulletin*, 61
(1965–1966): 10–19, illus. p. 11.
David Irwin, *English Neoclassical
Art* (London, 1966), pp. 48–51, pl.
38.
Lender: Yale University Art Gallery; gift of Louis M. Rabinowitz.
1947.16.

20
Benjamin West, 1738–1820
The Death of General Wolfe
1771. Oil on canvas.
H. 60 1/2″ (153.7 cm); w. 96 1/2″
(245.1 cm). There are additions
by West in this second version of
about 6 1/2″ on the left and about
6 1/2″ on the right, containing details not included in the first
version.
Replicas: The first version, signed
and dated 1770, is now in the

19
(detail)

National Gallery of Canada, Ottawa. For the most recent published discussion of the location of later replicas, see *Benjamin West, 1738–1820* (exhibition catalogue, Philadelphia Museum of Art, 1938), no. 20.
Provenance: Commissioned by King George III in 1771; in continuous possession of the British royal family (located in the Warm Room, Buckingham House, London, until Sept. 18, 1833, when it was removed to Hampton Court).
Exhibitions: Philadelphia, Pa., *Centennial Exhibition* (1876).
Bibliography: John Galt, *The Life, Studies and Works of Benjamin West, Esq., President of the Royal Academy of London* (London, 1820), II, 46–50, 207, 216. Edgar Wind, "The Revolution of History Painting," *Journal of the Warburg Institute*, 2 (1938–1939): 116–127. Charles Mitchell, "Benjamin West's 'Death of General Wolfe' and the Popular History Piece," *Journal of the Warburg and Courtauld Institutes*, 7, nos. 1–2 (1944), pp. 20–33. Edgar Wind, "Penny, West, and the 'Death of Wolfe,' " *Journal of the Warburg and Courtauld Institutes*, 10, nos. 3–4 (1947), pp. 159–162. Oliver Millar, *The Late Georgian Pictures in the Collection of Her Majesty the Queen* (London, 1969), vol. I, no. 1167.
Lender: Her Majesty the Queen.

21
Benjamin West, 1738–1820
The Artist's Family
1772 or 1773. Oil on canvas.
H. 20 1/2″ (52 cm); w. 26 1/4″ (66.7 cm).

Signature: "B West / 1772", middle right.
Provenance: Benjamin West,

London (ca. 1772–1820); descended in the artist's family to Aubyn Margary; with Thomas Agnew and Sons, London (1964).
Exhibitions: Royal Academy, London, *English Paintings 1700–1850* (1964–1965), no. 146, pl. 67. YUAG, *American Art from Alumni Collections* (1968), no. 8, (illus.). NG, *American Self-Portraits, 1670–1973* (1974), no. 5, illus. p. 25.
Bibliography: Charles Henry Hart, "Benjamin West's Family: The American President of the Royal Academy of Arts Not a Quaker," *PMHB*, 32 (1908): 1–33. Ann C. van Devanter, "Benjamin West and His Self-Portraits," *Antiques*, 103, no. 4 (1973), pp. 764–773, color pl. 2.
Lender: Collection of Mr. and Mrs. Paul Mellon.

22
Benjamin West, 1738–1820
The Three Sisters
1783. Pen and India ink wash drawing on paper.
H. 14 3/16″ (36 cm); w. 11″ (27.9 cm).

Signature: "Benj. West / 1783.", lower right.
Inscription: "The Three Sisters", lower center.
Provenance: Alden Galleries, Kansas City, Mo.
Exhibitions: DIA, *History of American Drawing from the Seventeenth Century to the Present* (1948).
Bibliography: Charles Eli Slatkin and Regina Shoolman, *Treasury of American Drawings* (New York, 1947), pp. 7–9, fig. 13. Ruth S. Kraemer, *Drawings by Benjamin West*, The Pierpont Morgan Library (New York, 1975).
Lender: Nelson Gallery–Atkins Museum, Kansas City, Mo.; Nelson Fund. 33–276.

23
John Singleton Copley, 1738–1815
Head of a Negro
1777–1783. Oil on canvas.
H. 21″ (53.3 cm); w. 16 1/4″ (41.3 cm).

Provenance: John Singleton Copley, London (1783–1815); his widow, Mrs. John Singleton Copley, London (1815–1836); her son, John Singleton Copley, Jr., The Rt. Hon. the Lord Lyndhurst, London (1836–1863); Lyndhurst Sale at Christie, Manson and Woods, London (March 5, 1864) [69], to Isaac for 11.11.0; J.W. Burnett Sale, Christie, London (May 23–24, 1938) [217], to Mann; sold at Christie, London (Feb. 24, 1951) [102], to Mason; M. Knoedler & Co., New York, N.Y. (1951).
Exhibitions: NGA, *Copley* (1965–1966), no. 69, fig. 69.
Bibliography: Bayley, *Copley*, pp. 34, 36, 184. Edgar P. Richardson, " 'Head of a Negro' by John Singleton Copley," *Art Quarterly*, 15, no. 4 (1952), pp. 351–52, illus. Prown, *Copley*, II, 274, 402, 433, fig. 381.
Lender: The Detroit Institute of Arts, Detroit, Mich.; Gibbs-Williams Fund. 52.118.

24
John Singleton Copley, 1738–1815
The Death of the Earl of Chatham
1779–1781. Oil on canvas.
H. 90″ (228.6 cm); w. 121″ (307.3 cm).

Provenance: John Singleton Copley, London (1781–1788); sale at Christie, London (April 8, 1788), no. 93; Alexander Davison (1806); Earl of Liverpool (1823–1828). National Gallery, London (1828–1929).

Exhibitions: British Institution, London (1806–1807), no. 16; (1817), no. 36; (1820), no. 52. MMA, *An Exhibition of Paintings by John Singleton Copley* (1936–1937), no. 38. NG, *Copley* (1965–1966), no. 70, illus. p. 97.
Bibliography: Bayley, *Copley*, pp. 16–17, 76. Prown, *Copley*, II, 275–291, 437–440, figs. 392–415, 417.
Lender: The Trustees of the Tate Gallery, London. 100.

25
John Singleton Copley, 1738–1815
Study for the Central Group for "The Death of the Earl of Chatham"
1779. Black and white chalk on gray-blue paper.
H. 10 1/4″ (26 cm); w. 12 7/16″ (31.6 cm).

Provenance: John Singleton Copley, London (1779–1815); his wife, Mrs. John Singleton Copley, London (1815–1836); her son, John Singleton Copley, Jr., The Rt. Hon. the Lord Lyndhurst, London (1836–1863); Lyndhurst Library Sale at Christie, Manson and Woods, London (Feb. 26–27, 1864) [probably no. 664]; purchased by Sir Edward Basil Jupp, London (1864–1878).
Bibliography: Oskar Hagen, *The Birth of the American Tradition in Art* (New York, 1940), fig. 112. Helen Comstock, "Drawings by John Singleton Copley in the Karolik Collection," *Connoisseur*, 109, no. 6 (1942), pp. 150–153; "Drawings by John Singleton Copley," *Panorama*, 2 (Harry Shaw Newman Gallery, New York), no. 5 (1947), pp. 97–108. Prown, *Copley*, II, 281, 439, fig. 401.
Lender: The British Museum, London.

26
John Singleton Copley, 1738–1815
*Study for Lord Mansfield for
"The Death of the Earl of
Chatham"*
1779–1780. Black and white chalk
on gray paper.
H. 27 7/8" (70.8 cm); W. 18 7/8"
(47.9 cm).

Inscriptions: "Lord Mansfield",
upper center; "Top of the fore-
head, Eye, Nose, Mouth, Chin",
scaled on left; "Scale of 2 feet—
Lord Mansfield", lower center.
Provenance: John Singleton Copley, London (1780–1815); his
widow, Mrs. John Singleton Copley, London (1815–1836); her son,
John Singleton Copley, Jr., The
Rt. Hon. the Lord Lyndhurst,
London (1836–63); Lyndhurst
Library Sale at Christie, Manson
and Woods, London (Feb. 26–27,
1864) [probably no. 664]; pur-
chased by Sir Edward Basil Jupp,
London (1864–1883); purchased
from Jupp Collection, London
(1883).
Exhibitions: MMA, *Franklin and
His Circle* (1936), no. 87. MFA,
John Singleton Copley, 1738–1815
(1938), no. 119. The Iveagh Be-
quest, Kenwood, London, *The
True Resemblance of Lord Mans-
field* (1971).
Bibliography: *Massachusetts Law
Quarterly*, 25, no. 1 (1940), p. 35.
Prown, *Copley*, II, 285, 439, fig.
406.
Lender: The Boston Athenaeum,
Boston, Mass.

27
Samuel King, 1748/49–1819
Ezra Stiles (1727–1795)
1770–1771. Oil on canvas.
H. 33 1/2" (85.1 cm); W. 27 1/2"
(69.9 cm).

Signature: "Sam¹ King Pinx /
.1770–", lower left (at base of
column) and "Sam¹ King / Pinx.

1771", lower left.
Inscribed: "EZRA STILES D. D. / AE.
44. 1771", lower left.
Provenance: Ezra Stiles, New
Haven, Conn. (1771–1795); his
descendants to Mrs. Charles C.
Foote, New Haven, Conn. (1901);
her son, Dr. Charles Jenkins
Foote, New Haven, Conn. (until
1955).
Exhibitions: YUAG, "Ezra Stiles
of Yale" (1957). University Art
Museum, Berkeley, Calif., *The
Hand and the Spirit* (1972), no. 8,
illus. fig. 8. NG, *In the Minds
and Hearts of the People* (1974),
color illus. p. 139.
Bibliography: Josephine Setze,
"Ezra Stiles of Yale," *Antiques*,
72, no. 4 (1957), pp. 348–351,
illus. p. 349. Edmund Sears Morgan, *The Gentle Puritan: A Life
of Ezra Stiles, 1727–1795* (New
Haven, Conn., 1962). William B.
Stevens, "Samuel King of Newport," *Antiques*, 96, no. 5 (1969),
pp. 728–733.
Lender: Yale University Art Gallery; bequest of Dr. Charles
Jenkins Foote, B.A. 1883, M.A. 1890.
1955.3.1.

28
Charles Willson Peale, 1741–1827
William Buckland (1734–1774)
1773–1787. Oil on canvas.
H. 36 5/8" (93 cm); W. 27 1/2"
(69.9 cm).

Provenance: The sitter's daughter,
Mrs. John Callahan, Annapolis,
Md.; her daughter, Mrs. Richard
Hammond, Annapolis, Md.; her
granddaughter, Miss Hester Ann
Hammond, Annapolis, Md.;
Russell Thorpe; purchased by
Francis P. Garvan, New York,
N.Y. (1926–1934).
Exhibitions: Cincinnati Art Mu-
seum, Ohio, *Paintings by the
Peale Family* (1954), no. 9. DIA,
The Peale Family (1967), no. 21,
illus. p. 49.

Bibliography: Sellers, *Portraits
and Miniatures by Peale*, pp. 43–
44, fig. 68. R. R. Beirne and J. H.
Scarff, *William Buckland* (Balti-
more, 1958), [illus.].
Lender: Yale University Art
Gallery; Mabel Brady Garvan
Collection. 1934.303.

29
Charles Willson Peale, 1741–1827
*George Washington at the Battle
of Princeton*
1780–1781. Oil on canvas.
H. 95" (241.3 cm); W. 61" (154.94
cm).

Signature: "C: WPeale pinxit
1781", lower left.
Provenance: Widow of a British
consul in Cadiz, Spain; purchased
by a banker in Cadiz; purchased
by J. Montaignac of the gallery
Georges Petit, Paris (Feb. 1896);
purchased by the American Art
Association, New York, N.Y.
(April 1896); Thomas E. Kirby,
New York, N.Y. (1917); Gustavus
Town Kirby, New York, N.Y.
(1925).
Exhibitions: Brooklyn Institute of
Arts and Sciences, N.Y., *Early
American Paintings* (1917), no.
64. PAFA, *Exhibition of Portraits
by Charles Willson Peale and
James Peale and Rembrandt
Peale* (1923), no. 209. RISD, *Old
and New England* (1945), no. 44,
illus. p. 61.
Bibliography: John Hill Morgan
and Mantle Fielding, *The Life
Portraits of Washington and
Their Replicas* (Philadelphia,
1931), p. 28, no. 8. Gustavus A.
Eisen, *Portraits of Washington*
(New York, 1932), II, 355, illus.
p. 607, pl. 108. Sellers, *Portraits
and Miniatures by Peale*, p. 231,
no. 917, illus. p. 357.
Lender: Yale University Art
Gallery; gift of the Maitland
Fuller Griggs Fund and Mrs.
Henry B. Loomis, in memory of

Henry Bradford Loomis, B.A.
1875. 1942.319.

30
Charles Willson Peale, 1741–1827
Walter Stewart (ca. 1756–1796)
1781. Oil on canvas.
H. 49" (124.4 cm); W. 39 1/2"
(100.3 cm).

Provenance: Descended in the
family of the sitter to Philip
Schuyler Church, Dayton, Ohio
(1952); Graham Gallery, New
York, N.Y.
Bibliography: Sellers, *Portraits
and Miniatures by Peale*, pp. 201–
202, fig. 107.
Lender: Private collection.

31
Charles Willson Peale, 1741–1827
Mrs. Walter Stewart (Deborah
McClenachan, 1763–1823)
1781–1782. Oil on canvas.
H. 49" (124.4 cm); W. 39 1/2"
(100.3 cm).

Signature: C: WPeale, pinxᵗ
1782", lower right.
Provenance: Same as its pendant,
no. 30.
Bibliography: Sellers, *Portraits
and Miniatures by Peale*, p. 202,
figs. 106, 108 (detail).
Lender: Private collection.

32
Charles Willson Peale, 1741–1827
George Walton (1741–1804)
1781. Watercolor on ivory (in
gold locket).
Oval: H. 1 3/8" (3.5 cm);
W. 1 1/16" (2.8 cm).

Provenance: The sitter's daughter,
Mrs. Octavia Walton, Augusta,
Ga.; her son-in-law, George Wal-
ton Reab, Augusta, Ga.; pur-
chased by his cousin, Mrs.
Charles (Blanche Walton) Hick-
man, Augusta, Ga.; purchased by
Mrs. Thomas Barrett, Jr., Au-

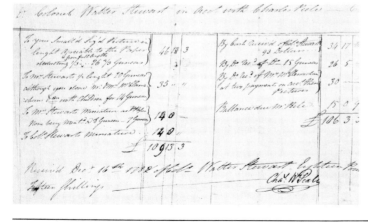

30 and 31

gusta, Ga.
Exhibition: Corcoran Gallery of Art, Washington, D.C., *Framers of the Constitution and Signers of the Declaration of Independence* (1937–1938).
Bibliography: Sellers, *Portraits and Miniatures by Peale*, p. 215, no. 892, illus. p. 367.
Lender: Yale University Art Gallery; Mabel Brady Garvan Collection. 1944.74.

33
Joseph Wright, 1756–1793
Benjamin Franklin (1706–1790)
1782. Oil on canvas.
H. 31 3/4″ (80.6 cm); w. 25 1/2″ (64 cm).

Inscriptions: "Mons. Oswald" and "Benjamin Franklin by J. S. Duplessis presented by Benjamin Franklin to Richard Oswald who negotiated on behalf of the government with Franklin in Paris 1782 and was chief negotiator of the treaty with the United States", on back.
Provenance: Richard Oswald, Auchencruive, Ayrshire, Scotland (1782–1784); his nephew, George Oswald, Auchencruive (1784–1819); his son, Richard Alexander Oswald, Auchencruive (1819–1841); his cousin, James Oswald, Glasgow (1841–1853); his son, Alexander Oswald, Auchencruive (1854–1868); his brother, George Oswald, Auchencruive (1868–1871); his son, Richard Alexander Oswald, Auchencruive (1871–1921); Gabriel Wells, New York, N.Y. (1922); William Smith Mason (1922–1936).
Bibliography: Charles Henry Hart, "An Original Portrait of Doctor Franklin," *PMHB*, 32, no. 3 (1908), pp. 320–334. Charles Coleman Sellers, *Benjamin Franklin in Portraiture* (New Haven, 1962), pp. 151–154, 415–417.

Lender: Benjamin Franklin Collection, Yale University Library; gift of William Smith Mason, PH.B. 1888, M.A. (hon.) 1924. 1935.163.

34
John Trumbull, 1756–1843
Governor Jonathan Trumbull and Mrs. Jonathan (Faith Robinson) Trumbull (1710–1785 and 1718–1780, resp.)
1777–1778. Oil on canvas.
H. 40″ (101.6 cm); w. 50″ (127 cm).

Signature: "IT 1778", lower left.
Provenance: Probably painted for the artist's brother Jonathan; the artist's brother David (probably 1779–1822); his son, Joseph (probably 1822–1861); Connecticut Historical Society (before 1876, probably bequest of Joseph Trumbull).
Exhibitions: CHS, *Bicentennial Celebration of the First Constitution of Connecticut* (1840). AIC, *From Colony to Nation* (1949), no. 120. WA, *John Trumbull* (1956), p. 11, no. 14.
Bibliography: Theodore Sizer, "An Early Check List of the Paintings of John Trumbull," *Yale University Library Gazette* (April 1948), p. 6; Sizer, ed., *Autobiography of Trumbull*, pp. 44, 55, no. 33; Sizer, *Works of Trumbull*, p. 75, fig. 76. Jaffe, *Trumbull*, pp. 34, 37, 313, fig. 27.
Lender: The Connecticut Historical Society, Hartford, Conn. 72.

35
John Trumbull, 1756–1843
The Death of General Warren at the Battle of Bunker's Hill, 17 June 1775
1786. Oil on canvas.
H. 24″ (61 cm); w. 36″ (91.4 cm).

Signature: "Jn.º Trumbull. / 1786", lower center.

Provenance: Bequest of the artist to Yale College, 1831.
Exhibitions: AAFA, *Paintings by Colonel Trumbull* (1831), no. 1. Picture Gallery of Yale College, New Haven, Conn., *Paintings by Colonel Trumbull* (1864), no. 4. YUAG, *Paintings by Trumbull and Morse* (1935), p. 6, illus. no. 6.
Bibliography: John Trumbull, *Explanation of the Two Prints Representing the Battle of Bunker's Hill, and the Attack of Quebec* (pamphlet, 1798). William Dunlap, *A History of the Rise and Progress of the Arts of Design in the United States* (New York, 1834; reprint, New York, 1969), I, 357ff; Sizer, ed., *Autobiography of Trumbull*, pp. 88ff; Sizer, *Works of Trumbull*, p. 95, figs. 145, 146–151 (key and details). Jaffe, *Trumbull*, pp. 84–91, 316–317, fig. 55, fig. 56 (key), color pl. 1.
Lender: Yale University Art Gallery. 1832.1.

36
John Trumbull, 1756–1843
The Death of General Montgomery in the Attack on Quebec, 31 December 1775
1786. Oil on canvas.
H. 24 5/8″ (62.6 cm); w. 37″ (94 cm).

Signature: "Jⁿ Trumbull / 1786", lower right.
Provenance: Bequest of the artist to Yale College, 1831.
Exhibitions: AAFA, *Paintings by Colonel Trumbull* (1831), no. 2. Picture Gallery of Yale College, New Haven, Conn., *Paintings by Colonel Trumbull* (1864), no. 5. YUAG, *Paintings by Trumbull and Morse* (1935), p. 9, no. 20.
Bibliography: John Weir, *John Trumbull* (New York, 1901), pp. 18ff., illus. facing p. 52. John Hill Morgan, *Paintings by John Trumbull at Yale University* (New

Haven, 1926), pp. 31–35, illus. p. 30. Sizer, *Works of Trumbull*, pp. 95–96, figs. 152, 153–156 (key and details). Jules David Prown, *American Painting: From Its Beginnings to the Armory Show* (Cleveland, Ohio, n.d.), I, 46–47. Jaffe, *Trumbull*, pp. 91–94, 317, fig. 60, fig. 61 (key), color pl. 2.
Lender: Yale University Art Gallery. 1832.2.

37
John Trumbull, 1756–1843
Reclining Female Nude, Back View
Probably 1789. Charcoal and white chalk on blue paper.
H. 13 3/4″ (34.9 cm); w. 22 1/2″ (57.2 cm).

Provenance: John Trumbull, New York, N.Y., and New Haven, Conn. (1789–1843); his niece's husband, Prof. Benjamin Silliman, New Haven, Conn. (1843–1864); sold by Silliman's grandson, Benjamin Silliman III, in the "First Silliman Sale," Philadelphia, Pa. (Dec. 17, 1896), no. 77.
Exhibitions: Musée des Beaux-Arts, Rouen, France, *American Drawings from the Eighteenth Century to the Present* (1954), no. 118. WA, *John Trumbull* (1956), p. 13, no. 24. John and Mabel Ringling Museum of Art, Sarasota, Fla., *Masterpieces from American Museums* (1967).
Bibliography: Charles E. Slatkin and Regina Shoolman, *Treasury of American Drawings* (New York, 1947), pl. 17. Sizer, *Works of Trumbull*, p. 123, fig. 242. Theodore E. Stebbins, Jr., *A History of American Drawings and Watercolors* (to be published by The Drawing Society, New York, 1976), chap. 3 [illus.]. Jaffe, *Trumbull*, p. 65.
Lender: Yale University Art Gallery; gift of the Associates in Fine Arts. 1938.273.

38
John Trumbull, 1756–1843
Hopothle Mico, (ca. 1759–1793)
1790. Pencil on paper.
H. 4 7/8″ (12.4 cm); w. 3 7/8″
(9.8 cm).

Inscription: "Hopothle [?] Mico:
or / The Talasee [?] King /
N York July 1790", on back.
Provenance: John Trumbull,
New York, N.Y., and New Haven,
Conn. (1790–1843); his niece's
husband, Prof. Benjamin Silli-
man, New Haven, Conn. (1843–
1864); sold by Silliman's grandson, Benjamin Silliman III, in the
"First Silliman Sale," Philadelphia, Pa. (Dec. 17, 1896), no. 66;
purchased by Charles Allen
Munn (1896–1923); Munn's niece,
Mrs. I. Shelden Tilney (1924–1943).
Exhibitions: Duane Library,
Fordham University, Bronx, N.Y.
(1943). WA, *John Trumbull*
(1956), p. 20, no. 58. Free Public
Library, Jersey City, N.J. (1957).
Bibliography: Stewart Mitchell,
ed., *New Letters of Abigail
Adams, 1788–1801* (Boston, 1947),
pp. 56–57. Sizer, ed., *Auto-
biography of Trumbull,* pp. 166–
167. Irma B. Jaffe, "Fordham
University's Trumbull Drawings:
Mistaken Identities in *The
Declaration of Independence* and
Other Discoveries," *The Ameri-
can Art Journal,* 3, no. 1 (1971),
pp. 14–19, fig. 12. Theodore E.
Stebbins, Jr., *A History of Ameri-
can Drawings and Watercolors*
(to be published by The Drawing
Society, New York, 1976), chap. 3
[illus.].
Lender: Fordham University
Library, Bronx, N.Y.

39
John Trumbull, 1756–1843
Major William Lithgow (1750?–
1796)
1791. Pencil on paper mounted
on card.

H. 4 3/4″ (12.1 cm); w. 2 15/16″
(7.5 cm).

Inscription: "Maj. Lithgow",
lower center (probably by a later
hand); "Maj. Lithgow / Blue &
White / Black Stock / Boston
10th [July '91?]", on back.
Provenance: Mrs. Winchester
Bennett, New Haven, Conn. (1931).
Exhibitions: YUAG, *Paintings by
Trumbull and Morse* (1935),
p. 8, E.e. Lyman Allyn Museum,
New London, Conn., *John Trum-
bull and His Contemporaries*
(1944), no. 8. WA, *John Trumbull*
(1956), p. 20, no. 55.
Bibliography: Theodore Sizer,
"The Trumbull Gallery, 1832–
1932," *BAFA* (Oct. 1932), illus.
p. 134; *Works of Trumbull,* p. 51.
Lender: Yale University Art
Gallery; gift of Mrs. Winchester
Bennett. 1931.63.

40
John Trumbull, 1756–1843
Five Miniatures Framed Together

Harriet Wadsworth (1771–1793)
1793. Oil on mahogany panel.
Oval: H. 3 7/8″ (9.8 cm); w. 2 7/8″
(7.3 cm).
Inscription: "Miss H: Wadsworth / died at Bermuda / April
1793. / painted from Memory /
by J. Trumbull / July of the same
year", on back.

Faith Trumbull (1769–1846)
1791. Oil on mahogany panel.
Oval: H. 3 5/8″ (9.2 cm); w. 3″
(7.6 cm).
Inscription: "Faith Trumbull /
eldest daughter of / Gov.ʳ Trumbull Esq. / of Lebanon / Painted
at Hartford / 179[1] By her
Uncle / John Trumbull", on back.

Mrs. Jonathan Trumbull (Faith
Robinson, 1718–1780)
1793. Oil on mahogany panel.
Oval: H. 3 7/8″ (9.8 cm); w. 2 7/8″

(7.3 cm).
Inscription: "Faith Trumbull /
Wife of Gov.ʳ Trumbull. / died at
Lebanon / May 1780. aged 62. /
Painted at Lebanon / by her
youngest Son / J. Trumbull 1793.
/ copied from one done by him /
from the life in 1779.", on back.

Catherine Wadsworth (1774–
1841)
1792. Oil on mahogany panel.
Oval: H. 3 7/8″ (9.8 cm); w. 3″
(7.6 cm).
Inscription: "Catherine Wadsworth / daughter of / Gen:
Wadsworth Esq.ʳ / of Hartford.
Connecticut / Painted at Phil.ª /
1792 by J. Trumbull", on back.

Julia Seymour (1769–1843)
1792. Oil on mahogany panel.
Oval: H. 3 7/8″ (9.8 cm); w. 3″
(7.6 cm).
Inscription: "Julia Seymour /
daughter of / Tho.ˢ Seymour
Esq.ʳ of / Hartford. Connecticut /
Painted at Lebanon / by J. Trumbull / 1792.", on back.

Provenance: Bequest of the artist
to Yale College, 1831.
Exhibitions: YUAG, *Paintings by
Trumbull and Morse* (1935), no.
45, A-E.
Bibliography: Theodore Bolton,
*Early American Portrait Painters
in Miniature* (New York, 1921),
pp. 159–164. John Hill Morgan,
*Paintings by John Trumbull at
Yale University* (New Haven,
1926), pp. 70–77. Theodore Bolton
and Harry L. Binsse, "Trumbull,
'Historiographer' of the Revolu-
tion," *Antiquarian,* 17, no. 7
(1931), pp. 13–18, 50ff. Frederic
Fairchild Sherman, "John Trum-
bull's Portrait Miniatures on
Wood," *Art in America,* 19, no. 10
(1931), pp. 257–61. No. 40 illus. in
Sizer, *Works of Trumbull,* fig. 115.
Jaffe, *Trumbull,* color pl. 13.
Lender: Yale University Art Gal-

lery. 1832.35–1832.39, respectively.

41
John Trumbull, 1756–1843
Five Miniatures Framed Together

Nathaniel Greene (1742–1786)
1792. Oil on mahogany panel.
Oval: H. 3 13/16″ (9.7 cm);
w. 2 7/8″ (7.3 cm).
Inscription: "Nath.¹ Green Esq.ʳ /
Maj. Genl in the American /
Service during the War of / their
independence: —& / last commander of their / armies in the
Southern / pasture / Painted by
J. Trumbull / Phil.ª 1792. from
the only / original picture remaining.", on back.

William Hull (1753–1825)
1790. Oil on mahogany panel.
Oval: H. 3 15/16″ (10 cm);
w. 3 1/8″ (7.9 cm).

Inscription: "William Hull Esq.ʳ /
[?] in the American / [?] at the
taking of Gen¹ / Burgoyne—[?] /
Colonel to the close of the /
War. / Painted at Boston / 6 Nᵒ
1790 by J. Trumbull", on back.

Ebenezer Stevens (1751–1823)
1790. Oil on mahogany panel.
Oval: H. 3 7/8″ (9.8 cm); w. 3 1/4″
(8.3 cm).
Inscription: "William Stevens
Esq.ʳ / Commander of the American / Artillery at the capture of /
Gen.¹ Burgoyne [?] / [?] / Colonel
to the close of the War / Painted
at New York / 1790. by John
Trumbull", on back.

Thomas Youngs Seymour (1757–
1811)
1793. Oil on mahogany panel.
Oval: H. 3 7/8″ (9.8 cm); w. 3 1/8″
(7.9 cm).
Inscription: "[?] Tho.ˢ Seymour /
Ae 35 − / [?] of Dragoons / at the
surrender of / Gen¹ Burgoyne. /
painted by / J. Trumbull at /

Hartford. 1793.", on back.

John Brooks (1752–1825)
1790. Oil on mahogany panel.
Oval: H. 3 7/8″ (9.8 cm); w. 3 1/8″
(7.9 cm).
Inscription: "John Brooks Esq.ʳ /
Colonel of a Regiment in / [?]
American Service / during the
War of their / independanc —&
present / at the capture of
General / Burgoyne. / Painted by
J. Trumbull / at Boston Octº
1790.", on back.

Provenance: Bequest of the artist
to Yale College, 1831.
Exhibitions: YUAG, *Paintings by
Trumbull and Morse* (1935), no.
37, A-E.
Bibliography: Same as no. 40.
No. 41 illus. in Sizer, *Works of
Trumbull*, fig. 104.
Lender: Yale University Art Gal-
lery. 1832.25–1832.29, respectively.

42
John Trumbull, 1756–1843
Five Miniatures Framed Together

Henry Laurens (1724–1792)
1791. Oil on mahogany panel.
Oval: H. 3 5/8″ (9.2 cm): w. 3″
(7.6 cm).
Inscription: "Henry Laurens

Esq.ʳ / President at Congress in /
1779. —confined in the Town of
London 1780 & 1 / & of the commissioners on the / part of America at the / Treaty with G Britain
1783 / Painted by J. Trumbull /
in Charleston S.º Carolina /
1791/", on back.

John Jay (1745–1829)
1793. Oil on mahogany panel.
Oval: H. 4″ (10.2 cm); w. 3 1/4″
(8.3 cm).
Inscription: "John Jay [Esq.] /
[Chief Jus]tice of the Uni / [-ted
States] of America & one / [of the]
Ministers at the / [concl]usion of
peace / [with] G Britain in 1783 /
[Painted] by J. Trumbull /
[P]hila. 1793.", on back.

John Adams (1735–1826)
1793. Oil on mahogany panel.
Oval: H. 3 7/8″ (9.8 cm); w. 3 1/4″
(8.3 cm).
Inscription: "John Adams. / first
Vice President of / the United
States of America / & one of her
Ministers at / the conclusion of
peace / with G Britain in 1783 /
Painted by J. Trumbull / at
Philadelphia 179[3].", on back.

George Hammond (1763–1853)
1793. Oil on mahogany panel.

Oval: H. 3 7/8″ (9.8 cm); w. 3 1/8″
(7.9 cm).
Inscription: "George Hammond /
first Minister Plenip. / of G.
Britain to America / & Sec.ʳʸ to
the commi[ssioners] / for con-
cluding Peace / between the two
countries / in 1783. / Painted in
Philᵃ / by J. Trumbull 1793.", on
back.

William Temple Franklin (ca.
1760–1832)
1790. Oil on mahogany panel.
Oval: H. 3 7/8″ (9.8 cm); w. 3 1/8″
(7.9 cm).
Inscription: "Wm. Temple
Franklin / Grandson of Doctʳ
Franklin / & Sec.ʳʸ of the Ameri-
can / commissioners at the
treaty / with G Britain 1783. /
Painted in Philᵃ / 1790 by J.
Trumbull", on back.

Provenance: Bequest of the artist
to Yale College, 1831.
Exhibitions: YUAG, *Paintings by
Trumbull and Morse* (1935), no.
35, A-E.
Bibliography: Same as no. 40.
No. 42 illus. in Sizer, *Works of
Trumbull*, fig. 108.
Lender: Yale University Art
Gallery. 1832.20–1832.24, respec-
tively.

43
John Trumbull, 1756–1843
Elevation and Plan of a Residence
1790–1794. Pencil, pen and ink,
and ink wash on blue paper.
H. 6 1/2″ (16.5 cm); w. 8 1/4″
(21 cm).

Inscription: "Lebanon 1790 to 94",
lower center; " # 19 / Sketch
from Col John Trumbull[']s
Collection", lower left (by a later
hand); various numerical calcula-
tions on back.
Provenance: John Trumbull,
New York, N.Y., and New Haven,
Conn. (1794–1843); his niece's
husband, Prof. Benjamin Silliman,
New Haven, Conn. (1843–1864);
sold by Silliman's grandson,
Benjamin Silliman III, in the
"First Silliman Sale," Philadel-
phia, Pa. (Dec. 17, 1896).
Exhibitions: WA, *John Trumbull*
(1956), p. 34, no. 129.
Bibliography: Theodore Sizer,
"A Tentative 'Short-Title' Check-
List of the Works of Col. John
Trumbull," *Art Bulletin*, 30
(1948): 222. Sizer, *Works of
Trumbull*, p. 128. Jaffe, *Trum-
bull*, pp. 290–296.
Lender: Yale University Art
Gallery; gift of the Associates in
Fine Arts. 1938.283.

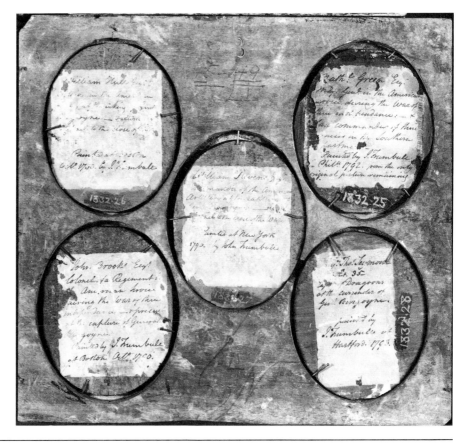

41

44
Gilbert Stuart, 1755–1828
The Skater (Portrait of William Grant), (dates unknown)
1782. Oil on canvas.
H. 96 5/8″ (245.4 cm); w. 58 1/8″ (147.6 cm).

Provenance: William Grant; his daughter, Mrs. Elizabeth Grant Pelham-Clinton (until 1899); her son, Charles Stapleton Pelham-Clinton (1899–1911); his widow, Mrs. Charles Stapleton Pelham-Clinton (1911–1913); her adopted niece, Georgiana Elizabeth May Pelham-Clinton, London (1913–1950).
Exhibitions: Royal Academy, London (1782), no. 190; *Works of the Old Masters* (1878), no. 128 (as *A Portrait of W. Grant, Esq., Congalton, Skating in St. James' Park*, attributed to "Thomas Gainsborough"[?]). Tate Gallery, London, *American Painting* (1946), no. 206. NG, *Gilbert Stuart* (1967), no. 8, illus. p. 49.
Bibliography: George C. Mason, *The Life and Works of Gilbert Stuart* (New York, 1879), pp. 187–190. Park, *Gilbert Stuart*, I, 358–359; illus. 3, p. 205. James Thomas Flexner, *Gilbert Stuart* (New York, 1955), pp. 61–64.
Lender: National Gallery of Art, Washington, D.C.; Andrew W. Mellon Collection, 1950.

45
Gilbert Stuart, 1755–1828
Portrait of the Artist (1755–1828)
Ca. 1786. Oil on canvas.
H. 10 5/8″ (26.9 cm); w. 8 7/8″ (22.6 cm).

Provenance: Gilbert Stuart, London, and Boston, Mass. (until 1828); his widow, Mrs. Gilbert Stuart, London; her daughter, Jane Stuart, Boston, Mass.; gift to Mrs. Harrison Gray Otis, Boston, Mass. (until 1883); the latter's estate (on deposit, Museum of Fine Arts, Boston, Mass., 1883–1922); Albert Rosenthal, Philadelphia, Pa. (1925); Ehrich Galleries, New York, N.Y. (1926).
Exhibitions: RISD, *Rhode Island Tercentenary Celebration* (1936), no. 27. Dayton Art Institute, Ohio, *The Artist and His Family* (1950). NG, *Gilbert Stuart* (1967), no. 13, illus. facing p. 9.
Bibliography: Park, *Gilbert Stuart*, II, 718; illus. 4, p. 494. Mount, *Gilbert Stuart*, p. 375. Gardner and Feld, *American Paintings*, I, 80–81, illus. p. 81.
Lender: The Metropolitan Museum of Art, New York, N.Y.; Fletcher Fund, 1926. 1926.16.

46
Gilbert Stuart, 1755–1828
Mrs. Richard Yates (Catherine Brass, 1735–after 1797)
1793/94. Oil on canvas.
H. 30 1/4″ (76.8 cm); w. 25″ (63.4 cm).

Provenance: Descendants of Mrs. Richard Yates, New York, N.Y. and New Orleans, La.; the sitter's great-great-great-granddaughter, Mrs. Louise Chiapella Formento, New Orleans, La. (until 1911); sold to Dr. Isaac M. Cline, New Orleans, La. (1911–1918); sold to Thomas B. Clarke, New York, N.Y. (1918–1931; his estate until 1937); sold to Andrew W. Mellon Educational and Charitable Trust, Pittsburgh, Pa. (1937–1940).
Exhibitions: MMA, *Life in America* (1939), no. 53. Tate Gallery, London, *American Painting* (1946), no. 207. BM, *Face of America* (1958), no. 25, fig. 20. NG, *Gilbert Stuart* (1967), no. 19, illus. p. 64.
Bibliography: Park, *Gilbert Stuart*, II, 837; illus. 4, p. 592. Margaret Bouton, *American Painting in the National Gallery of Art* (Washington, D.C., 1959), p. 20, color illus. p. 21. Mount, *Gilbert Stuart*, pp. 169–170 [illus.].
Lender: National Gallery of Art, Washington, D.C.; Andrew W. Mellon Collection, 1940.

47
Gilbert Stuart, 1755–1828
Matilda Stoughton de Jaudenes (1778–after 1822)
1794. Oil on canvas.
H. 50 5/8″ (128.6 cm); w. 39 1/2″ (100.3 cm).

Inscription: "G. Stuart, R.A. New York Sept. 8, / 1794", lower left (by a later hand); "Dona Matilde Stoughton, / de Jaudenes-Esposa / de Don Josef de Jaudenes, / y Nebot Comisario Ordena- / dor de los Reales Exercitos / de Su Magestad Catholica / y su Ministro Embiado cerca / de los Estados Unidos de / America- / Nacio / en la Ciudad de / Nueva-York en los Estados Unidos el 11 de / 1778.", upper left, below coat of arms.
Provenance: Don Josef Jaudenes, Philadelphia, Pa., and Palma, Majorca (1794–ca. 1819); the Jaudenes family, Spain; M. Knoedler and Co., Inc., New York, N.Y. (1907).
Exhibitions: MMA, *Fourteen American Masters* (1958–1959). NG, *Gilbert Stuart* (1967), no. 24, illus. p. 70.
Bibliography: Park, *Gilbert Stuart*, I, 433; illus. 3, p. 263. Mount, *Gilbert Stuart*, pp. 179ff., 349, [illus.]. Gardner and Feld, *American Paintings*, I, 84, illus. p. 83.
Lender: The Metropolitan Museum of Art, New York, N.Y.; Rogers Fund, 1907. 1907.76.

48
Gilbert Stuart, 1755–1828
Josef de Jaudenes y Nebot (1764–before 1819)
1794. Oil on canvas.
H. 50 1/4″ (127.6 cm); w. 39 1/2″ (100.3 cm).

Inscription: "G. Stuart, R.A. New York, Sept. 8 / 1794", lower right (by a later hand); "Don Josef de Jaudenes, y Nebot / Comisario Ordenador de los / Reales Exercitos y Ministro Em / biado de Su Magestad Catholi / ca cerca de los Estados Unidos / de America. / Nacio en la Ciudad de Valen- / cia Reyno de Espana el 25, de / Marzo de 1764.", upper right, below coat of arms.
Provenance: Same as its pendant, no. 47.
Exhibitions: MMA, *Fourteen American Masters* (1958–1959). NG, *Gilbert Stuart* (1967), no. 23, illus. p. 69.
Bibliography: Park, *Gilbert Stuart*, I, 432; illus. 3, p. 262. Mount, *Gilbert Stuart*, pp. 179ff., 349. Gardner and Feld, *American Paintings*, I, 82–83, illus. p. 83.
Lender: The Metropolitan Museum of Art, New York, N.Y.; Rogers Fund, 1907. 1907.75.

49
Ralph Earl, 1751–1801
Roger Sherman (1721–1793)
Ca. 1775. Oil on canvas.
H. 64 5/8″ (164.1 cm); w. 49 3/4″ (126.4 cm).

Provenance: Roger Sherman, New Haven, Conn. (until 1793); his son (?), Roger Sherman, New Haven, Conn. (until 1856); his daughter, Mrs. Henry White, New Haven, Conn. (ca. 1870–1888); her son, Charles A. White, New Haven, Conn. (1888); his son, Roger Sherman White, New Haven, Conn. (until 1918).
Exhibitions: YUAG, *Connecticut Portraits by Ralph Earl* (1935), no. 34, illus. p. 29. MMA, *Life in America* (1939), no. 30, illus. p. 21. WM, *Ralph Earl, 1751–1801* (1945–1946), no. 2, [illus.]. AIC, *From Colony to Nation* (1949), no. 47, illus. p. 36. NPG, *This New Man: A Discourse in Portraits* (1968), illus. p. 63.

Bibliography: Roger Sherman Boardman, *Roger Sherman, Signer and Statesman* (Philadelphia, 1938), frontispiece. Laurence B. Goodrich, *Ralph Earl: Recorder for an Era* (Albany, N.Y., 1967), pp. 1–12, 14, illus. p. 15. Harold Spencer, *The American Earls: Ralph Earl, James Earl, R. E. W. Earl*, The William Benton Museum of Art, University of Connecticut (Storrs, Conn., 1972), pp. xiii–xxxii, illus. p. xiv.
Lender: Yale University Art Gallery; gift of Roger Sherman White, B.A. 1899, LL.B. 1902. 1918.3.

50
Ralph Earl, 1751–1801
Major General Frederic Wilhelm Augustus, Baron von Steuben (1730–1794)
Ca. 1786. Oil on canvas.
H. 49 3/4″ (126.4 cm); w. 41 3/8″ (105.1 cm).

Inscription: "FIDELITA", center (on medal on the subject's coat).
Replicas: New York State Historical Association, Cooperstown, N.Y.
Provenance: Baron von Steuben, New York, N.Y. (ca. 1786–1794); his former aide-de-camp and adopted heir, Major William North, New York, N.Y.; North's great-granddaughter, Mrs. F. B. Austin, New York, N.Y. (1889–1929); purchased by M. Knoedler and Co., Inc., New York, N.Y.; purchased by William Randolph Hearst; purchased by Mrs. Paul Moore, New York, N.Y. (until 1939).
Exhibitions: Corcoran Gallery of Art, Washington, D.C., *Washington Bicentennial Exhibition of Portraits* (1932), no. 98. MMA, *Portraits of the Original Members of the Society of the Cincinnati* (1935), no. 24. WM, *Ralph Earl, 1751–1801* (1945–1946), no. 10, [illus.]. AIC, *From Colony to Nation* (1949), no. 48.
Bibliography: Theodore Sizer and Henry La Farge, "Earl's Portrait of Steuben," *BAFA*, 9, no. 1 (1939); pp. 13–14, illus. on cover. Laurence B. Goodrich, *Ralph Earl: Recorder for an Era* (Albany, N.Y., 1967), pp. 1–12, 46. Harold Spencer, *The American Earls: Ralph Earl, James Earl, R. E. W. Earl*, The William Benton Museum of Art, University of Connecticut (Storrs, Conn., 1972), pp. xiii–xxxii.
Lender: Yale University Art Gallery; gift of Mrs. Paul Moore in memory of her nephew Howard Melville Hanna, Jr., B.S. 1931. 1939.14.

51
Ralph Earl, 1751–1801
Mrs. William Moseley (Laura Wolcott) and Her Son Charles (1761–1814 and 1786–1815, resp.)
1791. Oil on canvas.
H. 86 7/8″ (220.6 cm); w. 68 3/8″ (173.6 cm).

Signature: "R. Earl Pinxt 1791–", lower left.
Provenance: William Moseley, Hartford, Conn.; his wife's younger brother, Frederick Wolcott, Hartford, Conn.; his son, Charles Moseley Wolcott, Fishkill-on-Hudson, N.Y.; his daughter, Katherine Rankin Wolcott, Fishkill-on-Hudson, N.Y. (until 1942).
Exhibitions: RISD, *Old and New England* (1945), no. 29, illus. p. 4. WM, *Ralph Earl, 1751–1801* (1945–1946), no. 27. Lyman Allyn Museum, New London, Conn., *Eighty Eminent Painters of Connecticut* (1947), no. 10.
Bibliography: Alice Elizabeth Chase, "Ralph Earl's Portrait of Mrs. William Moseley and her son Charles," *BAFA*, 12, no. 1 (1943), pp. 1–3, illus. p. 1. Laurence B. Goodrich, "Ralph Earl's Debt to Gainsborough and Other English Portraitists," *Antiques*, 78, no. 5 (1960), pp. 464–465; *Ralph Earl: Recorder for an Era*, Albany, N.Y. (1967), pp. 1–12, 72, illus. p. 73.
Lender: Yale University Art Gallery; bequest of Mrs. Katherine Rankin Wolcott Verplanck. 1942.64.

52
**Anonymous Artist
(The Beardsley Limner),** active 1780–1800
Dr. Hezekiah Beardsley (1748–1790)
Ca. 1788–1790. Oil on canvas.
H. 45″ (114.3 cm); w. 43″ (109.2 cm).

Provenance: Dr. Hezekiah Beardsley, New Haven, Conn. (until 1790); possibly his wife's sister, Abigail Davis Marshall; her daughter, Elizabeth Marshall Peck; her daughter, Elizabeth Peck Fairchild; Emma Lathrop Jones; her daughter, Gwendolen Jones Giddings, West Hartford, Conn.
Exhibitions: CHS, *Little-Known Connecticut Artists, 1790–1810* (1957–1958), no. 10, fig. 10. Abby Aldrich Rockefeller Folk Art Collection, Williamsburg, Va., *The Beardsley Limner and Some Contemporaries* (1972–1973), no. 2, color illus. p. 2.
Bibliography: Walter R. Steiner, "Doctor Hezekiah Beardsley," *Yale Journal of Biology and Medicine*, 6, no. 3 (1934), pp. 367–374. Frederick G. Kilgour, "Portraits of Doctor Hezekiah Beardsley and His Wife, Elizabeth," *Connecticut State Medical Journal*, 17, no. 4 (1953), pp. 298–300, illus. p. 299.
Lender: Yale University Art Gallery; gift of Gwendolen Jones Giddings. 1952.46.1.

53
**Anonymous Artist
(The Beardsley Limner),** active 1780–1800
Mrs. Hezekiah Beardsley (Elizabeth Davis, 1748/49–1790)
Ca. 1788–1790. Oil on canvas.
H. 45″ (114.3 cm); w. 43″ (109.2 cm).

Provenance: Same as its pendant, no. 53.
Exhibitions: CHS, *Little-Known Connecticut Artists, 1790–1810* (1957–1958), no. 11, fig. 11. Abby Aldrich Rockefeller Folk Art Collection, Williamsburg, Va., *The Beardsley Limner and Some Contemporaries* (1972–1973), no. 3, fig. 3.
Lender: Yale University Art Gallery; gift of Gwendolen Jones Giddings. 1952.46.2.

54
Anonymous Artist
Emma Van Name (dates unknown)
Ca. 1795. Oil on canvas.
H. 29″ (73.6 cm); w. 23″ (58.4 cm).

Provenance: Edgar William and Bernice Chrysler Garbisch, New York, N.Y. (1961–1969).
Exhibitions: MMA, *101 Masterpieces of American Primitive Painting from the Collection of Edgar William and Bernice Chrysler Garbisch* (organized and circulated under the auspices of The American Federation of Arts, New York, N.Y., 1961–1964), no. 28, color illus. p. 54. Grand Palais, Paris, *Peintures naïves américaines, XVIIe XIXe siècles: Cent onze tableaux de la Collection Edgar William et Bernice Chrysler Garbisch* (1968), no. 22, illus. p. 38.
Bibliography: Mary Black and Jean Lipman, *American Folk Painting* (New York, 1966), pp. 16–50.
Lender: Whitney Museum of American Art, New York, N.Y.; gift of Edgar William and Bernice Chrysler Garbisch. 69.142.

55
William Jennys, active 1790–1805
Nathaniel Lamson (b. 1781)
Ca. 1795. Oil on canvas.
H. 29 7/8″ (75.8 cm); W. 24 1/2″
(62.2 cm).

Inscription: "1795" on reverse of
stretcher, upper right (original
stretcher removed during con-
servation and inscription lost).
Provenance: Descendants of Na-
thaniel Lamson; Miss Frances B.
Russell, Stratford, Conn. (on
loan to Stratford Historical So-
ciety, 1932–1956).
Exhibitions: CHS, *Portraits of
Richard and William Jennys*
(1955–1956).
Bibliography: Frederic Fairchild
Sherman, "J. William and Wil-
liam Jennys," *Art in America*, 20,
no. 6 (1932), pp. 202–206. William
Lamson Warren, "The Jennys
Portraits," *Connecticut Historical
Society Bulletin*, 20, no. 4 (1955),
pp. 112–117, 127, fig. 18; "A
Checklist of Jennys Portraits,"
*Connecticut Historical Society
Bulletin*, 21, no. 2 (1956), pp. 33–
39, 57.
Lender: Mary Allis.

56
Winthrop Chandler, 1747–1790
*View of a River with Trees and
Figures*
Ca. 1779. Oil on wood panel.
H. 20″ (50.8 cm); W. 58″ (147.3 cm).

Provenance: Commissioned by
Ebenezer Waters for his house in
Sutton, Mass. (ca. 1779–before
1796); remained in the house
under various ownership until
removed and acquired by the
present owners: Mr. Hunt (ca.
1796–1805), Dr. Artemus Bullard
(1805–after 1837), the Rev. Mr.
Tuttle, and Mr. and Mrs. Gordon
Wood (1948–1972).
Bibliography: Nina Fletcher
Little, "Winthrop Chandler,
Limner of Windham County,

Connecticut," *Art in America*, 35,
no. 2 (1947), pp. 77–168; "Re-
cently Discovered Paintings by
Winthrop Chandler," *Art in
America*, 36, no. 2 (1948), pp. 81–
97, illus. p. 90; *American Decora-
tive Wall Painting, 1700–1850*
(New York, 1972), pp. 28, 53–55.
Lender: Mr. and Mrs. Bertram
K. Little.

57
James Peale, 1749–1831
The Ramsay-Polk Family
Ca. 1793. Oil on canvas.
H. 50″ (127 cm); W. 40″ (101.6 cm).

Provenance: Descendants of the
Peale family; Horace Wells
Sellers (1933); Mrs. Sellers Walton;
purchased by Lawrence Fleisch-
man, Detroit, Mich. (1955).
Exhibitions: PAFA, *Portraits by
Charles Willson Peale, James
Peale and Rembrandt Peale*
(1923), no. 5, [illus.]. DIA, *Collec-
tion in Progress* (1955), no. 2,
illus. p. 9. Milwaukee Art Center,
American Painting, 1760–1960
(1960), illus. p. 25.
Bibliography: Frederic Fairchild
Sherman, "Two Recently Dis-
covered Portraits in Oils by
James Peale," *Art in America*, 21,
no. 3 (1933), pp. 114–121, no. 5.
Charles Coleman Sellers, "James
Peale and Charles Willson Peale,"
in *The Peale Family: Three
Generations of American Artists*,
DIA (Detroit, 1967), pp. 25–28,
73–88; "James Peale: A Light in
Shadow, 1749–1831," in *Four
Generations of Commissions: The
Peale Collection*, The Maryland
Historical Society (Baltimore,
1975), pp. 28–41.
Lender: Private collection.

58
James Peale, 1749–1831
Rembrandt Peale (1778–1860)
1795. Watercolor on ivory.
Oval: H. 2 3/8″ (6.3 cm); W. 1 3/4″
(4.9 cm).

Signature: "I.P. / 1795", lower
right.
Provenance: Descendants of Rem-
brandt Peale; G. B. Wirgam;
Mrs. John Hill Morgan, Farming-
ton, Conn. (1921–1940).
Exhibitions: MMA, *Miniatures*
(1927), p. 41. BM, *Five Centuries
of Miniature Painting* (1936), no.
213. DIA, *The Peale Family:
Three Generations of American
Artists* (1967), no. 77.
Bibliography: Harry B. Wehle,
American Miniatures, 1730–1850
(New York, 1927), pp. 20–21, color
pl. 4. Jean Lambert Brockway,
"The Miniatures of James Peale,"
Antiques, 22, no. 3 (1932), pp.
130–134.
Lender: Yale University Art
Gallery; gift of Mrs. John Hill
Morgan. 1940.510.

59
John Ramage, ca. 1748–1802
Anthony Rutgers (dates un-
known)
Ca. 1780–1790. Watercolor on
ivory.
Oval: H. 1 7/8″ (4.5 cm); W. 1 3/8″
(3.5 cm).

Inscription: "Cornelia M
Rutgers", on reverse of case.
Provenance: Descendants of An-
thony Rutgers; Mrs. Thomas
Weckham; Mrs. Joseph C. Ring-
walt; Mrs. Elizabeth Morse; Mrs.
John Hill Morgan, Farmington,
Conn. (1921–1940).
Exhibitions: MMA, *Miniatures*
(1927), p. 45. BM, *Five Centuries
of Miniature Painting* (1936),
no. 224.
Bibliography: Harry B. Wehle,
American Miniatures, 1720–1850
(New York, 1927), pp. 29–30,
color pl. 15. Frederic Fairchild
Sherman, *John Ramage: A
Biographical Sketch and a List of
His Portrait Miniatures* (New
York, 1929), pp. 21–22, illus. no.
26. John Hill Morgan, *A Sketch
of the Life of John Ramage,

Miniature Painter* (New York,
1930), illus. facing p. 32.
Lender: Yale University Art
Gallery; gift of Mrs. John Hill
Morgan. 1940.515.

60
Archibald Robertson, 1765–1835
New York from Long Island
Ca. 1794–1796. Ink and color wash
on paper.
H. 17 1/4″ (43.8 cm); W. 24 1/2″
(62.2 cm).

Inscriptions: "by Archibald
Robertson / my father / Andrew
Robertson", lower right of image;
"NEW YORK FROM LONG ISLAND /
(Washingtons Headquarters—in
foreground)", lower center in
margin; "original drawing by
Archibald Robertson", lower left
in margin; "The watermark on
paper is 1794", lower right in
margin.
Provenance: J. Pierpont Morgan,
New York, N.Y. (before 1915).
Bibliography: Emily Robertson,
*Letters and Papers of Andrew
Robertson . . .* (London, 1895?).
I. N. Phelps Stokes, *The Iconog-
raphy of Manhattan Island, 1498–
1909* (New York, 1915–1928), I,
443, pl. 65. John E. Stillwell,
"Archibald Robertson, Miniaturist, 1765–1835," *New-York Historical Society Quarterly Bulletin*,
13 (1929), pp. 1–33.
Lender: Columbia University,
New York, N.Y.; gift of J. Pierpont Morgan; before 1915.
co0.805.

61
Raphaelle Peale, 1774–1825
A Deception
1802. Pencil and ink on paper.
H. 16″ (40.6 cm); W. 10 3/4″ (27.3
cm).

Inscription: "This done by pencil
& India ink / by Raphaelle Peale,
Phila, 1802", on back (inscribed
with notations by various de-

57
(detail)

scendants and owners, including the one here cited).
Provenance: Raphaelle Peale, Philadelphia, Pa. (until 1825); his wife, Martha Ann Peale, Philadelphia, Pa. (1825–1852); her nephew (son of Rubens Peale), Franklin Peale, Philadelphia, Pa.; his son, Robert R. Peale (1902); Calvin W. Stillman, Chicago, Ill.; J. William Middendorf II, New York, N.Y.; with Kennedy Galleries, Inc., New York, N.Y. (1967).
Exhibitions: Milwaukee Art Institute, Wis., *Raphaelle Peale* (1959), no. 17. DIA, *The Peale Family* (1967), no. 125, illus. pp. 96 and 141 (detail). YUAG, *American Art from Alumni Collections* (1968), no. 80, [illus.]. NG, *The Reality of Appearance* (1970), no. 2, illus. p. 33.
Bibliography: William H. Gerdts and Russell Burke, *American Still-Life Painting* (New York, 1971). p. 30, fig. 2–1.
Lender: Private collection.

62
Raphaelle Peale, 1774–1825
Still Life with Celery and Wine
1816. Oil on wood panel.
H. 12 3/8″ (31.4 cm); w. 17 1/8″ (43.5 cm).

Signature: "Raphaelle Peale 1816", lower right.
Provenance: Vose Galleries, Boston, Mass. (until 1966).
Exhibitions: DIA, *The Peale Family* (1967), no. 127, illus. p. 97.
Lender: Munson-Williams-Proctor Institute, Utica, N.Y. 66.30.

63
John Johnston, 1758–1818
Still Life with Fruit
1810. Oil on wood panel.
H. 14 5/8″ (37.1 cm); w. 18 1/8″ (46.1 cm).

Signature: "J. Johnston Pinx /

1810", lower right.
Provenance: L. P. L. C. Lapp; the Sohier family, Cohasset, Mass.; Emily and Mary Sohier; Mrs. Bertha Sohier, Concord, Mass. (until 1966).
Exhibitions: Coe Kerr Gallery, New York, N.Y., *150 Years of American Still-Life Painting* (1970), no. 2.
Bibliography: William H. Gerdts and Russell Burke, *American Still-Life Painting* (New York, 1971), pp. 48–49. color pl. 3. William H. Gerdts, "On the Tabletop: Europe and America," *Art in America*, 60, no. 5 (1972), pp. 63–64, color illus. p. 62.
Lender: The St. Louis Art Museum, St. Louis, Mo. 218:66.

64
John Vanderlyn, 1775–1852
Mrs. Edward Church and Child (dates unknown)
1799. Crayon on paper.
H. 8 3/8″ (21.3 cm); w. 6 3/8″ (16.2 cm).

Signature: "J. Vanderlyn. Fect.", lower right (on chair).
Provenance: The Church family; Ella Church Strobell (until 1917).
Exhibitions: University Art Gallery, State University of New York, Binghamton, *The Works of John Vanderlyn* (1970), no. 20, fig. 20.
Bibliography: Louise Hunt Averill, "John Vanderlyn, American Painter" (Ph.D. diss., Yale University, 1949), no. 41. John Davis Hatch, Jr., "The First American Artist to Study in Paris, 'John Vanderlyn,'" *International Congress on the History of Art*, Actes du XIX Congrès (Paris, 1959), pp. 505ff. Gardner and Feld, *American Paintings*, pp. 121–122.
Lender: The Metropolitan Museum of Art, New York, N.Y.; bequest of Ella Church Strobell, 1917. 1917.134.3.

65
John Vanderlyn, 1775–1852
Death of Jane McCrea
1804. Oil on canvas.
H. 32 1/2″ (82.6 cm); w. 26 1/2″ (67.3 cm).

Provenance: Possibly purchased by Robert Fulton, New York, N.Y. (until 1815); presented to the American Academy of Fine Arts, New York, N.Y. (1816–1842); purchased through Alfred Smith at the auction of the collection of the American Academy of Fine Arts, New York, N.Y. (1842).
Exhibitions: Salon, Paris (1804), no. 495 (as "Une Jeune Femme massacrée par deux sauvages au service des anglais dans la guerre d'Amérique"). AAFA (1816), no. 83; (1826), no. 18; (1827), no. 87. Museum of Modern Art, New York, N.Y., *Romantic Painting in America* (1943–1944), no. 198. MMA, *19th-Century America* (1970), no. 8, [illus.]. University Art Gallery, State University of New York, Binghamton, *The Works of John Vanderlyn* (1970), no. 63, fig. 63. Los Angeles County Museum of Art, Cal., *American Narrative Painting* (1974), no. 10, illus. p. 41.
Bibliography: Kathleen H. Pritchard, "John Vanderlyn and the Massacre of Jane McCrea," *Art Quarterly*, 12, no. 4 (1949), pp. 361–366, illus. p. 360. Samuel Y. Edgerton, Jr., "The Murder of Jane McCrea: The Tragedy of an American 'Tableau d'histoire,'" *Art Bulletin*, 47, no. 4 (1965), pp. 481–492, fig. 1. Elwood C. Parry III, *The Image of the Indian and the Black Man in American Art, 1590–1900* (New York, 1974), pp. 59–63, illus. p. 59.
Lender: Wadsworth Atheneum, Hartford, Conn.; purchased by subscription. 1855.4.

66
John Vanderlyn, 1775–1852

Marius amidst the Ruins of Carthage
1807. Oil on canvas.
H. 87″ (221 cm); w. 68 1/2″ (174 cm).

Signature: "J. Vanderlyn fec. Roma 1807", lower center.
Provenance: Purchased by Leonard Kip, Hartford, Conn. (1834–1847); his son, William Ingraham Kip, Hartford, Conn. (1847–1853/54), and California (1853/54–ca. 1883); Mrs. Edward Searles, California (ca. 1883–1891); her husband, Edward Searles, California (1891–1893); gift to Mark Hopkins Institute [San Francisco Art Institute] (1893–ca. 1917–1920); purchased by M. H. DeYoung Museum, San Francisco, Calif.
Exhibitions: Salon, Paris (1808), no. 595 (as "Caïs Marius sur les ruines de Carthage"). Senate House Museum, Kingston, N.Y., *Exhibition of the Work of John Vanderlyn* (1938), no. 12. MMA, *19th-Century America* (1970), no. 9, [illus.]. University Art Gallery, State University of New York, Binghamton, *The Works of John Vanderlyn* (1970), no. 51, fig. 51.
Bibliography: Marius Schoonmaker, *John Vanderlyn, Artist* (Kingston, N.Y., 1950). Salvatore Mondello, "John Vanderlyn," *New-York Historical Society Quarterly*, 52, no. 2 (1968), pp. 172ff.
Lender: The Fine Arts Museums of San Francisco, Calif.

67
Edward Greene Malbone, 1777–1807
Washington Allston (1779–1843)
Prior to 1801. Watercolor on ivory.
Oval: H. 3 3/8″ (8 cm); w. 2 7/8″ (6.5 cm).

Signature: "Malbone", middle

left (possibly by a later hand).
Provenance: Washington Allston, Cambridge, Mass. (ca. 1801–1843); his daughter, Miss Helen Allston (1843–1897).
Exhibitions: MMA, *Miniatures* (1927). p. 34. NG, *Miniatures and Other Works by Edward Greene Malbone, 1777–1807* (1929), no. 2. MFA, *New England Miniatures, 1750–1850* (1957), no. 4, fig. 3.
Bibliography: Jared B. Flagg, *The Life and Letters of Washington Allston* (New York, 1892), pp. 9, 12, 32, 35–36, 45. R. T. H. Halsey, "Malbone and His Miniatures," *Scribner's Magazine*, 67, no. 5 (1910), p. 565. Ruel Pardee Tolman, *The Life and Works of Edward Greene Malbone, 1777–1807* (New York, 1958), pp. 130–131, fig. 5.
Lender: Museum of Fine Arts, Boston, Mass.; Otis Norcross Fund. 97.599.

68
Washington Allston, 1779–1843
Samuel T. Coleridge (1772–1834)
1806. Oil on canvas.
H. 29 1/2″ (74.8 cm); W. 24 5/8″ (62.4 cm).

Provenance: Family of the artist; Henry Wadsworth Longfellow Dana, Cambridge, Mass. (1943).
Exhibitions: MMA, *Romantic Painting in America* (1943), no. 4. DIA, *Washington Allston* (1947), no. 10.
Bibliography: Edgar P. Richardson, *American Romantic Painting* (New York, 1944), pp. 6–8, 23, fig. 15; *Washington Allston* (Chicago, 1948), pp. 75, 77–78, no. 40, pl. 12. Thomas Leavitt, "Washington Allston at Harvard," *Harvard Alumni Bulletin*, 58, (April 21, 1956):552.
Lender: Fogg Art Museum, Harvard University, Cambridge, Mass.; loan of the Washington Allston Trust. 6.1955.

Prints

69
Peter Pelham, 1697–1751
Cotton Mather (1663–1728)
1728. Mezzotint. Only known state.
H. 13 5/8″ (34.6 cm); W. 9 13/16″ (24.9 cm).

Inscriptions: "Cottonus Matherus / S. Theologiae Doctor Regiae Societatis Londinensis Socius, / et Ecclesiae apud Bostonum Nov = Anglorum nuper Praepositus. / Ætatis Suae LXV, MDCCXXVII.", lower center; "P. Pelham ad vivum pinxit ab Origin Fecit et excud.", lower right.
Provenance: Francis P. Garvan, New York, N.Y.
Exhibitions: LC, *Garvan Prints* (1931), no. 10.
Bibliography: For other impressions see the following references: Stauffer, *American Engravers*, vol. II, no. 2469. Andrew Oliver, "Peter Pelham (c. 1697–1751) Sometime Printmaker of Boston," *Boston Prints*, pp. 135–138, 170, fig. 63. *American Printmaking*, pp. 20–21, fig. 17.
Lender: Yale University Art Gallery; Mabel Brady Garvan Collection. 1946.9.200.

70
Thomas Johnston, ca. 1708–1767
Quebec, The Capital of New-France
1759. Line engraving. First state of two.
H. 6 7/8″ (17.5 cm); W. 9″ (22.9 cm).

Inscriptions: "QUEBEC, the Capital of NEW-FRANCE, a Bishoprick, and / Seat of the Soverain COURT. / 1. The Citadel. 2. The Castel / 3. Magazine 4. yᵉ Recolets. / 5. Ursulines 6. Jesuits. 7. / 7Cathedral of Our Lady. /8. The Palace 9. yᵉ Seminary. / 10. The Hôtel Dieu. / 11. Sᵗ. Charles River. / 12. The Common Hos-pital. / 13. The Hermitage of the Recolets. / 14. The Bishop's House. 15. The / Parish Church of the Lower Town. / 16. The Upper Town 17. yᵉ Lower Town. / 18. The Platform & Battery of Cannon / 19. The Isle of Orleans 20. Point Lieve.", bottom; "Engrav'd & Printed By Thoˢ Johnston for Step. Whiting.", lower left; "Neuville / Cul de Sac / Beau Port / River Sᵗ Laurence / Sault de la Chaudierre", in image, from upper left to lower right.
Provenance: The Old Print Shop, New York, N.Y. (1951).
Bibliography: For other impressions and states see the following references: Stauffer, *American Engravers*, vol. II, no. 1505. Stokes and Haskell, *American Historical Prints*, p. 34, P. 1758–B–17. Sinclair Hitchings, "Thomas Johnston," *Boston Prints*, p. 91, fig. 49 (first state).
Lender: Yale University Art Gallery; Mabel Brady Garvan Collection. 1955.22.2.

71
Thomas Johnston, ca. 1708–1767
Bookplate of William P. Smith
Ca. 1730–1740. Line engraving. Possibly only known state.
H. 5 1/4″ (13.3 cm); W. 3 7/8″ (9.8 cm).

Inscriptions: "William P. Smith AM.", lower center; "DEUS NOBIS HÆC OTIA FECIT", in banner above; "Thomas Johnston Sculp:", center above banner and below cartouche with arms.
Bibliography: Allen, *American Book-Plates*, p. 44, illus. p. 45. Martha Gandy Fales, "Heraldic and Emblematic Engravers of Colonial Boston," *Boston Prints*, p. 204. Sinclair Hitchings, "Thomas Johnston," *Boston Prints*, pl. 60.
Lender: Yale University Art Gallery; Mabel Brady Garvan

Collection. 1948.264.

72
Nathaniel Hurd, 1729–1777
Bookplate of Thomas Child
Ca. 1765–1770. Line engraving.
One of two states.
H. 3 15/16″ (10 cm); W. 2 1/2″
(6.4 cm).

Inscriptions: "Thomas Child",
lower center; "FARI AUDE", in
banner above.
Bibliography: Allen, *American
Book-Plates*, no. 160. Hollis
French, *Jacob Hurd and his Sons
Nathaniel & Benjamin: Silver-
smiths 1702–1781* (Cambridge,
Mass., 1939), p. 98.
Lender: Bookplate Collection,
Yale University Library.

73
Nathaniel Hurd, 1729–1777
Bookplate of Francis Dana
Ca. 1770–1775. Line engraving.
Possibly only known state.
H. 4″ (10.2 cm); W. 2″ (5.1 cm).

Inscriptions: "N.H. Sc^p", lower
right; "Francis Dana", lower
center; "CAVENDOTUTUS", in ban-
ner above; "N°", upper left.
Bibliography: Allen, *American
Book-Plates*, no. 201. Hollis
French, *Jacob Hurd and his Sons
Nathaniel & Benjamin: Silver-
smiths 1702–1781* (Cambridge,
Mass., 1939), p. 99.
Lender: Bookplate Collection,
Yale University Library.

74
Nathaniel Hurd, 1729–1777
Danforth Bookplate
Ca. 1770–1775. Line engraving.
Possibly only known state.
H. 3 1/2″ (8.9 cm); W. 2 7/16″
(6.2 cm).

Inscriptions: "N.H. Sc^p", lower
right; "Danforth", lower center;
"UBI PLURA NITENT NON EGO

PAUCIS OFFENDAR MACULIS", in
banner above; "July", upper right
(not in plate).
Bibliography: Allen, *American
Book-Plates*, no. 203. Hollis
French, *Jacob Hurd and his Sons
Nathaniel & Benjamin: Silver-
smiths 1702–1781* (Cambridge,
Mass., 1939), p. 101.
Lender: Bookplate Collection,
Yale University Library.

75
Paul Revere, 1735–1818
Bookplate of David Greene
Ca. 1760–1770. Line engraving.
One of four known states (two
eighteenth-century and two
nineteenth-century).
H. 4 1/16″ (10.3 cm); W. 2 9/16″
(6.5 cm).

Inscriptions: "Revere Sc^p", lower
right; "David I. Greene", lower
center; "NEC TIMEO NEC SPERNO",
in banner above.
Bibliography: Allen, *American
Book-Plates*, no. 329. Brigham,
Paul Revere's Engravings, p. 161,
pl. 51.
Lender: Bookplate Collection,
Yale University Library.

76
Paul Revere, 1735–1818
Bookplate of Andrew Oliver
Ca. 1760–1770. Line engraving.
Possibly only known state.
H. 3 5/8″ (9.2 cm); W. 2 13/16″
(7.1 cm).

Inscriptions: "Andrew Oliver",
lower center; "PAX QUÆRITUR
BELLO", in banner above.
Bibliography: Allen, *American
Book-Plates*, no. 625. Brigham,
Paul Revere's Engravings, pp.
161–162, pl. 52.
Lender: Bookplate Collection,
Yale University Library.

77
Paul Revere, 1735–1818

Bookplate of Epes Sargent
1764. Line engraving. Only
known state.
H. 3 1/2″ (8.9 cm); W. 2 3/4″
(7 cm).

Inscriptions: "P. Revere Sculp",
lower left; "Epes Sargent", lower
center; "N°", upper left.
Bibliography: Allen, *American
Book-Plates*, no. 760. Bingham,
Paul Revere's Engravings, pp.
162–163, pl. 51.
Lender: Bookplate Collection,
Yale University Library.

78
Paul Revere, 1735–1818
Bookplate of Isaiah Thomas
Ca. 1765–1770. Line engraving.
Only known state.
H. 3 3/8″ (8.6 cm); W. 2 7/8″
(7.3 cm).

Inscriptions: "Isaiah Thomas",
lower center; "NEC • ELATUS NEC •
DEJECTUS", in banner above;
"N°", upper left.
Bibliography: Allen, *American
Book-Plates*, no. 853. Brigham,
Paul Revere's Engravings, p. 163,
pl. 52.
Lender: Bookplate Collection,
Yale University Library.

79
Paul Revere, 1735–1818
The Bloody Massacre
1770. Line engraving, colored.
Second state of two.
H. 10 3/16″ (25.9 cm); W. 8 15/16″
(22.7 cm).

Inscriptions: "Engrav'd Printed
& Sold by PAUL REVERE BOSTON",
inset in image, lower right; "The
BLOODY MASSACRE perpetrated in
King Street BOSTON on March 5th
1770, by a party of the 29th
REG^t", at top; "Unhappy
BOSTON! see thy Sons deplore, /
Thy hallow'd walks besmear'd
with guiltless Gore: / While
faithless P___n and his savage

Bands, / With murd'rous Ran-
cour stretch their bloody Hands; /
Like fierce Barbarians grinning
o'er their Prey, / Approve the
Carnage, and enjoy the Day. / If
scalding drops from Rage from
Anguish Wrung / If speechless·
Sorrows lab'ring for a Tongue, /
Or if a weeping World can ought
appease / The plaintive Ghosts
of Victims such as these; / The
Patriot's copious Tears for each
are shed, / A glorious Tribute
which embalms the Dead. / But
know, FATE summons to that
awful Goal, / Where JUSTICE
strips the Murd'rer of his Soul: /
Should venal C___ts the
scandal of the Land, / Snatch the
relentless Villain from her Hand,
/ Keen Execrations on this Plate
inscrib'd, / Shall reach a Judge
who never can be brib'd. / The
unhappy Sufferers were Mess^s
SAM^L GRAY, SAM^L MAVERICK, JAM^s
CALDWELL, CRISPUS ATTUCKS & PAT^K
CARR / Killed. Six wounded two
of them (CHRIST^R MONK & JOHN
CLARK) Mortally.", bottom.
Provenance: Rev. Joseph Lee,
Royalston, Mass. (until 1819);
Thomas Jones Lee; Thomas J.
Lee; Frederick W. French, Bos-
ton, Mass.; Alice Cheney Baltzell;
purchased by John Hill Morgan,
Farmington, Conn. (1943).
Exhibitions: Colby College Art
Museum, Waterville, Me., *Ameri-
can Arts of the Eighteenth Cen-
tury* (1967).
Bibliography: For other impres-
sions and states see the following
references. Stauffer, *American
Engravers*, vol. II, no. 2675.
Brigham, *Revere's Engravings*,
pp. 52–78, color pl. 14 (second
state). *Middendorf Collection*
(1967), pp. 88–90, illus. p. 90
(first and second states).
Lender: Yale University Art
Gallery; John Hill Morgan Collection.
1943.87.

80
Charles Willson Peale, 1741–1827
Mr. Pitt
1768. Mezzotint. Second state of two.
H. 21 11/16″ (55.1 cm); W. 14 5/8″ (37.1 cm).

Inscriptions: "Cha⁸ Willson Peale, pinx. et fects", lower right; "Worthy of Liberty, Mʳ Pitt scorns to invade the Liberties of other People", bottom; "Congress at New York", center left, on pedestal; "SANCTVS•AMOR / PATRIAE. / DAT. ANIMVM.", lower left, on plaque on foreground pedestal; "Sidney / Hamden", lower left, on busts on altar; "Magna Charta", center right, on scroll in subject's left hand.
Provenance: Francis P. Garvan, New York, N.Y.
Exhibitions: LC, *Garvan Prints* (1931), no. 28.
Bibliography: For other impressions and states see the following references. Stauffer, *American Engravers*, vol. II, no. 2426. Charles Henry Hart, "Charles Willson Peale's Allegory of William Pitt, Earl of Chatham," *Proceedings of the Massachusetts Historical Society*, 48 (Boston, 1915): 3–14, illus. (first state). R. T. H. Halsey, "America's Obligation to William Pitt, Earl of Chatham," *MMAB*, 13, no. 6 (1918), pp. 138–143, illus., p. 139 (first state). Frank H. Sommer III, "Thomas Hollis and the Arts of Dissent," *Prints in and of America to 1850* (Charlottesville, Va., 1970), pp. 142–155, fig. 13 (first state). Wendy J. Shadwell, "The Portrait Engravings of Charles Willson Peale," a paper read at the Colonial Williamsburg Print Conference, March 1974, to be published in the Spring of 1976, illus. (first and second states).

Lender: Yale University Art Gallery; Mabel Brady Garvan Collection. 1946.9.941.

81
Amos Doolittle, 1754–1832
A Display of the United States of America
1794. Stipple and line engraving, colored. Fourth state of five.
H. 20 3/4″ (52.7 cm); W. 17 1/8″ (43.5 cm) [sight].

Inscriptions: "GEORGE WASHINGTON, President of the UNITED STATES of AMERICA. The Protector of his COUNTRY, and the Supporter of the rights of MANKIND.", center, around roundel of Washington, reading from bottom; "BORN 11ᵗʰ FEB 1732", on scroll under shoulder; "The / UNITED STATES / were first declar'd / Free and Independent / July 4th 1776", upper left; "The Present / CONSTITUTION / was formd by the / Grand Convention / held at Philadelphia Sepᵗ 17ᵗʰ / 1787", upper right; "ARMS of the UNITED STATES / TOTAL of INHABITANTS 3,919,023 / E / Pluribus / Unum / ; NEW HAMPSHIRE 2 SENATORS, 4 REPRESENTATIVES. / 141,885 INHABITANTS. / INDEPENDENCE / MDCCLXXVI / ; MASSACHUSETTS 2 SENAT. 15 REPR. / 378,785 INHABITANTS. / Main 96,540 Inhabitants / ENSE PETIT PLACIDAM / SUB LIBERTATE QUIETEM / ; RHODE ISLAND 2 SENAT 2 REPR. / 68,825 INHABITANTS. / IN GOD WE HOPE / ; CONNECTICUT 2 SENAT. 7 REPR. / 237,946 INHABITANTS. / QUI TRANSTULIT / SUSTINET / ; NEW-YORK 2 SENAT. 11 REPR. / 340,120 INHABITANTS. / EXCELSIOR / FRUSTRA / ; NEW JERSEY 2 SENAT 5 REPR / 184, 139 INHABITANTS. / INDEPENDENCE / MDCCLXXVI / ; PENNSYLVANIA 2 SENAT. 14 REPR. / 434,373 INHABITANTS. / VIRTU LIBERTY / AND / INDEPENDENCE / ; DELAWARE 2 SENAT. 1 REPR. / 59,094 INHABITANTS. / INDEPENDENCE / MDCCLXXVI / ; MARYLAND 2 SENAT. 9 REPR. / 319,728 INHABITANTS. / INDEPENDENCE / MDCCLXXVI / ; VIRGINIA 2 SENAT. 23 REPR. / 747,610 INHABITANT / Kentucky 73,677 Inhabitants / INDEPENDENCE / MCCLXXVI [sic] / ; NORTH CAROLINA 2 SENAT. 11 REPR. / 393,751 INHABITANTS. / INDEPENDENCE / 1776 / O FORTUNATOS NIMIUM SUA / SI BONA / NORINT COLONOS / ; SOUTH CAROLINA. 2 SENAT. 6 REPR. / 240,000 INHABITANTS. / 1776 / ANIMIS OPIBUSQUE / PARATI / ; GEORGIA 2 SENAT. 2 REPR. / 82,584 INHABITANTS. / PRO BONO PUBLICO / 1777 / DEUS NOBIS HAEC / OCIA FECIT;", around and in coat-of-arms, reading clockwise from the top; "S.W. Territory / 30,000 Inhabitants / N.W. Territory / 5,000 Inhabitants / The number of Inhabitants in the / Several States are according to the returnes / made to the Secretary of State in / the year 1791;", lower left; "VERMONT / 85,000 Inhabitants / 2 Senat. 2 Repre. / The number of Senators and Representatives is what the Constitution alloweth / each State at Congress:", lower right; "A DISPLAY of the UNITED STATES OF AMERICA / To the Patrons of Arts and Sciences, in all parts of the World, this Plate / is most respectfully Dedicated by their most obedient humble Servant / Amos Doolittle / New Haven Marᶜʰ 1ˢᵗ 1794. / Printed & Sold by A. Doolittle New Haven where Engraving and Roling Press Printing is performed", bottom.
Bibliography: For other impressions and states see the following references. Charles Henry Hart, *Catalogue of Engraved Portraits of Washington* (New York, 1904), pp. 354–357, nos. 840, 840a, and 840b, illus. opp. p. 354 (first state), illus. opp. p. 356 (second state). Stauffer, *American Engravers*, vol. II, no. 521. Rev. William A. Beardsley, "An Old New Haven Engraver and his Work: Amos Doolittle," *Papers of the New Haven Colony Historical Society*, 8 (1914): 142–143. *Middendorf Collection* (1967), p. 102, illus. p. 103 (third state).
Lender: Yale University Art Gallery; gift of C. Sanford Bull, B.A. 1893. 1955.44.25.

82
Edward Savage, 1761–1817
Thomas Jefferson (1743–1826)
1800. Mezzotint. Second state of two.
H. 9 1/2″ (24.1 cm); W. 7 7/8″ (20 cm).

Inscriptions: "E Savage Pinx & fc.", lower left; "Philadᵃ Published June 1, 1800", lower right; "THOMAS JEFFERSON.", bottom.
Provenance: Francis P. Garvan, New York, N.Y.
Exhibitions: LC, *Garvan Prints* (1931), no. 109.
Bibliography: For other impressions and states see the following references. Charles Henry Hart, "Edward Savage, Painter and Engraver, and his Unfinished Copperplate of 'The Congress Voting Independence,'" *Proceedings of the Massachusetts Historical Society*, 19 (1905): 18. Stauffer, *American Engravers*, vol. II, no. 2746. *American Printmaking*, p. 47, fig. 90 (second state).
Lender: Yale University Art Gallery; Mabel Brady Garvan Collection. 1946.9.793.

83
Edward Savage, 1761–1817
Benjamin Rush (1745–1813)

1800. Mezzotint. Only known state.
H. 14 1/2″ (36.8 cm); w. 11 3/8″ (28.9 cm).

Inscriptions: "Painted & Engraved by E Savage / BENJAMIN RUSH, / Professor of Medicine in the University of Pennsylvania / Philadᵃ. Published by E. Savage Feb: 6, 1800.", bottom.
Provenance: Francis P. Garvan, New York, N.Y.
Exhibitions: LC, *Garvan Prints* (1931), no. 127.
Bibliography: For other impressions see the following references. Charles Henry Hart, "Edward Savage, Painter and Engraver, and his Unfinished Copperplate of 'The Congress Voting Independence,' " *Proceedings of the Massachusetts Historical Society*, 19 (1905): 18. Stauffer, *American Engravers*, vol. II, no. 2749. *American Printmaking*, p. 48, fig. 91.
Lender: Yale University Art Gallery; Mabel Brady Garvan Collection. 1946.9.893.

84
Edward Savage, 1761–1817
David Rittenhouse (1732–1796)
1796. Mezzotint. Only known state.
H. 20″ (50.8 cm); w. 14″ (35.6 cm).

Inscriptions: "C.W. Peale Pinxᵗ", lower left; "Philadᵃ Pub: Decʳ 10ᵗʰ 1796 by E. Savage.", lower center; "E: Savage Sculpᵗ", lower right; "DAVID RITTENHOUSE, L. L. D. F. R. S. / President of the American Philosophical Society.", bottom.
Provenance: Francis P. Garvan, New York, N.Y.
Exhibitions: LC, *Garvan Prints* (1931), no. 62.
Bibliography: For other impressions see the following references.

Charles Henry Hart, "Edward Savage, Painter and Engraver, and his Unfinished Copperplate of 'The Congress Voting Independence,' " *Proceedings of the Massachusetts Historical Society*, 19 (1905): 17. Stauffer, *American Engravers*, 2:no. 2748. *American Printmaking*, p. 46, fig. 85.
Lender: Yale University Art Gallery; Mabel Brady Garvan Collection. 1946.9.891.

85
William Rollinson, 1762–1842
Alexander Hamilton (1757–1804)
1804. Stipple. First state of two.
H. 21 1/2″ (54.6 cm); w. 17″ (43.2 cm).

Inscriptions: "Painted by Archᵈ. Robertson 79 Liberty Sᵗ.", lower left; "Engraved by Wᵐ. Rollinson 27 Pine Sᵗ.", lower right; "ALEXANDER HAMILTON, / Major General of the Armies of the United States of America. Secretary of the Treasury etc. etc. / New York Septʳ 1ˢᵗ 1804. Published at the Columbia Academy of Painting 79 Liberty Sᵗ. & by William Rollinson 27 Pine Street. / Entered according to Act of Congress the 28ᵗʰ Day of August 1804 by Archibald Robertson and William Rollinson of the State of New York Author and Proprietors", bottom.
Provenance: Francis P. Garvan, New York, N.Y.
Exhibitions: LC, *Garvan Prints* (1931), no. 76.
Bibliography: For other impressions and states see the following references. Stauffer, *American Engravers*, 2:no. 2709. Robert W. Reid and Charles Rollinson, *William Rollinson, Engraver* (New York, 1931), p. 44, illus. p. 45 (first state). *American Printmaking*, pp. 48–49, fig. 93 (second

state). *Made in America: Printmaking 1760–1860* (Philadelphia, Pa., 1973), pp. 16–17.
Lender: Yale University Art Gallery; Mabel Brady Garvan Collection. 1946.9.859.

86
Anonymous Artist
A Front View of Yale-College, and the College Chapel, New-Haven
1786. Woodcut. Only known state.
H. 20 1/2″ (52.1 cm); w. 17″ (43.2 cm).

Inscriptions: "A Front VIEW of YALE-COLLEGE, and the COLLEGE CHAPEL, in New-Haven. / A compendious History of Yale-College, and a general Account of the Course of Studies pursued by the Students.", lower center; "YALE-COLLEGE was founded / A. D. 1700; and subsisted at Killing- / worth, in Connecticutt, until the death of / Rector Pierson, 1707; then at Say-Brook, un- / til 1716, when it was removed and fixed at / NEW-HAVEN. Here the first College Edi- / fice was erected 1717, being 170 feet in length / and 22 feet in width, and three stories high, / containing about 50 studies in convenient / chambers, besides the Hall and Library. In / 1714 Mr. Agent DUMMER procured a dona- / tion of 800 volumes in London for the Libra- / ry; to which he afterwards obtained additions. / Governor YALE contributed to this donation, / and in 1717 added himself 300 volumes. — He / was born at New-Haven 1648; became Go- / vernor of Fort St. George, in the East-Indies, / where he lived about 20 years; and returning / to London the beginning of this century be- / came Governor of the

London East-India Com- / pany. He made so respectable a benefaction / to this academic institution, that the appella- / tion of Y A L E - C O L L E G E was / given to it, by the Governors of it at the public / commencement 1718. The present College / Edifice, which is of brick, was during / the Presidency of the Rev. THOMAS CLAP, / 1750, being 100 feet long, and 40 feet wide, / three stories high, containing 32 chambers and / 64 studies convenient for the reception of 100 / students. The College-Chapel also built of brick, / was erected 1761, being 50 feet and 40, with / a steeple 125 feet high. In this building is the / public Library consisting of about 2500 vo- / lumes. The first building of wood was taken / down 1782, when a dining-hall and kitchen / was built of brick 60 and 40 feet. /

This literary institution was incorporated / by the General Assembly of Connecticutt. The / first charter of incorporation was granted to / eleven Ministers 1701. The powers of the / Trustees were enlarged by the additional char- / ter 1723; and by that of 1745 the Trustees- / were incorporated by the name of the President / and Fellows of Yale-College, in New-Haven. / The corporation are empowered to hold estates; / continue their succession; make academic / laws, elect and constitute all officers of instruc- / tion and government usual in Universities, and / confer all the learned degrees. The ordinary / instruction and executive government is in the / hands of the President, Professors and Tutors. / Besides the four Tutors who give instruction / in the learned languages and the whole circle of the sciences, there have been three Professor-ships, (although one is now vacant) viz. / of *Mathematics & Natural Philoso- / phy, Ecclesiasti- / cal History, and Divinity.* In 1732 the Rev. / George Berkeley, D.D. then Dean of Derry, / and afterward Bishop of Cloyne in Ireland, made / a generous donation of 880 volumes, and an / estate in Rhode Island, being an house and 96 / acres of land: The annual rent of which be- / ing 100 ounces of silver, is divided into three / scholar-ships of the house, and annually appro- / priated to the three best scholars in the Latin / and Greek classics. This has proved a great / incentive among the students, to excel in clas- / sical learning. /

Major James Fitch made the first donation / in land about 600 acres in 1701, before the / first Charter. The honorable the General / Assembly in 1732, made a donation of 1500 / acres within this State. Dr. Daniel Lathrop / added a donation of 500l. to the college funds, / in 1781. These are the principal benefactions. /

The philosophic apparatus is not compleat; / it contains how-ever a reflecting Telescope, an / excellent microscope, a compleat and elegant / sett of surveying instruments, the hydrostatic / balance, an excellent brass astro-nomical qua- / drant fiitted with a nonius and spirit level, a / large planetarium and cometarium, a scioptic / glass for perspective views, an air-pump and / re-ceivers, with the other machines necessa- / ry for exhibiting the principal experiments in / the whole course of experimental philosophy / and astronomy. The college-musaeum con- / tains, though not a copious collection, yet / some great natural curiosities, and is constant- / ly

increasing. The number of ma-triculated / students or under-graduates has been for some / years from 150 to 250, and now is about 200, / divided into four classes. The course of edu- / cation in this University comprehends the / whole circle of literature. The three learned / languages are taught here, together with so / much of the sciences, as can be commu- / nicated in four years. It is expected that the youth at admission be found able to translate / Virgil, Tully, and the Greek Testament. / During their Collection residence they study, the / first year the Languages, Decimal Arithmetic, / the Proportions and Roots; they are also ex- / ercised in public speaking; The second year, / English Grammar, Rhetoric, Logic, Algebra, / and Geometry, together with English Com- / position, Oratory, Geography and the Classics: / The third is spent in Mathematics and natu- / ral Philosophy and Astronomy. In Mathema- / tics they are carried through the Conic Sec- / tions, the Mensuration of Superficies and So- / lids of all Figures, and Trigonometry with its / Applica-tion to Navigation and Astron-omy. / In Astronomy they have not only a general / systematical view of the Planets and Comets, / but are taught the Law of Gravity, the sesqui- / plicate Ratio of revolving Bodies, and their / description of equal Areas in equal times, with / the principia of the Astronomical Calculations, / whether of the heliocentric and geocentric / places of the Planets, the Eclipses of their Sa- / tellites, or the Tra-jectories of Comets: In / the fourth year they study Ethics and Metaphy- / sics or Moral Philoso-phy, Criticism, History, / and the Belles Letters. During the whole /

academic life, the students are daily exercised / in compositions, rehearsals, dialogues, and / other oratorial performances, tending to give / them a free elocution, and form them for public / speakers. Having finished this course, the / Degree of Bachelor of Arts is conferred upon / them at the anniversary Commence-ment in / September: and three years after, they / receive the Degree of Master of Arts. / Those who afterwards proceed to the high- / er Branches of Literature, and become emi- / nent for Erudition, are admitted to the / Doctorate in either or any of the Learned Pro- / fessions. About Nineteen Hun-dred have re- / ceived a Liberal Education here, and have / gone forth into the world with the honors of / this University. / YALE-COLLEGE, June 26, 1786.", lower center, text in seven columns; "NEW-HAVEN: PRINTED BY DANIEL BOWEN, in CHAPEL-STREET; where every Kind of PRINTING is performed with Dis-patch, and in the neatest Man-ner.", bottom.

Bibliography: Anson Phelps Stokes, *Historical Prints of New Haven* (New Haven, Conn., 1910), no. 10. *American Printmaking*, p. 43, fig. 78.

Lender: Yale University Art Gallery; gift of Jesse Lathrop Moss, B.A. 1869. 1940.317.

87

William Russell Birch, 1755–1834
Back of the State House, Philadelphia
1799. Line engraving, colored.
First state of four.
H. 10 3/4" (27.3 cm); w. 12 3/4" (32.4 cm).

Inscriptions: "Drawn Engraved & Published by W. Birch & Son",

lower left; "Sold by R. Campbell & Cº. Nº 30 Chestnut Street Philadª. 1799.", lower right; "BACK of the STATE HOUSE, PHILA-DELPHIA.", bottom.

Provenance: Francis P. Garvan, New York, N.Y.

Bibliography: For other impres-sions and states see the following references. Stauffer, *American Engravers*, vol. II, no. 182. Stokes and Haskell, *American Historical Prints*, p. 77, 1798–1800–D-2. Martin P. Snyder, "William Birch: his Philadelphia Views," *PMHB*, 73, no. 3 (1949), pp. 271–315 (includes checklist). *Phila-delphia Reviewed: The Print-maker's Record, 1750–1850* (Winterthur, Del., 1960), pp. 27–28. Martin P. Snyder, "William Birch: His Philadelphia Views," *PMHB*, 88, no. 2 (1964), pp. 164–173.

Lender: Yale University Art Gallery; Mabel Brady Garvan Collection. 1946.9.1970.

88

William Russell Birch, 1755–1834
Preparation for War to Defend Commerce
1800. Line engraving, colored.
Only known state.
H. 11 1/4" (28.3 cm); w. 13 1/2" (34.4 cm).

Inscriptions: "Drawn Engraved & Published by W. Birch & Son.", lower left; "Sold by R. Campbell & Cº Nº 30 Chestnut Street Philadª 1800.", lower right; "Preparation for WAR to defend Commerce. / The Sweedish Church Southwark with the building of the FRIGATE PHILA-DELPHIA.", bottom.

Bibliography: For other impres-sions see the following references. Stauffer, *American Engravers*, 2:no. 170. Stokes and Haskell, *American Historical Prints*, p. 77, 1798–1800—D-2. Martin P.

Snyder, "William Birch: his Philadelphia Views," *PMHB*, 73, no. 3 (1949), pp. 271–315 (includes checklist); "William Birch: his Philadelphia Views," *PMHB*, 88, no. 2 (1964), pp. 164–173.
Lender: The Athenaeum of Philadelphia; gift of Mrs. Charles Fearon, 1952. 18518.

Furniture

89
John L. Boqueta de Woiseri, active 1797–1815
A View of New Orleans Taken from the Plantation of Marigny. 1804. Aquatint, printed partially in color. Only known state.
H. 13 1/2″ (34.3 cm); W. 22 1/2″ (57.2 cm).

Inscriptions: "Boqueta de Woiseri fecit in New Orleans Novr 1803.", lower left; "A. Plantation of Marigny / B. Saw Mills", lower right; "A VIEW OF NEW ORLEANS TAKEN FROM THE PLANTATION OF MARIGNY", bottom; "UNDER MY WINGS EVERY THING PROSPERS", on ribbon held by eagle, center.
Provenance: Henry Graves, Jr., New York, N.Y. (until 1959); Kennedy Galleries, New York, N.Y. (1960).
Exhibitions: Kennedy Galleries, New York, N.Y., *Notable American Prints: The Collection of Henry Graves, Jr.* (1959), no. 14. MMA, *Middendorf Collection* (1967), no. 71, illus. p. 107. MGA, *American Printmaking* (1969–1971), no. 92, fig. 92.
Bibliography: For other impressions see the following references. Mantle Fielding, *American Engravers upon Copper and Steel* (Philadelphia, 1917), p. 293, no. 1743. J. William Middendorf II, "Notes on Collecting American Historical Prints," *The Walpole Society Notebook* (1958), pp. 33–34.
Lender: The Secretary of the Navy and Mrs. J. William Middendorf II.

90
Upholstered settee
Philadelphia, Pa., ca. 1740. American walnut, yellow pine; upholstered in red linen and green silk damask, probably eighteenth century.
O.H. 46″ (106.8 cm); O.W. 62″ (157.5 cm); O.D. 28 1/2″ (72.4 cm).

Provenance: Descended in the Smith family of Philadelphia, Pa., possibly from Hannah Logan Smith (1720–1761), Burlington, N.J. (daughter of James Logan, 1674–1751), in whose husband's inventory (1771) a "settee covered with damask £9.10.0" was listed; Louis Guerineau Myers.
Exhibitions: Winter Antiques Show, New York, N.Y., 1966.
Bibliography: Louis G. Myers, "Queen Anne Chairs of Colonial Days," *Antiques*, 22 (Dec. 1932): 215–217, fig. 7. Halsey and Cornelius, *The American Wing*, p. 113, fig. 53. Robert Bishop, *Centuries and Styles of the American Chair 1640–1970* (New York, 1972), p. 115, fig. 125.
Lender: The Metropolitan Museum of Art, New York, N.Y.; Rogers Fund (1925). 25.115.1.

91
Easy chair
Philadelphia, Pa., 1740–1750. Walnut; reproduction pale yellow silk damask, with eighteenth-century blue-green galloon.
O.H. 47 1/4″ (120 cm); S.H. 14 1/2″ (36.8 cm); O.W. 37 3/4″ (95.9 cm); O.D. 28 1/2″ (72.4 cm).

Provenance: Descended through six generations of a Philadelphia family to a descendant living on the eastern shore of Maryland; David Stockwell, Inc., Wilmington, Del.
Lender: Private collection.

92
Armchair
Philadelphia, Pa., 1730–1750. Walnut; yellow pine back of slip-seat frame; modern yellow wool upholstery.
O.H. 45″ (114.3 cm); S.H. 16 3/8″ (41.6 cm); O.W. 32 1/2″ (82.6 cm); O.D. 22 1/2″ (57.2 cm).

Inscription: The numeral "IIII" chiseled into slip-seat frame, front seat rail, and rear seat rail; the inscription "John & Mary Ann Bacon 1801 / Geo. B. Wood. 1859. / Mary May Dunn 1909" carved into slip-seat frame; "Wood" written in pencil on slip-seat frame; "G. B. WOOD" branded into underside of front and rear seat rails.
Provenance: John Bacon (b. 1779), m. Mary Ann Warder, Philadelphia, Pa.; their daughter Elizabeth H. Bacon (Mrs. Horatio C. Wood, b. 1807); her son, George Bacon Wood (b. 1832); his daughter, Mary May (Mrs. Harry Martyn Dunn, b. 1859); her daughter, Emelie (Mrs. Norman Henderson Donald, b. 1892).
Lender: Mr. Peter W. Eliot.

93
Side chair
Philadelphia, Pa., 1740–1750. Cherry.
O.H. 42 1/8″ (107 cm); S.H. 17 1/2″ (44.5 cm); O.W. 21″ (53.3 cm); O.D. 19″ (48.3 cm).

Provenance: Barclay Ivins, Penn's Manor; Howard Reifsnyder. Philadelphia, Pa.
Bibliography: Nutting, *Furniture Treasury*, vol. II, no. 2119 [illus.]. Bondome, "What Chairs for the Dining-Room," *Antiques*, 13 (June 1928): 499, fig. 3. *Colonial Furniture: The Superb Collection of the Late Howard Reifsnyder* (New York, 1929), p. 213, no. 653.
Lender: Mrs. Alfred Elliott Bissell.

94
Side chair
New York, N.Y., 1730–1750.
Walnut; crotch walnut splat
veneered on maple; pine corner
blocks; cherry slip-seat frame now
upholstered in modern gold silk
damask.
O.H. 38 1/2″ (97.8 cm); S.H. 16″
(40.6 cm); O.W. 20 1/2″ (52.1 cm);
O.D. 21 3/4″ (55.3 cm).

Provenance: Grizzell Eastwicke
(Mrs. Charles Apthorp, 1709–
1796); Elizabeth Symington
(until 1960).
Exhibitions: Victoria and Albert
Museum, London, *CINOA Ex-
hibit* (1962), no. 121.
Bibliography: Helen Comstock,
American Furniture (New York,
1962), no. 161 [illus.]. John T.
Kirk, *American Chairs: Queen
Anne and Chippendale* (New
York, 1972), no. 130, illus. p. 113.
Lender: Benjamin Ginsburg.

95
Tea table
New England, 1740–1760.
Mahogany, white pine, poplar.
O.H. 26 3/4″ (68 cm); O.W. 20″
(50.8 cm); O.D. 30″ (76.2 cm).

Provenance: Laight family, Salem,
Mass.
Lender: Mr. and Mrs. Stanley
Stone.

96
Tea table
Saybrook-Lyme area, Conn.,
1740–1780.
Maple, birch.
O.H. 27 1/4″ (69.2 cm); O.W. 30 1/2″

(77.5 cm); O.D. 26 1/4″ (66.7 cm).

Provenance: Purchased by the
donor's father, George L. Cheney,
in Essex, Conn.; Harriet Cheney
(Mrs. Augustus C. Downing).
Exhibitions: Lyman Allyn Mu-
seum, New London, Conn., *New
London County Furniture 1640–
1840* (1974), no. 17, illus. p. 23.
Lender: Wadsworth Atheneum,
Hartford, Conn.; gift of Mrs.
Augustus C. Downing. 1973.113.

97
Dressing table
Newport, R.I., 1740–1770.
Mahogany, pine, tulip poplar.
O.H. 30 3/8″ (77.2 cm); O.W. 34 1/4″
(87 cm); O.D. 22 1/2″ (57.2 cm).

Provenance: Cornelius C. Moore;
Israel Sack, Inc., New York, N.Y.
Exhibitions: The Rhode Island
Historical Society, Providence,
R.I., *The John Brown House
Loan Exhibition of Rhode Island
Furniture* (1965), no. 63, illus.
p. 99.
Bibliography: *Important Ameri-
can Furniture: Property from the
Estate of the Late Cornelius C.
Moore* (New York: Parke-Bernet
Galleries, Oct. 30, 1971), no. 129,
illus. p. 45.
Lender: Mrs. Thomas M. Cole.

98
Blockfront dressing table
Boston, Mass., 1730–1750.
Walnut, white pine.
O.H. 31 1/2″ (80 cm); O.W. 43 1/2″
(110.5 cm); O.D. 21″ (53.3 cm).

Provenance: Descended in the

Howland-Wellington-Ellery
families; Israel Sack, Inc., New
York, N.Y.
Bibliography: *American Antiques
from Israel Sack Collection*
(1972), vol. III, no. P3394, illus.
pp. 738–739; IV:861, no. P3394,
illus. p. 861.
Lender: The Dietrich Brothers
Americana Corporation.

99
Blockfront bureau table
Newport, R.I., 1760–1790.
Mahogany; tulip and chestnut.
O.H. 34″ (86.4 cm); O.W. 36″ (91.4
cm); O.D. 20 1/2″ (52.1 cm).

Provenance: Pascal Allen, Warren, R.I.; Pascal Allen Horton,
Stratham, N.H.; Higgins (a
dealer), Exeter, N.H.; H. Eugene
Bolles, Boston, Mass. (1907).
Bibliography: Luke V. Lockwood,
Colonial Furniture (New York,
1913), I, 124, fig. 122. Halsey and
Tower, *Homes of Our Ancestors*,
fig. 112, facing p. 145.
Lender: The Metropolitan Museum of Art, New York, N.Y.; gift
of Mrs. Russell Sage (1909).
10.125.83.

100
Blockfront desk and bookcase
Newport, R.I., 1765–1785.
Mahogany, tulip poplar, chest-
nut, white pine.
O.H. 106 3/4″ (271.1 cm);
O.W. 44 3/4″ (113.7 cm);
O.D. 25 1/4″ (64.1 cm).

Provenance: Made for John
Brown (1736–1803), Providence,
R.I.; his great-granddaughter,

Caroline L. H. (Mrs. A. S. Cheese-
brough), Bristol, R.I.; Collings
and Collings, New York, N.Y.;
Francis P. Garvan, New York,
N.Y. (1918); Mabel Brady Garvan,
New York, N.Y. (1937).
Exhibitions: American Art Gal-
leries, New York, N.Y., *Girl Scout
Loan Exhibition* (1929), no. 638.
Bibliography: Meyric R. Rogers,
"Garvan Furniture at Yale," *The
Connoisseur's Yearbook* (1960),
no. 10. Wendy A. Cooper, "The
Purchase of Furniture and
Furnishings by John Brown,
Providence Merchant," *Antiques*,
103 (Feb. 1973): 334, 338–39, pl. 2.
Kirk, *Early American Furniture*,
pp. 34–35, fig. 19.
Lender: Yale University Art
Gallery; Mabel Brady Garvan
Collection. 1940.320.

101
Chest-on-chest
Colchester, Conn., area, 1780–
1805.
Cherry, tulip poplar, pine.
O.H. 90″ (228.6 cm); O.W. 40 1/4″
(102.2 cm); O.D. 23 3/4″ (60.3 cm).

Provenance: Morgan Bulkeley;
Elinor B. Ingersoll.
Exhibitions: Morgan Memorial,
Hartford, Conn., *Three Centuries
of Connecticut Furniture 1635–
1935* (1935), p. 27, no. 223 (illus.).
Bibliography: Luke Vincent
Lockwood, *Colonial Furniture in
America* (New York, 1926), II,
120–123, fig. 120; Benjamin Gins-
burg, "The Barbour Collection
of Connecticut Furniture in the
Connecticut Historical Society,"
Antiques, 105 (May 1974): 1093

(illus.).
Lender: The Connecticut Historical Society, Hartford, Conn.; gift of Elinor B. Ingersoll.

102
Bombé desk and bookcase
Boston, Mass., 1770–1792.
Maker: George Bright (1726–1805).
Mahogany, white pine.
o.h. 99 1/2″ (252.7 cm); o.w. 43″ (109.2 cm); o.d. 24″ (61 cm).

Signature: "Ge [?] Bright" on bottom of left bottom drawer of interior; inscribed in chalk.
Provenance: Samuel Barrett (1738–1798), Boston, Mass.; acquired by Ann (Barrett) and Isaac Green, Windsor, Vt. (1792); preserved in Green homestead (until 1956).
Exhibitions: MFA, *A Bit of Vanity: Furniture of Eighteenth Century Boston* (1972), no. 24, illus. p. 24.
Bibliography: Richard H. Randall, Jr., "George Bright, Cabinetmaker," *Art Quarterly*, 27, no. 2 (1964), pp. 136, 144–146, figs. 1–4; *American Furniture in the Museum of Fine Arts Boston* (Boston, 1965), no. 64, illus. pp. 91–93. Gilbert T. Vincent, "The Bombé Furniture of Boston," *Boston Furniture of the Eighteenth Century* (Boston, 1974), pp. 176–178, figs. 124, 140.
Lender: Museum of Fine Arts, Boston; bequest of Miss Charlotte Hazen. 56.1194.

103
Side chair
Philadelphia, Pa., 1755–1785.
Mahogany; cedar corner blocks and slip-seat frame.
o.h. 39″ (99.1 cm); s.h. 17 1/4″ (43.8 cm); o.w. 22 1/4″ (56.5 cm); o.d. 17 1/4″ (43.8 cm).

Provenance: Joseph Kindig and Son, York, Pa.; Reginald M. Lewis.
Bibliography: *American Furniture Featuring Examples by Important XVIII Century Cabinetmakers Property of the Estate of the Late Reginald M. Lewis* (Parke-Bernet Galleries, New York, N.Y., March 24–25, 1961), no. 123, illus. p. 37.
Lender: Private collection.

104
Side chair
Philadelphia, Pa., 1760–1780.
Mahogany; upholstered with reproduction yellow silk damask.
o.h. 41″ (94.1 cm); s.h. 17″ (43.1 cm); w. 21 3/4″ (55.2 cm).

Provenance: L. Richmond, Freehold, N.J.; Mrs. J. Amory Haskell, Red Bank, N.J.; Israel Sack, Inc., New York; Cornelius C. Moore.
Bibliography: *Americana Collection of the Late Mrs. J. Amory Haskell* (New York: Parke-Bernet Galleries, May 17–20, 1944), pt. 2, p. 207, no. 743. *Important American Furniture: Property from the Estate of the Late Cornelius C. Moore* (New York: Parke-Bernet Galleries, Oct. 30, 1971), no. 125.
Lender: Department of State, Diplomatic Reception Rooms; gift of Mr. and Mrs. George M. Kaufman.

105
Side chair
Massachusetts, possibly Boston, ca. 1765.
Mahogany.
o.h. 38″ (96.5 cm); o.w. 23 1/2″ (59.7 cm); o.d. 22 1/8″ (56.2 cm).

Provenance: Henry V. Weil, New York, N.Y.; Mrs. J. Amory Haskell, Red Bank, N.J.; possibly one of a set of chairs that descended in the deWolfe family of Boston, Mass., and Bristol, R.I.
Exhibitions: Monmouth County Historical Association, Freehold, N.J. (n.d.).
Bibliography: *Americana Collection of the Late Mrs. J. Amory Haskell* (New York, Parke-Bernet Galleries, May 17–20, 1944), p. 214, fig. 753. Joseph Downs, "Recent Additions to the American Wing," *MMAB*, n.s. 3 (Nov. 1944): 81 (illus.). Helen Comstock, *American Furniture* (New York, 1962), p. 147, fig. 272.
Lender: The Metropolitan Museum of Art; Rogers Fund (1944). 44.55.

106
Side chair
East Windsor, Conn., ca. 1780.
Maker: Attributed to Eliphalet Chapin (1741–1807).
Cherry; white pine corner blocks; white oak seat frame.
o.h. 38 3/8″ (97.5 cm); s.h. 16 3/8″ (41.6 cm); o.w. 20 1/2″ (52.1 cm); o.d. 16 5/8″ (42.2 cm).

Provenance: Harry Arons, Ansonia, Conn.; Francis P. Garvan, New York, N.Y.
Exhibitions: WA, *Connecticut Furniture* (1967), no. 237, illus. p. 130.
Bibliography: Nutting, *Furniture Treasury*, II, 2192 [illus.]. Kirk, *Early American Furniture*, p. 123, fig. 114; *American Chairs: Queen Anne and Chippendale* (New York, 1972), p. 146, fig. 194.
Lender: Yale University Art Gallery; Mabel Brady Garvan Collection. 1930.2561.

107
Side Chair
Goffstown or Bedford, N.H., 1770–1790.
Maker: attributed to Major John Dunlap (1746–1792).
Maple, cherry.
o.h. 44 7/8″ (114 cm); s.h. 16 3/4″ (42.6 cm); o.w. 21 7/8″ (55.6 cm); o.d. 13 7/8″ (35.2 cm).

Provenance: Found by Mrs. DeWitt Howe in Goffstown, N.H.; purchased by Mrs. J. Insley Blair.
Exhibitions: Currier Gallery of Art, Manchester, N.H., *The Decorative Arts of New Hampshire 1725–1825* (1964), nos. 38, 39, illus. p. 37; *The Dunlaps and Their Furniture* (1970), p. 9, pl. 78.
Bibliography: "American Chairs," *Antiques*, 81 (May 1962): illus. p. 542.
Lender: The Metropolitan Museum of Art, New York, N.Y.; gift of Mrs. J. Insley Blair (1943). 43.149.1.

106
(detail)

108
Corner chair
Newport, R.I., ca. 1760.
Mahogany; maple slip-seat
frame; white pine corner blocks.
O.H. 31 1/4″ (79.4 cm); S.H. 17″
(43.2 cm); O.W. 29″ (73.7 cm);
O.D. 27″ (68.6 cm).

Inscription: The name "Brown"
written on slip-seat frame.
Provenance: One of a pair made
for John Brown (1736–1803),
Providence, R.I.; inherited by his
daughter Sarah (Mrs. Karl
Herreshoff) in 1783; Mrs. Sidney
Herreshoff, Bristol, R.I.; Israel
Sack, Inc., New York, N.Y.;
Lansdell K. Christie; Israel Sack,
Inc., New York, N.Y.
Exhibitions: MMA, *American
Art from American Collections*
(1963), pl. 57.
Bibliography: Luke Vincent
Lockwood, *Colonial Furniture*
(New York, 1926), II, 71–72,
fig. 521. *The Lansdell K. Christie
Collection of Notable American
Furniture* (New York: Sotheby
Parke Bernet, Oct. 21, 1972), p. 72,
no. 49, illus. pp. 71, 73. *American
Antiques from Israel Sack Col-
lection*, IV, P937, illus. pp. 966–
967.
Lender: Mr. Peter W. Eliot.

109
Chest-on-chest
Charleston, S.C., ca. 1770.
Maker: Attributed to Thomas
Elfe, ca. 1719–1775.
Mahogany; yellow popular;
cypress.
O.H. 87″ (220.9 cm); O.W. 44 1/2″
(113.0 cm); O.D. 24 3/8″ (61.9 cm).

Exhibitions: Virginia Museum of
Fine Arts, Richmond, *Southern
Furniture 1640–1820* (Jan.–March
1952), p. 15, fig. 8.
Bibliography: E. Milby Burton,
*Thomas Elfe, Charleston Cabinet-
Maker*, The Charleston Leaflet
No. 25 (Charleston, 1952), p. 9,
fig. 2; *Charleston Furniture
1700–1825* (Charlestown, S.C.,

1955), p. 45, fig. 36.
Lender: Colonial Williamsburg
Foundation, Williamsburg, Va.
1974.166.

110
High chest
Philadelphia, Pa., ca. 1770.
Mahogany, cedar, tulip poplar.
O.H. 91 1/2″ (232.4 cm);
O.W. 46 3/4″ (118.8 cm);
O.D. 24 1/4″ (61.6 cm).

Provenance: Barnes family;
George S. Palmer, New London,
Conn.
Exhibitions: MMA, *Masterpieces
of Fifty Centuries* (1970), no. 343,
p. 295, illus. p. 294.
Bibliography: R. T. H. Halsey,
"William Savery, the Colonial
Cabinetmaker and His Furni-
ture," *MMAB*, 13 (Dec. 1918):
262, fig. 7. Nutting, *Furniture
Treasury*, I, 364 (illus.). Joseph
Downs, "A Philadelphia Low-
boy," *MMAB*, 27 (Dec. 1932):
259–262, illus. p. 261.
Lender: The Metropolitan Mu-
seum of Art, New York, N.Y.;
Kennedy Fund (1918). 18.110.4.

111
Tea table
Philadelphia, Pa., 1760–1775.
Mahogany.
O.H. top down, 27 5/8″ (70.2 cm);
DIAM. top, 33 3/8″ (84.8 cm).

Provenance: Louis Guerineau
Myers.
Bibliography: Halsey and Tower,
Homes of Our Ancestors, p. 106,
fig. 90. Halsey and Cornelius, *The
American Wing*, p. 137, fig. 68.
Meyric R. Rogers, *American In-
terior Design* (New York, 1947),
p. 60, fig. 36.
Lender: The Metropolitan Mu-
seum of Art, New York, N.Y.;
Rogers Fund (1925). 25.115.31.

112
High chest
Connecticut, ca. 1780.
Cherry, pine, tulip poplar.

O.H. 87″ (221 cm); O.W. 37 1/2″
(95.3 cm); O.D. 19 5/8″ (49.9 cm).

Inscription: "Timothy Millet
[r?]" written in chalk on the back
of the third (counting from the
bottom) drawer of the upper
section.
Provenance: Israel Sack.
Exhibitions: WA; *Connecticut
Furniture* (1967), no. 85, illus. p.
51.
Bibliography: Nutting, *Furniture
Treasury*, I, 384 [illus.]. Charles
F. Montgomery, "Furniture,"
American Art Journal, 8 (May
1975): illus. p. 60.
Lender: Greenfield Village and
Henry Ford Museum, Dearborn,
Mich.

113
Chest-on-chest-on-frame
Henniker or Salisbury, N.H.,
1790–1795.
Maker: Attributed to the Dunlap
school of cabinetmakers.
Curly maple, white pine.
O.H. 82 1/2″ (209.6 cm); O.W. 41″
(104.1 cm); O.D. 18 3/4″ (47.6 cm).

Provenance: Found in Weare,
N.H.; Agnes Eastman; Albert
Marks; Israel Sack, Inc., New
York, N.Y.
Exhibitions: Currier Gallery of
Art, Manchester, N.H., *The
Decorative Arts of New Hamp-
shire, 1725–1825* (1964), p. 40, no.
46; *The Dunlaps and Their
Furniture* (1970), p. 77, no. 1.
Bibliography: Charles E. Buckley,
"A New Hampshire Double
Chest," *Currier Gallery of Art
Bulletin* (June–Sept. 1959).
Melvin E. Watts, "New England
Furniture in the Currier Collec-
tion," *Currier Gallery of Art
Bulletin* (July–Sept. 1969). Kirk,
Early American Furniture, p. 59,
fig. 44.
Lender: The Currier Gallery of
Art, Manchester, N.H.

114
Card table

Massachusetts, 1760–1780.
Mahogany, white pine, maple;
original needlework top.
O.H. 28 1/4″ (71.8 cm); O.W. 35 3/4″
(90.8 cm); O.D. 34 3/4″ (88.3 cm).

Provenance: Dr. William Samuel
Johnson (1727–1819), first presi-
dent of King's College, later
Columbia University; Johnson
family (until 1950s); John S.
Walton, Inc. (adv. *Antiques*, 102
[Nov. 1972]: 728).
Bibliography: Frances Clary
Morse, *Furniture of the Olden
Time* (New York, 1908), pp. 232–
233, illus. p. 199.
Lender: Mr. and Mrs. Stanley
Stone.

115
Pole screen
Massachusetts, 1760–1780.
Mahogany; original needlework.
O.H. 53 1/2″ (135.9 cm); H. screen
22 1/2″ (57.2 cm); W. screen
20 1/2″ (52.1 cm).

Provenance: See no. 114.
Bibliography: Frances Clary
Morse, *Furniture of the Olden
Time* (New York, 1908), p. 308,
illus. p. 257.
Lender: Mr. and Mrs. Stanley
Stone.

116
Card table
New York, N.Y., 1765–1785.
Mahogany; white pine drawer
supports; white oak fly rail; red
gum back rail and drawer linings.
O.H. 27 3/4″ (70.5 cm);
O.W. 35 1/4″ (89.5 cm); O.D. 17 3/4″
(45.1 cm).

Inscription: "H. TIBATS" stamped
on left hinge of the top.
Bibliography: *Yale Alumni
Magazine* (Jan. 1962), illus. p. 11.
Kirk, *Early American Furniture*,
pp. 36–37, fig. 21. Charles F.
Montgomery, "Furniture,"
American Art Journal, 8 (May
1975): illus. p. 65.
Lender: Yale University Art

Gallery; Mabel Brady Garvan Collection. 1936.308.

117
Stool
New York, 1760–1780.
Mahogany.
O.H. 18″ (45.7 cm); O.W. 22″ (55.9 cm); O.D. 16″ (40.6 cm).

Exhibitions: MMA, *American Art from American Collections* (1963), no. 44.
Lender: Mr. and Mrs. Stanley Stone.

118
Painted Chest
Yellow pine, tulip poplar.
O.H. 28 5/8″ (72.7 cm); O.W. 52 1/2″ (133.4 cm); O.D. 23″ (58.4 cm).

Provenance: Mrs. R. W. deForest.
Bibliography: Henry Kauffman, *Pennsylvania Dutch American Folk Art* (New York, 1946), illus. p. 118. Helen Comstock, *American Furniture* (New York, 1962), no. 292 [illus.]. Dean A. Fales, Jr., *American Painted Furniture 1660–1880* (New York, 1972), pp. 256–257, illus. no. 447.
Lender: The Metropolitan Museum of Art, New York, N.Y.; Rogers Fund (1923). 23.16.

119
Windsor armchair
Probably Philadelphia, Pa., or possibly New York, N.Y., 1760–1780.
Red oak arm rail; tulip seat; maple legs, stretchers, arm supports, and spindles.
O.H. 28 1/2″ (72.4 cm); O.W. 27 1/8″ (68.9 cm); O.D. 20 3/4″ (52.7 cm).

Inscription: "PVR" branded on underside of seat.
Provenance: "PVR" is the brand of Philip Van Rensselaer of Cherry Hill, Albany, N.Y. (1747–1798), who was probably the original owner. Van Rensselaer married Maria Sanders in 1768,

and the chair then descended through the family: probably to their daughter Elizabeth, who married Peter Edmond Elmendorf; to their daughter Maria and her husband Peter Sanders; to their son Charles P. Sanders; to his son Charles P. II; to his son J. Glen; to his widow, Pearl (1961). Colonial Williamsburg then purchased the Glen-Sanders collection of furnishings.
Exhibitions: MMA, *A Loan Exhibition of New York State Furniture* (1934), no. 75. Colonial Williamsburg, *The Glen-Sanders Collection from Scotia, New York* (1966), p. 24.
Bibliography: John M. Graham II, "Scotia Furnishings," *Antiques*, 89 (1966): illus. p. 101. Dean Fales, Jr., *American Painted Furniture, 1660–1880* (New York, 1972), p. 85, fig. 135.
Lender: Colonial Williamsburg Foundation, Williamsburg, Va. 1964.252.

120
Windsor high chair
Philadelphia, Pa., 1755–1775.
White oak crest rail, spindles, and arm rail; sycamore seat; hickory arm supports, legs, and stretchers.
O.H. 38 3/4″ (98.4 cm); S.H. 19 7/8″ (50.5 cm); O.W. 14 3/8″ (36.5 cm); O.D. 10 1/4″ (26 cm).

Provenance: Wallace Nutting, Framingham, Mass. (sale New York, John Wanamaker, Sept. 1918); Francis P. Garvan, New York, N.Y.
Bibliography: Wallace Nutting, *A Windsor Handbook* (Saugus, Mass., 1917), p. 101, illus. p. 100; *Furniture Treasury*, II, no.

2530 [illus.].
Lender: Yale University Art Gallery; Mabel Brady Garvan Collection. 1930.2364.

121
Windsor Armchair
Massachusetts, 1780–1800.
White oak crest rail and spindles; white pine seat; beech stiles, arms, arm supports, legs, and stretchers.
O.H. 43 1/4″ (109.9 cm); S.H. 17 1/4″ (43.8 cm); O.W. 21 1/4″ (54 cm); O.D. 20″ (50.8 cm).

Provenance: Capt. Obadiah Pease (1743–1831), Edgartown, Mass.; Maria Thurston Pease; Laura M. Pease; Charles W. Lyon, New York, N.Y.; Francis P. Garvan, New York, N.Y. (1919).
Bibliography: Meyric R. Rogers, "The Mabel Brady Garvan Collection of Furniture," *Yale Alumni Magazine*, 25 (Jan. 1962): illus. p. 13. Kirk, *Early American Furniture*, p. 142, fig. 144.
Lender: Yale University Art Gallery; Mabel Brady Garvan Collection. 1930.2360.

122
Windsor armchair
Lisbon, Conn., 1785–1795.
Maker: Ebenezer Tracy (1744–1803).
White oak crest rail, spindles, arm supports, and stretchers; chestnut seat; hard maple legs.
O.H. 38 5/8″ (98.1 cm); S.H. 17 5/8″ (44.8 cm); O.W. 17 1/4″ (43.8 cm); O.D. 20″ (50.8 cm).

Inscription: "EB: TRACY" branded on underside of seat.
Provenance: Irving W. Lyon, Hartford, Conn.; Francis P.

Garvan, New York, N.Y.
Bibliography: Kirk, *Early American Furniture*, p. 140, fig. 143.
Lender: Yale University Art Gallery; Mabel Brady Garvan Collection. 1930.2377.

123
Chest-on-chest
Salem, Mass., 1796.
Makers: Cabinetwork by William Lemon (1763–1827); carving by Samuel McIntire (1757–1811).
Mahogany, ebony, satinwood, white pine.
O.H. 102 1/2″ (260.4 cm); O.W. 46 3/4″ (118.8 cm); O.D. 23″ (58.4 cm).

Inscription: Scratched on top of lower case "J. Shaw 1809, July 14."
Provenance: Probably owned by Elizabeth Crowninshield Derby (1736–1799); descended in Derby family of Salem and Curtis family of Boston.
Exhibitions: MMA, *19th-Century America* (1970), no. 1 [illus.].
Bibliography: Fiske Kimball, "Chest-on-Chest with Carvings by Samuel McIntire," *Old-Time New England*, 22 (Oct. 1930): 87–89; "Furniture Carvings by Samuel McIntire," *Antiques*, 9 (March 1931): 209, figs. 4–5. Mabel M. Swan, "McIntire: Check and Countercheck," *Antiques*, 21 (Feb. 1932): 86–87. Hipkiss, *Karolik Collection*, pp. 74–75, fig. 41. Dean A. Fales, Jr., "The Furniture of McIntire," *Samuel McIntire: A Bicentennial Symposium 1757–1957* (Salem, Mass., 1957), p. 58, fig. 26.
Lender: Museum of Fine Arts, Boston; M. and M. Karolik Collection. 41.580.

123
(detail)

124

Gentleman's secretary and bookcase
Salem, Mass., 1800–1810.
Mahogany; light and dark wood inlay; white pine.
o.h. 96″ (243.8 cm); o.w. 68 ″ (172.7 cm); o.d. 20″ (50.8 cm).

Provenance: Israel Sack, Inc., New York, N.Y. (adv. *Antiques*, 95 [June 1969]).
Bibliography: "Recent Accessions," *MMAB*, 29 (April 1971): illus. p. 371.
Lender: The Metropolitan Museum of Art, New York, N.Y.; purchase, by exchange. 1971.9.

125

Side chair
Salem, Mass., ca. 1795.
Maker: Carving attributed to Samuel McIntire (1757–1811).
Mahogany; ebony; ash front and side-seat rails; birch, veneered with mahogany rear-seat rail.
o.h. 39 3/8″ (100 cm); s.h. 17″ (43.2 cm); o.w. 21 3/4″ (55.3 cm); o.d. 18 1/2″ (47 cm).

Provenance: Made for Elias Hasket Derby (1739–1799); inherited by his daughter, Elizabeth Derby (Mrs. Nathaniel West, 1762–1814); Martha Codman (Mrs. Maxim Karolik), until 1923.
Bibliography: Fiske Kimball, "Furniture Carvings by Samuel McIntire," *Antiques*, 19 (Jan. 1931): 30–31, fig. 3. Hipkiss, *Karolik Collection*, pp. 156–157, fig. 92. Richard H. Randall, Jr., *American Furniture in the Museum of Fine Arts, Boston* (Boston, 1965), pp. 205, 207, fig. 166.

Lender: Museum of Fine Arts, Boston; M. and M. Karolik Collection. 23.27.

126

Painted chair
Philadelphia, Pa., or Salem, Mass. ca. 1796.
Maple; one ash seat rail; three birch seat rails; pine and cedar corner blocks.
h. 38 3/4″ (98.4 cm); w. of seat 19″ (48.3 cm); d. of seat 17 3/4″ (45.1 cm).

Provenance: Descended in the Derby, West, and Lander families to Mrs. Karolik.
Bibliography: Hipkiss, *Karolik Collection*, p. 166, no. 104 [illus.].
Lender: Museum of Fine Arts, Boston; M. and M. Karolik Collection. 39.108.

127

Card table
Boston (or Salem?), Mass., ca. 1800.
Mahogany with light and dark wood inlay; bird's-eye maple; white pine; birch fly rail.
o.h. 28 3/8″ (72.1 cm); o.w. 35 13/16″ (91 cm); o.d. 17 5/16″ (44 cm).

Inscription: "No 1" written in pencil on underside of top.
Provenance: Mr. and Mrs. Giles Whiting, New York, N.Y.
Exhibitions: American Art Galleries, New York, *Girl Scout Loan Exhibition* (1929), no. 734 [illus.].
Bibliography: *Important American Furniture from the Estate of the Late Flora E. [Mrs. Giles] Whiting* (New York, Parke-Bernet Galleries, April 14–22, 1972), no. 751, illus. p. 125.

Lender: Mr. and Mrs. George M. Kaufman.

128

Tambour desk
Boston, Mass., 1795–1805.
Makers: Attributed to John (ca. 1738–ca. 1818) and Thomas (1771–1848) Seymour.
Mahogany inlaid with light wood; curly maple; white pine.
o.h. 41 3/4″ (106.1 cm); o.w. 37 1/2″ (95.3 cm); o.d. 19 1/2″ (49.5 cm).

Provenance: Israel Sack, Inc.; Mr. and Mrs. Andrew Varick Stout.
Bibliography: Mabel M. Swan, "John Seymour & Son, Cabinetmakers," *Antiques*, 32 (Oct. 1937): 176, fig. 1. Vernon C. Stoneman, *John and Thomas Seymour: Cabinetmakers in Boston 1794–1816* (Boston, 1959), pp. 56–57, fig. 11. *Americana Week* (New York, Parke-Bernet Galleries, Jan. 24–27, 1973), no. 943, illus. p. 225.
Lender: Mr. and Mrs. George M. Kaufman.

129

Armchair
Philadelphia, Pa., 1806–1807.
Maker: Ephraim Haines (1775–after 1811).
Ebony; ash seat rails; yellow poplar block.
o.h. 35 1/2″ (90.2 cm); o.w. 20 1/4″ (51.4 cm); o.d. 18 1/2″ (47 cm).

Provenance: Stephen Girard (1750–1831); bequeathed by him to Girard College collection, Philadelphia, Pa.
Exhibitions: PMA, *A Loan Exhibition of Authenticated Furniture of the Great Philadelphia Cabinetmakers* (1935), no. 60; *Furniture by Connelly and Haines* (1953), nos. 34, 35 [illus.].
Bibliography: Esther Singleton, *The Furniture of Our Forefathers* (New York, 1901), II, 625 [illus.]. William Macpherson Hornor, Jr., *Blue Book, Philadelphia Furniture* (Philadelphia, 1935), pp. 242–244, 274. Marian Stadtler Carson, "Connelly and Haines: Two Philadelphia Sheraton Makers and the Key to Their Individuality," *Philadelphia Museum Bulletin* (Spring 1953), pp. 39, 43, no. 34, illus. p. 42.
Lender: Girard College; estate of Stephen Girard, deceased.

130

Sofa
Baltimore, Md., 1790–1800.
Mahogany; satinwood inlay.
o.h. 37″ (94 cm); o.w. 78″ (198.1 cm); o.d. 32″ (81.3 cm).

Provenance: Ginsburg and Levy, New York, N.Y.; George Horace Lorimer.
Lender: Mr. and Mrs. Edward A. Kilroy, Jr.

131

Candlestand
Connecticut, ca. 1805.
Cherry; mahogany and light colored wood inlay.
o.h. 28 1/2″ (12.4 cm); o.w. 17″ (43.18 cm); o.d. 20 1/2″ (51.3 cm).

Provenance: Israel Sack Inc., N.Y.
Lender: Mr. and Mrs. Christopher Ireland Granger.

132

Lolling chair
New England (probably Portsmouth, N.H.), 1800–1810.

Mahogany; light wood inlay; white pine; green silk upholstery.
O.H. 47 1/2" (120.7 cm); S.H. 16 3/4" (42.6 cm); O.W. 25" (63.5 cm); O.D. 20" (50.8 cm).

Provenance: H. Eugene Bolles; Mrs. Russell Sage.
Bibliography: Halsey and Tower, *Homes of Our Ancestors*, fig. 164. Halsey and Cornelius, *The American Wing*, fig. 101.
Lender: The Metropolitan Museum of Art, New York, N.Y.; gift of Mrs. Russell Sage (1909). 10.125.313.

133
Sideboard
New York, N.Y., ca. 1790.
Mahogany; satinwood inlay; tulip poplar drawer linings; white pine; ash.
O.H. 39 5/16" (99.9 cm); O.W. 72 7/16" (184 cm); O.D. 29 5/16" (74.5 cm).

Provenance: Robert Doughty Weeks; James Weeks; the Weeks family, Oyster Bay, Long Island, N.Y. (1937); Ginsburg and Levy, Inc., New York, N.Y.
Bibliography: Hipkiss, *Karolik Collection*, pp. 80–81, fig. 44.
Lender: Museum of Fine Arts, Boston; M. and M. Karolik Collection. 39.141.

134
Work table
Boston, Mass., 1800–1810.
Maker: Attributed to John (ca. 1738–ca. 1818) and Thomas (1771–1848) Seymour.
Mahogany, satinwood, maple.
O.H. 30" (76.2 cm); O.W. 21 1/4" (54 cm); O.D. 17" (43.2 cm).

Provenance: Mitchell Taradash collection; Israel Sack, Inc., New York, N.Y.
Bibliography: "Tables and Chairs: Some Significant Examples From the Collection of Mr. and Mrs. Mitchell Taradash," *Antiques*, 59 (June 1946): illus. p. 360. *American Antiques From Israel Sack Collection*, IV, P3971, illus. p. 867.
Lender: Mr. and Mrs. Eric M. Wunsch.

135
Patent timepiece, or banjo clock
Boston, Mass., ca. 1805.
Maker: Simon Willard, 1753–1848.
Mahogany with light wood stringing.
O.H. 34 1/2" (77.5 cm); O.W. 10" (25.4 cm); O.D. 3 1/2" (8.9 cm).

Inscriptions: "WILLARDS PATENT" painted on throat; "S. WILLARD's/ PATENT" painted on lower panel.
Provenance: Israel Sack, Inc.
Lender: Private collection.

136
Bentwood side chair
Boston, Mass., 1808–1812.
Maker: Samuel Gragg (1772–ca. 1855).
Oak, beech.
O.H. 34 7/8" (88.6 cm); O.W. 17 1/2" (44.5 cm); O.D. 20" (50.8 cm).

Signature: "S. GRAGG / BOSTON. PATENT", branded on underside of front seat rail.
Provenance: Found in Boston.
Exhibitions: MMA, *American Art from American Collections* (1963).
Lender: Mr. and Mrs. Bertram K. Little.

Silver
and Gold

137
Teapot
New York, N.Y., ca. 1715–1725.
Maker: Peter Van Dyck (1684–1751).
Silver; wooden handle.
H. 7 3/4" (197 mm); DIAM. lip 2 7/8" (72 mm); DIAM. base 3 5/16" (84 mm); L. 8 1/8" (206 mm).
WT. 18 oz (558 gm).

Marks: "P·V·D" in oval, at lip on each side of handle.
Inscription: "IVB" cipher on each side; "IVBM" on bottom.
Provenance: Johannes Van Brugh (m. 1695), New York; his sister, Catherine (Van Brugh) Rensselaer (m. 1689); Kiliaen Van Rensselaer (m. 1742); Kiliaen Van Rensselaer (m. 1791); John Van Rensselaer (m. 1816); Ann Elizabeth (Van Rensselaer) Hoff (m. 1847); Elizabeth Dunkin (Hoff) Greene (m. 1880); Ann Dunkin (Greene) Bates (m. 1908); Elizabeth Munsell Bates, Summit, N.J. (1930).
Exhibitions: MCNY, *Silver by New York Makers* (1937–1938), p. 34, no. 339, [illus.]. MFA, *Colonial Silversmiths* (1956), no. 261. VMFA, *Masterpieces of American Silver* (1960), no. 224.
Bibliography: J. M. Phillips, "Captain Van Brugh's Teapot," *BAFA* (June 1938), pp. 66–67, illus. p. 67. Buhler and Hood, *American Silver*, II, no. 593, illus. p. 47.
Lender: Yale University Art Gallery; Mabel Brady Garvan Collection. 1938.30.

138
Teapot
New York, N.Y., 1720–1735.
Maker: Peter Van Dyck (1684–1751).

134

Silver; pear wood.
H. 7 1/8" (181 mm); DIAM. lip
2 7/8" (73 mm); DIAM. base 3 1/2"
(89 mm); L. 9" (229 mm).
WT. 21 oz, 18 dwt (679 gm).

Marks: "P•V•D" in oval, at lip
to left of handle.
Inscription: "T^WI" engraved on
bottom; "P^BM" added later on
bottom.
Provenance: S. J. Phillips Co.,
London (1933); James Robinson,
New York, N.Y. (1935); Francis P.
Garvan, New York, N.Y. (1935).
Exhibitions: MCNY, *Silver by
New York Makers* (1937–1938),
p. 34, no. 340. AIC, *From Colony
to Nation* (1949), no. 215, illus.
p. 116. MFA, *Colonial Silver-
smiths* (1956), no. 262.
Bibliography: Mrs. Russel
Hastings, "Peter Van Dyck of
New York, Goldsmith, 1684–1750,"
Antiques, 31 (May 1937): 236–
239, fig. 7. Buhler and Hood,
American Silver, II, no. 595,
illus. p. 50.
Lender: Yale University Art
Gallery; Mabel Brady Garvan
Collection. 1935.230.

139
Covered sugar bowl
New York, N.Y., 1738–1745.
Maker: Simeon Soumain (1685?–
1750).
Silver.
H. 4 3/16" (106 mm); DIAM. bowl
at top, 4 11/16" (119 mm); DIAM.
bowl at base, 2" (51 mm).
WT. 9 oz, 6 dwt (288 gm).

Marks: "ss" in rectangle, on
bottom of bowl and inside top of
handle.
Inscriptions: Engraved cipher "EC"
on side of bowl; repeated in
smaller form on the top.
Provenance: Cruger family, New
York, N.Y.; Luke V. Lockwood,
Greenwich, Conn.; Francis P.
Garvan, New York, N.Y. (1929).
Exhibitions: MMA, *Silver Used
in New York, New Jersey and the*

South (1911), pp. 49–50, no. 104;
*An Exhibition of Early New York
Silver* (1931–1932), no. 67. MCNY,
Silver by New York Makers
(1937–1938), p. 29. no. 284.
Bibliography: Buhler and Hood,
American Silver, II, no. 603,
illus. p. 56.
Lender: Yale University Art
Gallery; Mabel Brady Garvan
Collection. 1930.1056.

140
Teapot
Boston, Mass., ca. 1735–1745.
Maker: Jacob Hurd (1702/03–
1758).
Silver; wooden handle and finial.
H. 5 1/8" (130 mm); D. base 3 1/8"
(79 mm); L. including handle,
8 7/8" (225 mm). WT. 15 oz, 6 dwt
(474 gm).

Marks: "IHURD" in cartouche on
bottom.
Inscription: Pepperell arms en-
graved on side; "RB" on bottom.
Provenance: Pepperell family,
Kittery, Maine; Francis H. Bige-
low, Cambridge, Mass.; R. T. H.
Halsey, New York, N.Y.; Francis
P. Garvan, New York, N.Y.
Exhibitions: MFA, *American
Silversmiths* (1906), no. 150, pls.
8, 18. MMA, *The Hudson-Fulton
Celebration* (1909), II, 111, no.
378. YUAG, *Masterpieces of New
England Silver* (1939), pp. 60–61,
no. 132.
Bibliography: Hollis French,
*Jacob Hurd and His Sons,
Nathaniel and Benjamin, Silver-
smiths, 1702–1781* (Cambridge,
Mass., 1939), p. 47, no. 267.
Buhler and Hood, *American
Silver*, no. 140, illus. p. 121.
Lender: Yale University Art
Gallery; Mabel Brady Garvan
Collection. 1930.1350.

141
Salver
Boston, Mass., 1740–1750.
Maker: Jacob Hurd (1702/03–
1758).

Silver.
H. 1 13/16" (46 mm);
DIAM. 12 9/16" (319 mm).
WT. 34 oz, 8 dwt (1066 gm).
Marks: "HURD" in small rectangle,
on face.
Inscription: Clarke arms and crest
in cartouche engraved on face;
"34-12-0" scratched on bottom.
Provenance: Major William
Clarke (b. 1728), Boston, Mass.;
his granddaughter, Hepzibah
(Clarke) Swan; her daughter,
Mrs. John Turner Sargent; her
daughter, Mrs. Whitney; her
daughter, Mrs. Harold A. Pitman,
Boston, Mass.; Mrs. F. S. Whit-
well, Boston, Mass. (until 1940).
Exhibitions: YUAG, *Masterpieces
of New England Silver* (1939),
p. 61, no. 134. AIC, *From Colony
to Nation* (1949), no. 183, illus.
p. 112. ESU, *American Silver*
(1960), no. 48.
Bibliography: Hollis French,
*Jacob Hurd and His Sons, Na-
thaniel and Benjamin, Silver-
smiths 1702–1781* (Cambridge,
Mass., 1939), p. 50, no. 296, pl. 11.
Buhler and Hood, *American
Silver*, I, no. 151, illus. p. 130.
Lender: Yale University Art
Gallery; Mabel Brady Garvan
Collection. 1940.125.

142
Two-handled covered cup
Boston, Mass., 1744.
Maker: Jacob Hurd (1702/03–
1758).
Silver.
H. 15 1/16" (383 mm); DIAM. lip
7 3/4" (197 mm); DIAM. base 6 1/4"
(159 mm); W. 13 3/4" (349 mm).
WT. 96 oz, 5 dwt (2984 gm).

Marks: "HURD" in small rectangle
at lip and twice on bezel of cover;
"Jacob Hurd" in two lines, in
cartouche, on bottom.
Inscription: "To / EDWARD TYNG
Esqr. / Commander of ye SNOW /
Prince of Orange / As an
Acknowledgement of / his good
Service done the / TRADE in

Taking ye First / French
Privateer / on this Coast the 24th
of June / 1744 This Plate is
presented / BY Several of ye
Merchts. / in Boston New /
England", in shield, with a trophy
of arms engraved on front.
Provenance: Edward Tyng, Bos-
ton, Mass.; his son, William Tyng,
Falmouth, Mass.; stolen during
the Revolution; restored to Tyng's
mother-in-law, Mrs. Ross; the
Tyng family; Timothy Hilliard,
Portland, Maine (?); his son,
William Tyng Hilliard; his
granddaughter, Miss Mabel Har-
low; Francis P. Garvan, New
York, N.Y.
Exhibitions: MFA, *American
Church Silver* (1911), no. 643.
AIC, *From Colony to Nation*
(1949), no. 178, illus. p. 114. MFA,
Paul Revere's Boston (1975), p.
35, no. 32, illus. p. 34.
Bibliography: John Marshall
Phillips, "Mr. Tyng's Bishop,"
BAFA, 4 (Oct. 1932): 147–149,
illus. p. 148. Buhler and Hood,
American Silver, I, no. 157, illus.
p. 134.
Lender: Yale University Art
Gallery; Mabel Brady Garvan
Collection. 1932.48.

143
Admiralty Oar
Boston, Mass., ca. 1740.
Maker: Jacob Hurd (1702/03- 1758).
Silver.
L. 23 1/2" (597 mm). WT. slightly
over 12 oz (373 gm).

Marks: "HURD" in rectangle,
in center of anchor ring.
Inscription: The royal arms of
England engraved on one side of
blade, between the initials "G"
and "R"; the admiralty anchor on
the reverse.
Provenance: Made for the Vice-
Admiralty Court of Boston,
probably during the judgeship of
Robert Auchmuty; used there
by Arodi Thayer; to his daughters,
Charlotte and Mary Thayer; to

the Dorchester Antiquarian and Historical Society (1855); Massachusetts Historical Society, Boston (1931).
Exhibitions: MFA, *Colonial Silversmiths* (1956), no. 98. ESU, *American Silver* (1960), no. 46, pl. 10. National Maritime Museum, Greenwich, England, Charles Oman and K. C. McGuffie, *Oar Maces of Admiralty* (1966). MFA, *Paul Revere's Boston* (1975), p. 31, no. 30, illus. p. 30.
Bibliography: *Massachusetts Historical Society Proceedings*, 64 (Nov. 1931): 388–391.
Lender: Massachusetts Historical Society, Boston, Mass.

144
Punch bowl
Boston, Mass., 1763.
Maker: William Homes (1716/17–1783).
Silver.
H. 4 7/8″ (124 mm); DIAM. base 5 1/4″ (133 mm); DIAM. lip 9 7/8″ (251 mm). WT. 32 oz, 17 1/2 dwt (1022 gm).

Marks: "HOMES" in italic script in rectangle below center point, over "W.H." in rectangle.
Inscription: "The Gift / of the Field Officers and / Captains of the Regiment / of the Town of BOSTON. to / THOMAS DAWES Esqʳ / for his past Services as Ad- / jutant to said Re- / giment Sepᵗ 13/1763", within a medallion; on other side, the Dawes arms.
Provenance: Thomas Dawes (d. 1808); his grandson Thomas Dawes; Mrs. Ambrose Dawes.
Exhibitions: MFA, *American Church Silver* (1911), no. 566, pl. 18. Victoria and Albert Museum, London, and Manchester Gallery, *Exhibition Honoring the Ancient and Honorable Artillery Company* (1954). MFA, *Paul Revere's Boston* (1975), p. 226, no. 204.
Bibliography: Kathryn C. Buhler, "Silver 1640–1820," in Helen Comstock, ed., *The Concise Encyclopedia of American Antiques* (New York, 1958), I, 90, fig. 18; *American Silver*, I, no. 231, illus. p. 276.
Lender: Museum of Fine Arts, Boston, Mass.; gift of Mrs. Ambrose Dawes in memory of her husband. 13.381.

145
Punch strainer
Providence, R.I., 1765.
Maker: Jonathan Clarke (1705(?)–1770).
Silver.
H. 1 13/16″ (46 mm); DIAM. 4 11/16″ (119 mm); L. 11 7/8″ (302 mm). WT. 5 oz, 13 dwt (175 gm).

Marks: "CLARK" in cartouche, on back of each handle.
Inscription: "JABEZ BOWEN PROVIDENCE JANUARY 1765" in lettering of pierced holes.
Provenance: Bowen family, Providence, R.I.; Philip Flayderman, Boston, Mass.; Francis P. Garvan, New York, N.Y. (1930).
Exhibitions: RISD, *Rhode Island Tercentenary Celebration* (1936), no. 83. YUAG, *Masterpieces of New England Silver* (1939), p. 23, no. 25. RISD, *The New England Silversmith* (1965), no. 255.
Bibliography: *Philip Flayderman Collection* (American Art Association, New York, N.Y., Jan. 4, 1930), no. 387. Buhler and Hood, *American Silver*, I, no. 471, illus. p. 283.
Lender: Yale University Art Gallery; Mabel Brady Garvan Collection. 1930.1001.

146
Teakettle on stand
Philadelphia, Pa., ca. 1745–1755.
Maker: Joseph Richardson (1711–1784).
Silver; wooden insulation on handle.
Kettle: H. 11 1/16″ (281 mm); D. base 3 1/8″ (79 mm); L. 11 1/8″ (283 mm). WT. 62 oz, 10 dwt (1938 gm). Stand: H. 4 1/4″ (108 mm). WT. 29 oz, 19 dwt (929 gm).

Marks: "IR" in large rectangle with leaf above, twice on bottom of kettle and lamp.
Inscription: The Plumstead arms and crest engraved on each side of kettle; weight "62.14" scratched on bottom of kettle, and "30.16" on bottom of lamp.
Provenance: Made for Clement Plumstead (1680–1745), Philadelphia, or his wife, Mary Curry Plumstead (d. 1755); bequeathed by Mary to her step-granddaughter, Elizabeth (Plumstead) Elliot (1734–99); Elizabeth's half-brother, George Plumstead (1765–1805); his daughter Anna (Mrs. John H. Scheetz, 1800–1878); her daughter, Helena R. Scheetz; her niece, Mrs. Sidney Bradford; her children, J. H. Bradford and Frances M. Bradford; Frances P. Garvan (1932).
Exhibitions: PMA, *Philadelphia Silver* (1956), no. 389, [illus.]. MIA, *French, English and American Silver* (1956), no. 276, fig. 46. MFA, *Colonial Silversmiths* (1956), no. 314.
Bibliography: Buhler and Hood, *American Silver*, II, no. 843, Fales, *Joseph Richardson*, pp. 87–89, figs. 44, 44a.
Lender: Yale University Art Gallery; Mabel Brady Garvan Collection. 1932.93.

147
Teapot
Baltimore, Md., ca. 1760–1770.
Maker: Gabriel Lewyn (active ca. 1768–1780).
Silver; wooden handle.
H. 6″ (152 mm); DIAM. base 3″ (76 mm); L. 9 1/4″ (235 mm). WT. 18 oz, 7 dwt (569 gm).

Marks: "GL" in rectangle, five times on bottom.
Inscription: "MS" monogram engraved in shield on side; initials "DT" scratched on bottom; weight scratched on bottom (illegible).
Provenance: Sidney T. Manning; Walter M. Jeffords, Glen Riddle, Pa.
Exhibitions: ESU, *American Silver* (1960), no. 180. Museum of Fine Arts, Houston, Texas, *Southern Silver* (1968), no. G-14-A.
Bibliography: J. Hall Pleasants and Howard Sill, *Maryland Silversmiths, 1715–1830* (Baltimore, 1930), p. 157, pl. 32. Buhler and Hood, *American Silver*, II, no. 959, illus. p. 247.
Lender: Yale University Art Gallery; John Marshall Phillips Collection. 1955.10.4.

148
Pair of candlesticks
New York, N.Y., ca. 1760–1775.
Maker: Myer Myers (1723–1795).
Silver.
H. of one stick, 10 1/8″ (257 mm); H. of other, 9 7/8″ (251 mm); W. base (both sticks) 5 1/2″ (140 mm). WT. 20 oz, 4 dwt (626 gm), and 19 oz, 13 dwt (609 gm).

Marks: "MM" conjoined serifs, in rectangle, on drip pan and socket of each candlestick.
Inscription: "THE GIFT OF PETER & SARAH Vᴺ BRUGH TO CATHAᴱ LIVINGSTON" engraved under foot of each.
Provenance: Catharine (Livingston) Lawrence; her niece, Lady Mary Watts; her son, DeLancey Watts; Miss Inglis Griswold, New York, N.Y.; Francis P. Garvan, New York, N.Y. (1936).
Exhibitions: AIC, *From Colony to Nation* (1949), no. 191, illus. p. 120. BM, *Works in Silver and Gold by Myer Myers* (1954), nos. 19–20.
Bibliography: Jeanette W. Rosenbaum, *Myer Myers, Goldsmith* (Philadelphia, 1954), p. 104, pl. 7. Buhler and Hood, *American Silver*, II, no. 658, illus. p. 101.
Lender: Yale University Art Gallery; Mabel Brady Garvan Collection. 1936.148 a,b.

146

149
Salver
Boston, Mass., 1761.
Maker: Paul Revere (1735–1818).
Silver.
H. 1 7/8″ (48 mm); DIAM. 13 1/16″ (331 mm). WT. 29 oz, 9 1/2 dwt (917 gm).

Marks: "·REVERE" in rectangle.
Inscription: "L. Chandler" on back in semiscript, below maker's mark; "30 oz." scratched on back; Chandler arms engraved on front.
Provenance: Lucretia Chandler (Mrs. John Murray, 1728–1768), Rutland, Mass.; her daughter Lucretia (d. 1836); bequeathed by her to Joseph Willard.
Exhibitions: MIA, *French, English, and American Silver* (1956), no. 269, fig. 45. VMFA, *Masterpieces of American Silver* (1960), no. 112. MFA, *Paul Revere's Boston* (1975), p. 219, no. 10.
Bibliography: Jones, *Old Silver*, pp. 39–40. Buhler, *American Silver*, II, no. 343, illus. p. 393.
Lender: Museum of Fine Arts, Boston; gift of Henry Davis Sleeper in memory of his mother, Maria Westcote Sleeper. 25.592.

150
Snuffbox
Philadelphia, Pa., ca. 1750–1770.
Maker: Joseph Richardson (1711–1784).
Silver.
H. 9/16″ (14 mm); L. 3 1/16″ (78 mm); W. 2 5/16″ (59 mm). WT. 2 oz, 4 dwt (68 gm).

Marks: "IR" in rectangle, with leaf below, inside bottom.
Provenance: Willoughby Farr, Edgewater, N.J.; Francis P. Garvan, New York, N.Y. (1922).
Exhibitions: PMA, *Philadelphia Silver* (1956), no. 376.
Bibliography: Buhler and Hood, *American Silver*, II, no. 837, illus. p. 187. Fales, *Joseph Richardson*, pp. 133–134, fig. 117.

Lender: Yale University Art Gallery; Mabel Brady Garvan Collection. 1930.1281.

151
Coral and bells
New York, N.Y., ca. 1760–1770.
Maker: Daniel Christian Fueter (active ca. 1754–1776).
Gold, coral.
L. 5 3/16″ (132 mm). WT. 2 oz, 6 dwt (71 gm).

Marks: "DCF" in oval and "N: YORK" in two lines, in conforming punch, on underside of mouthpiece.
Inscription: "THE GIFT OF Mʳˢ MARY LIVINGSTON / TO HER GRAND-DAUGHTER MARY DUANE" engraved on end above coral.
Provenance: Mary (Duane) North, New York, N.Y.; her granddaughter, Mrs. F. B. Austin, New York, N.Y.; her son, William Austin, New York, N.Y.; James Graham and Sons, New York, N.Y.
Exhibitions: MFA, *Colonial Silversmiths* (1956), p. 76, no. 182. YUAG, *American Gold 1700–1860* (1963), pp. 11, 30, no. 24, illus. p. 10.
Bibliography: Berenice Ball, "Whistles with Coral and Bells," *Antiques*, 80 (Dec. 1961): 552–555, fig. 8. Buhler and Hood, *American Silver*, II, no. 716, illus. p. 134.
Lender: Yale University Art Gallery; gift of Mrs. Francis P. Garvan, James R. Graham, Walter M. Jeffords, and Mrs. Paul Moore. 1942.91.

152
Shoe buckle
New York, N.Y., ca. 1760–1775.
Maker: Myer Myers (1723–1795).
Gold, with steel chape and tongue.
L. 2 5/16″ (59 mm); W. 1 3/4″ (44 mm). WT. 1 oz, 9 dwt (45 gm).

Marks: "MM" conjoined serifs in rectangle, on back of each end.
Inscription: "The Gift of Robt.

Arcdeckne Esqr. to Danl. McCormick", engraved on back.
Provenance: Francis P. Garvan, New York, N.Y.
Exhibitions: MCNY, *Silver by New York Makers, Late Seventeenth Century to 1900* (1937–1938), p. 22, no. 208. Johns Hopkins University, Baltimore, Md., *History in Gold and Silver* (1940). BM, *Works in Silver and Gold by Myer Myers* (1954), no. 165.
Bibliography: Jeanette W. Rosenbaum, *Myer Myers, Goldsmith* (Philadelphia, 1954), p. 103, pl. 6. Buhler and Hood, *American Silver*, II, no. 657, illus. p. 100.
Lender: Yale University Art Gallery; Mabel Brady Garvan Collection. 1936.166.

153
Torah bells
New York, N.Y., 1772.
Maker: Myer Myers (1723–1795).
Silver.
H. 13″ (330 mm); WT. (each) 14 oz, 11 dwt, 16 gr (346 gm).

Marks: "Myers" in script, on end of handle of each.
Provenance: Made for Congregation Mikveh Israel, Philadelphia, Pa.
Exhibitions: BM, *Works in Silver and Gold by Myer Myers* (1954).
Bibliography: Guido Schoenberger, "The Ritual Silver made by Myer Myers," *Publication of the American Jewish Historical Society*, 43 (1953): 1–9; Jeanette W. Rosenbaum, *Myer Myers, Goldsmith 1723–1795* (Philadelphia, Pa., 1954), pp. 33–34, 100, pl. 2.
Lender: Kahal Kadosh Mikveh Israel in the City of Philadelphia, Pa.

154
Communion dish
Boston, Mass., 1764.
Maker: John Coburn (1725–1803).
Silver.

DIAM. 13 3/16″ (335 mm). WT. 25 oz, 5 dwt (730 gm).

Marks: "J. Coburn" in rectangle, on bottom at center point and upside down on rim of left wing framing cherub.
Inscription: "The Gift of the Honᵇˡᵉ THOMAS HANCOCK ESQ ᴿ / to the CHURCH in Brattle Street Boston 1764", around brim in semiscript and block letters; "No. 2 wt 26ᵒᶻ" scratched on bottom; Hancock arms engraved on brim.
Provenance: The Benevolent Fraternity of Churches (until 1913).
Exhibitions: MFA, *American Silversmiths* (1906), no. 57; *American Church Silver* (1911), no. 215, 216, or 217; *Paul Revere's Boston* (1975), p. 42, no. 42, illus. p. 42.
Bibliography: E. Alfred Jones, *The Old Silver of American Churches* (Letchworth, England, 1913), pp. 68–69, pl. 27. Kathryn C. Buhler, "Some Engraved American Silver," *Antiques*, 48, no. 6 (Dec. 1945): 350–351, fig. 8; *American Silver*, I, no. 272, illus. p. 316.
Lender: Museum of Fine Arts, Boston, Mass.; gift of the Benevolent Fraternity of Churches. 13.394.

155
Chocolate pot
Boston, Mass., ca. 1755.
Maker: Zachariah Brigden (1734–1787).
Silver; wooden handle.
H. including finial, 9 7/8″ (251 mm); DIAM. base 4 11/16″ (119 mm). WT. 27 oz, 7 dwt (851 gm).

Marks: "Z·Brigden", in cartouche, in script on bottom and left of handle; "Z·B", in rectangle, on edge of cover.
Inscription: Engraved with coat of arms used by Ebenezer Storer,

in cartouche; added to bottom, "Storer / 1720", and in script "EHS / 1863".
Provenance: Ebenezer and Mary Storer (m. 1723); their daughter Elizabeth Storer (Mrs. Isaac Smith); their son William; his son Thomas Carter; his sister, Elizabeth Hall Smith; her sister Frances (Mrs. Thomas Davis Townsend); her son William Smith Townsend, father of the donors.
Exhibitions: MFA, *American Church Silver* (1911), no. 78; *Colonial Silversmiths* (1956), no. 5, fig. 60. VMFA, *Masterpieces of American Silver* (1960), no. 2, illus. p. 46. MFA, *Paul Revere's Boston* (1975), p. 222, no. 89.
Bibliography: Jones, *Old Silver*, pp. 35–36. Buhler, *American Silver*, I, no. 326, illus. p. 373.
Lender: Museum of Fine Arts, Boston, Mass.; gift of the Misses Rose and Elizabeth Townsend. 56.676.

156
Porringer
Boston, Mass., ca. 1740–1750.
Maker: Paul Revere, Sr. (1702–1754).
Silver.
H. 1 13/16″ (46 mm); D. bowl 4 13/16″ (122 mm); L. handle 2 3/4″ (70 mm). WT. 7 oz. 15 dwt (240 gm).

Marks: "P·Revere" in cartouche (in bowl).
Inscription: "IP" (originally "I^PM") engraved on handle toward tip; "7 oz-19" scratched on bottom.
Provenance: William Inglis Morse; his daughter, Susan Morse Hilles.
Bibliography: Buhler and Hood, *American Silver*, I, no. 133, illus. p. 116.
Lender: Yale University Art Gallery; gift of the daughter of William Inglis Morse, Mrs. Frederick W. Hilles. 1959.17.1.

157
Tankard
Boston, Mass., 1762.
Maker: Paul Revere (1735–1818).
Silver.
H. 8 5/8″ (219 mm); DIAM. lip 3 3/16″ (81 mm); DIAM. base 5 1/8″ (130 mm). WT. 30 oz, 5 dwt (938 gm).

Marks: "REVERE" in rectangle, at lip to left of handle; "PR" in small rectangle on bottom.
Inscription: Greene arms and crest, in cartouche engraved on front; "T G / to / M G" on handle; "30 oz 14" scratched on bottom.
Provenance: Thomas Greene (1706–1763); Crichton Bros., New York, N.Y.; Francis P. Garvan, New York, N.Y. (1916).
Exhibitions: YUAG, *Masterpieces of New England Silver* (1939), p. 73, no. 168.
Bibliography: Buhler and Hood, *American Silver*, I, no. 240, illus. p. 186.
Lender: Yale University Art Gallery; Mabel Brady Garvan Collection. 1930.1196.

158
Tankard
New York, N.Y., 1765–1780.
Maker: Ephraim Brasher (1744–1810).
Silver.
H. 8 3/4″ (222 mm); DIAM. base 4 13/16″ (123 mm).

Marks: "BRASHER", "N YORK", each in rectangle on underside.
Inscription: "40 oz. 16 dwt" scratched on underside.
Exhibitions: MMA, *American Art from American Collections* (1963), p. 57, no. 118 [illus.].
Lender: Mr. and Mrs. James H. Halpin.

159
Dish
Philadelphia, Pa., ca. 1775.
Maker: Joseph Richardson, Jr. (1752–1831).
Silver.
L. 11 1/8″ (283 mm); W. 8 1/4″ (210 mm). WT. 17 oz, 14 dwt (550.5 gm).

Marks: "JR" in rectangle, twice, on bottom.
Inscription: Engraved with the Powel crest on inside rim; "17 oz, 14 dwt, 12 grs" scratched on bottom.
Provenance: Samuel Powel (1739–1793), Philadelphia, Pa.
Exhibitions: PMA, *Philadelphia Silver* (1956), no. 419 or 420.
Bibliography: Fales, *Joseph Richardson*, pp. 191–192, fig. 174.
Lender: Philadelphia Museum of Art; McIlhenny Fund (1956).

160
Coffeepot
Boston, Mass., 1781.
Maker: Paul Revere (1735–1818).
Silver; wooden handle.
H. 12 7/8″ (328 mm); DIAM. base 4 7/8″ (124 mm). WT. 40 oz, 5 dwt (1252 gm).

Marks: "·REVERE" in rectangle, on bottom near center point.
Inscription: Engraved with Sargent arms; "oz.39·3" scratched in lower curve under foot.
Provenance: Paul Dudley Sargent (1745–1827); inherited by Evelina Augusta Rust (Mrs. Jesse W. Mighels, 1802–1878) in 1846; her son Henry Rust Mighels; his son Henry Rust, Jr. (until 1930).
Exhibitions: ESU, *American Silver* (1960), no. 72, pl. 17. MFA, *Paul Revere's Boston* (1975), p. 233, no. 381.
Bibliography: Buhler, *American Silver*, II, no. 367, illus. p. 419.
Lender: Museum of Fine Arts, Boston, Mass.; gift of Mrs. Nathaniel Thayer. 31.139.

161
Waiter
Boston, Mass., 1797.
Maker: Paul Revere (1735–1818).
Silver.
W. 13 1/4″ (337 mm); L. 17″ (432 mm). WT. 39 oz, 16 dwt (1219 gm).

Marks: "REVERE" in rectangle, with clipped lower corner and uneven lower line, on bottom.
Inscription: "EHD" monogram in oval medallion of leaves, on face.
Provenance: Elias Hasket Derby (1739–1799), Salem, Mass.; his daughter, Lucy Derby (Mrs. Samuel Richard Fuller); Francis P. Garvan, New York, N.Y.
Exhibitions: MFA, *American Church Silver* (1911), no. 894, pl. 31; *Colonial Silversmiths* (1956), no. 122; *Paul Revere's Boston* (1975), p. 191, no. 296, illus. p. 190.
Bibliography: Buhler and Hood, *American Silver*, I, no. 259, illus. p. 199.
Lender: Yale University Art Gallery; Mabel Brady Garvan Collection. 1930.958.

156

157

162
Freedom box
New York, N.Y., 1784.
Maker: Samuel Johnson (1726–1796); engraved by Peter Maverick (1755–1811).
Gold.
H. 3/4″ (19 mm); L. 3 1/4″ (83 mm); W. 1 15/16″ (49 mm). WT. 2 oz, 12 dwt (80 gm).

Marks: "SJ" in rectangle, on inside bottom.
Inscription: Arms, crest, and motto of New York, "SIGILLUM CIVITAT·NOV EBORAC", engraved on cover; "Maverick Sct" engraved below; "PRESENTED BY THE CORPORATION OF THE CITY OF NEW·YORK·WITH THE FREEDOM·OF THE CITY" on sides; "Oct. 11th 1784 / Frederick Wm, Baron de Steuben / to / William North / to / William Augustus Steuben North" on bottom (last line added later).
Provenance: Baron Steuben; bequeathed to his former aide-de-camp William North; Francis P. Garvan, New York, N.Y.
Exhibitions: MCNY, *Silver by New York Makers* (1937–1938), p. 17, no. 161, [illus.]. Johns Hopkins University, Baltimore, Md., *History in Gold and Silver* (1940). YUAG, *American Gold, 1700–1800* (1963), p. 28, no. 16, illus. p. 4.
Bibliography: John Marshall Phillips, "Marked Gold in the Garvan Collection," *BAFA*, 8 (June 1937): 19–20, illus. p. 20. Harrold E. Gillingham, "New York Common Council Lavish with Gold Boxes," *New York Sun* (on file at Yale University Art Gallery, American Arts Office). Buhler and Hood, *American Silver*, II, no. 667, illus. p. 107.

Lender: Yale University Art Gallery; Mabel Brady Garvan Collection. 1930.1100.

163
Indian peace medal
New York, N.Y., 1766.
Maker: Daniel Christian Fueter (active ca. 1754–1776).
Silver.
DIAM. 2 3/16″ (56 mm); WT. 50.26 gm.

Marks: "DCF" in oval and N:YORK" in two lines, in conforming punch on face.
Inscription: In relief around edge "HAPPY WHILE UNITED" on the obverse; "GEORGIUS III · D·G·M·BRI·FRA·ET·HIB·REX·F·D" on the reverse.
Provenance: Thomas A Hendricks, 1941.
Exhibitions: NPG, *In the Minds and Hearts of the People* (1974), p. 60, illus.
Bibliography: Harrold E. Gillingham, "Indian and Military Medals from Colonial Times to Date," PMHB 51 (1927): 104–105.
Lender: American Numismatic Society, New York, N.Y.

164
Indian peace medal
Philadelphia, Pa., 1793.
Maker: Joseph Richardson, Jr. (1752–1831).
Silver.
H. 6 3/4″ (171 mm); W. 5″ (127 mm).

Marks: The initials "JR" appear at the bottom of the reverse.
Inscription: A scene of peacemaking engraved on the obverse, with "GEORGE WASHINGTON/PRESIDENT 1793" in exergue; on reverse, engraved, seal of the United States.
Provenance: Given to Chief Jean Baptiste Ducoigne (Du Quoin) of

the Kaskaskia Indians by President George Washington in 1793 at the time when Washington made his proclamation protecting the Kaskaskia Indians. On July 7, 1817, Ninian Edwards, governor of the Illinois Territory and superintendent of Indian Affairs, presented this same medal to the chief's son, Louis Jefferson Ducoigne, when he became chief after the death of his father. The Washington proclamation, with Edwards's endorsement on its reverse, accompanied the medal.
Bibliography: Bauman L. Belden, *Indian Peace Medals Issued in the United States, 1789–1889* (2d ed., New York, 1966), p. 16, no. 5 A pls. 6, 7. Harrold E. Gillingham, "Indian Silver Ornaments," *PMHB*, 58, no. 2 (1934): 97ff.
Lender: Chicago Historical Society; Gunther Collection.

165
Indian armband
Philadelphia, Pa., ca. 1792–1796.
Maker: Joseph Richardson, Jr. (1752–1831).
Silver.
H. 2 1/2″ (64 mm); L. 9 3/16″ (233 mm); WT. 2 oz, 8 dwt (74 gm).

Marks: "J·R" in rectangle, inside.
Provenance: Philip H. Dilg, Chicago (after discovery in an Indian mound in Emmet County, Mich., ca. 1898); Titus C. Geesey, Wilmington, Del.
Exhibitions: PMA, *Philadelphia Silver* (1956), no. 400.
Bibliography: Harrold E. Gillingham, "Indian Trade Silver Ornaments Made by Joseph Richardson, Jr.," *PMHB* 67 (1943): 87. Buhler and Hood, *American Silver*, II, no. 861, illus. p. 198.

Lender: Yale University Art Gallery; Mabel Brady Garvan Collection. 1948.270.

166
Cake basket
New York, N.Y., 1790–1795.
Maker: Simeon Bayley (active 1785–1797).
Silver.
L. 13 7/8″ (352 mm); H. 5 1/4″ (133 mm). WT. 40 oz, 10 dwt (1259.7 gm).

Marks: "BAYLEY" in capitals of two sizes, in conforming rectangle on base with two pseudo marks.
Inscription: Bright-cut and engraved cartouche of draped ermine form with script initials "EMD" inside of basket.
Provenance: Made for Edward and Mary (Elsworth) Dunscombe, married in 1787; descended to George Elsworth Dunscombe.
Exhibitions: MCNY, *Silver by New York Makers* (1937–1938), no. 21, illus. p. 45.
Bibliography: Graham Hood, *American Silver* (New York, 1971), p. 166, fig. 180.
Lender: Museum of the City of New York, New York, N.Y.; gift of George Elsworth Dunscombe. 32.237.6.

167
Tea service
Philadelphia, Pa., 1797–1800.
Makers: Samuel Richards and Samuel Williamson (partnership 1797–1800).
Silver; wood handle on teapot.
Teapot: H. 12 1/2″ (318 mm); O.L. 11″ (279 mm). Sugar urn: H. 11″ (279 mm); DIAM. at top, 4 5/8″ (117 mm). Creamer: H. 8 3/4″ (222 mm). Slop bowl: H. 6 9/16″ (167 mm); DIAM. of top,

162

6 1/4" (159 mm).

Marks: "RICHARDS & / WILLIAMSON" in rectangle on opposite sides of teapot base, one stamped upside down; same mark stamped on opposite sides of sugar urn base and stamped upside down on opposite sides of slop bowl base; "WILLIAMSON" stamped upside down on creamer base.
Inscription: Monogram "JJA" in script on all four pieces; "oz /29– dwts/ 4" scratched on bottom of teapot (in bell of stem); "20 oz" on bottom of sugar urn base; "oz /17 – dwts /9" on edge of slop bowl base.
Provenance: Descended in the Slaymaker family, Lancaster, Pa., until 1959, when it was purchased by present owner.
Exhibitions: 103rd Engineers' Armory, Philadelphia, *The University Hospital Antiques Show* (1969), p. 57, nos. 59–63.
Bibliography: Ellen Beasley, "Samuel Williamson; Philadelphia Silversmith, 1794–1813" (M.A. thesis, University of Delaware, 1964), pp. 32–33.
Lender: Private collection.

168
Sugar tongs
Philadelphia, Pa., 1797–1800.
Makers: Samuel Richards and Samuel Williamson (partnership 1797–1800).
Silver.
L. 6 3/4" (171 mm).

Marks: "RICHARDS & / WILLIAMSON" in rectangle, stamped inside arch.
Inscription: "IMR" monogram in script, in bright-cut cartouche on outside of arch.
Provenance: Purchased in Philadelphia.

Lender: Private collection.

169
Coffee urn
Boston, Mass., 1793.
Maker: Paul Revere (1735–1818).
Silver; ivory spigot handle.
H. 18" (457 mm); W. base 4 5/8" (117.6 mm); DIAM. lip 4 1/4" (108 mm). WT. 52 oz, 16 1/2 dwt (1643 gm).

Marks: "•REVERE" in rectangle at edge of plinth, on back.
Inscription: Script monogram "BAC" in ellipse on back.
Provenance: Burrell Carnes (d. 1805), Lancaster, Mass.; Benjamin Lincoln (1733–1810); Mrs. W. B. Rogers (by 1911); Mrs. Charles Russell; bequeathed to the Misses Porter, Boston.
Exhibitions: MFA, *American Silversmiths* (1906), no. 239, pls. 21, 22, 25; *American Church Silver* (1911), no. 865, pl. 30. Society of Colonial Dames, Philadelphia, *Three Centuries of Historic Silver* (1938), p. 73, figs. 67–68. MFA, *Paul Revere's Boston* (1975), p. 230, no. 303.
Bibliography: Jones, *Old Silver*, p. 37. Kathryn C. Buhler, "Three Teapots with Some Accessories," *Bulletin of the Museum of Fine Arts, Boston*, 61 (1963): 58–62, no. 324, fig. 9; *American Silver*, II, no. 392, illus. p. 442.
Lender: Museum of Fine Arts, Boston, Mass.; gift of Henry Davis Sleeper in memory of his mother, Maria Westcote Sleeper, by exchange. 60.1419.

170
Teapot
Boston, Mass., 1796.
Maker: Paul Revere (1735–1818).
Silver, fruitwood.

H. 6 1/4" (159 mm); L. base, 5 7/8" (149 mm); O.L. 11 1/2" (292 mm). WT. 20 oz, 14 dwt (489 gm).

Mark: "REVERE" in rectangle on bottom.
Inscription: "H" engraved on body, pourer's side. Other side gothic "G" added later. "2²0-3" scratched on bottom.
Provenance: Made for Jonathan Hunnewell; subsequent history unknown.
Bibliography: Kathryn C. Buhler, "Some Engraved American Silver, Part II," *Antiques*, 48, no. 6 (Dec. 1945): 351, fig. 14; *American Silver*, II, no. 405, illus. p. 456.
Lender: Museum of Fine Arts, Boston, Mass.; Pauline Revere Thayer Collection. 35.1779.

171
Sugar basket
Boston, Mass., ca. 1798.
Maker: Paul Revere (1735–1818).
Silver.
H. inc. handle, 6 3/4" (171 mm); L. bowl 6 5/32" (156 mm). WT. 8 oz, 18 dwt (277 gm).

Marks: "REVERE" in rectangle, on top of bail handle.
Inscription: Script "ET / to / EHT" in a panel of one side; "KENNARD / 1870" on opposite side in Old English lettering.
Provenance: Possibly Edward Tuckerman; his wife, Elizabeth (Harris) Tuckerman; probably his son Edward (1775–1843); the Hon. Martin P. Kennard (1891); his family.
Exhibitions: MFA, *American Church Silver* (1911), no. 885, pl. 31; *Paul Revere's Boston, 1735–1818* (1975), p. 232, no. 341.
Bibliography: Elbridge Henry Goss, *The Life of Colonel Paul*

Revere (Boston, 1891), illus. p. 15. Francis Hill Bigelow, *Historic Silver of the Colonies and Its Makers* (New York, 1917), p. 405, fig. 294. Buhler, *American Silver*, II, no. 413, illus. p. 463.
Lender: Museum of Fine Arts, Boston, Mass.; Helen and Alice Colburn Fund. 39.39.

172
Pitcher
Boston, Mass., 1802–1806.
Maker: Paul Revere (1735–1818).
Silver.
H. 6" (152.4 mm); DIAM. lip 4" (101.6 mm).

Marks: "REVERE" in rectangle at bottom.
Inscription: "PRESENTED / -by- / The Government of the Mechanic Association, / -TO- / Mr. SAMUEL GILBERT. / As compensation for his faithful / and extra services while their / SECRETARY / Boston Janʸ 1st 1806 / Jona. Hunnewell, Presᵗ / Benjⁿ Russell, Vice Presᵗ" engraved below spout in script and capital letters.
Provenance: Purchased by the Paul Revere Life Insurance Company in 1958.
Exhibitions: VMFA, *Richmond, Masterpieces of American Silver* (1960), no. 114, illus. p. 63. ESU, *American Silver* (1960), no. 114, illus. p. 63. *American Silver* (1960), no. 77, pl. 27. Worcester Art Museum, Worcester, Mass., *Paul Revere, 1735–1818* (1965), no. 9, illus. p. 75.
Bibliography: Martha Gandy Fales, "Samuel Gilbert's Revere Pitcher," *Antiques*, 75 (May 1959): 476–477, illus. p. 477.
Lender: The Paul Revere Life Insurance Company, Worcester, Mass.

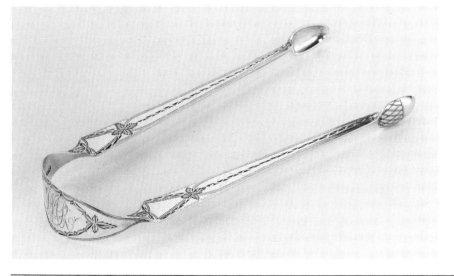

168

Pewter

173
Deep dish
Hartford, Conn., 1795–1816.
Maker: Samuel Danforth (1774–1816; active 1795–1816).
Pewter.
DIAM. 13 1/4″ (33.7 cm).

Marks: L.397a, 400 with X, 404.
Exhibitions: The M. H. de Young Memorial Museum, San Francisco, Calif. (1936).
Bibliography: Hood, *American Pewter*, p. 22, no. 75. Laughlin, *Pewter in America*, I, 118–119; III, 77.
Lender: Yale University Art Gallery; Mabel Brady Garvan Collection. 1931.270.

174
Plate
New York, N.Y., 1752–1774.
Maker: John Will (1701–ca. 1774; active 1752–1774).
Pewter.
DIAM. 9 1/8″ (23.2 cm).

Marks: L. 478, 479, 480.
Provenance: Louis Guerineau Myers.
Bibliography: Louis Guerineau Myers, *Some Notes on American Pewterers*, p. 68. Hood, *American Pewter*, p. 35, no. 141.
Lender: Yale University Art Gallery; Mabel Brady Garvan Collection. 1931.237.

175
Plate
Middletown, Conn., ca. 1755–1782.
Maker: Thomas Danforth II (1731–1782; active 1755–1782).

Pewter.
DIAM. 7 3/4″ (19.7 cm).

Marks: L. 364, 363 a.
Bibliography: Hood, *American Pewter*, p. 13, no. 6.
Lender: Yale University Art Gallery; Mabel Brady Garvan Collection. 1931.224.

176
Footwarmer
New York or Albany, N.Y., ca. 1761–1793.
Maker: Henry Will (ca. 1735–ca. 1802; active 1761–1793).
Pewter.
H. 10 11/16″ (27.1 cm); L. 12″ (30.5 cm); w. of base 5 7/8″ (14.9 cm); H. of body 6 11/16″ (17 cm).

Marks: L. 487a, 492.
Bibliography: Laughlin, *Pewter in America*, I, pl. XLII, fig. 272. Hood, *American Pewter*, p. 45, no. 161. Montgomery, *American Pewter*, p. 195, fig. 12–8.
Lender: Yale University Art Gallery; Mabel Brady Garvan Collection. 1931. 302.

177
Plate
Philadelphia, Pa., ca. 1795–1819.
Maker: Parks Boyd (1771/2–1819; active 1795–1819).
Pewter.
DIAM. 7 7/8″ (19 cm).

Marks: L. 544.
Bibliography: Hood, *American Pewter*, p. 56, no. 195.
Lender: Yale University Art Gallery; Mabel Brady Garvan

Collection. 1931.238.

178
Spoon
New York, N.Y., 1787–1811.
Maker: George Coldwell (d. 1811; active 1787–1811).
Pewter.
O.L. 7 9/16″ (19.2 cm).

Marks: L. 509.
Inscription: "LIBERTY, FEDERAL CONSTITUTION, PEACE".
Bibliography: Laughlin, *Pewter in America*, as in I, pl. 25, fig. 173; II, 23–26; III, 38, 111–113. Montgomery, *American Pewter*, as in p. 160, fig. 10-3 D.
Lender: The Metropolitan Museum of Art, New York, N.Y.; Rogers Fund, 1963. 63.95.

179
Spoon
New York, N.Y., 1787–1811.
Maker: George Coldwell (d. 1811; active 1787–1811).
Pewter.
O.L. 7 3/4″ (19.7 cm).

Marks: L. 510.
Inscription: "PEACE & AMITY".
Exhibitions: MMA (1939).
Bibliography: Laughlin, *Pewter in America*, as in I, pl. 25, fig. 174. Montgomery, *American Pewter*, as in p. 160, fig. 10-3C.
Lender: The Metropolitan Museum of Art, New York, N.Y.; gift of Mrs. Blair in memory of her husband, J. Insley Blair, 1941. 41.34.18.

180
Porringer

Hartford, Conn., ca. 1805–1820.
Maker: Thomas D. Boardman (1784–1873).
Pewter.
H. 1 13/16″ (4.6 cm); DIAM. at rim 4 7/8″ (12.4 cm).

Marks: L. 427, 427 a.
Bibliography: Hood, *American Pewter*, p. 24, no. 90.
Lender: Yale University Art Gallery; Mabel Brady Garvan Collection. 1931.173.

181
Porringer
Newport, R.I., 1793–1796.
Maker: Attributed to Thomas Melville (d. 1796; active 1793–1796).
Pewter.
O.H. 1 5/8″ (4.1 cm); DIAM. rim 5″ (12.7 cm).

Marks: L. 324, 325 ("TM" cast on bracket of handle).
Bibliography: Hood, *American Pewter*, p. 23, no. 79. Laughlin, *Pewter in America*, I, 92–94.
Lender: Yale University Art Gallery; Mabel Brady Garvan Collection. 1930.747.

182
Porringer
Providence, R.I., 1773–1810.
Maker: Samuel Hamlin (1746–1801; active 1773–1801), or Samuel E. Hamlin (1774–1864; active 1801–1856).
Pewter.
O.H. 1 7/8″ (4.8 cm); DIAM. rim 5 5/16″ (13.5 cm).

Marks: L.336.
Exhibitions: The M. H. de Young Memorial Museum, San Francisco, Calif. (1936). The Westport Public Library, Westport, Conn. (1954).
Bibliography: Hood, *American Pewter*, p. 15, no. 21. Laughlin, *Pewter in America*, I, 95–97; III, 55–57.
Lender: Yale University Art Gallery; Mabel Brady Garvan Collection. 1931.167.

183
Porringer

Springfield, Vt., 1788–1820.
Maker: Richard Lee, Sr. (1747–1823) or Richard Lee, Jr. (b. 1775). Father and son active 1788–1820.
Pewter.
O.H. 3/4″ (1.9 cm); DIAM. rim 2 5/16″ (5.9 cm).

Marks: L. 412.
Provenance: Thomas D. Williams, Litchfield, Conn.
Bibliography: Laughlin, *Pewter in America*, as in I, 13, fig. 68; pp. 121–124.
Lender: Private collection.

184
Nursing bottle
Pennsylvania, 1750–1800.
Maker: Unknown.
Pewter.
O.H. 6 1/4″ (15.9 cm); DIAM. body 3 1/2″ (8.9 cm).

Marks: None.
Provenance: Howard Reifsnyder, Philadelphia, Pa.
Bibliography: *Colonial Furniture: The Superb Collection of the Late Howard Reifsnyder* (American Art Association, Inc., New York, April 24–27, 1929), no. 232, illus. p. 57.
Lender: Yale University Art Gallery; Mabel Brady Garvan Collection. 1930.810.

185
Quart mug
Providence, R.I., 1794–1810.
Maker: Samuel Hamlin (1746–1801; active 1773–1801) or Samuel E. Hamlin (1774–1864; active 1801–1856).
Pewter.
O.H. 6″ (15.2 cm); DIAM. body 4 3/4″ (12.1 cm); DIAM. rim 4 1/16″ (10.3 cm).

Marks: L.330.
Exhibitions: The Westport Public Library, Westport, Conn. (1954).
Bibliography: Hood, *American Pewter*, p. 15, no. 20. Laughlin, *Pewter in America*, as in I, pl. 19, fig. 117.
Lender: Yale University Art Gallery; gift of Mrs. James C.

Greenway. 1942.148.

186
Quart mug
Charlestown, Mass., 1763–1807.
Maker: Nathaniel Austin (1741–1816; active 1763–1807).
Pewter.
O.H. 5 3/4″ (14.6 cm); DIAM. body 4 9/16″ (11.6 cm); DIAM. rim 3 13/16″ (9.7 cm).

Marks: L.296.
Provenance: Louis Guerineau Myers.
Exhibitions: MMA (1939).
Bibliography: Louis Guerineau Myers, *Some Notes on American Pewterers* (New York, 1926), p. 42. Hood, *American Pewter*, p. 14, no. 13. Laughlin, *Pewter in America*, I, pl. 20, fig. 122; pp. 75–76.
Lender: Yale University Art Gallery; Mabel Brady Garvan Collection. 1930.735.

187
Quart tankard
New York, N.Y. 1720–1761.
Maker: John Bassett (1696–1761; active 1720–1761).
Pewter.
O.H. 7 11/16″ (19.5 cm); DIAM. base 5 1/2″ (14 cm); DIAM. *rim* 4 13/16″ (12.2 cm).

Marks: L.458.
Bibliography: Laughlin, *Pewter in America*, as in I, pl. 14, fig. 80; II, 5–7; III, 98–100.
Lender: Helen and Harvey Muehlenbeck.

188
Three-and-one-half-pint tankard
New York, N.Y., 1720–1761.
Maker: John Bassett (1696–1761; active 1720–1761).
Pewter.
O.H. 7 11/16″ (19.5 cm); DIAM. base 5 1/2″ (14 cm); DIAM. *rim* 4 13/16″ (12.2 cm).

Marks: L.458.
Inscription: "EHD" engraved on front between fillet and base.
Bibliography: Hood, *American Pewter*, p. 35, no. 139, illus. p. 34.

Laughlin, *Pewter in America*, as in I, pl. 15, fig. 85.
Lender: Yale University Art Gallery; Mabel Brady Garvan Collection. 1931.162.

189
Quart tankard
Philadelphia, Pa., 1764–1798.
Maker: William Will (1742–1798; active 1764–1798).
Pewter.
O.H. 7 7/8″ (20 cm); DIAM. base 4 7/16″ (11.3 cm); DIAM. rim 4″ (10.2 cm).

Marks: L.539 with crowned X.
Provenance: Louis Guerineau Myers.
Exhibitions: The M. H. de Young Memorial Museum, San Francisco, Calif. (1936). The Westport Public Library, Westport, Conn. (1954).
Bibliography: Louis Guerineau Myers, *Some Notes on American Pewterers* (New York, 1926), p. 73. Hood, *American Pewter*, p. 51, no. 187. Laughlin, *Pewter in America*, II, 51–55; III, 133–134. Suzanne Hamilton, "The Pewter of William Will: A Checklist," *Winterthur Portfolio*, 7 (Charlottesville, Va., 1972): 156, no. 159.
Lender: Yale University Art Gallery; Mabel Brady Garvan Collection. 1930.720.

190
Quart tankard
Philadelphia, Pa., 1764–1798.
Maker: William Will (1742–1798; active 1764–1798).
Pewter.
O.H. 7 11/16″ (19.5 cm); DIAM. base 4 11/16″ (11.9 cm); DIAM rim 3 7/8″ (9.8 cm).

Marks: L.539 with crowned X.
Bibliography: Hood, *American Pewter*, p. 53, no. 188. Suzanne Hamilton, "The Pewter of William Will: A Checklist," *Winterthur Portfolio*, 7 (Charlottesville, Va., 1972): 154, no. 145.
Lender: Yale University Art Gallery; Mabel Brady Garvan Collection. 1930.806.

188   189

191
Teapot
Philadelphia, Pa., 1764–1785.
Maker: William Will (1742–1798;
active 1764–1798).
Pewter.
O.H. 7″ (17.8 cm); O.W. 8″ (20.3 cm).

Marks: L.539.
Provenance: Dr. and Mrs. Irving
Berg.
Bibliography: Dr. Robert Mallory
III, "An American Pewter Col-
lection," *Antiques*, 72, no. 1 (July
1957): 40–43. Laughlin, *Pewter
in America*, I, pl. 28, fig. 190.
Suzanne Hamilton, "The Pewter
of William Will: A Checklist,"
Winterthur Portfolio, 7 (Char-
lottesville, Va., 1972): 158, no. 174.
Lender: Dr. and Mrs. Robert
Mallory III.

192
Teapot
Philadelphia, Pa., 1788–1798.
Maker: William Will (1742–1798;
active 1764–1798).
Pewter.
O.H. 7 1/8″ (18.1 cm).

Marks: L.540.
Provenance: Judge Wharton
Sinkler; John F. Ruckman.
Exhibitions: PMA (1971).
Bibliography: Charles V. Swain,
"On the Collecting of Teapots,"
PCCA, Bull. 53, vol. 5, no. 4
(Dec. 1965), p. 81, fig. 1. Suzanne
Hamilton, "The Pewter of Wil-
liam Will: A Checklist," *Winter-
thur Portfolio*, 7 (Charlottesville,

Va., 1972): 156, no. 163.
Lender: Charles V. Swain.

193
Teapot
Philadelphia, Pa., 1785–1798.
Maker: William Will (1742–1798;
active 1764–1798).
Pewter.
O.H. 6″ (15.2 cm); O.W. 9 7/8″
(25.1 cm); DIAM. 5 3/4″ (14.6 cm).

Marks: L.542.
Bibliography: Dr. Robert Mallory
III, "An American Pewter Col-
lection," *Antiques*, 72, no. 1 (July
1975): 41–43. Laughlin, *Pewter
In America*, as in I, pl. 29, fig. 195.
Suzanne Hamilton, "The Pewter
of William Will: A Checklist,"
Winterthur Portfolio, 7 (Char-
lottesville, Va., 1972): 159, no. 180.
Lender: Dr. and Mrs. Robert
Mallory III.

194
Creamer
Philadelphia, Pa., 1785–1798.
Maker: William Will (1742–1798;
active 1764–1798).
Pewter.
O.H. 5 3/8″ (13.7 cm); O.W. 5 3/8″
(13.7 cm).

Marks: L. 538 ("X" mark only).
Provenance: John F. Ruckman.
Bibliography: Laughlin, *Pewter
in America*, III, pl. 95, fig. 777.
Suzanne Hamilton, "The Pewter
of William Will: A Checklist,"
Winterthur Portfolio, 7 (Char-
lottesville, Va., 1972): 137, no. 30.

Montgomery, *American Pewter*,
p. 128, fig. 7-2.
Lender: Charles V. Swain.

195
Covered sugar bowl
Philadelphia, Pa., 1764–1798.
Maker: Attributed to William
Will (1742–1798; active 1764–
1798).
Pewter.
O.H. 4 13/16″ (12.2 cm).

Marks: None.
Provenance: John F. Ruckman.
Exhibitions: PMA (1971).
Bibliography: Charles V. Swain,
"Interchangeable Parts in Early
American Pewter," *Antiques*, 83,
no. 2 (Feb. 1963): 212–213, fig. 2.
Suzanne Hamilton, "The Pewter
of William Will: A Checklist,"
Winterthur Portfolio, 7 (Char-
lottesville, Va., 1972): 150, no. 131.
Lender: Charles V. Swain.

196
Coffeepot
Philadelphia, Pa., 1785–1798.
Maker: William Will (1742–1798;
active 1764–1798).
Pewter.
O.H. 15 3/4″ (40 cm); width of
plinth 4 1/4″ (10.8 cm).

Marks: L.541.
Bibliography: Laughlin, *Pewter
in America*, III, pl. 91, fig. 760.
Suzanne Hamilton, "The Pewter
of William Will: A Checklist,"
Winterthur Portfolio, 7 (Charlottesville, Va., 1972): 136, no. 21.

Lender: Dr. and Mrs. Robert
Mallory III.

197
Two-handled cup
Boston, Mass., 1731–1763.
Maker: Attributed to Robert
Bonynge (active 1731–1763).
Pewter.
O.H. 4 3/16″ (10.6 cm); O.W. 7″
(17.8 cm); DIAM. rim 4″ (10.2 cm);
DIAM base 2 13/16″ (7.1 cm).

Marks: L. 292.
Provenance: John Carl Thomas,
Hanover, Conn.
Exhibitions: Flint Institute of
Arts, Flint, Mich., *American
Pewter* (1973).
Bibliography: Laughlin, *Pewter
in America*, I, 66–67; III, 36–38.
Lender: Dr. and Mrs. Melvyn D.
Wolf.

198
Beaker
Boston, Mass., 1731–1763.
Maker: Robert Bonynge (active
1731–1763).
Pewter.
O.H. 5 3/16″ (13.2 cm); DIAM. base
2 15/16″ (7.5 cm); DIAM. rim 3 1/2″
(8.9 cm).

Marks: L.292.
Inscription: "Dwight / MDCCXXXX"
engraved on front.
Provenance: Daniel Dwight (1780–
1865), Dudley, Mass.; Mary E.
Dwight, Spokane, Wash.
Bibliography: Hood, *American
Pewter*, as on p. 13, no. 2, illus. at
p. 14. Laughlin, *Pewter in
America*, III, 36–38.
Lender: Yale University Art
Gallery; gift of Mary E. Dwight
to Sterling Memorial Library.
1965.10.4b.

199
Flagon
Lancaster, Pa., 1771.
Maker: Johann Christoph Heyne
(1715–1781; active 1756–1780).
Pewter.
O.H. 11 1/4″ (28.6 cm); DIAM. base
5 7/8″ (14.9 cm); DIAM. rim
3 7/16″ (8.7 cm).

Marks: L.530, 531, 532.
Inscription: "for / The Peters Kirche / in Mount Joy Town Ship / von John Dirr / 1771" engraved on the body.
Provenance: The Peter's Church, Mt. Joy Township, Lancaster County, Pa.; Howard Reifsnyder.
Exhibitions: MMA (1939).
Bibliography: "The Frontispiece," *Antiques*, 13, no. 2 (Feb. 1928): 110, 112–113. *Colonial Furniture: The Superb Collection of the Late Howard Reifsnyder* (American Art Association, Inc., New York, April 24–27, 1929), p. 56, no. 231, illus. p. 57. John J. Evans, Jr., "I. C. H., Lancaster Pewterer," *Antiques*, 20, no. 3 (Sept. 1931): 150–153. Hood, *American Pewter*, p. 51, no. 186, illus. p. 52. Laughlin, *Pewter in America*, II, 44; III, 123–130. John H. Carter, Sr., "A Checklist of the Extant Pewter of Johann Christoph Heyne," *PCCA*, Bull. 70, vol. 7, no. 1 (Dec. 1974), p. 29, no. 49.
Lender: Yale University Art Gallery; Mabel Brady Garvan Collection. 1930.725.

200
Standing cup with cover
Lancaster, Pa., 1756–1780.
Maker: Johann Christoph Heyne (1715–1781; active 1756–1780).
Pewter.
O.H. 8 3/4" (22.2 cm); DIAM. base 4 9/16" (11.6 cm); DIAM. rim 4 3/16" (10.6 cm).

Marks: L.533.
Provenance: Carl Jacobs, Deep River, Conn.
Bibliography: John H. Carter, Sr., "A Checklist of the Extant Pewter of Johann Christoph Heyne," *PCCA*, Bull. 70, vol. 7, no. 1 (Dec. 1974), p. 28, no. 28.
Lender: Yale University Art Gallery; Mabel Brady Garvan Collection. 1966.1.

201
Chalice
Albany, N.Y., 1775–1795.
Maker: Peter Young (1749–1813; active 1775–1795).
Pewter.
O.H. 8 1/2" (21.6 cm); DIAM. base 4 3/8" (11.1 cm); DIAM. at lip 4" (10.1 cm).

Marks: L.515.
Bibliography: Laughlin, *Pewter in America*, I, pl. 36, fig. 242; p. 44; II, pp. 22–23; III, pp. 108–109.
Lender: Dr. and Mrs. Robert Mallory III.

202
Baptismal basin
Hartford, Conn., 1795–1816.
Maker: Samuel Danforth (1774–1816; active 1795–1816).
Pewter.
O.H. 3 5/16" (8.4 cm); DIAM. rim 7 9/16" (19.2 cm).

Marks: L.403, 404 with X.
Provenance: Charles F. Hutchins collection.
Exhibitions: The M. H. de Young Memorial Museum, San Francisco, Calif. (1936).
Bibliography: Laughlin, *Pewter in America*, I, pl. 73, fig. 245. Hood, *American Pewter*, p. 22, no. 74. Montgomery, *American Pewter*, p. 62, fig. 4–6.
Lender: Yale University Art Gallery; Mabel Brady Garvan Collection. 1930.760.

203
Flagon
Hartford, Conn., 1795–1816.
Maker: Samuel Danforth (1774–1816; active 1795–1816).
Pewter.
O.H. 13" (33 cm); DIAM. base 6 5/16" (16 cm); DIAM. rim 4" (10.2 cm).

Marks: L. 403, 404.
Exhibitions: The M. H. de Young Memorial Museum, San Francisco, Calif. (1936).
Bibliography: Hood, *American Pewter*, pp. 20–22, no. 68, illus. p. 21. Montgomery, *American Pewter*, p. 62, fig. 4–7.
Lender: Yale University Art Gallery; Mabel Brady Garvan Collection. 1930.723.

Brass

204
Pair of andirons
Possibly Rhode Island, 1740–1760.
Brass, wrought iron.
O.H. 20" (50.8 cm); W. base 12" (30.5 cm).

Provenance: Purchased in Hartford, Conn. (1943); Charles F. Montgomery.
Lender: Mr. and Mrs. Stanley Stone.

205
Pair of andirons
America, 1760–1785.
Brass, wrought iron.
O.H. 25 1/4" (64.1 cm); O.W. 13" (33 cm); O.D. 22" (55.9 cm).

Provenance: Quentin H. Bowers.
Lender: Mr. and Mrs. George M. Kaufman.

206
Pair of andirons
America, 1760–1780.
Brass, wrought iron.
O.H. 24 7/8" (63.2 cm); O.W. 12 3/4" (32.4 cm); O.D. 21 1/4" (54 cm).

Provenance: Paul N. and Olive Louise Dann.
Lender: Yale University Art Gallery; bequest of Olive Louise Dann. 1962.31.58 A and B.

207
Pair of andirons
New York, N.Y. 1795–1805.
Maker: R. Wittingham, Sr. (1748–1821).
Brass, wrought iron.
O.H. 21 3/4" (55.3 cm); O.W. 10 7/8" (27.6 cm); O.D. 18 13/16" (47.8 cm).

Marks: "R• WITTINGHAM / N• YORK" stamped on the rear faces of the plinths.
Provenance: Quentin H. Bowers.
Bibliography: Henry J. Kauffman and Quentin H. Bowers, *Early American Andirons* (New York, 1974), pp. 50–52, illus. p. 51.
Lender: Mr. and Mrs. George M. Kaufman.

Ceramics

208
Pickle stand or sweetmeat dish
Philadelphia, Pa., 1770–1772.
Maker: Bonnin and Morris factory (Gousse Bonnin, ca. 1741–?, and George Anthony Morris, ca. 1744–1773; active 1770–1772).
Soft-paste porcelain.
O.H. 5 7/16″ (13.8 cm); DIAM. 7 1/2″ (19.1 cm).

Bibliography: Graham Hood, *Bonnin and Morris of Philadelphia: The First American Porcelain Factory, 1770–1772* (Chapel Hill, 1972), fig. 37. *Britannica Encyclopedia of American Art* (Chicago, 1973), p. 107, fig. 5. Gordon A. Rust, *Collection Guide to Antique Porcelain* (New York, 1973), p. 119.
Lender: The National Museum of History and Technology, Smithsonian Institution, Washington, D.C.; gift of the Barra Foundation, Inc. 70.597.

209
Fruit basket
Philadelphia, Pa., 1770–1772.
Maker: Bonnin and Morris factory (Gousse Bonnin, ca. 1741–?, and George Anthony Morris, ca. 1744–1773; active 1770–1772).
Soft-paste porcelain.
O.H. 2 3/16″ (5.6 cm); DIAM. 6 3/4″ (17.1 cm).

Marks: "P" on center bottom.
Lender: Mr. and Mrs. Richard Stiner.

210
Dish
Montgomery County, Pa., 1793.
Maker: Probably Henry Roudebuth.
Lead-glazed earthenware with incised and slip decoration.
O.H. 1 7/8″ (4.8 cm); DIAM. 12 1/4″ (31.1 cm).

Marks: "1793·H R" on front.
Bibliography: Frances Lichten, *Folk Art of Rural Pennsylvania* (New York, 1949), illus. p. 31. Guilland, *Pennsylvania German*

Arts and Crafts: A Picture Book (New York, 1949 rev. ed.) fig. 25, illus. p. 288. Guilland, *Folk Pottery*, illus. p. 288.
Lender: The Metropolitan Museum of Art, New York; gift of Mrs. Robert W. de Forest. 34.100.124.

211
Dish
Bucks County, Pa., ca. 1800.
Maker: David Spinner (1758–1811).
Earthenware.
DIAM. 11 1/2″ (29.4 cm).

Inscription: "DEERS CHASE" inscribed on the front.
Bibliography: Barber, *Tulip Ware*, pp. 130–132, figs. 40, 42. Guilland, *Folk Pottery*, illus. p. 157.
Lender: Philadelphia Museum of Art; gift of John T. Morris. 00-74.

212
Dish
Bucks County, Pa., ca. 1800.
Maker: David Spinner (1758–1811).
Earthenware.
DIAM. 11 1/2″ (29.4 cm).

Bibliography: Barber, *Tulip Ware*, pp. 130–132, figs. 41–42. Guilland, *Folk Pottery*, illus. p. 156.
Lender: Philadelphia Museum of Art; gift of John T. Morris. 00-76.

213
Dish
Bucks County, Pa., ca. 1800.
Maker: David Spinner (1758–1811).
Earthenware.
DIAM. 9 1/4″ (23.7 cm).

Bibliography: Barber, *Tulip Ware*, fig. 43. Guilland, *Folk Pottery*, illus. p. 270.
Lender: Philadelphia Museum of Art; gift of John T. Morris. 00-72.

214
Dish

Bucks County, Pa., ca. 1800.
Maker: David Spinner (1758–1811).
Earthenware.
DIAM. 11 1/2″ (29.4 cm).

Marks: "Sholder Firelocke" inscribed on front of plate.
Bibliography: Barber, *Tulip Ware*, fig. 44.
Lender: Philadelphia Museum of Art; gift of John T. Morris. 00-199.

215
Dish
Southern Wachovia, N.C., ca. 1795.
Maker: Friedrich Rothrock (1772–after 1839).
Earthenware.
DIAM. 11 1/2″ (29.2 cm).

Mark: "FR", impressed stamp, on back.
Inscription: The initials "G R" on the front are probably those of the potter's brother, George Rothrock.
Provenance: Descended in the family of George Rothrock, the potter's brother.
Bibliography: John Bivins, Jr., *The Moravian Potters in North Carolina* (Chapel Hill, 1972), pl. facing p. 242, fig. 263; "The Moravian Potters in North Carolina, 1756–1821," *Ceramics in America*, ed. Ian M. G. Quimby (Charlottesville, Va., 1973), fig. 28b.
Lender: Old Salem, Inc.

216
Jug
Bennington, Vt., 1798.
Maker: Abel Wadsworth (active 1798), potter at the works of Captain John Norton (1758–1827).
Earthenware.
O.H. 5 1/8″ (13 cm); DIAM. 3 5/8″ (9.2 cm).

Provenance: Made for Ominidia Armstrong (Mrs. Jethro Gerry, 1788–1880); given by her to George Wadsworth Robinson (March 22, 1878); acquired from him by John Spargo.

Bibliography: John Spargo, *The Potters and Potteries of Bennington* (Boston, 1926), pp. 5–6, pl. 2. Richard Carter Barret, *Bennington Pottery and Porcelain* (New York, 1958), pl. 1.
Lender: Bennington Museum, Inc., Bennington, Vt.

217
Dish
New England, possibly Conn., late 18th or early 19th century. Lead glazed earthenware with yellow slip-trailed decoration and spots of green.
O.H. 3 1/2″ (8.9 cm); W. 18 5/8″ (50.0 cm); D. 12 3/4″ (32.4 cm).

Provenance: Bought from the Boston dealer Stainforth for $5 in November 1918.
Lender: The Society for the Preservation of New England Antiquities; gift of William Sumner Appleton. 1918.1385.

218
Jar
New York, N.Y., ca. 1800. Stoneware.
O.H. 12 1/4″ (31.1 cm); W. 11 3/8″ (28.9 cm).

Bibliography: Donald Blake Webster, *Decorated Stoneware Pottery of North America* (Rutland, Vt., 1971), figs. 44, 161.
Lender: Mr. and Mrs. John Paul Remensnyder.

219
Jar
New York, 1775–1800. Stoneware.
O.H. 11″ (27.9 cm); DIAM. top 4 7/8″ (12.4 cm); DIAM. base 4 1/2″ (11.4 cm).

Provenance: Purchased from a dealer in Wallingford, Conn., who had bought it in Cheshire, Conn.
Lender: Yale University Art Gallery; gift of Mr. and Mrs. Charles F. Montgomery. 1973.138.12.

Glass

220
Candlestick
Wistarburg, Salem County, N.J. ca. 1740–1780.
Maker: Attributed to the glassworks of Caspar Wistar (1694–1752).
Light green nonlead glass.
O.H. 7 9/16″ (19.2 cm); DIAM. foot 4″ (10.2 cm).

Provenance: Purchased from a Dilkes family, Woodbury, N.J., in 1936; George William Collins, Woodbury, N.J.; George S. McKearin.
Bibliography: G. S. McKearin, "This is How it Happened," *Antiques*, 58 (Oct. 1950): 291, illus. *Glass from The Corning Museum of Glass* (Corning, N.Y., 1955), no. 72, illus. p. 66; 1974 ed., no. 108, illus. p. 86.
Lender: The Corning Museum of Glass, Corning, N.Y. 50.4.1A.

221
Jug
Eastern United States, 1790–1810. Olive green nonlead glass.
O.H. 8 3/4″ (22.2 cm); DIAM. (max.) 7 3/8″ (18.7 cm); DIAM. rim 3 7/8″ (9.8 cm).

Provenance: Minnie I. Meacham; George S. McKearin.
Bibliography: McKearin and McKearin, *American Blown Glass*, p. 192, pl. 36.
Lender: The Corning Museum of Glass, Corning, N.Y. 55.4.128.

222
Jar
Eastern United States, 1790–1810. Olive green ("black") nonlead glass.
O.H. 9 1/8″ (23.2 cm); DIAM. shoulder 6 1/2″ (16.5 cm).

Provenance: George S. McKearin.
Bibliography: McKearin and McKearin, *American Blown Glass*, p. 230, pl. 55.
Lender: The Corning Museum of Glass, Corning, N.Y. 55.4.126.

223
Flask
Probably Manheim, Pa., 1767–1774.
Maker: Attributed to the glasshouse of Henry William Stiegel (1729–1785; active 1763–1774). Blown pattern-molded amethyst lead glass.
O.H. 4 13/16″ (12.2 cm); O.D. 3 9/16″ (9 cm).

Provenance: Montague collection, no. 151.
Lender: Yale University Art Gallery; Mabel Brady Garvan Collection. 1930.1502.

224
Flask
Possibly Manheim, Pa., or Ohio, 1770–1810.
Maker: Possibly by the glasshouse of Henry William Stiegel (1729–1785; active 1763–1774). Blown pattern-molded amethyst lead glass.
O.H. 5 11/16″ (14.4 cm); O.W. 4″ (10.2 cm).

Provenance: Henry V. Weil.
Lender: Yale University Art Gallery; Mabel Brady Garvan Collection. 1930.1568.

225
Sugar bowl
Probably Manheim, Pa., 1767–1774.
Maker: Attributed to the glasshouse of Henry William Stiegel (1729–1785; active 1763–1774). Blown pattern-molded cobalt lead glass.
O.H. 7 1/2″ (19.1 cm); O.W. 4 7/8″ (12.4 cm).

Provenance: Montague collection, no. 195.
Lender: Yale University Art Gallery; Mabel Brady Garvan Collection. 1930.1501.

226
Pitcher
Probably Manheim, Pa., 1767–1774.

Maker: Attributed to the glass-house of Henry William Stiegel (1729–1785; active 1763–1774). Blown pattern-molded cobalt lead glass.
O.H. 3 3/4″ (9.5 cm); O.W. 3 5/16″ (8.4 cm).

Provenance: Montague collection, no. 190.
Lender: Yale University Art Gallery; Mabel Brady Garvan Collection. 1930.1800.

227
Salt
Probably Manheim, Pa., 1767–1774.
Maker: Attributed to the glass-house of Henry William Stiegel (1729–1785; active 1763–1774). Blown pattern-molded cobalt lead glass.
O.H. 2 3/4″ (7 cm); DIAM. rim 2 1/8″ (5.4 cm); DIAM. foot 2 1/16″ (5.2 cm).

Provenance: Montague collection, no. 215.
Lender: Yale University Art Gallery; Mabel Brady Garvan Collection. 1930.1512.

228
Salt
Probably Manheim, Pa., 1767–1774.
Maker: Attributed to the glass-house of Henry William Stiegel (1729–1785; active 1763–1774). Blown pattern-molded amethyst lead glass.
O.H. 2 3/4″ (7 cm); DIAM. rim 2 1/8″ (5.4 cm); DIAM. base, 1 13/16″ (4.6 cm).

Lender: Yale University Art Gallery; Mabel Brady Garvan Collection. 1930.1565.

229
Covered bowl
Probably Manheim, Pa., 1772–1774.
Maker: Attributed to the glass-

house of Henry William Stiegel (1729–1785; active 1763–1774). Colorless lead glass.
O.H. 5 11/16″ (14.4 cm); DIAM. rim 4 1/4″ (10.8 cm); DIAM. foot 2 3/8″ (6 cm).

Provenance: Descended in the John Deacon and Charles Read families of New Jersey; purchased from a Deacon family in the 1940s; George S. McKearin.
Bibliography: McKearin and McKearin, *American Blown Glass*, pl. 30, no. 2.
Lender: The Corning Museum of Glass, Corning, N.Y. 55.4.69.

230
Tumbler
Probably Manheim, Pa., 1772–1774.
Maker: Attributed to the glass-house of Henry William Stiegel (1729–1785; active 1763–1774). Colorless glass with enamel decoration.
O.H. 3 3/4″ (9.5 cm); DIAM. rim 3″ (7.6 cm); DIAM. base 2 3/16″ (5.6 cm).

Inscription: "We two will be true" on the reverse.
Provenance: George S. McKearin.
Exhibitions: East Side Antiques Show, New York, N.Y. (1968).
Lender: The Corning Museum of Glass, Corning, N.Y. 55.4.67.

231
Goblet
New Bremen, Md., 1793.
Maker: Glass manufactory of John Frederick Amelung (d. 1798; active New Bremen 1784–1795).
Colorless nonlead glass.
O.H. 8 5/8″ (21.9 cm); DIAM. rim 4 15/16″ (12.5 cm); DIAM. foot 4 7/8″ (12.4 cm).

Inscription: "George Trisler 1793" engraved on bowl.
Provenance: Grace Thomas, Wytheville, Va.

Exhibitions: U.S. National Museum, Washington, D.C., Amelung exhibit case (1952).
Bibliography: "Famous Firsts," *Antiques*, 62 (Dec. 1952): 489, illus. p. 488. "In the Museums," *Antiques*, 69 (March 1956): 262 (illus.).
Lender: The Corning Museum of Glass, Corning, N.Y. 55.4.34A.

232
Bowl
New Geneva, Pa., 1798–1807.
Maker: Attributed to Baltzer Kramer, overseer, the New Geneva Glass Works.
Blown pattern-molded glass.
O.H. 5″ (12.7 cm); DIAM. rim 8 3/8″ (21.3 cm); DIAM. foot 4 1/8″ (10.5 cm).

Provenance: George S. McKearin.
Bibliography: George S. and Helen McKearin, *American Glass* (New York, 1948), pl. 45, no. 6; *American Blown Glass*, p. 146, pl. 13, no. 2.
Lender: The Corning Museum of Glass, Corning, N.Y. 55.4.93.

233
Pair of candlesticks
Probably southern New Jersey, ca. 1800–1820.
Blue-green nonlead glass.
O.H. 9 1/8″ (23.2 cm).

Provenance: Alfred B. Maclay.
Exhibitions: MMA, *Nineteenth-Century America* (1970), no. 47.
Bibliography: Helen McKearin, *The Alfred B. Maclay Collection of ... American Glass* (sale catalogue, American Art Association, New York, N.Y., Dec. 5–7, 1935), no. 469. Joseph Downs, "Three Examples of Early American Glass," *MMAB*, 31 (Feb. 1936): 34 (illus.). McKearin and McKearin, *American Blown Glass*, pl. 93, no. 1.
Lender: The Metropolitan Museum of Art; Rogers Fund (1935). 35.124.1.

Textiles

234
Embroidered picture,
"The Fishing Lady"
New England, mid-18th century.
Maker: Possibly by Eunice
Bourne, wife of Col. Sylvanus
Bourne, Barnstable, Mass.
Wool, silk, metal yarns, and
beads, embroidered on linen
canvas.
o.h. 24 8/10" (63 cm); o.w.
50 4/10" (128 cm).

Exhibitions: MFA, *Exhibition of
New England Embroidery before
1800* (1941).
Bibliography: Helen Bowen, "The
Fishing Lady and Boston Com-
mon," *Antiques*, 4, no. 2 (Aug.
1923): 70–73, fig. 3. Nancy Graves
Cabot, "The Fishing Lady and
Boston Common," *Antiques*, 40,
no. 1 (July 1941): 28, fig. 1.
Lender: Museum of Fine Arts,
Boston; Seth Kettell Sweetser
Fund. 21.2233.

235
Bed hangings
York, Me., ca. 1745.
Maker: Mary Bulman (b. 1715).
Wool and linen.
Top valance, left: o.l. 72 1/4"
(183.5 cm); o.w. 7 3/8" (18.7 cm).
Top valance, foot: o.l. 55"
(139.7 cm); o.w. 8 1/8" (20.6 cm).
Top valance, right: o.l. 75"
(190.5 cm); o.w. 7 3/4" (19.7 cm).
Backcloth: o.l. 61 1/2" (156.2
cm); o.w. 59" (149.9 cm). Head
curtain: o.l. 78" (198.1 cm);
o.w. 73" (185.4 cm). Head
curtain: o.l. 77" (195.6 cm);
o.w. 73 1/4" (186.1 cm). Foot
curtain: o.l. 77 1/4" (196.2 cm); o.w. 35 1/4"
(89.5 cm). Foot curtain: o.l.
77 1/2" (196.9 cm); o.w. 37"
(94 cm). Coverlet with bases:
o.l. 79" (200.7 cm); o.w. 73 1/4"
(186.1 cm).

Provenance: York, Maine.
Exhibitions: MFA, *New England
Crewel Embroidery* (1971–1972).
Bibliography: Abbott Lowell

Cummings, *Bed Hangings* (Bos-
ton, 1961), p. 56, figs. 39, 40, 41,
45, 48. Safford and Bishop, *Quilts
and Coverlets*, pp. 52–55, fig. 52.
Anne Pollard Rowe, "Crewel
Embroidered Bed Hangings in
Old and New England," *Boston
Museum Bulletin*, 71, nos. 365–
366 (1973): 104, 135, fig. 1.
Lender: Old Gaol Museum, York,
Me.

236
Coverlet
Kingston, N.Y., ca. 1728–1748.
Maker: Clarissa Stokradt (or
Stokraad) Deyo.
Wool embroidery on linen.
o.l. 101" (256.5 cm); o.w. 98"
(248.9 cm).

Bibliography: Mildred J. Davis,
*Early American Embroidery
Designs* (New York, 1969), illus.
facing p. 48. Safford and Bishop,
Quilts and Coverlets, fig. 54.
Lender: Colonial Williamsburg
Foundation. 1959.55.

237
Coverlet
New York or New England,
ca. 1770.
Crewel-embroidered glazed
worsted.
o.l. 102" (259.1 cm); o.w. 84"
(213.4 cm).

Lender: Colonial Williamsburg
Foundation. 1974.193.

238
Bed rug
Lebanon, Conn., 1802.
Maker: Philena McCall, 1783–
1822.
Wool.
o.l. 101" (256.5 cm); o.w. 91"
(231.1 cm).

Provenance: Philena McCall
(Mrs. Eliphalet Abell), Lebanon,
Conn.; descended in Abell
family (until 1970).
Exhibitions: WA, *Bed Ruggs /*

1722–1833 (1972), pl. IV.
Bibliography: Homer Eaton
Keyes, "A Note on Certain Early
Coverlets," *Antiques*, 12 (Nov.
1927): 389, fig. 4. William L.
Warren, "Bed Rugs: An Exhibi-
tion at the Wadsworth Athe-
neum," *Antiques*, 102 (Dec. 1972):
1039, pl. 4. Safford and Bishop,
Quilts and Coverlets, p. 19, fig. 13.
Lender: Wadsworth Atheneum,
Hartford, Conn.
1972.11.

239
Coverlet
Charles City Co., Va., ca. 1770.
Maker: Members of the Byrd
and Harrison families of Westover and Berkeley plantations,
Charles City Co., Va.
Unbleached cotton, red and white
calico, chintz.
o.l. 105 1/2" (268 cm); o.w.
97 3/4" (248.3 cm).

Provenance: Family of Mary
Willing Harrison of Berkeley
plantation; Susan McGuire
Ellett (until 1956).
Exhibitions: Valentine Museum,
Richmond, Va., *When Richmond
Became the Capital* (1957).
Woodlawn Plantation, Mount
Vernon, Va. (1965).
Bibliography: Mildred J. Davis,
*Early American Embroidery
Designs* (New York, 1969), pp.
96–98. Safford and Bishop,
Quilts and Coverlets, pp. 145–
148, fig. 208. Mildred J. Davis,
"Textiles in the Valentine Mu-

seum," *Antiques*, 103, no. 1 (Jan.
1973): 176, pl. 5. Myron and
Patsy Orlofsky, *Quilts in Amer-
ica* (New York, 1974), pls. 4–6.
Lender: Valentine Museum,
Richmond, Va.; gift of Susan
McGuire Ellett. 56.203.1.

240
Coverlet
Philadelphia, Pa., and Springfield, Mass., 1774–1809.
Maker: Cotton printed by John
Hewson, Philadelphia; quilting
formerly attributed to Fanny
Glover of Springfield, Mass.;
possibly by unidentified "E.C."
Cotton, both printed and plain;
quilting.
o.l. 116 1/2" (295.9 cm); o.w.
112 1/4" (285.1 cm).

Inscription: "E.C. 1807" in black
cross stitch in upper left corner on
back; "E.C. 1809" quilted in
medallion, center top of quilt
face.
Provenance: Misses Clementina
and Lizzie Black, Springfield, Ill.
Exhibitions: St. Louis Art Museum, *2000 Years of Textiles*
(1972).
Bibliography: Florence Montgomery, *Printed Textiles* (New
York, 1970), p. 86, fig. 57. Safford
and Bishop, *Quilts and Coverlets*,
fig. 94. Myron and Patsy Orlofsky,
Quilts in America (New York,
1974), p. 46 (illus.).
Lender: The St. Louis Art Museum, St. Louis, Mo.; gift of Miss
Mildred Petrie. 61.48.

240
(detail)

Index

Photograph Credits
(Numbers without prefix are catalogue numbers; photographs not listed were lent by the collector.)

American Antiquarian Society, figs. 11, 15, 18, 19, 20, 21
Wayne Andrews, fig. 2
Gilbert Ask, 57 (det.)
E. Irving Blomstrann, 65, 96, 106 (det.), 121, 137, 138, 140-2, 145, 147, 148, 150, 151/162 (color), 152, 156, 157 (det.), 158, 159, 161, 162, 165, 174, 175, 177, 180, 183, 184/5, 191, 192, 199/200 (color), 202, 218a,b, 219, 223–8 (color), 238, figs. 1, 3, 4, 7, 19, 81, 82, 85.
Richard Cheek, Cambridge, 2, 5, 6, 7, 92, 100, 108, 128, 187.
Chicago Historical Society, 164
Colonial Williamsburg, 107, 119, 236, 237
George M. Cushing, Boston, 26, 143a,b
Davis-Dunlop, Inc., Washington, D. C., 104
Daniel Farber, 198, 203
John R. Freeman, London, 25
Frick Art Reference Library, 38, fig. 52
Fogg Museum, figs. 10, 13
Edmund B. Gilchrist, Jr., Philadelphia, 103
Hildebrand Studio, fig. 86
Kennedy Galleries, New York, 61
Richard Merrill, Saugus, Mass., 136
Photo Studios Limited, London, 20
Jeremy Ross, 173, 181, 182, 188, 189, 202
Israel Sack, Inc., New York, 98, 131, 134, 134 (det.), 135
Smithsonian Institution, 208
Willard Stewart, Wilmington, 91
Joseph Szaszfai, 10, 19, 29, 36, 41, 41 (det.), 42, 49, 50, 54, 69, 70-87, 120, 209a,b, figs. 6, 40, 51, 63, 64
Charles Uht, New York, 106
Terry Vanderplas, Deerfield, Mass., 156 (det.)
Henry Francis duPont Winterthur Museum, 207, fig. 25
A. J. Wyatt, Philadelphia Museum, fig. 58

Composed in 11 on 12 Baskerville by Maryland Linotype Composition Company, Baltimore, Maryland.
Printed by Eastern Press, Inc., New Haven, Connecticut.
Bound by A. Horowitz and Son, Fairfield, New Jersey.